MILITARY Living's™

# MILITARY SPACE-A AIR OPPORTUNITIES

## Around the World


**William "Roy" Crawford, Sr., Ph.D.**
**President, Military Marketing Services, Inc.**
**and Military Living Publications**

**L. Ann Crawford, Vice-President, Military Marketing Services, Inc.**
**and Publisher, Military Living Publications**



**Vice President - Marketing - R J Crawford**

EDITORS - Kenneth Kaizer and Emily Peraro
ASSISTANT EDITOR - Leon Russ
COVER DESIGN - Chris Harris

CHIEF OF STAFF - Nigel Fellers

OFFICE STAFF - Timothy Brown, Eula Mae Brownlee,
Maureen Fleegal, Irene Kearney, Rose McLain, Lourdes Medina,
Donna Russell, Joel Thomas, MSG, USA (Ret)

Military Living Publications
P.O. Box 2347
Falls Church, Virginia 22042-0347
**TEL: (703) 237-0203**
FAX: (703) 237-2233

# NOTICE

The information in this directory has been compiled and edited either from the activity/ facility listed, its superior headquarters, or from other sources that may or may not be noted. All listed facilities, their locations, hours of operation, and telephone/telefax numbers could change. Flight schedules, including destinations, routings, frequency, time in route and stop overs of flights, and aircraft used, are always subject to change; however, many of the flights listed in this guide have followed the same routes for over 50 years. Changes in air routes occur largely with the repositioning and redeployment of United States Military Forces around the world. Space-A passenger eligibility could change; however, we have published the most up-to-date passenger eligibility and other information available. The "how to travel Space-A" supporting information in the appendices is subject to change, but the latest changes to these appendices were included at press time. The elementary "how to travel Space-A" supporting information ,among other things, are contained in our book **MILITARY SPACE-A AIR BASIC TRAINING AND READER TRIP REPORTS** and in our map **MILITARY SPACE-A AIR OPPORTUNITIES AIR ROUTE MAP.** This book should be used as a guide to Space-A air travel with all of the above in mind. **Please forward any corrections or additions to the publisher.**

This directory/guide is published by **Military Marketing Services Inc. and Military Living Publications** (T/A) a private firm in no way connected with the U.S. Federal or other governments. The directory is copyrighted by William Roy, Sr. and L. Ann Crawford. Opinions expressed by the publishers and writers herein are not to be considered an official expression by any government agency or official.

The information and statements contained in this directory have been compiled from sources believed to be reliable and to represent the best current opinion on the subject. No warranty, guarantee, or representation is made by **Military Marketing Services, Inc.** and **Military Living Publications,** as to the absolute correctness or sufficiency of any representation contained in this or other publications and we can assume no responsibility.



**First Printing - August 1995**



**Library of Congress Cataloging-in-Publication Data**

Crawford, William Roy, 1932 -
Military living's military space-A air opportunities around the world / William "Roy" Crawford, Sr., L. Ann Crawford ; editors Kenneth E. Kaizer, Emily Peraro, Leon G. Russ.
p. cm.
ISBN 0-914862-55-3
1. United States—Armed Forces—Transportation—Directories.
2. United States—Armed Forces—Facilities—Directories. 3. Air travel—Directories. I. Crawford, Ann Caddell. II. Kaizer. Kenneth E. III. Peraro, Emily H. IV. Russ, Leon G. V. Military living.
UC333.C73 1995
355.3'4—dc20 95-31142
CIP

**ISBN 0-914862-55-3**

# INTRODUCTION

**Military Living's Military Space-A Air Opportunities Around the World** is a comprehensive guide to military Space-A air opportunities worldwide, which are provided by all of the military departments (US ARMY, US NAVY, USMC, USCG AND US AIR FORCE). **This edition has been completely revised,** and contains more than **260** Space-A departure/arrival stations/locations worldwide. In response to our readers' needs, we have provided information regarding Space-A air opportunities for active duty, guard/reserve, and retired uniformed services (US ARMY, US NAVY, USMC, USCG, US AIR FORCE, USPHS AND NOAA) personnel and their families. These Space-A air opportunities are provided by the active Army, Navy, USMC, Air Force, and Coast Guard, as well as the National Guard and Reserve. You can save thousands of $$$ with this directory.

## HOW THIS DIRECTORY IS ORGANIZED

This directory is divided into **four major sections: Section I** - Continental United States (CONUS); **Section II** - Outside the Continental United States (OCONUS); **Section III** - Foreign Countries; and **Section IV** - Detailed appendices, containing information essential to Space-A travelers. This particular organization of the materials has been selected because it matches the CONUS, OCONUS and Foreign Country organization of the Space-A Travel Regulation, Chapter 6, (and selected relative portions of other chapters) DoD 4515.13-R at appendix A in this book.

Listings within each section are alphabetized by state, territory, foreign country, and/or departure geographic areas. This last group, which have changing departure locations and limited Space-A air opportunities, have been placed in composite (roll-up) listings. These departure stations are easily identified in the contents.

This directory also provides **country and state abbreviations; the three letter Federal Aviation Administration (FAA) coordinated and four letter International Civil Aviation Organization (ICAO) Location Identifiers;** the new Space-A travel regulations; personnel entrance requirements; a station cross-reference index; A brief description of aircraft on which most Space-A travel occurs, authentication of reserve status for travel eligibility; remote sign-up form and other Space-A support information. The contents pages also serve as the book's index. Several sample listings follow which explain in detail **how to use this directory.**

## HOW TO USE THIS DIRECTORY

**Departure Location (Official Name of Station) and**
**Three letter Location Identifier (LI)**
**Mailing Address of Unit Responsible for Space-A Passenger Activities**

**LOCATION**: Here you'll find specific driving instructions to the departure location from local major cities, interstate/country highways and routes. More than one routing may be provided. **USMRA**: Coordinates in **Military Living's UNITED STATES MILITARY ROAD ATLAS** which are given for each CONUS and OCONUS location. **ML-ARM:** Coordinates on **Military Living's MILITARY SPACE-A AIR OPPORTUNITIES AIR ROUTE MAP** for each Foreign Country station/location. **NMC**: is the nearest major city. Distance in miles and directions from the departure station/location to the nearest major city are provided.

**Main installation telephone numbers:** **C**-commercial. This is the installation's main or information/operator assistance telephone number accessed via the civilian/commercial telephone system, when dialed from CONUS (North America Dial Area) and **D**-defense is the Defense Switched Network **(DSN),** which is the DoD worldwide telephone voice system. The number given is, in most cases, for information/operator assistance. When dialing into the following geographic areas using the DSN system, the following prefixes must be used: **312 (CONUS); 314 (Europe); 313 (Caribbean); 315 (Pacific); 317 (Alaska). (CAUTION-these information numbers are not the passenger information numbers, in most cases).**

The telephone information section of the listings in this book, contains detailed civilian and defense telephone numbers and prefixes and for dialing from a civilian telephone to a military telephone (where this capability exists). These numbers as listed, as well as other numbers in each listing, assumes that the call is being placed from a commercial or defense telephone respectively in, North America for civilian systems and in the CONUS for DSN. By way of example, the telephone information section for Ramstein Air Base in Germany looks like this: Main installation numbers: **C**-011-49-6371-47-1110, **D**-314-480-1110. All telephone information sections for Germany and for most installations in other countries with civilian to military dialing capabilities follow this same basic pattern. The main civilian number breaks down as follows: the first number **(011)** is the international dialing access number for North America; the second number **(49)** is the country code for Germany: the third number **(6371)** is local area/city code within Germany; the fourth number **(47)** is the civilian to military conversion number; and the last number **(1110)** is the line or extension number. **IMPORTANT:** All local area codes in Germany and several other countries begin with a **"0"** which is not used when dialing into the country but must be added if dialing within the country. In Germany, if you are within the boundaries of the local area code, you will not need to dial the local area code when dialing a civilian number or a defense number, dial the military conversion number and the military extension when dialing from a local commercial telephone.

Visitors to foreign countries should keep in mind that telephone systems in North America are the best and most reliable in the world. They are also the easiest to use. Don't expect your knowledge of American telephone systems, especially civilian telephone systems, to be of much use to you in foreign countries. Most foreign country telephone systems can be quite baffling when first encountered. For instance, in the United Kingdom, when dialing a particular location, the number you should dial is determined not only by the location you are dialing to, but by the location you are dialing from. When calling someone from within the U. K., we recommend that you consult the local telephone directory for the proper dialing codes or use operator assistance.

**PAX TERM INFO:** Commercial and defense telephone numbers, recording numbers, (and when the recorded information is updated), and remote sign-up C and D FAX numbers. Complete information is given to dial these numbers from the CONUS. Terminal building number and hours of operation are given. Driving directions to the passenger service area and other pertinent information is also provided. **Pax Service Office**: Location, hours, telephone number(s), staffing and other useful information. **Pax Paging**: Location, hours, telephone number(s), how to request paging service.

**PAX LOUNGES**: General information about available lounge facilities. **General**: Locations, hours, telephone number(s), facilities & services. **Family**: Location, hours, telephone number(s), services & restrictions. **DV/VIP**: Location, hours, telephone number(s), facilities & services. Grades served. **Protocol Service**: Location, hours, telephone number(s), facilities & services. Grades served.

**FOOD SERVICE**: **Cafeteria**: Locations, hours, telephone number(s), other pertinent information. **Dining Hall**: Location, hours, telephone number(s). **In-Flight Kitchen:** Location, hours, telephone number(s). **Enlisted Club**: Location, hours, telephone number(s), facilities and services. **O'Club**: Location, hours, telephone number(s). Grades served. **NCO/CPO Club**: Location, hours, telephone number(s). Grades served. **Restaurants**: Location(s), hours,telephone number(s). **Snack Bar**:

Location(s), hours, telephone number(s), other pertinent information. **Vending:** Location(s), hours, telephone number(s), useful information.

**TRANSPORTATION**: **Air Tickets**: Location(s), hours, telephone number(s). **Bus (Commercial, Shuttle/Government):** Location, hours, telephone number(s). **Car Rental**: Location, hours, telephone number(s), agencies and information. **Taxi**: Location, hours, telephone number(s), commercial, shuttle, and/or government. **Trains**: Location, hours, telephone number(s), call for local train info. **Parking**: Location(s), hours, telephone number(s), short & long term information.

**TML**: Location, hours, telephone number(s) and telefax (FAX) numbers when available. All ranks, Navy Lodges & DV/VIP, **information is given for each departure station and at nearby installations when not available at the departure station.**

**TRAVELERS AID**: **American Red Cross**: Location, hours, telephone number(s), duty & 24-hour telephone numbers. **Chaplain**: Location, hours, telephone number(s), duty & 24-hour emergency telephone number. **Emergency Relief**: Location, hours, telephone number(s), type of relief organization. **Lost/Found**: Location, hours, telephone number(s), agency providing service. **Security Police**: Location, hours, telephone number(s), other pertinent information. **USO**: Location, hours, telephone number(s) may be off base.

**OTHER SERVICES**: **Exchange**: Location, hours, telephone number(s), other pertinent information. **Bank/Money Exchange**: Location, hours, telephone number(s), information on currency conversion. **Hair Styles**: Location, hours, telephone number(s), barber & beauty shops. **Laundry/Dry Cleaning**: Location, hours, telephone number(s), self-served laundry facility. **Medical**: Location, hours, telephone number(s) (commercial & defense), emergency care for AD and retired. **Postal**: Location, hours, telephone number(s). **US Postal Service/Commercial Package/Telegraph facilities:** Location, hours, telephone number(s).

**ATTRACTIONS**: Key attractions at the station/location or in the nearby area.

Note: All of the above support facilities may not be listed due to the availability of some services or limited Space-A air opportunities from some stations/locations.

## SCHEDULED FLIGHTS

The **Air Mobility Command (AMC), regular scheduled flights** have been listed in tables for easy reference and use. These scheduled flights originate largely in the CONUS. A limited number of AMC flights originate in Foreign Countries. These flights travel from their originating or home station on a trip/mission, stopping at few to many stations in route for varried periods of time. In almost most all cases these flights/missions return to the originating or home station. The limited number of missions which do not immediately return to their home station, remain overseas at a station for staging to participate in a future mission or for scheduled mainentance and return to service. The all new schedules in this edition are greately improved and have been simplified for your use.

**ORIGINATING SCHEDULES:** All of the originating schedules at each station/location are listed under/at that station, i.e. all the scheduled flights originating at Charleston AFB/IAP, SC (CHS) are listed under/at Charleston AFB/IAP, SC. The Originating Schedules have been placed in a table for ease in understanding and use. The heading of the table is "ORIGINATING SCHEDULES", next (first line) in the center of the table is the Military Living air route/mission number assigned to that mission. This first mission is APM/CHS-1 which means that this is a mission originating in the Atlantic Region **(A)** (there is also a Pacific Region) , Passenger schedule **(P)**, Mixed (passenger and cargo) mission **(M)**, Charleston AFB/IAP **(CHS)**, and First mission of this type at CHS, **(1). A complete explanation of all air route/mission numbers is at Appendix H General Abbreviations Used in this Book.** On this same line, we have listed the days each month that this flight/mission operates/departs the originating station: **2nd TUE** (see Appendix H, General abbreviations used in this book for an explanation of the date abbreviations). The last item on this first line is the designation of the equipment/aircraft used on this mission: **C-141B.** See Appendix D: A Brief Description of Aircraft on Which Most Space-A Travel Occurs, for a discription of Space-A aircraft.

| ORIGINATING SCHEDULES | | | |
|---|---|---|---|
| | **APM/CHS-1 2nd TUE C-141B** | | |
| **Location ID** | **Airport (Station)** | **Country/State** | **Days Out** |
| CHS | Charleston AFB/IAP | SC | +0 |
| BSB | Brasilia APT | BR | +1 |
| **BUE** | **Ezeiza APT** | **AG** | **+1** |
| MVD | Carrasco IAP | UG | +2 |
| BSB | Brasilia APT | BR | +2 |
| CHS | Charleston AFB/IAP | SC | |

The heading for each mission table is as follows: **Location ID**=this is the Federal Aviation Administration coordinated three letter location identifier for Stations/Airports in the United States, its possessions and Canada. Foreign country three letter LI's have been coordinated by the Department of Defense. The International Civil Aviation Organization (ICAO) has established an international location indicator which is a four letter code used in international aviation and commuunications. Many military stations in foreign countries have converted to this indicator. For a complete list of both types of indicator, see **Military Space-A Air Basic Training (Appendix C). Airport (Station)**=this is the airport or takeoff/landing facility along with the terminal/passenger processing facility. **Country/State**=The two letter abbreviation for foreign Countries and U. S. States is used. Please see Appendix G State, Possession and Country Abbreviations. **Days Out**=this is the number of days or lapse time measured from the departure from the originating station. In our example **(APM/CHS-1),** the flight departs (CHS) at +0 or TUE, departs BSB at +1 or WED, departs BUE at +1 or WED (note that this area is shaded to signify the turnaround point of this mission. This is important for the purpose of "Continuious Sign-up Priority"), departs MVD at +2 or THR, departs BSB at +2 or THR, and returns safely to CHS on +2 or THR. Some missions/trips like CONUS MEDEVAC are accomplished in one day, others take 2 to 5 days to fly their missions and a few may take up to 20 or more days to complete their missions. There are zero days out for CONUS MEDEVAC since each mission is completed in one day.

| IN ROUTE SCHEDULES | | | |
|---|---|---|---|
| **McGuire AFB** | APM/WRI-3 | ACC/WRI-4 | APM/WRI-5 |

In addition to the tables for **ORIGINATING SCHEDULES,** we have included tables which show the IN ROUTE SCHEDULES that apply to Charleston AFB/IAP, SC (CHS). These are schedules which originate at other stations in the system and transit (CHS). We have listed the originating station and the mission number for each **IN ROUTE SCHEDULE.** For example, the following flights originate at McGuire AFB, NJ (WRI) and transit CHS and other stations during these missions (APM/WRI-3; ACC/WRI-4; APM/WRI-5). We have shown the **In Route Schedules** at each station in the system. **This technique allows us to detail the complete schedule for a mission only once at the originating station.** However it does require the reader to refer to (look up) the **In Route Schedules at other stations** to determine where **In Route flights are coming from and more importantly where they are going.**

There are **UNSCHEDULED FLIGHTS**, which in most cases, show the destinations from the listing station, the type equipment flown in some cases and the frequency of the flights. You should always call to confirm unscheduled flights. We have listed below, as an example, the UNSCHEDULED FLIGHTS informatiion from the Washington Naval Air Facility, DC (NSF), located at Andrews AFB, MD, ADW, east side of main runways.

**UNSCHEDULED FLIGHTS**

There are no scheduled flights from the Washington NAF. Most flights are planned 24 hours prior to departure. Call for information. There are frequent unscheduled flights to the following locations: Brunswick NAS, ME (**NHZ**); Cherry Point MCAS, NC (**NKT**); Dallas NAS, TX (**NBE**); Jacksonville NAS, FL (**NIP**); Memphis NAS, TN (**NQA**); New Orleans NAS, LA (**NBG**); Norfolk NAS, VA (**NGU**); Pensacola NAS, FL (**NPA**); South Weymouth NAS, MA (**NZW**). Equipment flown varies with flights and distances. Most aircraft are C-9A, C-12, C-130, P-3C and T-39.

In some cases we have combined the schedules of minor departure located in a central region, in order to conserve space, without diluting the value of the information. See the below listing.

## US PACIFIC ISLANDS

(Not listed separately in this book)

The stations listed below have Space-A air opportunities. Base support facilities are very limited. Billeting and mess arrangements for extended visits should be made and confirmed in advance of your planned visit.

**JOHNSTON ATOLL, JO (JON) (USA),** FCDNA Term Ops JQ/AMC REP, Johnston Atoll, APO AP 96558-5000. *ML-ARM: (160°30'W/16°00'N).* **C-011-808-621-3044-X-2252. D-312-441-2252, FAX 808-621-3044/2343, D FAX 312-441-2343.** *NOTE: Permission/official approval required to visit Johnston Atoll (see Appendix B).*

| IN ROUTE SCHEDULES | |
|---|---|
| **Hikam AFB** | PPP/HIK-1 |
| **March AFB** | PCM/RIV-4 |
| **Travis AFB** | PPM/SUU-9 |

**KWAJALEIN ATOLL, U.S. Army, KA (KWA) (USA), Republic of the Marshall Islands,** Kwajalein Missile Range, ATTN: CSSD-KA-P, PO Box 26, APO AP 96555-2526. *ML-ARM: (167°45'E/8°45'N).* **C-011-805-238-7994, EX 2169, D-315-254-1110 (from CONUS), C-480-1110 (from Pacific locations) PAC D 480-2169, DSN 254-2169 PAC D FAX 480-1215, PAC D FAX (TERM) 480-3421.** *Note: Permission/official approval required to visit KWA (see Appendix B).*

| IN ROUTE SCHEDULES | |
|---|---|
| **Hikam AFB** | PPP/HIK-1 |
| **March AFB** | PCM/RIV-4 |
| **Travis AFB** | PPM/SUU-9 |

*****IMPORTANT NOTE*****

Scheduled Military Services (U S ARMY, U S NAVY, USMC, USAF, USCG) flights by Service owned and operated aircraft and contractor furnished and operated aircraft change often with respect to the key elements of destination, routing, schedules, aircraft equipment, and mission. There are frequent, minor (and sometimes not so minor) adjustments made in these key elements with very limited prior notice. These unannounced changes are particularly true of MEDEVAC flight missions which are very sensitive to patient requirements. Many of the CONUS, OCONUS, and foreign country routes have been flown for more than 50 years with constant modification of some or all of these key elements to meet the needs of the Uniformed Services. We have provided the most current reported information concerning these key elements for this edition. Subsequent printings will contain the most current information at that press time. We encourage you to keep current on changes in **MILITARY SPACE-A AIR OPPORTUNITIES AROUND THE WORLD** by subscribing to our worldwide travel newsletter **Military Living's R & R SPACE-A REPORT** (Please see the central order coupons in the back of this book). Lastly, we encourage you to call or visit your intended Space-A departure location prior to registering for Space-A travel to obtain the latest information regarding the key elements of Space-A travel.

## BASE CLOSURES

The President approved on 13 July 1995 the recommendations of the 1995 Defense Base Closure and Realignment Commission (BRAC) and forwarded the Commission's report to Congress. The President noted that the recommendations meet important national security and budgetary goals and that savings resulting from the report are essential to maintain the operational readiness and modernization of our military forces. The Congress will have 45 legislative days to reject the entire package or it becomes law. Final action by the Congress is expected by early September 1995.

Previous directed closures in the Base Closure and Realignment Acts of October 1988, 1991 and September 1993 are so noted at the beginning of each listing affected with the DoD estimated date of closure. Some bases have already closed and consequently have been deleted from this directory. It should also be noted that all final closure dates will be established and may change as the DoD completes the final closure plans and funding becomes available to effect the closures. Also, only the bases with Space-A Passenger service have been addressed. There are no channel bases (major flights) contained in the 1995 base closure recommendations.

Lastly, it should be noted that all BRAC recommendations and actions apply only to domestic United States Bases (CONUS and OCONUS not foreign countries). The Secretary of Defense, acting within his authority, announced on 23 February 1995 the further reduction or realignment of United States Military Sites Overseas (in foreign countries). Any Space-A Passenger operations affected by this and previous announcements have been included/noted in this edition.

## - PHOTO CREDITS -

**Front Cover:** C-17 GLOBEMASTER III in flight.

Photograph provided courtesey Public Affairs Office, Air Mobility Command (AMC), Scott AFB, IL.

The C-17 is the newest, most flexible cargo aircraft to enter the airlift force. McDonnell Douglas Aerospace of Long Beach, CA, a division of McDonnell Douglas, is the prime contractor for the C-17 development and production. The C-17 is operated by the Air Mobility Command with initial operations at Charleston AFB/IAP, SC (CHS).

# CONTENTS

## CONTINENTAL UNITED STATES (CONUS)

NEW MEXICO



NEW YORK



NORTH CAROLINA



NORTH DAKOTA



OHIO



OKLAHOMA



OREGON



PENNSYLVANIA



RHODE ISLAND



SOUTH CAROLINA



SOUTH DAKOTA

## CARIBBEAN, CENTRAL & SOUTH AMERICA



## CUBA



## CYPRUS



## DENMARK



## EGYPT



## GERMANY



## GREECE

## SAUDI ARABIA



## SINGAPORE



## SPAIN



## THAILAND



## TURKEY



## UNITED ARAB EMIRATES



## UNITED KINGDOM



# APPENDICES

## RECENT MAJOR IMPROVEMENTS IN SPACE-A AIR OPPORTUNITIES

The below listed improvements in Space-A air travel are covered in the all new chapter 6 and relevant portions of chapter 1, Space-Available Travel, DoD 4515.13R, dated November 1994, issued February 1995.

### BOOKING FEE

The Space-A **Air Passenger Fee of $10.00 was eliminated** by the Assistant Secretary of Defense for all Space-A passengers on 1 February 1993. Since that time Space-A has been truly free except for in-flight meals and commercial airport departure and arrival processing fees at some Airports/Stations which are explained in **Appendix B Personnel Entrance Requirements.**

### ONE TIME SIGN-UP

Space-A passengers are now able to use their originating date of sign-up for Space-A eligibility when they change missions in route. Example: An active duty person signs up at Incirlik Apt, (Adana)TU (ADA) to go to Travis AFB, CA (SUU). The mission he/she takes goes only to Germany. Now, when he/she signs up at Ramstein AB, GE (RMS) for a different flight, **they will be able to use their originating sign-up date.** If they only get to Dover AFB, DE (DOV) and must sign up for another mission to go further, their sign up date will be the first sign-up date in Turkey. This will help Space-A personnel get to their destination with the knowledge they will not be stuck in a terminal because others had signed up earlier.

### REMOTE SIGN-UP

To compete for Space-A travel, eligible personnel must sign up on the Space-A roster in person and present all required documentation. The DoD Components/Services (and USCG) **may also accept sign up information in writing from eligible space-A travelers through mail, telefax transmission and courier.** The required telefax numbers are listed within each station listing where available. A copy of the Space Available Travel Request form is at Appendix F. You may photocopy this form. All categories of Space-A travelers may stay on the Space-A roster for 60 days after which they will be removed. All Space-A passengers dropped from the register may sign up again in their respective categories.

### SPACE-A CATEGORIES OF TRAVEL AND PRIORITIES OF MOVEMENT

Based on the new Space-A regulation, there are six categories of Space-A travel. Space-A travelers are placed in one of the six categories based on their status, e. g. active duty, retired and their situation, e.g. emergency leave, ordinary leave (vacation). Once accepted for movement, a Space-A passenger regardless of category, may not be 'bumped' by another Space-A passenger. The numerical order of Space-A categories indicates the precedent of movement. The order in which travelers are listed in a particular category does not indicate priority of movement in that category. In each category, transportation is furnished on a first-in, first-out basis. When the issue may arise, the local installation commander may change the priority of movement of any Space-A traveler for emergency or extreme humanitarian reason when the facts provided fully support such an exception.

### MILITARY LIVING'S R & R SPACE-A REPORT

The best way to find out what the news is on Space-A air travel is to become a subscriber to Military Living's *R&R Space-A Report®*. (See the Central Order Coupon in the back of this book) This all-ranks travel newsletter is a clearinghouse for all ranks. Information is included on Space-A Air opportunities around the world, temporary military lodging, military RV, camping and rec areas, and discounts in the civilian sector which enable military and their families to splurge and yet get high quality accommodations for less in the civilian sector.

# CONTINENTAL UNITED STATES

# ALABAMA

## BIRMINGHAM MUNICIPAL AIRPORT (BHM)

117th ARW/OTM, Air National Guard,
5401 Eastlake Blvd
Birmingham, AL 35217-3595

**LOCATION:** Exit I-59/20 at Tallapoosa St, north for 1/2 mile to a right on East Lake Blvd to Installation. *USMRA: Page 36 (D,E-4)*. NMC: located in the northeast section of Birmingham. Main installation numbers: C-205-841-9200, D-312-778-2210.

**PAX TERM INFO: C-205-841-9441, D-312-778-2441. FAX: 205-841-9219**, Bldg Base Ops. Hours vary Tue-Sun. Closed Mon. Call for flight information.

**PAX LOUNGES:** None. See Base Operations.

**FOOD SERVICE:** Vending machine: Hrs: 24 hours daily. Food services at Birmingham Municipal Airport.

**TRANSPORTATION: Bus (Comm):** Birmingham Municipal Airport, C-205-252-7171/205-323-1678. **Car rentals, Limo & Taxi:** Birmingham Municipal Airport, See telephone directory. Parking: None on ANG Base, use public parking at Birmingham Municipal Airport.

**TRAVELERS AID: American Red Cross:** 2225 3rd Ave N, Hrs: daily 0800-1200, C-205-322-5661. **Security Police:** located at main gate, Hrs: 24 hours daily, C-205-841-9240.

**ATTRACTIONS:** Vulcan (iron man statue) on Red Mountain in city and largest shopping mall in southeast.

| IN ROUTE SCHEDULES | |
|---|---|
| **Keesler AFB** | BIX/MEDEVAC-1 |

### UNSCHEDULED FLIGHTS

Few MEDEVAC Flights (1-2 weekly) via transient aircraft to CONUS. New KC-135E tankers will begin Space-A flights in late 1995.

*ALABAMA*

# CAIRNS ARMY AIRFIELD (OZR)

Building 30501
Fort Rucker, AL 36362-5000

**LOCATION:** Ninety miles SE of Montgomery, and 7 miles south of Ozark, off US-231 on Rt 249. Clearly marked. *USMRA: Page 36 (F,G-8)*. NMC: Dothan, 26 miles southeast. Main Installation Numbers: C-205-255-3156, D-312-558-1110.

**PAX TERM INFO: C-205-255-8564, D-312-558-8564.** Bldg: 30501, Hrs: daily 0730-1630 (L). Directions: From the main gate (Daleville), continue on AL-85 to Air Traffic Control tower/Base Ops, right turn to Bldg 30501.

**PAX LOUNGES: General:** Bldg 3010l, Hrs: 24 hours daily, C-205-255-8361, D-312-558-8361. A/C, telephone (commercial), TV, O/S seats. Also, pilot's lounge. DV/VIP: Bldg: 3010l, Hrs: Daily: 24hrs, C-205-255-8361, D-312-558-8361. A/C, telephones (commercial and defense), TV, restrooms, O/S seats. **Protocol Service:** D-312-558-3100.

**FOOD SERVICE: Cafeteria:** Bldg: 30101, C-205-598-6384-EX-69. **NCO/CPO Club:** Bldg 2908, C-205-598-2491. **O'Club:** Bldg 113, C-205-598-2426.

**TRANSPORTATION: Bus (Commercial):** Main gate. Greyhound C-205-774-5500 (in Ozark); Trailways C-205-598-2375 (Fort Rucker). **Limo Service:** (in Dothan): C-205-792-8100. Dothan to Ozark. **Taxi (Commercial):** Located in Daleville: C-205-598-2000.

**TML:** Lodging Office (Bldg 308), Hrs: 24 hours daily, C-205-255-3780, D-312-558-3780. All ranks. **DV/VIP:** C-205-255-3100, D-312-558-3100.

**TRAVELERS AID:** American Red Cross: Bldg 5315, C-205-255-1055/1101. **Military Police:** Bldg Main gate, C-205-255-2351.

**OTHER SERVICES:** Many support services. **Exchange:** Bldg 9214, C-205-598-0221. **Bank/Exchange:** C-205-598-2401. **Medical (Emergency):** Lyster Army Hospital, C-205-255-7900.

## UNSCHEDULED FLIGHTS

Unscheduled flights only. Most flights are via C-12C and U-21A aircraft. Most frequent destinations are: Washington DC/Baltimore, MD areas; Davison AAF, VA (**DAA**); and Langley AFB, VA (**LFI**) for Fort Monroe, VA. Most missions posted 12 hours in advance. Call for destinations and seat availability. Baggage limit is 30 lbs. Call Alabama OSA Flight Det, C-205-255-8563/8532, D-312-558-8563/8532.

# MAXWELL AIR FORCE BASE (MXF)

502nd LSS/LGTCP
Maxwell AFB, AL 36112-5000

**LOCATION:** In the west section of city. Take I-85 to I-65, exit on Day Street which leads to main gate of Base. *USMRA: Page 36 (E-6)*. NMC: Montgomery, 1.5 miles southeast. Main Installation Numbers: C-205-953-1110, D-312-493-1110.

**PAX TERM INFO: C-205-953-6454, D-312-493-6454, FAX: 205-953-4564, D-312-493-4564. Recording: C-205-953-6760, D-312-493-6760.** Bldg 844, Hrs: Mon-Fri 0700-1700, weekends and holidays as needed. Schedule received 24 hours in advance. Directions: Day Street to left on Ash Street, right on 1st Street. **Pax Service Office:** Same as PAX Terminal, C-205-953-7372, D-312-493-7372.

**PAX LOUNGES: General:** Bldg 844, Hrs: Mon-Fri 0700-1700, C-205-953-6454, D-312-493-6454. A/C, telephones (commercial and defense), TV, restrooms, P/C seats. DV/VIP: Bldg 844, Hrs: daily 0700-2300, C-205-953-5374, D-312-493-5374. A/C, coffee/tea served, telephones (commercial and defense), TV, restrooms, O/S seats (06+,GS15+). **Protocol Service:** Bldg 800, Hrs: Mon-Fri 0800-1700, C-205-953-2095, D-312-493-2095

**FOOD SERVICE: Cafeteria:** Bldg 1090, C-205-953-5720. Breakfast/lunch served. **Dining Hall:** Bldg 668/1420. C-205-953-5127, D-312-493-5127. **NCO Club:** Bldg 742, C-205-262-8364. **O'Club:** Bldg 144, C-205-264-6423. **Vending:** Bldg 844, C-205-953-5946.

**TRANSPORTATION:** Car rental, limo service and taxi off base. Telephone numbers at Terminal. **Air Tickets:** SATO, Bldg 924, offical travel: C-205-953-0076, leisure travel: C-205-263-5500. **Bus (Commercial):** Bldg 927, C-205-953-5038 (Maxwell AFB to Montgomery). **Taxi (Gov):** Bldg 927, C-205-953-5038 (duty passengers only). **Parking:** Bldg 843 (in front and across the street-short & long term).

**TML:** Lodging Office (Bldg 157, 351 West Dr.) Hrs: 24 hours daily, C-205-953-2401, D-312-493-2401, Fax: C-205-953-5696, d-312-493-5696. Extensive facilities. All ranks. **DV/VIP:** C-205-953-2095, D-312-493-2095.

**TRAVELERS AID: American Red Cross:** Bldg 18, C-205-953-5626. After duty hours, C-205-953-7333. **Chaplain:** Bldg 155, C-205-953-2111. After duty hours, C-205-953-2862. **Emergency Relief:** Bldg 500, C-205-953-2353. **Security Police:** Bldg 837, C-205-953-7222.

**OTHER SERVICES: Exchange:** Bldg 1090, C-205-834-5946. **Bank/Exchange:** Bldg 1081, C-205-832-8190. **Hair Styles:** Bldg 1090: Barber: C-205-263-3444; Beauty: C-

*ALABAMA*
*Maxwell Air Force Base*

205-263-3010. **Laundry/Dry Cleaning:** Bldg 1090, C-205-263-7826. **Medical:** Bldg 50, Hrs: Daily: 24hrs, C-205-953-2333.

**ATTRACTIONS:** Air University, W.H. Gayle Planetarium, state capital & historical homes in Montgomery including the Zoo, and the First White House of the Confederacy.

| IN ROUTE SCHEDULES | | |
|---|---|---|
| **Keesler AFB** | BIX/MEDEVAC-1 | BIX/MEDEVAC-2 |

**UNSCHEDULED FLIGHTS**

Frequent flights to: Andrews AFB, MD (**ADW**); Offutt AFB, NE (**OFF**); Randolph AFB, TX (**RND**); Scott AFB, IL (**BLV**); Wright-Patterson AFB, OH (**FFO**) and other CONUS locations. Note: Baggage limit is 30 pounds on all executive aircraft (C-12 & C-21).

## MOBILE COAST GUARD AVIATION TRAINING CENTER (MOB)

Commanding Officer
Mobile, AL 36608-9682

**LOCATION:** Take Airport Blvd exit, west from I-65, 8 miles from Base. Turn right on Schillinger Road, then left on Tanner Williams Road, 1 mile. Clearly marked. *USMRA: Page 36 (B-9)*. NMC: Mobile, 1 mile northwest. Main Installation Numbers: C-205-639-6110, D-312-436-3635, Flight Operations: D-312-436-3635.

**PAX TERM INFO: C-205-639-6161, D-312-436-3635, FTS-537-6161, FAX 205-639-6435**, Main hangar, Hrs: M-F: 0800-1600, Directions: North side of Bates Municipal Airport, 2nd deck on ramp side. No Pax lounge. Restrooms, vending machines available.

**TML:** Lodging Office C-205-639-6361.

**OTHER SERVICES: Exchange:** C-205-639-6390. **Enlisted Club:** C-205-639-6359. **Barber:** C-205-639-6494. **Medical:** C-205-639-6401.

**UNSCHEDULED FLIGHTS**

Infrequent flights only to East and Midwest. No overseas or helicopter Space-A.

## REDSTONE ARSENAL ARMY AIRFIELD (HUA)

Flight Ops Div, Attn: AMSMI-RA-FO
Redstone Arsenal, AL 35898-5320

**LOCATION:** Off US-231 on Martin Rd for main gate with visitor control. For uniformed personnel, Gate #8 is on Drake Ave. Take I-565 onto Jordan Lane, then west on Drake Ave. Drake Ave becomes Goss Rd on the Arsenal. *USMRA: Page 36 (E-1)*. NMC: Huntsville, adjacent north and east sides. Main Installation Numbers: C-205-876-2151, D-312-746-0011, F-876-1916.

*ALABAMA*
*Redstone Arsenal Army Airfield*

**PAX TERM INFO: C-205-876-1916, D-312-746-4290. FAX: 205-842-0562, D-312-788-0562**. Bldg 4809, Hrs: Mon-Fri 0700-1700, closed all national holidays. Directions: From Gate 8, take Goss Rd to Rideout Rd., left on Rideoute Rd to Hale Rd, right on Hale Rd to Base Ops.

**PAX LOUNGES:** Bldg 4809, Hrs: daily: 0630-1730, C-205-876-4290, D-312-746-1916. A/C, read/write room, telephones (commercial and defense), TV, restrooms, O/S seats. **Protocol Service:** Bldg 5250, Hrs: Duty hours, C-205-876-7135 (06+).

**FOOD Service: None on Airfield. Cafeteria:** Bldg 4488, C-205-876-9973. **Enlisted Club: Sports Haven:** Bldg 3479, C-205-881-6595. **NCO/CPO Club:** Bldg 1500, C-205-837-0750. **O'Club:** Bldg 130, C-205-830-2582. **Restaurants:** Bldg 3231, C-205-882-9631. **Snack Bars:** Bldg 3220, C-205-881-1591.

**TRANSPORTATION: Bus** (Commercial): Main gate. Greyhound C-205-536-5349, Trailways C-205-534-1681. **Taxi** (Gov): Bldg 3664, C-205-876-2261. Duty passengers only. **Car Rentals:** HUA, Jetplex, Avis C-205-772-9301, Hertz C-205-772-9331, National C-205-772-9336. **Parking:** limited, short term only.

**TML:** Lodging Office (Bldg 244), Hrs: daily 0700-1630, C-205-876-5713/8028, D-312-746-5713/8028, **FAX**: C-205-876-2929, D-312-746-2929. All ranks. DV/VIP: C-205-876-7135, D-312-746-7135.

**TRAVELERS AID: American Red Cross:** Bldg 3491, C-205-876-4427. **Chaplain:** Bldg 376, C-205-876-2409. **Security Police:** C-205-876-2222.

**OTHER SERVICES: Exchange:** Bldg 3220, C-205-883-6100. **Bank/Exchange:** C-205-883-0173. **Emergency Medical:** Fox Army Hospital, C-205-876-8621, D-312-746-8621.

**ATTRACTIONS:** Space & Rocket Center on Highway 20, Tennessee River.

| IN ROUTE SCHEDULES | |
|---|---|
| **Keesler AFB** | BIX/MEDEVAC-2 |

## UNSCHEDULED FLIGHTS

All flights are unscheduled. Missions are posted 24 hours in advance when possible. Most flights are to Wright-Patterson AFB, OH (**FFO**), Huntsville IAP (**NSV**) and to the Midwest, including Lambert-St Louis IAP, MO (**STL**), Kansas City Downtown Airport, MO (**MKC**), and Kansas City IAP, MO (**MCI**). Call for availability of flights and seats. Baggage limit is 30 pounds.

# ARIZONA

## DAVIS-MONTHAN AIR FORCE BASE (DMA)

355 TRNS/TRTI
5275 E. Granite St.
Davis-Monthan AFB, AZ 85707-3017

**LOCATION:** Southeast of Tucson. Exit I-10 North Kolb Rd, left on Golflinks Rd., left on Craycroft Rd to main gate. *USMRA: Page 108 (F-9)*. NMC: Tucson, 3 miles northwest. Main Installation Number: C-602-750-3900, D-312-361-1110.

**PAX TERM INFO: C-602-750-3641, D-312-361-3641, FAX/Remote Sign-up: C-602-750-7229, D-312-361-7229**. Bldg 4819, Hrs: Mon-Fri 0700-1600, Recording operated after hours. Directions: Continue on Craycroft Rd to Tempe St to right on Phoenix St, Pax Term on left next to Base Ops. **Pax Service Office:** Same as PAX Terminal.

**PAX LOUNGES:** No family lounge. **General:** Bldg 4819, Hrs: Mon-Fri 0700-1600, C-602-750-3641, D-312-361-3641. A/C, baggage check, (commercial and defense) telephones, restrooms, TV, O/S seats. **DV/VIP:** Bldg 4820, Hrs: 24 hours daily, C-602-750-4315, D-312-361-4315. A/C, TV, telephones (commercial and defense), showers, O/S seats, restrooms, coffee/tea served. Contact Base Ops in advance (06+ and VIP). **Protocol Service:** Bldg 2300, Hrs: Mon-Fri 0700-1600, C-602-750-3600, D-312-361-3600 (06+ and VIP). Air Combat Command sponsored.

**FOOD SERVICE: Burger King:** Bldg 2521, C-602-745-2878. **Desert Inn:** Bldg 4100, C-602-750-3072, D-312-361-3072. **In-Flight Kitchen:** Bldg 5428, Hrs: Mon-Fri: 1030-1330, 1730-2030, C-602-750-3532. **NCO Club:** Bldg 4455, C-602-750-3100, D-312-361-3100. **Cabana Pizza:** Dine-in/Take-out/Delivery: C-602-747-3234. **O'Club:** Bldg 2050, C-602-750-3301. **Snack Bar:** (AAFES) Bldg 2441, C-602-790-6150.

**TRANSPORTATION:** Commercial Air Tickets: **SATO (Offical Travel)** Bldg 2300, Mon-Fri, Hrs: 0700-1600, C-602-750-4841, D-312-361-4841. **SATO (Leisure travel)** Bldg 4430, Mon-Fri, Hrs: 0900-1800, Sat 1000-1500, C-602-748-1942. **Bus (Comm):** Base Exchange parking lot, Bldg 2441, C-602-792-9222. **Rental Car:** Enterprise Rent-A-Car: (AAFES) Bldg 4432, C-602-571-0886. **Taxi (Comm):** ABC: C-602-623-7979, Allstate: C-602-881-2227, Checker: C-602-623-1133, Yellow Cab, C-602-624-6611. **Parking:** Bldg 4819, C-602-750-3641, D-312-361-3641.

**TML:** Bldg 2350, Hrs: 24 hours daily, C-602-748-3230, D-312-361-3230. All ranks. DV/VIP: Wing Protocol: Bldg 2300, Hrs: Mon-Fri 0700-1600, C-602-750-3600, D-312-361-3600.

**TRAVELERS AID: American Red Cross:** Bldg 4300, C-602-750-3205, D-312-361-3205. **Chaplain:** Bldg 3205, C-602-750-5411, D-312-361-5411. **Emergency Relief:** Family Support Center: (Air Force Aid Society) Bldg 3210, C-602-750-3891, D-312-361-

3891. **Lost/Found:** Bldg 4819, C-602-750-3641, D-312-361-3641. **Security Police:** Bldg 4413, C-602-750-3517, D-312-361-3517.

**OTHER SERVICES: Exchange:** Bldg 2441, C-602-748-7887. **Bank/Exchange:** Bank of America: Bldg 2317, C-602-792-7025. **Hair Styles:** Bldg 2441, Barber: C-602-571-1604; Beauty: C-602-748-8334. **Laundry:** Bldg 5000 (near Civilian Base Personnel Office (CBPO)), Hrs: 24 hours daily. **Medical:** Bldg 400, Hrs: 24 hours daily, C-602-750-3878 (Emergency). **Postal/Wire:** Military: Bldg 2240, C-602-750-4571, D-312-361-4571. Civilian: Bldg 2240, C-602-748-1651.

**ATTRACTIONS:** Old movie sets, Pima Air Museum, Arizona-Sonora Desert Museum, Zoo, Colossal Cave, Saguaro National Monument.

| IN ROUTE SCHEDULES | |
|---|---|
| **Scott AFB** | BLV/MEDEVAC-8 |
| **Travis AFB** | SUU/MEDEVAC-1 |

**UNSCHEDULED FLIGHTS**

Flights to: Kirtland AFB, NM (**ABQ**); North Island NAS, CA (**NZY**); Phoenix IAP, AZ (**PHX**); Travis AFB, CA (**SUU**) and other CONUS locations.

## LIBBY ARMY AIRFIELD (FHU)

Fort Huachuca, AZ 85613-6000

**LOCATION:** From I-10 take AZ-90 south to Sierra Vista and main gate of post. *USMRA: Page 108 (F,G-9,10)*. NMC: Tucson, 75 miles northwest. Main installation numbers: C-602-538-7111, D-312-879-0111.

**PAX TERM INFO: C-602-538-2860.** Call for flight information.

**FOOD SERVICE: O'Club:** C-602-533-2193. **Snack Bar:** C-602-533-5759. **NCO Club:** C-602-533-3802.

**TML:** Lodging office (Bldg 43083, Service Rd), Hrs: 24 hours daily, C-602-533-2222/5361, D-312-821-5950. FAX: C-602-458-0459. DV/VIP: C-602-533-1231, D-312-821-1231

**TRAVELERS AID: Security Police:** Located at main gate, Hrs: 24 hours daily, C-602-533-2181/3000.

**ATTRACTIONS:** Fort museum. Original cantonment a National Historical Landmark. Tombstone, 25 minute drive on Charleston Road.

**UNSCHEDULED FLIGHTS**

Flights to Midwestern and Farwest locations via Army executive aircraft. Baggage limit is 30 lbs. Call for destinations, routings and schedules.

*ARIZONA*

# LUKE AIR FORCE BASE (LUF)

56th OSS/OSAA, 7254 N. Fighter Country Ave., Suite 2,
Luke AFB, AZ 85309-1215

**LOCATION:** From Phoenix, west on I-10 to Litchfield Rd. North on Litchfield Rd, approximately 7 miles. Also, from Phoenix on US-60 to AZ-89 to Glendale Avenue. West on Glendale Ave to intersection of Glendale Ave and Litchfield Rd, approximately 10 miles. *USMRA: Page 108 (D-6,7)*. NMC: Phoenix, 20 miles southeast. Main installation numbers: C-602-856-7411, D-312-853-0111.

**PAX TERM INFO: C-602-856-7131, D-312-853-7131, REC: C-602-856-7016, D-312-853-7016.** Bldg 453, Hrs: Mon-Fri 0630-2230, Sat-Sun-Hol: 0730-1800. Directions:From main gate west on Eagle St to left on Fighter Country Ave to Terminal on flight line.

**PAX LOUNGES: General:** Bldg 453. See Pax Term, C-602-856-7016/7131. A/C, baggage check, read/write room, telephones (commercial and defense), TV, restrooms, P/C seats. **DV/VIP:** Bldg 453. See Pax Term, C-602-856-6087, D-312-853-6087. Located in the rear wing of the Terminal. **Protocol Service:** Bldg 11, Hrs: Mon-Fri 0730-1630, D-312-853-5840 (07+). AETC.

**FOOD SERVICE:** Many support services on and off Base. **Dining Hall:** Bldg 543, C-602-856-6420/7097, D-312-853-6420/7097. **NCO/CPO Club:** Bldg 161, C-602-856-7136. **O'Club:** Bldg 750, C-602-856-6446. **Run-In-Chef:** Bldg 1540, C-602-935-4029. **Vending:** Bldg 453, Hrs: 24 hours daily, C-602-269-5879.

**TRANSPORTATION: Air Tickets:** SATO: Bldg 1150 Hrs: Mon-Fri 0730-1630, C-602-856-6891. **Taxi (Gov):** Bldg 330, C-602-856-6866, other hours C-602-856-3702. **Parking:** Bldg 453, C-602-856-7131, D-312-853-7131. Unlimited parking.

**TML:** Lodging Office (Bldg 660, Bong Lane), Hrs: 24 hours daily, C-602-856-3941, D-312-853-3941. All ranks. **DV/VIP:** C-602-856-5840, D-312-853-5840.

**TRAVELERS AID: American Red Cross:** Bldg 1150, C-602-856-7823. **Chaplain:** Bldg 799, C-602-856-6211. **Security Police:** Bldg 179, C-602-856-6322.

**OTHER SERVICES: Exchange:** Bldg 1540, C-602-935-2671, D-312-863-2671. **Bank/Exchange:** 1st Natl Bank of AZ, C-602-935-3382. Located directly across from main gate. **Hair Styles:** Bldg 1540: Barber: C-602-935-3466; Beauty: C-602-935-5850. **Laundry/Dry Cleaning:** Bldg 1540, C-602-935-9554. **Medical:** Bldg 1130, Hrs: 24 hours daily, C-602-856-7506, D-312-853-7506. **Postal:** Bldg 550, C-602-935-1343.

**ATTRACTIONS:** Colorful Scottsdale nearby, fairgrounds and coliseum in Phoenix (state capital), Arizona State University in Tempe, Sun City—largest retirement center in the world.

| IN ROUTE SCHEDULES | |
|---|---|
| **Scott AFB** | BLV/MEDEVAC-8 |
| **Travis AFB** | SUU/MEDEVAC-1 |

## SKY HARBOR INTERNATIONAL AIRPORT (PHX)

161st ARG/DO
2001 South 32nd Street
Phoenix, AZ 85034-6098

**LOCATION:** Exit 152 off I-10 or I-17 north. *USMRA: Page 108 (DE-7)*. NMC: Phoenix, 3 miles northwest. Main installation numbers: C-602-231-8000, D-312-853-9000.

**PAX TERM INFO: C-602-231-8162, D-312-853-9162, REC: C-602-231-8058, D-312-853-9058, FAX: C-602-231-8288, D-312-853-9288**, Operations, Tue-Fri, Hrs: 0630-1600.

**OTHER SERVICES:** Facilities of an IAP available. Commercial taxi/hotel shuttle available from ANGB to IAP. **SATO:** ANG Hq, Hrs: Mon-Fri: 0730-1530, C-602-220-0774. **Security Police:** Hrs: Daily: 24hrs, C-602-231-8133.

**UNSCHEDULED FLIGHTS**

Space-A flights are available via KC-135E aircraft to CONUS and OCONUS locations. Call prior to arrival for flight info and specific directions.

## YUMA MARINE CORPS AIR STATION (YUM)

Traffic Management Officer,
Marine Corps Air Base, Western Area
Yuma MCAS, AZ 85369-5000

**LOCATION:** From I-8 take Exit 3E South for 1 mile to Base on right, adjacent to Yuma IAP. *USMRA: Page 108 (A-8)*. NMC: Yuma, 3 miles northwest. Main installation numbers: C-602-341-2011, D-312-951-2011.

**PAX TERM INFO: C-602-341-2729, D-312-951-2729**. Bldg 151, Hrs: Mon-Fri 0600-1530, weekends as needed. Directions: From main gate straight on Quitter St to a right on O'Neill St. Pax Term is on the left. **Pax Service Office:** Bldg 151, Hrs: Mon-Fri 0600-1530, weekends as needed, C-602-341-2729. NCO on duty. **Pax Paging:** Bldg 151, Hrs: Mon-Fri: 0600-1530, C-602-341-2729.

**PAX LOUNGES:** No family lounges. **GENERAL:** Bldg 151, Hrs: Mon-Fri: 0600-1530, weekends as needed, C-602-341-2729. A/C, bag check, restrooms, P/C seats, telephones. **DV/VIP:** Bldg 151, Hrs: daily: 0600-1530, C-602-341-2729. A/C, bag check, restrooms, P/C seats, telephones. **Protocol Service:** Bldg 980, Hrs: Mon-Fri: 0600-1530, C-602-341-2252, D-312-951-2252.

**FOOD SERVICE: Cafeteria:** C-602-341-2369. **Enlisted Club:** C-602-341-2457. **O'Club:** C-602-341-2711. **Restaurants:** Godfather's Pizza: C-602-341-0150, **Burger King:** C-602-341-0490, **Deli:** C-602-725-5706. **Vending:** C-602-341-2294/5.

*ARIZONA*
*YUMA MARINE CORPS AIR STATION*

**TRANSPORTATION:** Limited on Base. **Air Tickets:** C-602-341-2755. Major airline counters. **Car Rentals:** Avis: C-602-341-0104. Additional car rental companys at Yuma IAP. **Taxi (Comm):** Yuma IAP, Hrs: Daily: 24hrs, C-602-782-0111.

**TML:** Lodging Office (Bldg 1020, Thomas Ave), Hrs: 24 hours daily, C-602-341-3578, D-312-951-3578. All Ranks. **DV/VIP:** C-602-341-2262.

**TRAVELERS AID: American Red Cross:** C-602-341-2427. **Chaplain:** C-602-341-2371. **Emergency Relief:** C-602-341-2373/4 (Navy Relief). **Security Police:** Bldg 950, C-602-341-2205/2361.

**OTHER SERVICES: Exchange:** C-602-341-2256. **Bank/Exchange:** First Interstate, C-602-343-7840. **Hair Styles:** Barber: C-602-341-2364; Beauty: C-602-341-2364. **Laundry/Dry Cleaning:** C-602-341-2356. **Medical:** Bldg 1175, Hrs: Daily: 24hrs, C-602-341-2772. **Postal:** C-602-341-2033. **Wire:** C-602-341-3567.

**ATTRACTIONS:** Desert climate, greyhound racing, major league baseball training, Territorial Prison.

**UNSCHEDULED FLIGHTS**

Flights to: Beaufort MCAS, SC (**NBC**); Camp Pendelton MCAF, CA (**NFG**); Cherry Point MCAS, NC (**NKT**); El Toro MCAS, CA (**NZJ**)(Weekly); Fallon NAS, NV (**NFL**); North Island NAS, CA (**NZY**); Twentynine Palms MCAS, CA (**NXP**); and other locations as needed. Call for destinations, routings, and schedules.

# ARKANSAS

## LITTLE ROCK AIR FORCE BASE (LRF)

314th TRNS/LGTAP
3911 Avenue B
Little Rock AFB, AR 72099-5000

**LOCATION:** Use US-67/167 to Jacksonville, AR, take AFB exit to main gate. *USMRA: Page 76 (D,E-5)*. NMC: Little Rock, 18 miles southwest. Main installation numbers: C-501-988-3131, D-312-731-1110.

**PAX TERM INFO: C-501-988-3684, D-312-731-3684**, Recording after hours. Bldg 430, Hrs: daily 0730-1630. Directions: Main gate on Vandenberg Blvd for 1.2 miles to a left on 3rd St for a block, to Thomas Ave. Pax terminal located at the corner of Thomas and 3rd Streets. **Pax Service Office:** Bldg 430, Hrs: Mon-Fri 0730-1630, C-501-988-3933/3342, D-312-731-3933/3342. **Remote FAX Sign-up:** (501)-988-6726.

**PAX LOUNGES:** Bldg 272. General lounge restricted to passengers awaiting processing. Lobby, A/C, couch, restrooms, TV. DV/VIP: Bldg 120, Hrs: 24 hours daily, C-501-988-6123. A/C, restrooms, O/S seats.

**FOOD SERVICE: Dining Hall:** Bldg 864, Hrs: daily 0530-1800, C-501-988-6268/3427. **Bowling Alley:** Bldg 956 Hrs: Sun-Thu 0900-2200, Fri-Sat 0900-2400, C-501-988-3338. **Champs Snack Bar:** Bldg 868, Hrs: Mon-Fri 1100-2200, Sat 1200-2400, Sun: 1200-2200, C-501-988-3908. **Enlisted Club:** Bldg 1080. Hrs: Sun, Tue-Thu 1000-2200, Fri-Sat 1030-2300 (closed Monday), C-501-988-4121. **O'Club:** Bldg 1030, Hrs: Mon-Sat: 1000-2200, Sun: 1000-1400, C-501-988-1111.

**TRANSPORTATION: Worldwide Travel,** C-501-982-7551. **Air Tickets:** SATO: Bldg 1255, Hrs: Mon-Fri 0730-1630, C-501-988-4117. **Car Rentals:** No car rentals on base. **Taxi (Comm):** Off Base, Hrs: 24 hours daily, Jacksonville Taxi Co.: C-501-982-1500, Black & White: C-501-374-0333. $25+ to Little Rock. **Taxi (Gov):** Bldg 551, Hrs: 24 hours daily, C-501-988-6086 (duty passengers only). **Parking:** Bldg 430, Hrs: 24 hours daily, short-term terminal; long term-contact Security Police, C-501-988-3221, or use unsecured long-term at Bldg 430.

**TML:** Lodging Office (Bldg 1192), Hrs: 24 hours daily, C-501-988-6753/1141, D-312-731-6552, FAX: C-501-988-7769, D-312-731-7769. All ranks. DV/VIP: C-501-988-6828/3588, lodging available to retirees on a space-a basis.

**TRAVELERS AID: American Red Cross:** Bldg 840, Hrs: Mon-Fri 0730-1630, C-501-988-3249. After hours, call the operator. **Chaplain:** Bldg 950, Hrs: Mon-Fri 0730-1630, C-501-988-6014. After hours, call the operator. **Lost/Found:** Bldg 430, Hrs: daily 0730-1630, C-501-988-3933. **Security Police:** Bldg 480, Hrs: 24 hours daily, C-501-988-3221.

***ARKANSAS***
***Little Rock Air Force Base***

**OTHER SERVICES: Exchange:** Bldg 940, Hrs: Mon-Sat 0900-2100, Sun: 1100-1800, C-501-988-1150. **Bank/Exchange:** Bldg 970, Hrs: Mon-Thu 0900-1600, Fri 0900-1800, C-501-982-4521. **Hair Styles:** Bldg 959, Hrs: Mon-Fri 1000-1800, Sat-Sun 1000-1700, C-501-988-1150. **Laundry/Dry Cleaning:** Bldg 959, Hrs: daily 0700-1800, C-501-988-1150. **Medical:** Base Hospital, Hrs: daily 0730-2000, C-501-988-8811. **Postal:** Bldg 966, Hrs: Mon-Fri 0900-1630, Sat 0830-1200, C-501-988-3695.

**ATTRACTIONS:** Little Rock, Governor's Mansion, Arkansas River, Ozark Mountains, Burns Park, Hot Springs and Lake Conway.

| ORIGINATING SCHEDULES | | | |
|---|---|---|---|
| | **ACC/LRF-1 2nd TUE C-130E** | | |
| **Location ID** | **Airport (Station)** | **Country/State** | **Days Out** |
| LRF | Little Rock AFB | AR | +0 |
| NGU | Norfolk NAS | VA | +1 |
| **NRR** | **Roosevelt Roads NAS** | **PR** | **+2** |
| NGU | Norfolk NAS | VA | +3 |
| LRF | Little Rock AFB | AR | |
| | **ACC/LRF-2 3rd THU C-130E** | | |
| LRF | Little Rock AFB | AR | +0 |
| NGU | Norfolk NAS | VA | +0 |
| **NRR** | **Roosevelt Roads NAS** | **PR** | **+1** |
| NGU | Norfolk NAS | VA | +1 |
| LRF | Little Rock AFB | AR | |
| | **ACC/LRF-3 2nd THU C-130E** | | |
| LRF | Little Rock AFB | AR | +0 |
| NGU | Norfolk NAS | VA | +0 |
| NRR | Roosevelt Roads NAS | PR | +1 |
| **KIN** | **Norman Manley IAP** | **JM** | **+1** |
| NRR | Roosevelt Roads NAS | PR | +2 |
| NGU | Norfolk NAS | VA | +2 |
| LRF | Little Rock AFB | AR | |
| | **ACM/LRF-4 3rd SUN C-130E** | | |
| LRF | Little Rock AFB | AR | +0 |
| NGU | Norfolk NAS | VA | +1 |
| NRR | Roosevelt Roads NAS | PR | +1 |
| **SJH** | **V C Bird IAP** | **AN** | **+2** |
| NRR | Roosevelt Roads NAS | PR | +2 |
| NGU | Norfolk NAS | VA | +3 |
| LRF | Little Rock AFB | AR | |

| IN ROUTE SCHEDULES | |
|---|---|
| **Scott AFB** | BLV/MEDEVAC-10 |

**UNSCHEDULED FLIGHTS**

Flights to CONUS, OCONUS and foreign countries. Including flights to: St. Croix, VI;(STX) Hickam AFB, HI (HIK); and Norfolk NAS, VA (NGU).Weekly schedule is received each Friday for the Fr-Sa flights. Call for destinations, routings and schedules.

**—— NOTES ——**

# CALIFORNIA

## ALAMEDA NAVAL AIR STATION (NGZ)

Operations Department
Alameda NAS, CA 94501-5000
**Scheduled to close 12/31/97**

**LOCATION:** From Nimitz Freeway, I-880 South, take the Broadway/Alameda exit. I-880 North, take Broadway Exit (I-880 North does not say Alameda). Directions to NAS clearly marked. *USMRA: Page 119 (D-5)*. NMC: Oakland, 2 miles northeast. Main installation numbers: C-510-263-0111, D-312-993-0111.

**PAX TERM INFO: C-510-263-3346, D-312-686-3346, REC: C-510-263-3347, D-312-686-3347,** updated daily. Bldg 77, Hrs: Mon-Fri: 0930-1800, call for Space-A register info. Directions: South end of Taxiway, 2 blocks north of East Gate and 5 blocks west of main gate. **Pax Service Office:** Bldg 77, Hrs: Mon-Fri: 0930-1800, C-510-263-3343. **Pax Paging:** Bldg 77, Hrs: Mon-Fri: 0930-1800, C-510-263-3346.

**PAX LOUNGES:** No family lounge at Air Terminal. **General:** Bldg 77, Hrs: Mon-Fri 0930-1800, C-510-263-3346, telephones (local, long distance and defense), restrooms, P/C seats.

**FOOD SERVICE: Cafeteria:** Bldg 2, C-510-263-6306. **Anchor Lounge:** Bldg 264, C-510-263-4639. **Enlisted Club:** Bldg 4, C-510-263-2931. **NCO/CPO Club:** Bldg 285, C-510-263-4441. **O'Club:** Bldg 60, C-510-263-3241. **Restaurants:** McDonalds: Bldg 119, C-510-521-4700. **Snack Bars:** Bowling Alley: Bldg 2, C-510-263-6308. **Vending:** Bldg 77, C-510-263-3530.

**TRANSPORTATION: Air Tickets:** Bldg 271, C-510-263-3208/3 (SATO). **Bus (Comm):** Bldg 77, C-510-839-2882. NGZ to OAK, Greyhound: C-510-834-3212, Trailways: C-510-444-5600. **Car Rentals:** All major rentals within 6 miles of Base. **Taxi (Comm):** Bldg 77, (Goodwill, Veterans, & Yellow). **Parking:** Bldg 77, short term-Lot 158, south of Bldg 77 (15 spaces); long term-Lot 120, 1 block from Term (10 days). Call Security Police for info/assistance, C-510-263-3053.

**TML:** Lodging Office (Bldg 17, "B" St), Hrs: Mon-Fri: 0800-1600, C-510-263-3649, D-312-993-3649. Navy Lodge: C-510-523-4917 or 1-800-NAVY-INN. DV/VIP: C-510-263-3000, O7+.

**TRAVELERS AID: American Red Cross:** Bldg 135, C-510-263-2615, after hours C-510-834-6656. **Chaplain:** Bldg 135, C-510-263-3740. **Emergency Relief:** Bldg 135, C-510-263-3740 (Navy Relief). **Lost/Found:** Bldg 77, C-510-263-3754. **Security Police:** Bldg 30, C-510-263-3756. **USO:** OAK IAP, C-510-562-3448.

**OTHER SERVICES: Exchange:** Bldg 118, C-510-748-8140. **Credit Union:** Bldg 62, C-510-865-3500. No bank on Base. **Hair Styles:** Bldg 118: Barber: C-510-263-6238; Beauty: C-510-523-1400. **Laundry/Dry Cleaning:** Bldg 118, Hrs: Tue-Sat 0900-1700, C-510-748-8139. **Medical:** Bldg 16, Hrs: 24 hours daily, C-510-263-2761. **Postal:** Bldg 18, C-510-263-4269.

**ATTRACTIONS:** San Francisco Bay area.

**UNSCHEDULED FLIGHTS**

Frequent daily flights to: Fallon NAS, NV (**NFL**); Lemoore NAS, CA (**NLC**); McChord AFB, WA (**TCM**); North Island NAS, CA (**NZY**); San Diego CGAS, CA (**SAN**); and Whidbey Island NAS, WA (**NUW**). Infrequent flights to: Dallas NAS, TX (**NBE**); Glenview NAS, IL (**NBU**); Jacksonville NAS, FL (**NIP**); Memphis NAS, TN (**NQA**); Norfolk NAS, VA (**NGU**); Salt Lake City IAP, UT (**SLC**); and Willow Grove NAS, PA (**NXX**). There are very few flights & seats available for overseas stations.

# BEALE AIR FORCE BASE (BAB)

9th TRANS/LGTX-A
Beale AFB, CA 95903-1615

**LOCATION:** From CA-70 north, exit south of Marysville, to North Beale Rd, continue for 10 miles until road dead-ends at main gate. *USMRA: Page 110 (C,D-5,6)*. NMC: Sacramento, 40 miles southwest. Main installation numbers: C-916-634-3000, D-312-368-3000, F-634-XXXX.

**PAX TERM INFO: C-916-634-8388, D-312-368-8388.** Bldg 1062, Hrs: Mon-Fri 0700-1600. Directions: One block north of ATC tower. Main gate: Beale Rd to left on J St, to left on Doolittle Dr to Pax Term on left. **Pax Service Office:** Same as Pax Term. **Pax Paging:** Same as Pax Term.

**PAX LOUNGES:** Bldg 1062, Hrs: Mon-Fri 0700-1600, C-916-634-8387, D-312-368-8387. Bag check, telephones (commercial and defense), TV, restrooms. **Protocol Service:** Bldg 1086, Hrs: Mon-Fri 0730-1630, C-916-634-2564, D-312-368-2564.

**FOOD SERVICE: NCO/CPO Club:** Bldg 5800, C-916-788-0286 (Also EM Club). **O'Club:** Bldg 2340, C-916-788-0292. **Snack Bars:** Bldg 1060, C-916-788-1550.

**TRANSPORTATION:** Limited. POV (Privately Owned Vehicle) desirable. **Air Tickets:** Bldg 2432, C-916-634-2940 (SATO). **Bus (Shuttle):** Bldg 1060 (across street from Term), C-916-634-2543. **Taxi (Comm):** Marysville, C-916-743-4661. **Taxi (Gov):** Bldg 2491, C-916-634-2543. **Parking:** Bldg 1060, short & long term, adjacent to Term, C-916-634-8387.

**TML:** Lodging Office (Gold Country Inn, Bldg 24112, "B" St), 24 hrs daily, C-916-634-2953, D-312-368-2953, FAX 916-634-3674, DSN FAX 312-368-3674. All ranks. DV/VIP: C-916-634-2120, O6+.

**TRAVELERS AID: American Red Cross:** Bldg 2179, C-916-634-2078, After duty hours, call Operator. **Chaplain:** Bldg 5700, C-916-634-2306, After duty hours call

*CALIFORNIA*
***Beale Air Force Base, continued***

Operator. **Lost/Found:** Bldg 1062, C-916-634-8387. **Security Police:** Bldg 2440, C-916-634-2131.

**OTHER SERVICES: Exchange:** Bldg 2434, C-916-788-0221. **Bank/Exchange:** Bldg 2433, C-916-634-2251. **Hair Styles:** Bldg 2434, C-916-788-0053. **Laundry/Dry Cleaning:** Bldg 2434, C-916-788-0192. **Medical:** Bldg 5700, Hrs: 24 hours daily, C-916-634-4444/2333 (Emergency). **Postal:** Bldg 2483, C-916-634-2766.

**ATTRACTIONS:** Sutter's Fort, zoo, Old Sacramento (rebuilding Chinatown).

**UNSCHEDULED FLIGHTS**

Infrequent flights to CONUS and OCONUS locations. Call for destinations, routings and schedules.

## CHINA LAKE NAVAL WEAPONS CENTER (NID)

Air Terminal, Code 6111
China Lake NWC, CA 93555-6001

**LOCATION:** From US-395 or CA-14, take CA-178 to Ridgecrest and the main gate. *USMRA: Page 111 (G-10,11,12 & H-11, 12)*. NMC: Los Angeles, 150 miles south. Main installation numbers: C-619-939-9011, D-312-437-9011.

**PAX TERM INFO: C-619-939-5301/5282, D-312-437-5308/5267, FAX: 616-446-7204.** Bldg 20002, Hrs: Mon-Fri 0630-2200, Sat-Sun 0730-1600, (only if flight ops are open, otherwise secured during non-flight ops hours). **Pax Service Office:** Bldg 20002, Hrs: Mon-Fri: 0700-1600, C-619-939-5301/5282, D-312-437-5308/5267.

**TML:** Lodging Office, Bldg 1395, C-619-939-3146/2383/3039. DV/VIP: C-619-939-1364, D-312-437-1364, O6+.

**UNSCHEDULED FLIGHTS**

Daily flights to Point Mugu NAS, CA (**NTD**). Unscheduled flights to civilian and military locations in CA, NM, NV, and AZ.

## EDWARDS AIR FORCE BASE (EDW)

412 OSS/OSAM
85 S. Flightline Rd.
Edwards AFB, CA 93524-5000

**LOCATION:** Eighteen miles east of Rosamond, and 30 miles northeast of Lancaster, off CA-14. Also, 10 miles southwest of Boron, off CA-58. *USMRA: Page 111 (F,G-12)*.

NMC: Los Angeles, 90 miles southwest. Main installation numbers: C-805-277-1110, D-312 527-1110.

**PAX TERM INFO: C-805-277-4412/4185, D-312-527-2222, FAX: C-805-277-5544.** Bldg 1200, Hrs: daily 0600-2200. Direction: From west gate, Rosamond Blvd, right on Fitzgerald Blvd, left on Wolfe Ave. **Pax Service Office:** Bldg 1200, Hrs: daily: 0600-2200, C-805-277-3571, D-312-527-3571. **Pax Paging:** Bldg 1200, Hrs: daily: 0600-2200, C-805-277-7667.

**PAX LOUNGES:** No separate family lounge. **General:** Bldg 1200, Hrs: Daily: 0600-2200, C-805-277-2222, D-312-527-2222. A/C, bag check, telephones, TV, restrooms, O/S seats. **DV/VIP:** Bldg 1200, Hrs: daily 0600-2200, C-805-277-3326, D-312-527-3326 (06+). A/C, telephones, O/S seats. **Protocol Service:** Bldg 2650, Hrs: Mon-Fri 0730-1630, C-805-277-3326, D-312-527-3326.

**FOOD SERVICE: NCO Club:** Bldg 5620, C-805-277-3230. **O'Club:** Bldg 5600, C-805-277-2830. **Snack Bars:** Bldg 1200, C-805-258-5696. **Burger King:** Bldg 6005, C-805-258-5987. **Vending:** Bldg 1200, C-805-277-2222.

**TRANSPORTATION:** Limited on Base. **Air Tickets:** SATO: Bldg 2670, C-805-277-3160. **Bus (Shuttle):** Bldg 1200, C-805-277-2620 (on Base). **Car Rentals:** Bldg 2110, C-805-258-8023. **Taxi (Gov):** Bldg 3510, C-805-277-2620 (duty Pax only). **Parking:** Bldg 1200, C-805-277-2222.

**TML:** Lodging Office (Bldg 5602), Hrs: 24 hours daily, C-805-277-3394/4101, D-312-527-3394/4101, FAX 805-277-2517, DSN FAX 312-527-2517. All ranks. DV/VIP: C-805-277-3326, O7+/SES .

**TRAVELERS AID: American Red Cross:** Bldg 2500, C-805-277-2845. **Chaplain:** Bldg 2700, C-805-277-6976. **Security Police:** Bldg 2860, C-805-277-3340.

**OTHER SERVICES:** Full Base support facilities available. **Exchange:** Bldg 7210, C-805-258-6573. **Medical:** Bldg 5500, Hrs: 24 hours daily, C-805-277-2330, D-312-527-2330 (Emergency).

**ATTRACTIONS:** NASA Space Shuttle Landing Site, Mojave Desert area, historic mining, and ghost towns.

| IN ROUTE SCHEDULES | |
|---|---|
| **Travis AFB** | SUU/MEDEVAC-3 |

# EL CENTRO NAVAL AIR FACILITY (NJK)

El Centro, CA 92243-5001

**LOCATION:** Take I-8, 2 miles west of El Centro to Forrester Rd exit. Right on Forrester Road. Continue 1.5 miles to left on Even Hewes Hwy (west) for 4 miles, then right on Bennet Road to main gate. *USMRA: Page 111 (H-15,16)*. NMC: El Centro, 7 miles east. Main installation numbers: C-619-339-2408, D-312-958-8408.

**PAX TERM INFO: C-619-339-2426, D-312-958-8426.** Bldg 519, Hrs: Mon-Sat 0700-2300.

**TML:** Lodging Office, (Bldg 270, B & 2nd St), C-619-339-2535, D-312-958-8535, FAX 619-339-2943. Navy Inn: C-619-339-2478 or 1-800-NAVY-INN. DV/VIP: C-619-339-8535.

**OTHER SERVICES:** Good Pax lounge and Full Base support facilities.

**UNSCHEDULED FLIGHTS**

Two to three days notice on Space-A flights. Most flights via C-009/B aircraft to CONUS locations. Call before going to Base.

## EL TORO MARINE CORPS AIR STATION (NZJ)

Air Freight/Passenger Terminal
El Toro MCAS, CA 92709-5001
**Scheduled to close 7/31/99.**

**LOCATION:** Off I-5, take the Sand Canyon Road exit. Follow signs to the MCAS. *USMRA: Page 111 (F-14); Page 117 (G,H-7,8)*. NMC: Los Angeles, 40 miles northwest. Main installation numbers: C-714-726-3011, D-312-997-3011.

**PAX TERM INFO: C-714-726-3920, D-312-997-3920.** Bldg 624, Hrs: Mon 0800-2200, Tue-Thu 0700-2200, Fri 0700-1800, Sat-Sun 0900-1700, Closed Holidays. Directions: Main gate straight on Trabuco Road to a left on West Marine Way for .25 mi, then turn right to Pax Term. **Pax Service Office:** Bldg 624, Hrs: Mon-Fri 0730-1630, C-714-726-3920. OIC/SNCOIC, D-312-726-4687. **Pax Paging:** Same as Pax Term.

**PAX LOUNGES:** No family lounge. **General:** Bldg 624, Hrs: See Pax Term, C-714-726-3920. Bag check, restrooms, TV, P/C seats. **DV/VIP:** Bldg 624, Hrs: Same as Pax Term, C-714-726-3920. A/C, restrooms, TV, O/S seats. Opened per request of Pax Service OIC. **Protocol Service:** Bldg 65, Hrs: Mon-Fri 0800-1700, C-714-726-3736, D-312-997-3736.

**FOOD SERVICE: Cafeteria:** Bldg 649, C-714-726-3340/3438. **Dining Hall:** Bldg 364, C-714-726-2312/4919. **Enlisted Club:** Bldg 718, C-714-726-2477. **NCO/CPO Club:** Bldg 718, C-714-726-2477. **O'Club:** Bldg 791, C-714-726-2464/5/6. **Snack Bars:** Ops Tower, Hrs: daily 0630-1700. **Vending:** Bldg 624, C-714-726-3920.

**TRANSPORTATION: Air Tickets:** SATO: Bldg 58, C-714-559-3339/1511. **Bus (Comm):** Bldg 924, C-714-636-RIDE (Orange County). **Car Rentals:** Orange County Airport, Avis: C-714-546-9420, Hertz: C-714-475-1150, Budget: C-714-540-6511. **Limo Service:** Bldg 624, C-714-776-9210 (NZJ to LAX $13-minimum 5 people). **Taxi (Comm):** El Toro: C-714-770-2828; Santa Ana: C-714-542-1133. **Taxi (Gov):** Commercial pool: C-714-726-2156. **Parking:** Bldg 624, C-714-726-3920, 30 day limit. For stays longer than 24 hours park in long term lot.

**TML:** Lodging Office (Bldg 58), Hrs: daily 0730-2130, C-714-726-2381/6000/3001, D-312-997-2381/6000/3001, FAX 714-726-3308. All ranks. Hostess House: C-714-726-2095. DV/VIP: C-714-726-3624, O6+.

**TRAVELERS AID: American Red Cross:** Bldg 60, C-714-726-2471/2, After hours, C-714-835-5381. **Chaplain:** Bldg 83, C-714-726-3824/5. **Emergency Relief:** Bldg 60, C-714-726-2473 (Navy Relief). **Lost/Found:** Bldg 624, C-714-726-4435. **Security Police:** Main gate, C-714-726-3527/8. **USO:** LAX, Term 4, C-213-642-0188. Also, Greyhound Bus Terminal C-213-624-0066.

**OTHER SERVICES: Exchange:** Bldg 649, C-714-726-3340. **Bank/Exchange:** Bldg 743, C-714-726-2564. **Hair Styles:** Bldg 649: Barber: C-714-726-3356; Beauty: C-714-559-1077. **Laundry/Dry Cleaning:** Bldg 649, C-714-726-3340. **Medical:** Bldg 439, Hrs: 24 hours daily, C-714-726-3172/2731, D-312-997-3172/2731. **Postal:** Bldg 273, C-714-726-3808.

**ATTRACTIONS:** Los Angeles, Disneyland, Anaheim Stadium, Crystal Cathedral (Garden Grove).

### UNSCHEDULED FLIGHTS

Frequent flights to Kadena AB, JA (**DNA**), North Island NAS, CA (**NZY**) and Yuma MCAS, AZ (**YUM**). Many unscheduled flights. Call 24 to 48 hours before requested departure date. Note: No civilian dependents allowed on some USMC aircraft.

## LEMOORE NAVAL AIR STATION (NLC)

Air Terminal, Bldg 184
Lemoore NAS, CA 93246-5001

**LOCATION:** On CA-198, 24 miles east of I-5, 30 miles west of CA-99 in the south central part of the state. *USMRA: Page 111 (D-10)*. NMC: Fresno, 40 miles north /northeast. Main installation numbers: C-209-998-0100, D-312-949-1110.

**PAX TERM INFO: C-209-998-1680/1/3, D-312-949-1680/1/3, FAX 209-998-3046, DSN FAX 949-3046.** Bldg 184, Hrs: daily 0800-2400. Directions: From main gate straight on Enterprise Ave, left on Franklin Ave for 5 miles to Ops area and Pax Term on right. **Pax Service Office:** Same as Pax terminal. **Pax Paging:** Same as Pax terminal.

*CALIFORNIA*
***Lemoore Naval Air Station, continued***

**PAX LOUNGES:** Limited lounge space. No DV/VIP or family lounge. **General:** Bldg 180, Hrs: 24 hours daily, C-209-998-1680. Only for scheduled flights originating at NLC. A/C, P/C seats, pay commercial telephones. **Protocol Service:** Hangar 1, Hrs: Mon-Fri 0800-1700, C-209-998-3360, 06+.

**FOOD SERVICE: Cafeteria:** C-209-998-3084, **Enlisted Club:** Bldg 920, C-209-998-3331. **In-flight Meals:** C-209-998-3236. **NCO/CPO Club:** C-209-998-3130. **O'Club:** C-209-998-3550. **Snack Bar:** McDonalds: Mainside, C-209-998-3222. **Vending:** Bldg 184, Hrs: 24 hours daily.

**TRANSPORTATION:** Limited on Base. **Bus (Shuttle):** C-209-998-4196. **Taxi (Comm):** At main gate.

**OTHER SERVICES: Exchange:** C-209-998-3611 (ask for information). **Medical:** 911 (Emergency).

**TML:** Lodging Office (Bldg 852, Hancock Cir), 24 hrs daily, C-209-998-4783, D-312-949-4783, FAX 209-998-3236. **Navy Lodge:** C-209-998-5791 or 1-800-NAVY-INN. DV/VIP: C-209-998-3344, O6+.

**TRAVELERS AID: American Red Cross:** C-209-998-3388/584-5015. **Chaplain:** C-209-998-3496. **Navy Relief:** C-209-998-4045. **Security Police:** C-209-998-3306 (24 hours at main gate).

**ATTRACTIONS:** Sequoia National Park, 70 miles east of LNAS. Ski areas nearby.

**UNSCHEDULED FLIGHTS**

Frequent flights to: China Lake NWC, CA (**NID**), Fallon NAS, NV (**NFL**), Miramar NAS, CA (**NKX**), North Island NAS, CA (**NZY**) and Whidbey Island NAS, WA (**NUW**). Call for information.

## LOS ALAMITOS ARMY AIRFIELD (SLI)

11200 Lexington Dr., Bldg. 1
Armed Forces Reserve Center (AFRC)
Los Alamitos AAF, CA 90720-5001

**LOCATION:** Off I-605 east of Long Beach. Clearly marked. *USMRA: Page 117 (E-6,7)*. NMC: Los Angeles, 5 miles north. Main installation numbers: C-310-795-2000, D-312-972-2000.

**PAX TERM INFO: C-310-795-2571, D-312-972-2571 ask for passenger service, FAX 310-795-2566.** Bldg Base Ops, Hrs: Tue-Fri 0600-2200, Sat-Mon: 0600-1630. Ask guard at Gate for directions to the airfield. **Pax Service Office:** Same as Pax Term. NOTE: No services available at terminal. No ground transportation available at terminal.

**TML:** Lodging Office, (Bldg 19), C-310-795-2124, D-312-972-2124, FAX 310-796-2125.

**OTHER SERVICES: Exchange:** C-213-430-1077. **Air Tickets:** SATO: C-213-493-8052.

**ATTRACTIONS:** Los Angeles, Hollywood, Orange County.

| IN ROUTE SCHEDULES | |
|---|---|
| Travis AFB | SUU/MEDEVAC-3 |

# LOS ANGELES INTERNATIONAL APT (LAX)

Det 1, 60 APS (AMC)
200 World Way, Suite 1067
Los Angeles, CA 90045-5810

**LOCATION:** The AMC ticket/processing counter is located at the Los Angeles International Airport, Terminal 2 on the departure level just to the left of Hawaiian Airlines. LAX is one mile west of the I-405 (take the Century Blvd. exit) or one mile north of the I-105 (take the Sepulveda Blvd. north exit), and is clearly marked. *USMRA: Page 117 (B-5).* NMC: Los Angeles (downtown), 10 miles northeast. NMI: Los Angeles Air Force Base(LAAFB), 3 miles south of LAX at 200 Douglas Street. Main installation numbers: C-310-363-0714/0715, D-312-833-0714/0716.

**PAX TERM INFO: C-310-363-0714/0715/0716, D-312-833-0714/0715/0716, FAX 310-216-2670, Space-A FAX 213-363-2790, D FAX 312-833-2790,** Tom Bradley International Terminal, Hrs: Mon-Sat 0630-1830, Sun 0630-1700, **Pax Paging:** Same as Pax Term.

**PAX LOUNGES:** No separate DV/VIP or family lounges. **General:** LAX Pax Term, Hrs: 24 hours daily. All IAP facilities available. **Protocol Service:** Hrs: daily 0730-2230, C-310-363-2030, D-312-833-2030 (see Pax NCO).

**FOOD SERVICE:** At LAX, LAAFB and off Base. **Cafeteria:** Bldg Terms 1-7, Hrs: 24 hours daily, C-310-363-0715, See Pax Service for assistance. **The Club:** LAAFB Area A, Bldg 120, Hrs: daily 0600-2000, C-310-363-2230. **Vending:** Term 4, Hrs: 24 hours daily.

**TRANSPORTATION:** Extensive facilities and means at LAX and LAAFB. **Air Tickets:** SATO: LAAFB Area B, Bldg 243, Hrs: Mon-Fri 0800-1600, C-310-363-1130. **Bus (Comm):** City Bus: RTD: C-310-626-4455; Greyhound: C-310-620-1200. **Car Rentals:** Thrifty: C-310-645-1880; Hertz: C-310-646-4861; Avis: C-310-646-5600; Budget:

*CALIFORNIA*
*Los Angeles International Airport, continued*

C-310-645-4500; Ajax: C-1-800-367-2529; Tropical: C-310-216-9130. **Limo Service:** Apt Express: C-310-679-5603, Hrs: 24 hours daily; Apt Limo Service: C-310-645-4346. **Taxi (Comm):** Apt Taxi Service: C-310-837-7252; A-1 Cab: C-310-222-1234; United Independent: C-310-653-5050; Red Top: C-310-822-4100. **Trains:** Los Angeles, AMTRAK: C-310-624-0171. **Parking:** Near LAX, Hrs: Daily: 24 hrs, Long term available with shuttle service. May be available at LAAFB. Coordinate with Security Police C-310-363-2122/3.

**TML:** Fort MacArthur, 22 miles from LAX, Hrs: daily 0715-1600, C-310-363-0260. Long Branch NS, Navy Lodge: C-310-833-2541 or 1-800-Navy-Inn.

**TRAVELERS AID: American Red Cross:** 100 World Way, Room 330, Los Angeles CA 90045, C-310-646-2271. **Chaplain:** LAAFB Bldg 219, duty hours: C-310-363-1956, after hours: C-310-363-0486. **Emergency Relief:** LAAFB Bldg 219, Hrs: Mon-Fri 0800-1600, C-310-363-1121 (AF Aid Society). **Lost/Found:** Term 4, Hrs: daily 0730-2230, C-310-417-1603. **Security Police:** LAAFB Bldg 241, Hrs: 24 hours daily, C-310-363-2122/3 (Desk Sgt). **USO:** Term 4 (at American Airlines), hours vary, C-310-642-0188.

**OTHER SERVICES:** Most support services available at LAX or LAAFB. **Exchange:** LAAFB Bldg 244, Hrs: Mon-Fri 1000-1730, Sat-Sun 1000-1600, C-310-640-0129. **Bank/Exchange:** Pax Term, hours posted, check-cashing at LAAFB clubs and BX. **Hair Styles:** Unisex: BX at LAAFB Bldg 244, Hrs: Mon-Fri 0830-1730, C-310-640-0379. **Laundry/Dry Cleaning:** LAAFB Bldg 244, Hrs: Mon-Fri 0900-1700, Sat: 0900-1500, C-310-322-1333. **Medical:** LAAFB Bldg 200, Hrs: daily 0700-1500, C-310-363-0964, D-312-833-0964. **Postal/Wire:** LAX, Bradley International Terminal, USPS, Hrs: Mon-Fri 0800-1700, American Express: Hrs: 0600-2100. **POV Shipment:** All State Auto Delivery, Inc., Hrs: Mon-Fri 0800-1700, C-310-678-5111.

| IN ROUTE SCHEDULES | | |
|---|---|---|
| **Lambert , St. Louis IAP** | PPP/STL-1 | PPP/STL-2 |

# MARCH AIR FORCE BASE (RIV)

TMO Passenger Terminal
610 Meyer Dr.
March AFB, CA 92518-2113
**Scheduled to close 3/3/96**

**LOCATION:** Off CA-60 and on I-215 which bisects AFB. *USMRA: Page 111 (G-14)*. NMC: Riverside, 7 miles northwest. Main installation numbers: C-909-655-1110, D-312-947-1110.

**PAX TERM INFO: C-909-655-2397/4621, D-312-947-2913/4, FAX 909-655-3887, DSN FAX 947-3887.** Bldg 265, Hrs: Mon-Fri 0730 1630 & during flight processing. Directions: From West Gate, Ellsworth Street to left on Graeber Street to Base Ops on right. **Pax Service Office:** Same as Pax Term.

**PAX LOUNGES:** Very limited lounge facilities. **General:** Bldg 265, Hrs: Mon-Fri 0730-1630, C-909-655-2913/4. Limit 25-40 people - most wait in snack bar next door. Restrooms, O/S seats. **Protocol Service:** Bldg 3403, Hrs: Mon-Fri 0800-1700, C-909-655-2213 (HQ 15th AF).

**FOOD SERVICE: Dining Hall:** Bldg 962, Hrs: daily 0500-0100, C-909-655-3266. **NCO/CPO Club:** Bldg 2706, Hrs: daily 1100-2300, C-909-653-1153. **O'Club:** Bldg 110, Hrs: daily 1000-0100, C-909-653-2121.

**TRANSPORTATION:** Air Tickets: Bldg 2405, Hrs: Mon-Fri 0800-1600, C-909-655-5116. **Car Rentals:** Riverside: Hrs: Mon-Sat 0800-1600, C-909-682-2610. **Taxi (Comm):** Main gate, Hrs: 24 hours daily, C-909-247-6191.

**TML:** Lodging Office (Bldg 100, 655 M St), 24 hrs daily, C-909-655-5241, D-312-947-5241, FAX 909-655-4574, DSN FAX 312-947-4574. All ranks. DV/VIP: C-909-655-4764, O6+.

**TRAVELERS AID:** Action Line: Bldg 470, Hrs: 24 hours daily, C-909-655-2244. **American Red Cross:** Bldg 641, Hrs: Mon-Fri 0800-1600, C-909-655-4189/4180, After hours C-909-655-1110. **Chaplain:** Bldg 2600, Hrs: Mon-Fri 0800-1800, C-909-655-4751, After hours C-909-655-4689. **Security Police:** Bldg 394, Hrs: 24 hours daily, C-909-655-4689. **USO:** LAX Term 4, Hrs: Daily: 24hrs, C-909-642-0188.

**OTHER SERVICES: Exchange:** Bldg 758, Hrs: Mon-Fri 1000-2100, Sat-Sun 1000-1800, C-909-653-3111. **Bank/Exchange:** Bldg 659, Hrs: Mon-Fri 1000-1500, C-909-653-1121. **Hair Styles:** Barber: Bldg 758, Hrs: Mon-Fri 0900-1800, Sat 0900-1600, C-909-653-7814. **Laundry/Dry Cleaning:** Bldg 758, Hrs: Mon-Fri 0900-1800, Sat 0900-1600, C-909-653-3003. **Medical:** Bldg 2990, Hrs: 24 hours daily, C-909-655-4266, Ambulance: C-909-655-2433. **Postal:** Bldg 323, Hrs: Mon-Fri 0800-1500, C-909-655-3010.

**ATTRACTIONS:** Greater Los Angeles, Palm Springs resorts and golf courses.

| **ORIGINATING SCHEDULES** | | | |
|---|---|---|---|
| | **APM/RIV-1 2nd/4th SUN KC10A** | | |
| **Location ID** | **Airport (Station)** | **Country/State** | **Days Out** |
| RIV | March AFB | CA | +0 |
| NGU | Norfolk NAS | VA | +2 |
| RTA | Rota NAS | SP | +3 |
| SIZ | Sigonella NAS | IT | +3 |
| BAH | Bahrain IAP | BA | +4 |

*CALIFORNIA*
*March Air Force Base, continued*

| | | | |
|---|---|---|---|
| **FUJ** | **Fujairah IAP** | **UA** | **+5** |
| BAH | Bahrain IAP | BA | +5 |
| SIZ | Sigonella NAS | IT | +6 |
| RTA | Rota NAS | SP | +7 |
| NGU | Norfolk NAS | VA | +8 |
| RIV | March AFB | CA | |
| | **PCC/RIV-2 1st/2nd WED KC010A** | | |
| RIV | March AFB | CA | +0 |
| SUU | Travis AFB | CA | +1 |
| EDF | Elmendorf AFB | AK | +2 |
| **OKO** | **Yokota AB** | **JA** | **+3** |
| SUU | Travis AFB | CA | +4 |
| RIV | March AFB | CA | |
| | **PCC/RIV-3 2nd SAT KC135R** | | |
| RIV | March AFB | CA | +0 |
| SUU | Travis AFB | CA | +1 |
| EDF | Elmendorf AFB | AK | +2 |
| **OKO** | **Yokota AB** | **JA** | **+3** |
| SUU | Travis AFB | JA | +4 |
| RIV | March AFB | CA | |
| | **PCM/RIV-4 TUE C-141B** | | |
| RIV | March AFB | CA | +0 |
| SUU | Travis AFB | CA | +1 |
| HIK | Hikam AFB | HI | +2 |
| KWA | Bucholz AAF KMR | KA | +2 |
| HIK | Hikam AFB | HI | +4 |
| **JON** | **Johnston Atoll AFB** | **JO** | **+4** |
| MDY | Midway NAF | MW | +4 |
| HIK | Hikam AFB | HI | +5 |
| SUU | Travis AFB | CA | +6 |
| RIV | March AFB | CA | |
| | **IN ROUTE SCHEDULES** | | |
| **Travis AFB** | SUU/MEDEVAC-3 | | |

**UNSCHEDULED FLIGHTS**

Frequent flights on KC-10 to Hickam AFB, HI (**HIK**), and Orlando IAP, FL (**MCO**). Also other CONUS, OCONUS and foreign country locations. Call after 1400 Friday for following week's destinations, routings and schedules.

# McCLELLAN AIR FORCE BASE (MCC)

77 ABW/LGTR
4443 Dudley Blvd.
McClellan AFB, CA 95652-1003

**LOCATION:** Off I-80 North. From I-80 take Madison Ave exit. Clearly marked. *USMRA: Page 110 (C-6).* NMC: Sacramento, 10 miles southwest. Main installation numbers: C-916-643-4113, D-312-633-1110.

**PAX TERM INFO: C-916-643-3944/4105, D-312-633-3944/4105, REC: C-916-643-4105 (after hours),** updated 1530 daily, FAX 916-643-5616, DSN FAX 633-5616. Bldg 251, Hrs: Mon-Fri 0700-1530. Directions: Gate 1 straight on Peacemaker Way to Pax Term on left. Also USCG flight via C-130 aircraft to CONUS and OCONUS locations. Call C-916-643-2081, F-533-3237, and D-312-633-2081. **Pax Service Office:** Same as Pax Term.

**PAX LOUNGES:** No family lounge. **General:** Bldg 251, Hrs: Mon-Fri 0700-1530, C-916-643-3944. A/C, bag check, telephones (commercial), TV, restrooms, P/C seats. **DV/VIP:** Bldg 251, Hrs: 24 hours daily, C-916-643-2845. A/C, coffee/tea, telephones (commercial and defense), TV, restrooms, O/S seats (06+). **Protocol Service:** Bldg 200, Hrs: Mon-Fri 0730-1615, C-916-643-2845 (06+).

**FOOD SERVICE: Cafeteria:** C-916-927-3829. **Dining Hall:** C-916-643-5092. **Enlisted Club:** C-916-643-4139. **NCO/CPO Club:** C-916-922-9657. **O'Club:** C-916-927-5013. **Snack Bars:** C-916-920-9394.

**TRANSPORTATION:** Very limited ground transportation from terminal. **Air Tickets:** SATO: C-916-643-4410. **Bus (Comm):** Gates 1,3,&4, hours vary, C-916-321-BUSS. **Limo Service:** Presidential: C-916-920-1123. **Taxi (Comm):** Yellow: C-916-444-2222. **Parking:** Behind main cafeteria. Long term at Bank of America.

**TML:** Lodging Office (Bldg 89, 5405 O'Malley Ave), 24hrs daily, C-916-643-3267, D-312-633-3267, all ranks. DV/VIP: C-916-643-4311, O6+.

**TRAVELERS AID: American Red Cross:** C-916-643-4013, weekends C-916-643-1110. **Chaplain:** C-916-643-3598, after hours C-916-643-6023. **Emergency Relief:** C-916-643-3815 (Family Services). **Lost/Found:** C-916-643-3460. **Security Police:** Bldg 948, C-916-643-6160 (Police Desk).

**OTHER SERVICES: Exchange:** C-916-920-0537. **Bank/Exchange:** Bank Of America: C-916-924-6582. **Hair Styles:** Barber: C-916-927-7521; Beauty: C-916-925-3374. **Laundry/Dry Cleaning:** C-916-922-0389. **Medical:** McClellan Medical Clinic, Bldg. 98, Mon-Fri 916-646-8420. **Ambulance:** EX-115. **Postal:** C-916-643-3971. No wire service.

*CALIFORNIA*
*McClellan Air Force Base, continued*

**ATTRACTIONS:** Lake Tahoe, CA and Reno, NV nearby (2 hour drive northeast). San Francisco Bay area (1.5 hours drive southwest).

**UNSCHEDULED FLIGHTS**

A schedule is posted each day at 0830 hours for flights for the next 24 hour period. Ocasional flights to: March AFB, CA (**RIV**); as well as other CONUS locations. Baggage limit for C-21A aircraft is 30 pounds. No regular scheduled flights.

## MIRAMAR NAVAL AIR STATION (NKX)

Operations Maintenance Division
Miramar NAS, CA 92145-5399

**LOCATION:** Take Miramar Way exit off I-15. *USMRA: Page 118 (C,D-2,3,4; E,F-2,3)*. NMC: San Diego CA, 15 miles southwest. Main installation numbers: C-619-537-1011, D-312-577-1011.

**PAX TERM INFO: C-619-537-4284, D-312-577-4284, FAX 619-537-4261.** Bldg 476, Hrs: Open 2 hours prior to scheduled departures. Directions: From main gate, straight on Miramar Way to left on Mitscher Way, right on Regulus Road and left at fork in road to front of Pax Term. **Pax Service Office:** Same as Pax Term, C-619-537-4284, NCO on duty. **Pax Paging:** Same as Pax Term.

**PAX LOUNGES:** Limited facilities. No separate family lounge. **General:** Same as Pax Term, restrooms, TV, W & P/C seats. **DV/VIP:** Bldg K-211, Hrs: Daily: 0700-2400, C-619-537-4279, restrooms, TV, O/S seats. **Protocol Service:** Bldg 402, Hrs: 24 hours daily, C-619-537-1657.

**FOOD SERVICE: Snack Bar:** Bldg K-211, C-619-695-7275 (Flight Line). **Dining Hall:** Bldg M-305, C-619-537-7086. **Enlisted Club:** Bldg M-309, C-619-537-4821/20. **NCO/CPO Club:** Bldg M-309, C-619-537-4799. **O'Club:** Bldg 472, C-619-537-4816. **Vending:** C-619-537-4808/4809.

**TRANSPORTATION:** Limited on Base. **Air Tickets:** SATO: Bldg 524, Hrs: Mon-Fri 0800-1700, C-619-578-3049. **Bus (Comm):** Main gate, C-619-233-3004. **Shuttle:** Bldg K-211, runs every 30 minutes, C-619-537-1142. **Car Rentals:** Bldg 257, C-619-695-7549. **Limo Service:** San Diego, C-619-291-9002. **Taxi (Base):** Main gate, C-619-537-1142. **Parking:** Bldg K-211, C-619-537-4279, no restrictions.

**TML:** Lodging Office (Bldg M-312), C-619-537-4235, D-312-577-4235, FAX 619-537-4243, DSN FAX 312-577-4243. Check in facility; check out 1200 daily. **Navy Lodge:** C-619-271-7111 or 1-800-NAVY-INN. DV/VIP: C-619-537-1221, O6+.

**TRAVELERS AID: American Red Cross:** Bldg 273, C-619-291-2620. **Chaplain:** Bldg 332, C-619-537-1333/38. **Emergency Relief:** Bldg 273, C-619-537-1807 (Navy Relief). **Lost/Found:** Bldg 476, C-619-537-4283. **Security Police:** Bldg M-310, C-619-

573-4059. **USO:** San Diego, C-619-235-6503.

**OTHER SERVICES: Exchange:** Bldg 660, C-619-695-7217. **Bank/Exchange:** California 1st Bank: Bldg 513, C-619-230-4717. **Hair Styles:** Barber: Bldg 600, C-619-695-7295; Beauty: Bldg 660, C-619-695-7227. **Laundry/Dry Cleaning:** Bldg 660, C-619-695-7238. **Medical:** Bldg 495, Hrs: 24 hours daily, C-619-537-4630, D-312-577-4630. **Postal:** Bldg 257, C-619-537-4578.

**ATTRACTIONS:** San Diego, beautiful beaches, Sea World, San Diego Zoo.

| IN ROUTE SCHEDULES | | |
|---|---|---|
| **Travis AFB** | SUU/MEDEVAC-1 | SUU/MEDEVAC-3 |

**UNSCHEDULED FLIGHTS**

Frequent flights to the following destinations: Alameda NAS, CA (**NGZ**); Cecil Field NAS, FL (**NZC**); Dallas NAS, TX (**NBE**); Memphis NAS, TN (**NQA**); Pensacola NAS, FL (**NPA**); Point Mugu NAS, CA (**NTD**); Travis AFB, CA (**SUU**); Whidbey Island NAS, WA (**NUW**); & Willow Grove NAS, PA (**NXX**). Call Pax Terminal 1 to 3 days prior to flight for info on unscheduled flights.

## NORTH ISLAND NAVAL AIR STATION (NZY)

Air Terminal Officer
North Island NAS, CA 92135-0001

**LOCATION:** From I-5 north or south exit at Coronado Bridge (toll). In city of Coronado. *USMRA: Page 118 (B,C-6,7)*. NMC: San Diego, 4 miles northeast. Main installation numbers: C-619-545-1011, D-312-735-0444.

**PAX TERM INFO: C-619-545-9567, D-312-735-9567, REC: C-619-545-8273/8278,** updated daily. Bldg 700, Hrs: 24 hours daily. Directions: Main gate on McCain Blvd, left on Roosevelt Blvd to Pax Term on right. **Pax Service Office:** Bldg 700, Hrs: 24 hours daily, C-619-545-9530. **Pax Paging:** Bldg 700, Hrs: 24 hours daily, C-619-545-9530.

**PAX LOUNGES:** No separate family lounge. **General:** Bldg 700, Hrs: 24 hours daily, C-619-545-9567. A/C, bag check, restrooms, telephones, TV, O/S seats. **DV/VIP:** Bldg 516, Hrs: 24 hours daily, C-619-545-8269, A/C, bag check, restrooms, local and defense telephones, TV, O/S seats. **Protocol Service:** Bldg 8, Hrs: 24 hours daily, C-619-545-2017.

**FOOD SERVICE: Cafeteria:** Bldg 700, C-619-522-7438. **Dining Hall:** Bldg 794, C-619-545-7514. **Enlisted Club:** Bldg 417, C-619-545-2881 (Windjammer). **McDonalds:** C-619-435-0074 (on Base). **NCO/CPO Club:** Bldg 864, C-619-545-7205. **O'Club:** Bldg X, C-619-545-6945. **Restaurants:** Bldg 243, C-619-522-7267 (civilian cafe). **Snack Bars:** Bowling Alley: Bldg 772, C-619-545-7240. **Vending:** Bldg 700, C-619-545-7438.

*CALIFORNIA*
*North Island Naval Air Station, continued*

**TRANSPORTATION: Air Tickets:** Bldg 11, C-619-545-7199. **Bus (Comm):** Bldg 700, C-619-233-3004. **Bus (Shuttle):** Bldg 493, C-619-437-7731. **Taxi (Comm):** Coronado, C-619-435-6211. **Parking:** Bldg 700, (very limited), Long Term parking available.

**TML:** Lodging Office (Bldg 1 (BOQ), Bldg 773 (BEQ)), 24 hrs daily, BOQ C-619-524-7545, FAX 619-545-9220, BEQ C-619-545-9551. **Navy Lodge:** C-619-545-6940. DV/VIP: C-619-437-6011.

**TRAVELERS AID: American Red Cross:** Bldg 607, C-619-435-3195. **Chaplain:** Bldg 665, duty hours, C-619-545-8213. Other hours call OOD, C-619-545-8123. **Emergency Relief:** Bldg 607, C-619-437-7649 (Navy Relief Society). **Lost/Found:** Bldg 700, C-619-545-8278. **Security Police:** Main gate, C-619-545-9449. **USO:** 433 Harbor Dr, C-619-235-6503.

**OTHER SERVICES: Exchange:** Bldg 483, C-619-522-7215. **Bank/Exchange:** Bldg 318, C-619-435-5417/8 (Credit Union). **Hair Styles:** Bldg 483, C-619-522-7272. **Laundry/Dry Cleaning:** Bldg 483, C-619-522-7231. **Medical:** Bldg 600, Hrs: 24 hours daily, C-619-545-4263, D-312-735-4263. Ambulance: C-619-545-4380. **Postal:** Bldg 124, C-619-437-7698.

**ATTRACTIONS:** Beaches, Old San Diego, Sea World, Mexico nearby.

**UNSCHEDULED FLIGHTS**

Frequent flights to CONUS stations: Alameda NAS, CA (**NGZ**); Fallon NAS, NV (**NFL**); Lemoore NAS, CA (**NLC**); McChord AFB, WA (**TCM**); Whidbey Island NAS, WA (**NUW**). Call for destinations, routings and schedules.

## POINT MUGU NAVAL AIR WEAPONS STATION/ CHANNEL ISLAND AIR NATIONAL GUARD BASE (NTD)

Air Operations Department,
Air Terminal Division
Point Mugu, CA 93042-5000

**LOCATION:** 2 miles north of Point Mugu, at the intersection of California Highway One (Pacific Coast Highway) and Hueneme Road. *USMRA: Page 111 (D, E-13).* NMC: Los Angeles, 50 miles southeast. Main installation numbers: C-805-989-1110, D-312-351-1110.

**PAX TERM INFO: NAVY: C-805-989-7731, D-312-351-7731.** Air Terminal: Hrs: Mon-Fri 0700-2200, Sat-Sun 0930-1800, Closed holidays. Reduced hours during Christmas and New Years. Enter gate 2, follow signs to Naval Air Warfare Center Air Terminal on 11th Street, Building 339. **Pax Service Office:** Same as Pax Term.

*CALIFORNIA*
***Point Mugu Naval Air Weapons Station***

**ANGB PAX TERM: C-805-986-7997, D-312-893-7997.** Bldg 106, Hrs: Tue-Fri 0700-1530. Operations building second entry on left side of main road.

**PAX LOUNGES:** Limited lounge facilities. No DV/VIP lounge. **General:** Air Terminal, Hrs: Mon-Fri: 0700-2200, C-805-989-7731. Bag check, rest-rooms, TV, P/C seats. **Protocol Service:** Bldg 1, Hrs: 24 hours daily, C-805-989-7209. No Lounge facilities at ANGB.

**FOOD SERVICE: Cafeteria:** Bldg 366, C-805-989-7189. **Mugu's Pizza:** NAS, C-805-989-8420/8714. **NCO/CPO Club:** NAS, C-805-989-8570. **O'Club:** NAS, C-805-989-7507. **Snack Bars:** Golf course, C-805-989-4620. No services available at ANGB.

**TRANSPORTATION: Air Tickets:** Bldg 1, C-805-989-8378. **Bus (Shuttle):** Air Terminal, C-805-989-7406. **Car Rentals:** Budget: C-805-483-2326, Avis: C-805-487-9429. **Taxi (Comm):** C-805-483-2444. **Parking:** Security, C-805-989-7907. Commercial taxi only from ANGB.

**TML:** Lodging Office (Bldg 27, D St), 24 hrs daily, C-805-989-8255/8235, D-312-351-8255/8235/7510, FAX 805-989-7470, DSN FAX 312-351-7470. All ranks. **DV/VIP:** C-805-989-8672, O6+. No quarters available at ANGB.

**TRAVELERS AID: American Red Cross:** Port Hueneme, C-805-989-4424. **Chaplain:** NAS, C-805-989-7967. **Emergency Relief:** NAS, C-805-989-8918 (Navy Relief). **Security Police:** Main gate, Hrs: 24 hours daily, C-805-989-7907. **USO:** LAX IAP, Term 4, C-213-642-0188. Limited services available at ANGB.

**OTHER SERVICES:** BX Complex has Hair Styles and Laundry/Dry Cleaning. **Exchange:** BX Complex, C-805-989-7189. **Bank/Exchange:** MFCU: Mugu Road, C-805-989-8787. **Medical:** Dispensary, Hrs: 24 hours daily, C-805-989-8821/3331. **Postal:** NAS, C-805-989-8253. No services available at ANGB.

**ATTRACTIONS:** Beaches, Los Angeles, Disneyland within 2 hour drive.

**UNSCHEDULED FLIGHTS**

Flights to:Andrews AFB MD (**ADW**); Kadena AB JA (**DNA**); Rota NAS SP (**RTA**); Sigonella Apt IT (**SIZ**); and Yokota AB JA (**OKO**) via various contract aircraft. Also, *Antarctic Dev Sqd 6 (VXE-6) and the Naval Construction Battalion Center Support "Operation Deep Freeze" with flights from (NTD) to Christchurch NZ (**CHC**) from August through February via C-141B and LC-130 aircraft. Dial direct C-805-989-7129/7585 for VXE-6 flights.*

*CALIFORNIA*

# TRAVIS AIR FORCE BASE (SUU)

60th APS/TRP
90 Ragsdale Rd.
Travis AFB, CA 94535-2216

**LOCATION:** Fifty miles northeast of San Francisco, 35 miles southeast of Sacramento and 7 miles east of Fairfield. From I-80 take Air Base Parkway exit ramp. *USMRA: Page 110 (B, C-7)*. NMC: San Francisco, 50 miles southeast. Main installation numbers: C-707-424-1110/5000, D-312-837-1110.

**PAX TERM INFO: C-707-424-1854, 1-800-787-2534, D-312-837-1854, REC: C-707-424-1854, D-312-837-1854 (updated 2200 hours), FAX: C-707-424-2048.** Bldg 3, Hrs: 24 hours daily. Directions: From main gate take Travis Ave, turn right on 2nd Ave, Pax Term is 2 1/2 blocks on left, adjacent to control tower (Bldg 4). **Pax Paging:** Same as Pax Term.

**PAX LOUNGES: General:** Bldg 3, Hrs: 24 hours daily, C-707-424-1854, D-312-837-1854. No smoking in terminal. Showers, free TV, bag check/lockers, restrooms. **DV/VIP:** Between Buildings 3 and 4, C-707-424-3185, D-312-837-3185 (06+). Staffed Mon-Fri 0600-1700, Sat-Sun 0600-1300. Ask for Protocol Service. A/C, O/S seats, showers, restrooms, TV, coffee/tea served. **Family:** Bldg 3 (USO), Hrs: daily 0800-2000, C-707-424-3316, D-312-837-3316. A/C, O/S seats, crib room (24 hrs daily), game rooms, restrooms, TV.

**FOOD SERVICE: Cafeteria:** Bldg 3, Hrs: daily 0500-2300, C-707-424-2092. **Dining Hall:** Bldg 1301 (half mile from Pax Term), Hrs: Mon-Sat 0600-1800, 4th meal: Mon-Fri 2230-0200, C-707-424-2155 (no retirees). **Enlisted Club:** Bldg 660, Hrs: Mon-Wed 0900-2300, Fri-Sat 0900-0100, Thu & Sun 0900-2400, C-707-437-3711. **O'Club:** Bldg 480, Hrs: Mon-Wed 0900-2300, Fri-Sat 0900-0100, Sun & Thr 0900-2400, C-707-437-3368. **Vending:** Bldg 3, Hrs: 24 hours daily, C-707-437-4655.

**TRANSPORTATION: Air Tickets:** Bldg 3, Hrs: 24 hours daily, C-1-800-521-4086 (E & J Travel). **Bus (Comm):** Bldg 3, Hrs: Mon-Fri 0430-2330, Sat-Sun & Hol: 0430-2100 (SUU-SFO-SF). See E&J Travel. $20 1-way, C-1-800-521-4086. **Bus (Shuttle):** Bldg 3, Hrs: daily 0700, 0800, 1100, 1200 & 1500-2100 (fare 25 cents). **Car Rentals:** Budget: C-707-437-4411, Hertz: C-1-800-654-3131, National: C-707-437-2529. **Taxi (Comm):** Bldg 3, 24 hrs daily, C-707-437-2961 (outside customs area). **Parking:** Short term-in front of Bldg 3 (2 hour limit); long term parking available through MWR.

**TML:** Lodging Office (Bldg 404, Sevedge Dr), Reservations: C-707-424-2987, D-312-837-2987, FAX 707-424-5489. All ranks. DV/VIP: C-707-424-3185/6, D-312-837-3185, O6+.

**TRAVELERS AID: American Red Cross:** Bldg 3, Hrs: Mon-Fri 0800-1700, C-707-424-2262 and C-707-824-0722. **Chaplain:** Bldg 438, Hrs: duty hours, C-707-424-2593, other hours C-707-824-0722. **Emergency Relief:** Bldg 246, C-707-424-4085 (Air Force Aid Society). **Lost/Found:** Bldg 3, Hrs: Mon-Fri 0800-1700, C-707-424-2180, weekends/holidays C-707-424-1854. **Security Police:** Bldg 850, Hrs: 24 hours daily, C-707-424-3293, (Emergency - 911).

**OTHER SERVICES: Exchange:** Bldg 650, Mon-Sun, C-707-437-4654. **Hair Styles:** Barber: Bldg 4, C-707-437-9926; Beauty: Blg: 650, C-707-437-2848. **Laundry/Dry Cleaning:** Bldg 690 C-707-437-2733. **Laundromat:** Bldg 651, Hrs: 24 hours daily, **Medical:** Bldg 777, Hrs: 24 hours daily, C-707-423-7300 D-312-837-7300 (Emergency - 911). **Postal:** Bldg 542, Hrs: Mon-Fri 0800-1630, C-707-437-2889. **POV Shipment:** OAK Army Base, C-707-466-3365 (turn in and pick up yourself). Commercial service at Travis - Union Garage, C-707-437-3394.

**ATTRACTIONS:** Marine World, Napa Valley wine country, San Francisco, Chinatown, Fisherman's Wharf, Golden Gate Bridge, and cable cars.

| **ORIGINATING SCHEDULES** | | | |
|---|---|---|---|
| | **PCC/SUU-1 1st/5th THU KC10A** | | |
| **Location ID** | **Airport (Station)** | **Country/State** | **Days Out** |
| SUU | Travis AFB | CA | +0 |
| EDF | Elmendorf AFB | AK | +1 |
| **OKO** | **Yokota AB** | **JA** | **+2** |
| SUU | Travis AFB | CA | |
| | **PCC/SUU-2 3rd MON, 3rd WED, 4th SAT C-141B** | | |
| SUU | Travis AFB | CA | +0 |
| EDF | Elmendorf AFB | AK | +1 |
| **OKO** | **Yokota AB** | **JA** | **+23** |
| EDF | Elmendorf AFB | AK | +23 |
| SUU | Travis AFB | CA | |
| | **PCC/SUU-3 1st/2nd/4th MON C-141B** | | |
| SUU | Travis AFB | CA | +0 |
| EDF | Elmendorf AFB | AK | +1 |
| **OKO** | **Yokota AB** | **JA** | **+2** |
| HIK | Hikam AFB | HI | +2 |
| SUU | Travis AFB | CA | |
| | **PCC/SUU-4 2nd/4th THU C141B** | | |
| SUU | Travis AFB | CA | +0 |
| EDF | Elmendorf AFB | AK | +1 |
| OKO | Yokota AB | JA | +2 |
| **OSN** | **Osan AB** | **RK** | **+3** |
| OKO | Yokota AB | JA | +3 |

*CALIFORNIA*
*Travis Air Force Base, continued*

| | | | |
|---|---|---|---|
| EDF | Elmendorf AFB | AK | +4 |
| SUU | Travis AFB | CA | |
| | **PCC/SUU-5 3rd SAT KC10A** | | |
| SUU | Travis AFB | CA | +0 |
| HIK | Hikam AFB | HI | +1 |
| **OKO** | **Yokota AB** | **JA** | |
| | **PCC/SUU-6 TUE C-5A/B** | | |
| SUU | Travis AFB | CA | +0 |
| HIK | Hikam AFB | HI | +1 |
| UAM | Andersen AFB | GU | +2 |
| DNA | Kadena AB | JA | +3 |
| **OKO** | **Yokota AB** | **JA** | **+4** |
| EDF | Elmendorf AFB | AK | +5 |
| SUU | Travis AFB | CA | |
| | **PPM/SUU-7 FRI DC 862** | | |
| SUU | Travis AFB | CA | +0 |
| HIK | Hikam AFB | HI | +0 |
| UAM | Andersen AFB | GU | +1 |
| **OKO** | **Yokota AB** | **JA** | |
| | **PCC/SUU-8 3rd TUE C-141B** | | |
| SUU | Travis AFB | CA | +0 |
| HIK | Hikam AFB | HI | +1 |
| UAM | Andersen AFB | GU | +2 |
| **OKO** | **Yokota AB** | **JA** | **+23** |
| UAM | Andersen AFB | GU | +23 |
| HIK | Hikam AFB | HI | +24 |
| SUU | Travis AFB | CA | |
| | **PPM/SUU-9 SUN C-141B** | | |
| SUU | Travis AFB | CA | +0 |
| HIK | Hikam AFB | HI | +1 |
| KWA | Bucholz AAF KMR | KA | +1 |
| HIK | Hikam AFB | HI | +2 |
| **JON** | **Johnston Atoll** | **JO** | **+2** |
| HIK | Hikam AFB | HI | +3 |
| AWK | Wake Island AFB | WK | +4 |
| HIK | Hikam AFB | HI | +5 |
| SUU | Travis AFB | CA | |

| | **PCC/SUU-10 FRI C-141** | | |
|---|---|---|---|
| SUU | Travis AFB | CA | +0 |
| HIK | Hikam AFB | HI | +2 |
| PPG | Pago Pago IAP | AS | +2 |
| RCM | Richmond RAAFB | AU | +3 |
| **ASP** | **Alice Springs** | **AU** | **+4** |
| RCM | Richmond RAAFB | AU | +4 |
| PPG | Pago Pago IAP | AS | +5 |
| HIK | Hikam AFB | HI | +6 |
| SUU | Travis AFB | CA | |
| | **PCC/SUU-11 2nd/4th FRI KC10A** | | |
| SUU | Travis AFB | CA | +0 |
| HIK | Hikam AFB | HI | +1 |
| **OKO** | **Yokota AB** | **JA** | **+15** |
| HIK | Hikam AFB | HI | +17 |
| SUU | Travis AFB | CA | |
| | **SUU/MEDEVAC-1 SUN, TUE, FRI C-9A** | | |
| SUU | Travis AFB | CA | |
| NKX | Miramar NAS | CA | |
| LUF | Luke AFB | AZ | |
| DMA | Davis-Monthan AFB | AZ | |
| BIF | Biggs AAF | TX | |
| IKR | Kirtland AFB | NM | |
| CVS | Cannon AFB | NM | |
| SKF | Kelly AFB | TX | |
| **BLV** | **Scott AFB** | **IL** | |
| | **SUU/MEDEVAC-2 SUN, THU C-9A** | | |
| SUU | Travis AFB | CA | |
| SKF | Kelly AFB | TX | |
| BIX | Keesler AFB | MS | |
| **ADW** | **Andrews AFB** | **MD** | |
| BLV | Scott AFB | IL | |
| | **SUU/MEDEVAC-3 THU C-9A** | | |
| SUU | Travis AFB | CA | |
| LSV | Nellis AFB | NV | |
| EDW | Edwards AFB | CA | |
| RIV | March AFB | CA | |
| **NKX** | **Miramar NAS** | **CA** | |

*CALIFORNIA*
*Travis Air Force Base, continued*

| | | | |
|---|---|---|---|
| SLI | Los Alamitos AAF | | CA |
| VBG | Vandenberg AFB | | CA |
| MRY | Monterey Peninsula APT | | CA |
| SUU | Travis AFB | | CA |
| | **SUU/MEDEVAC-4** | **FRI** | **C-9A** |
| SUU | Travis AFB | | CA |
| TCM | McChord AFB | | WA |
| SKA | Fairchild AFB | | WA |
| GFA | Malmstrom AFB | | MT |
| MIB | Mountain Home AFB | | ID |
| HIF | Hill AFB | | UT |
| BKF | Buckley ANGB | | CO |
| **BLV** | **Scott AFB** | | **IL** |

| **IN ROUTE SCHEDULES** | | | |
|---|---|---|---|
| **Altus AFB** | PCC/LTS-2 | PCC/LTS-3 | |
| **Bangor IAP** | PCC/BGR-2 | | |
| **Fairchild AFB** | PCC/SKA-2 | | |
| **Lincoln MAP** | PCC/LNK-1 | | |
| **Malmstrom AFB** | PCC/GFA-1 | | |
| **March AFB** | PCC/RIV-2 | PCC/RIV-3 | PCM/RIV4 |
| **McChord AFB** | PPM/TCM-1 | PCC/TCM-3 | PCC/TCM-4 |
| | PCC/TCM-5 | PPM/TCM-6 | PCC/TCM-7 |
| | PPM/TCM-8 | | |
| **McConnell AFB** | PCC/IAB-1 | | |
| **McGuire AFB** | PCC/WRI-23 | PCC/WRI-24 | |
| **O'Hare IAP/ARS** | PCC/ORD-1 | | |
| **Robins AFB** | PCC/WRB-2 | | |
| **Wright-Patterson AFB** | PCC/FFO-3 | | |
| **Yokota AB** | PPM/OKO-2 | | |

# VANDENBERG AIR FORCE BASE (VBG)

30 TRNS/LGTTA
1221 California Blvd.
Vandenberg AFB, CA 93437-5079

**LOCATION:** From the south on US-101, west on CA-246, north on CA-S20 to AFB. From north on US-101, west on US-1 from Gaviota, north on CA-S20 to AFB. *USMRA: Page 111 (C-12)*. NMC: Lompoc, 6 miles south. Main installation numbers: C-805-734-8232, D-312-276-8232.

**PAX TERM INFO: C-805-734-8232 EX 6-1854/6-7742, D-312-276-1854/7742, FAX 805-734-8232 EX 6-8038.** Bldg 1749, Hrs: daily 0800-1700. Directions: From main gate on CA Blvd to right on 13th St, left on Airfield Rd. Pax Term is on the left. **Pax Service Office:** Same as Pax Term (NCO on duty).

**PAX LOUNGES:** Limited lounge facilities. **General:** Bldg 1749, Hrs: daily 0800-1700, C-805-866-7742. Coffee/tea served, restrooms, P/C seats. **DV/VIP:** Adjacent to Bldg 1749, Hrs: daily 0800-1700, C-805-866-4129. Restrooms, TV, coffee/tea service, O/S seats. **Protocol Service:** Bldg 10577, Hrs: 24 hours daily, C-805-866-3711.

**FOOD SERVICE: Cafeteria:** Bldg 1749, C-805-734-2977. **Dining Hall:** Bldg 13330, C-805-866-9571. **Enlisted Club:** Bldg 10252, C-805-734-4375. **O'Club:** Bldg 11070, C-805-734-4311. **Burger King:** Bldg 1749, C-805-734-4263.

**TRANSPORTATION: Air Tickets:** SATO: Bldg 10364, Hrs: Mon-Fri 0730-1630. **Bus (Gov):** Bldg 10004, C-805-866-1843. **Car Rentals:** Bldg 10600, C-805-734-2185. **Parking:** Bldg 1749, C-805-866-7742.

**TML:** Lodging Office (Vandenberg Lodge, Bldg 13005, Oregon & L St), 24hrs daily, C-805-734-8232-EX-6-2245, FAX 805-734-8232-EX-6-0720, DSN FAX 312-276-0720. All ranks. DV/VIP: C-805-734-3711, O7/GS-16.

**TRAVELERS AID: American Red Cross:** Bldg 11012, Hrs: 24 hours daily, C-805-866-1855 or C-805-734-5110. **Chaplain:** Bldg 16200, Hrs: 24 hours daily, C-805-866-1859/6655. **Security Police:** Hrs: 24 hours daily, C-805-866-3911 (Desk Sgt).

**OTHER SERVICES: Exchange:** Bldg 10400, C-805-734-5521. **Bank/Exchange:** Bldg 10375, C-805-734-4365. **Hair Styles:** Bldg 10400, Barber: C-805-734-1259; Beauty: C-805-734-1264. **Laundry/Dry Cleaning:** Bldg 11193, C-805-734-3039. **Medical:** Bldg 13850, Hrs: 24 hours daily, C-805-866-6206, D-312-276-6206. **Postal:** Bldg 10373, C-805-866-3223. **Wire:** Bldg 10400, C-805-734-5521.

**ATTRACTIONS:** Great beaches, historic missions, and Hearst Castle.

| IN ROUTE SCHEDULES | |
|---|---|
| **Travis AFB** | SUU/MEDEVAC-3 |

**UNSCHEDULED FLIGHTS**

Occasional unscheduled flights to Offutt AFB, NE (**OFF**) via C-21 aircraft.

# Other California Installations with Possible Space-A Air Opportunities.

**PRESIDIO OF MONTEREY AIRPORT (MRY)**
c/o California Medical Detachment, ATTN: Regional Administrator, Presidio of Monterey, CA 93944-5006. C-408-242-7651, D-312-929-7651, FAX 408-242-0501. Very limited MEDEVAC flights.

| IN ROUTE SCHEDULES | |
|---|---|
| **Travis AFB** | SUU/MEDEVAC-3 |

—— NOTES ——

# COLORADO

## BUCKLEY AIR NATIONAL GUARD BASE (BKF)

Aircrew Support Section/140 TW/OTMP
Buckley ANGB, CO 80011-9599

**LOCATION:** On East 6th Ave off I-225. *USMRA: Page 109 (G-3, 4); Page 116 (C,D-3,4)*. NMC: Denver CO, 21 miles west. Main installation numbers: C-303-340-9011, D-312-877-9011. (Main Installation number works only on duty days (Tue-Fri).

**PAX TERM INFO: C-303-340-9663, D-312-877-9663. REC: C-303-340-9662, D-312-877-9662.** Bldg 809, Hrs: daily 0700-1900. Directions: From main gate south to a left at the fire station to 3rd building on the right. Army Flight Ops, Bldg 1500, Hrs: Mon-Fri 0600-2200, C-303-340-9847, D-312-877-9847. **Pax Service Office:** Same as Pax Terminal.

**PAX LOUNGES:** Limited lounge space. No separate family lounges. **VIP:** Lounge, Bldg 909. **General:** Bldg 809, Hrs: daily 0700-1900, C-303-340-9663, D-312-877-9663. Snack bar svc, telephones, TV, restrms, O/S seats. Bldg 909.

**TML:** Lodging Office, Fizsimons AMC, approximately 12 miles northwest (Bldg 400), C-303-361-8903, D-312-943-8903. DV/VIP: C-303-361-8824.

**TRANSPORTATION:** Parking at Bldg 850. Check with Security Police, C-303-340-9930, they must approve overnight/extended parking. Very limited off base transportation available to Space-A passengers. City bus schedule three hours in the morning until 0930 daily, bus resumes at 1530 until 1930 hours.

**OTHER SERVICES:** Limited Base support facilities. **Barber:** Bldg 809, Hrs: 0830-1500 duty days. All Ranks Club and Limited Exchange Services available (on duty days only).

**ATTRACTIONS:** Denver nearby, snow sports. Pro sports teams. National Western Stock Show and Rodeo in January. Fitzsimmons Army Medical Center 5 miles NW of Buckley ANGB.

| BKF/MEDEVAC-1 TUE C-9A | | |
|---|---|---|
| BKF | Buckley ANGB | CO |
| RCA | Ellsworth AFB | SD |
| RDR | Grand Forks AFB | ND |
| MIB | Minot AFB | ND |
| BKF | Buckley ANGB | CO |
| IAB | McConnell AFB | KS |
| **BLV** | **Scott AFB** | **IL** |

*COLORADO*

| IN ROUTE SCHEDULES | |
|---|---|
| **Scott AFB** | BLV/MEDEVAC-3 BLV/MEDEVAC-7 BLV/MEDEVAC-9 |
| | BLV/MEDEVAC-11 |
| **Travis AFB** | SUU/MEDEVAC-4 |

**UNSCHEDULED FLIGHTS**

Army flights and T-43 flights to CONUS locations as mission requires. Also host to Navy/USMC aircraft & reserve units, and ARNC and USAF units. Peterson AFB, CO (**COS**). New IAP at Denver, 12 miles NE of Buckley ANGB.

## PETERSON AIR FORCE BASE (COS)

21st LSS/LGTTS
621 W. Stewart Avenue
Peterson AFB, CO 80914-2420

**LOCATION:** Off US-24 (Platte Ave) east of Colorado Springs. Clearly marked. *USMRA: Page 109 (G-5)*. NMC: Colorado Springs, 6 miles northwest. Main installation numbers: C-719-556-7321, D-312-834-7011.

**PAX TERM INFO: C-719-556-4521, D-312-834-4521, REC: C-719-556-4707, D-312-834-4707, FAX 719-556-4979.** Bldg 122, Hrs: Mon-Fri: 0600-2200, Sat-Sun: (not open except for show times and to meet inbounds). Directions: From main gate, straight on Peterson Blvd to flight line & Pax Term directly ahead. **Pax Service Office:** Bldg 122, Hrs: Mon-Fri: 0600-2200. **Pax Paging:** Bldg 122, Hrs: Mon-Fri: 0600-2200, C-719-556-4521. (Flight Line is closed 2200-0600, if flight comes in there is no service available).

**PAX LOUNGES:** No separate family lounge. **General:** Bldg 122, Hrs: See Pax Term for hours, C-719-556-4707/4521. Telephones, TV, restrooms, O/S seats. **Protocol Service:** Bldg 122, Hrs: Mon-Fri: 0700-1630, 24 hours on call, C-719-556-4225, D-312-834-4225 (06+).

**FOOD SERVICE: Dining Hall:** Bldg 1160, Hrs: daily 0530-1730, C-719-556-4727 (In-flight meals). **NCO/CPO Club:** Bldg 725, Hrs: daily 0700-2330, C-719-556-4194/597-7876. **O'Club:** Bldg 1013, Hrs: daily 0630-2330, C-719-556-4181. **Restaurants:** Bowling Alley: Bldg 406, Hrs: daily 0900-2330, C-719-556-4607. Golf: C-719-556-4454. **Vending:** Bldg 172, 24 hrs daily, C-719-556-4707.

**TRANSPORTATION: Air Tickets:** Bldg 910, Hrs: Mon-Fri 0730-1630, C-719-556-4732 (Professional Travel Corp). **Bus (Comm):** Bldg 122, Hrs: daily 0554-1722, C-719-475-9733 (COS to Ft Carson). **Bus (Gov):** Bldg 1229, 24 hrs daily, C-719-556-4717. **Car Rentals:** Bldg 122, 24 hrs daily, Avis: C-719-596-2751, Hertz: C-719-596-1863,

Budget: C-719-574-7400, National: C-719-596-1519. **Limo Service:** Bldg 122, Hrs: 24 hours daily. Through Colorado Springs Municipal Airport. **Taxi (Comm):** Bldg 122, Hrs: 24 hours daily, Airport: C-719-596-7300, Yellow: C-719-634-6601. **Taxi (Gov):** Bldg 122, Hrs: 24 hours daily, C-719-554-4307 (duty Pax only). **Parking:** Short term: Bldg 122, long term: Bldg 1326, C-719-554-4000.

**TML:** Lodging Office (Bldg 1042, Stewart Ave), 24hrs daily, C-719-556-7851/4513, D-312-834-7851/4513. All ranks. DV/VIP: C-719-556-5077, O7+.

**TRAVELERS AID:** On Base and at Fort Carson. **American Red Cross:** Bldg 1470, Hrs: Mon-Fri 0800-1600, C-719-554-7590. **Chaplain:** Bldg 1410, Hrs: Mon-Fri 0715-1600, C-719-556-4442. **Emergency Relief:** Fort Carson, Hrs: Mon-Fri 0800-1600, C-719-579-2311. **Lost/Found:** Bldg 122, Hrs: daily 0630-1730, C-719-556-4521 (Pax Services).

**Security Police:** Bldg 1376, Hrs: 24 hours daily, C-719-556-4000. **USO:** Colorado Springs Municipal Airport, C-303-574-9626.

**OTHER SERVICES: Exchange:** Bldg 1425, Hrs: Mon-Sat 0900-2100, Sun 1000-1800, C-719-596-7270. **Bank/Exchange:** Bldg 1485, Hrs: Mon-Thu 0900-1500, Fri 0900-1700, C-719-475-6387. **Hair Styles:** Bldg 1425, Hrs: Mon-Sat 0800-1730, Barber: C-719-597-0300, Beauty: C-719-596-0579. **Laundry/Dry Cleaning:** Bldg 1425, Hrs: Mon-Sat 0830-1730, C-719-597-3050. **Medical:** Bldg 959, Hrs: 24 hours daily, Emergency: C-719-556-4333, D-312-834-4333, Other: C-719-556-7712. **Postal:** Bldg 1466, Hrs: Mon-Fri 0830-1630, Sat: 0830-1130, C-719-556-4596.

**ATTRACTIONS:** Ski resorts, U.S. Olympic Training Center, Air Force Academy.

## UNSCHEDULED FLIGHTS

Andrews AFB MD (**ADW**)(3 per week); Kelly AFB TX (**SKF**)(1 per month); Los Angeles IAP, CA (**LAX**)(6 per month); March AFB CA (**RIV**)( 2 per month); McClellan AFB CA (**MCC**)(2 per week); Offutt AFB NE (**OFF**)(3 per week); Randolph AFB TX (**RND**)(1 per week); Scott AFB IL (**BLV**)(1 per week); Wright-Patterson AFB OH (**FFO**)(2 per week). Most flights utilize C-21 or C-130 aircraft. Note: 24 hour notice available on all scheduled and unscheduled flights. Thirty pound luggage limit on C-21 aircraft.

# CONNECTICUT

## BRADLEY INTERNATIONAL AIRPORT (BDL)

103rd FG, Bradley ANG BASE
100 Nicholson Road
East Granby, CT 06026-9309

**LOCATION:** From I-91 north or south, Exit 40 west on Route 20 and follow signs to the Air National Guard, it will lead to the front gate. *USMRA: Page 16 (E-5,6).* NMC: Hartford CT, 12 miles south. Main installation numbers: C-203-292-2526, D-312-636-8310.

**PAX TERM INFO: C-203-292-2356, D-312-636-8356.** Bldg: IAP Departures, Hrs: Tue-Fri 0700-1730. Serves New London Naval Submarine Base and Newport Naval Education and Training Center, RI. Activated primarily during exercise periods. For more information contact 438th APS/TROP, McGuire AFB, NJ 08641-5000, C-609-724-3655, D-312-440-3655. For full details, see Military Living's *U.S. Forces Travel & Transfer Guide U.S.A. and Caribbean Areas.*

**ATTRACTIONS:** New England Air Museum, Historic Newgate Prison, Homes of Samuel Clemens (Mark Twain) and Harriet Beecher Stowe within 1 hour drive.

### UNSCHEDULED FLIGHTS

Very limited CONUS flights. Occasional flights to Andrews AFB, MD (**ADW**). Call for destinations, routings and schedules.

—— NOTES ——

# DELAWARE

## DOVER AIR FORCE BASE (DOV)

436th APS/TROP/ 505 Atlantic St., Rm 214
Dover AFB, DE 19902-5501

**LOCATION:** Off US-113. Clearly marked. *USMRA: Page 42 (I-3)*. NMC: Dover, 3 miles northwest. Main installation numbers: C-302-677-3000, D-312-445-1110. Base Information: C-302-677-2113,

**PAX TERM INFO: C-302-677-2854/4088, D-312-445-2854/4088, REC: C-302-677-4091, D-312-445-4091, (updated 2000 daily), FAX: C-302-677-2953.** Bldg 500, Hrs: 24 hours daily. Directions: From main gate on 13th St to left on 18th St, right after Wing Hq Building to Pax Term in ATC Bldg 500. **Pax Service Office:** Bldg 500, Hrs: Mon-Fri 0730-1630, C-302-677-4076/77/78 (NCO on duty). **Pax Paging:** Bldg 500, Hrs: 24 hours daily, C-302-677-2854/4088. **FAX remote sign-up: C-302-677-2953.**

**PAX LOUNGES:** USO Delaware, 2nd floor. **General:** Bldg 500, 1st floor, Hrs: 24 hours daily, C-302-677-6905. A/C, bag check, telephones (Commercial, defense & long distance), TV, restrooms, P/C seats. *Non-smoking building*. No sleeping in lounge area. **DV/VIP:** Bldg 500, Hrs: 24 hours daily, C-302-677-2854/4088. Not staffed. A/C, telephones (commercial & defense), TV, O/S seats (06+). **Protocol Service:** Bldg 201, Hrs: Mon-Fri 0800-1600, C-302-677-4366, D-312-445-4366.

**FOOD SERVICE:** In-Flight meals available at check-in. **Cafeteria:** Bldg 501, Hrs: 24 hours daily, (closed 0430-0530 M-F), C-302-674-3380. **Dining Hall:** Bldg 403, Hrs: daily 0600-0045, C-302-677-3923. **All Ranks Club:** Bldg 479, Hrs: Mon-Fri 0700-2400, Sat-Sun 0800-2400, C-302-677-6351. **O'Club:** Bldg 813, Hrs: Mon-Sat 1130-2300, C-302-677-6023. **Snack Bars:** Bldg 266, Hrs: Mon-Sat 0900-1500, C-302-677-3380.

**TRANSPORTATION: Air Tickets:** Rogers Travel Agency: Bldg 502, Hrs: Mon-Fri 0830-1630, C-302-736-1668. **Bus (Comm):** Dover, Hrs: 24 hours daily, Trailways: C-302-734-1417. **Car Rentals:** Bldg 500, Hrs: daily 0800-1700, National: C-302-734-5774 or 1-800-227-7368, Avis: C-302-734-5550 or 1-800-331-1212, Budget: C-1-800-527-0700, C-302-734-5688, Enterprise: C-302-674-5553 or 1-800-325-8007, Holden: C-302-734-5708, Hertz: C-302-678-0700 or 1-800-654-3131. **Limo Service:** Bldg 500, Hrs: daily 24hrs, JG Exec: C-302-697-3173. **Taxi (Comm):** City Cab: Bldg 500, Hrs: 24 hours daily, C-302-734-5968. **Trains:** AMTRAK: Wilmington, 45 miles, Hrs: 24 hours daily, C-1-800-872-7245. **Parking:** Bldg 500, Hrs: 24 hours daily, C-302-678-6892. Lot in front of Terminal limited to 12 hours (cars left longer will be towed at owner's expense). Long term lots 1, 2 and 3 are marked and have a pay and honor system. One to eight weeks $5.00 for cars, small trucks and motorcycles. Vans, motorhomes and buses (Lot 3 only) $7.50. Longer period prices available at parking lots. Notification not required.

***DELAWARE***
***Dover Air Force Base, continued***

**TML:** Lodging Office (Bldg 805, 14th St), 24hrs daily, C-302-677-2841, D-312-445-2841. FAX: C-302-677-2963, DSN FAX-312-445-2963. All ranks. DV/VIP: C-302-677-4366.

**TRAVELERS AID: American Red Cross:** Bldg 447, Hrs: Mon-Fri: 0730-1630, C-302-678-2855. After hours C-302-678-3000. **Chaplain:** Bldg 419, Hrs: Mon-Fri: 0745-1645, C-302-677-3931/2. **Emergency Relief:** Bldg 520, Hrs: Mon-Fri: 0730-1630, C-302-677-6930 (Air Force Aid). **Locator:** 677-3000. **Lost/Found:** Bldg 500, Hrs: Daily: 24hrs, C-302-677-4081 (See Pax Term NCO). **Security Police:** Bldg 727, Hrs: Daily: 24hrs, C-302-677-6666 (see SP to park RVs). **Retiree Desk:** Bldg 500, Near flight hours, C-302-677-4612 (unique service-volunteers).

**OTHER SERVICES: Exchange:** Bldg 266, Hrs: Mon-Fri 0900-2100, Sat 0900-1600, C-302-674-4862. **Bank/Exchange:** Mellon Bank: Bldg 267, Hrs: Mon-Fri 0900-1500, C-302-734-0281. **Hair Styles:** Barber: Bldg 266, Hrs: Mon-Fri 0800-1800, Sat 0800-1400, C-302-678-3562; Beauty: Bldg 266, Hrs: Mon-Fri 0830-1700, Sat 0830-1500, C-302-734-1747. Locator: duty hrs, Bldg 442, C-302-677-2841. **Medical:** Bldg 300, 24hrs daily, C-302-677-2500, D-312-445-2500 (Hospital). **Postal:** Bldg 442, Hrs: Mon-Fri 0730-1630, C-302-677-6195. **Valet/Dry Cleaning:** Bldg 266, Hrs: Mon-Fri 0800-1800, Sat 0900-1300, C-302-678-8835.

**ATTRACTIONS:** State capital, great beaches, and the Delaware Bay.

| **ORIGINATING SCHEDULES** | | | |
|---|---|---|---|
| **ACC/DOV-1 4th WED C-5A/B** | | | |
| **Location ID** | **Airport (Station)** | **Country/State** | **Days Out** |
| DOV | Dover AFB | DE | +0 |
| CHS | Charleston AFB | SC | +0 |
| **HOW** | **Howard AFB** | **PN** | **+1** |
| CHS | Charleston AFB/IAP | SC | +2 |
| DOV | Dover AFB | DE | |
| **APM/DOV-2 1st/3rd MON C-5A/B** | | | |
| DOV | Dover AFB | DE | +0 |
| NGU | Norfolk NAS | VA | +0 |
| RTA | Rota NAS | SP | +2 |
| SIZ | Sigonella NAS | IT | +2 |
| BAH | Bahrain IAP | BA | +3 |
| **FUJ** | **Fujairah IAP** | **UA** | **+4** |
| BAH | Bahrain IAP | BA | +4 |
| SIZ | Sigonella NAS | IT | +4 |
| RTA | Rota NAS | SP | +5 |
| LGS | Lajes AB | PO | +6 |

| | | | |
|---|---|---|---|
| NGU | Norfolk NAS | VA | +6 |
| DOV | Dover AFB | DE | |
| | **ACM/DOV-3 1st/3rd/5th THU C-5A/B** | | |
| DOV | Dover AFB | DE | +0 |
| NGU | Norfolk NAS | VA | +1 |
| RTA | Rota NAS | SP | +2 |
| SIZ | Sigonella NAS | IT | +2 |
| BAH | Bahrain IAP | BA | +3 |
| **FUJ** | **Fujairah IAP** | **UA** | **+4** |
| BAH | Bahrain IAP | BA | +4 |
| SIZ | Sigonella NAS | IT | +4 |
| RTA | Rota NAS | SP | +5 |
| LGS | Lajes AB | PO | +6 |
| NGU | Norfolk NAS | VA | +6 |
| DOV | Dover AFB | DE | |
| | **ACC/DOV-4 2nd/4th SUN C-5A/B** | | |
| DOV | Dover AFB | DE | +0 |
| RMS | Ramstein AB | GE | +2 |
| **TLV** | **Ben Gurion APT** | **IS** | **+2** |
| RMS | Ramstein AB | GE | +3 |
| DOV | Dover AFB | DE | |
| | **APM/DOV-5 SUN C-5A/B** | | |
| DOV | Dover AFB | DE | +0 |
| RMS | Ramstein AB | GE | +1 |
| **DHA** | **Dhahran IAP** | **SA** | **+2** |
| RUH | Riyadh IAP | SA | +2 |
| RMS | Ramstein AB | GE | +4 |
| DOV | Dover AFB | DE | |
| | **ACM/DOV-6 SUN C-5A/B** | | |
| DOV | Dover AFB | DE | +0 |
| RMS | Ramstein AB | GE | +1 |
| **DHA** | **Dhahran IAP** | **SA** | **+2** |
| RUH | Riyadh IAP | SA | +2 |
| RMS | Ramstein AB | GE | +4 |
| KEF | Keflavik APT | IC | +4 |
| DOV | Dover AFB | DE | |
| | **APM/DOV-7 1st/3rd TUE C-5A/B** | | |
| DOV | Dover AFB | DE | +0 |

***DELAWARE***
***Dover Air Force Base, continued***

| | | | |
|---|---|---|---|
| RMS | Ramstein AB | GE | +1 |
| **ADA** | **Incirlik APT** | **TU** | **+2** |
| RMS | Ramstein AB | GE | +3 |
| KEF | Keflavik APT | IC | +3 |
| DOV | Dover AFB | DE | |
| | **ACC/DOV-8 1st/2nd/4th WED C-5A/B** | | |
| DOV | Dover AFB | DE | +0 |
| RMS | Ramstein AB | GE | +2 |
| KWI | Kuwait IAP | KW | +2 |
| **DHA** | **Dhahran IAP** | **SA** | **+3** |
| RMS | Ramstein AB | GE | +4 |
| DOV | Dover AFB | DE | |
| | **ACC/DOV-9 3rd SUN C-5A/B** | | |
| DOV | Dover AFB | DE | +0 |
| **RMS** | **Ramstein AB** | **GE** | **+2** |
| LGS | Lajes AB | PO | +3 |
| DOV | Dover AFB | DE | |
| | **APM/DOV-10 SUN DC862** | | |
| DOV | Dover AFB | DE | +0 |
| RMS | Ramstein AB | GE | +0 |
| SIZ | Sigonella NAS | IT | +0 |
| KWI | Kuwait IAP | KW | +1 |
| BAH | Bahrain IAP | BA | +1 |
| **FUJ** | **Fujairah IAP** | **UA** | **+2** |
| BAH | Bahrain IAP | BA | +2 |
| KWI | Kuwait IAP | KW | +2 |
| SIZ | Sigonella NAS | IT | +2 |
| RMS | Ramstein AB | GE | +2 |
| DOV | Dover AFB | DE | |

| | **IN ROUTE SCHEDULES** | | |
|---|---|---|---|
| **Allen C Thompson Field** | ACC/JAN-1 | | |
| **Altus AFB** | ACC/LTS-1 | | |
| **Andrews AFB** | ACC/ADW-1 | ACC/ADW-2 | |
| **Charleston AFB/IAP** | ACC/CHS-3 | ACC/CHS-4 | ACC/CHS-5 |
| | APM/CHS-6 | ACC/CHS-7 | ACM/CHS-8 |
| | ACC/CHS-15 | | |
| **Fairchild AFB** | ACC/SKA-1 | | |
| **Kelly AFB** | ACC/SKF-1 | | |

| | | | |
|---|---|---|---|
| **McGuire AFB** | ACC/WRI-6 | ACC/WRI-7 | ACC/WRI-8 |
| | APM/WRI-9 | ACC/WRI-10 | ACC/WRI-11 |
| | ACM/WRI-13 | ACC/WRI-14 | ACC/WRI-15 |
| **Memphis IAP** | ACM/MEM-1 | | |
| **Robins AFB** | ACC/WRB-1 | | |
| **Stewart ANGB** | ACC/SWF-1 | ACC/SWF-2 | |
| **Tinker AFB** | ACC/TIK-1 | | |
| **Westover ARB** | ACC/CEF-2 | APM/CEF-2 | ACC/CEF-3 |
| **Wright-Patterson AFB** | ACC/FFO-1 | ACC/FFO-2 | PCC/FFO-2 |

# NEW CASTLE COUNTY AIRPORT (ILG)

166th AG/ILG, (ANG)
New Castle, DE 19720-2495

**LOCATION:** From I-95 north or south, take Exit 5 to DE-41 south for 1 mile to the intersection of DE-37 (Commons Blvd) where entrance to ANGB is well marked. *USMRA: Page 42 (I-1, 2)*. NMC: Wilmington DE, 7 miles NE. Main installation numbers: C-302-323-3525, D-312-445-7525.

**PAX TERM INFO: C-302-323-3525, D-312-445-7525, FAX: C-302-323-3330, D-312-445-7330.** Bldg 2812, Base Ops, Hrs: Mon-Fri 0800-1630 and during flight processing. Directions: Entrance off DE-41 and straight to ANG Base Ops. Also, DE ANG Flight Ops, Bldg 2812. All facilities of a regional airport are available at the Commercial Airport Term. **Pax Service Office:** Bldg 2812, Hrs: Mon-Fri 0800-1630, C-302-323-3525.

**PAX LOUNGES:** Limited lounge facilities. No DV/VIP or family lounges. **General:** Bldg 2812, Hrs: Mon-Fri 0800-1630, C-302-323-3525. A/C, restrooms, P/C seats.

**TRANSPORTATION: Car Rentals:** New Castle County Airport. Call for hours. Dollar: *C-302-655-7117*, National: *C-302-328-5636*. **Parking:** Behind Bldg 2812, Hrs: Daily: 24hrs, *C-302-323-3525* (no restrictions).

**TML:** Aberdeen Proving Ground, MD. Lodging Office (Bldg 2207, Bel Air St), C-410-278-5148/49, D-312-298-4373, FAX 410-273-6500-EX-7740. DV/VIP-TECOM protocol C-410-278-5156. O6+.

**ATTRACTIONS:** Historic section of Wilmington.

**UNSCHEDULED FLIGHTS**

Some flights to CONUS and OCONUS locations via C-130H aircraft. Call for destinations, routings and schedules.

# FLORIDA

## CECIL FIELD NAVAL AIR STATION (NZC)

Air Operations Officer
Cecil Field NAS, FL 32215-5000
**Scheduled to close 9/30/98.**

**LOCATION:** Take Normandy exit west off I-295 and follow Normandy (FL-228) to main gate. *USMRA: Page 38 (G-3).* NMC: Jacksonville, 13 miles east. Main installations numbers: C-904-778-5626, D-312-860-5626.

**PAX TERM INFO: C-904-778-5536/5448, D-312-860-5536/5448, FAX: C-904-778-5833.** Bldg 47, Hrs: Mon-Fri 0700-1600, weekends as needed. Directions: From main gate, straight on "D" Ave to left on 1st St to Air Processing Term on the right. **Pax Service Office:** Same as Pax Terminal.

**PAX LOUNGES:** Same as Pax terminal. (limited facilities).

**FOOD SERVICE: Dining Hall:** Bldg 91, C-904-778-5312. **Enlisted Club:** Bldg 220, C-904-778-6154. **CPO Club:** Bldg 340, C-904-778-5390. **O'Club:** Bldg 331, C-904-778-5255. **McDonalds:** C-904-771-7887. **Pizza:** Bldg 220, C-904-770-6107. **Snack Bars:** Bldg 905, C-904-778-5225.

**TRANSPORTATION: Air Tickets:** SATO: Bldg 26, Hrs: Mon-Fri 0800-1600, C-904-778-0063. **Taxi (Comm):** Main gate, C-904-778-5627 (Security Police for assistance). **Taxi (Gov):** Public works, Hrs: Mon-Fri 0730-1600, C-904-778-5487 (duty Pax only).

**TML:** Lodging Office (Bldg 331, D Ave & 4th St), 24hrs daily, C-904-771-0641, D-312-860-5255/5258 (Guest House), FAX C-904-778-6730. DV/VIP: C-904-771-5255, D-312-860-5255.

**TRAVELERS AID: American Red Cross:** Bldg 204, C-904-778-1550. **Chaplain:** Bldg 800, C-904-778-5340/9, After hours: C-904-778-5626. **Navy Relief:** Bldg 204, C-904-778-6170/1. **Security Police:** Bldg 327, C-904-778-5381/2/3 (Desk Sgt). **USO:**(JAX NAS), C-904-778-2821 (also, JAX Beach).

**OTHER SERVICES: Exchange:** Bldg 905, C-904-778-3176. **Hair Styles:** Bldg 905, Barber: C-904-778-3198; Beauty: C-904-771-0351. **Medical:** Bldg 808, Emerg, C-904-778-5212, D-312-772-5212. Inpatient at NAS Jacksonville.

**ATTRACTIONS:** Beaches, Disney World (Orlando area), Cypress Gardens, Universal Studios, Sea World.

**UNSCHEDULED FLIGHTS**

Weekly flights to: Brunswick NAS, ME (**NHZ**); Charleston AFB/IAP, SC (**CHS**); Jacksonville NAS, FL (**NIP**); and Norfolk NAS, VA (**NGU**) via P-3 and C-009A aircraft/missions. The best Space-A air opportunities in the area are at Jacksonville NAS, FL (**NIP**). Flight information available up to 72 hours in advance.

## CLEARWATER COAST GUARD AIR STATION (PIE)

Commanding Officer
15000 Rescue Way
Clearwater, FL 34622-5000

**LOCATION:** At the St Petersburg-Clearwater IAP, take the FL-686 exit from I-275 and go for 1 mile west. *USMRA: Page 38 (E-8)*. NMC: St Petersburg, 5 miles south. Main installation numbers: C-813-535-1437, D-312-968-4273.

**PAX TERM INFO: C-813-535-1437 EX 1181, D-312-968-4273 EX 1181, FAX: C-813-535-4256.** USCG Hangar, Hrs: Mon-Fri 0800-1600. Ask Security Police for directions. Parking—west of hangar.

**OTHER SERVICES:** Many support facilities available to include: Barber, Exchange, and Emergency Medical.

**UNSCHEDULED FLIGHTS**

Infrequent flights to CONUS and OCONUS locations via C-130 aircraft. No Space-A on helicopter aircraft. Call for destinations, routings and schedules.

## EGLIN AIR FORCE BASE (VPS)

96th TRANS/LGTRM
601 W. Choctawatchee Ave, Suite 78
Eglin AFB, FL 32542-5000

**LOCATION:** Exit I-10 at Crestview and follow posted direction signs to Niceville and Valparaiso (Eglin AFB). *USMRA: Page 39 (B,C,D-13); Page 53 (E,F,G,H-1,2,3,4)*. NMC: Fort Walton Beach, 7 miles south. Main installation numbers: C-904-882-1110, D-312-872-1110.

**PAX TERM INFO: C-904-882-4757, D-312-872-4757, FAX (Remote sign-up) 904-882-2655, D FAX 312-872-2655, Rec: C-904-882-3332.** Bldg 60, Hrs: Mon-Fri 0700-1600, Sat-Sun 0800-1600. Directions: From west gate straight on Eglin Blvd to left on 7th Street to a left onto Choctawhatchee Avenue to Pax Term on right. **Pax Service Office:** Same as Pax Terminal (NCO on duty). Pax Paging: Same as Pax Terminal, C-904-882-5313.

*FLORIDA*
*Eglin Air Force Base, continued*

**PAX LOUNGES:** No separate family lounge. **General:** Bldg 60, Hrs: 24 hours daily, C-904-882-5732. A/C, restrooms, TV, P/C seats. **DV/VIP:** Bldg 60, Hrs: 24 hours daily, C-904-882-5732 (no host). A/C, coffee/tea service, restrooms, separate read/write rooms, O/S seats. **Protocol Service:** Bldg 1, Hrs: Mon-Fri 0715-1600, C-904-882-3011.

**FOOD SERVICE: Cafeteria:** Bldg 1759, C-904-651-4821 ("Run-in-Chef"). **Dining Hall:** Bldg 18-D, C-904-882-5053. **Flight Kitchen:** C-904-882-5014. **NCO/CPO Club:** Bldg 860, C-904-678-5127. **O'Club:** Bldg 10870, C-904-651-1010. **Snack Bars:** Bldg 100, C-904-678-5932.

**TRANSPORTATION: Air Tickets:** (Ortega) Bldg 350, C-904-882-8016. **Taxi (Gov):** Bldg 509, C-904-882-3791 (duty Pax only). **Parking:** Bldg 60, C-904-882-2502 (in front of building).

**TML:** Lodging Office (Eglin Inn, Bldg 11001, Boatner Rd), 24hrs daily, C-904-882-4534/5, D-312-872-8761, FAX 904-882-2708. All ranks. DV/VIP: C-904-882-3011/3238.

**TRAVELERS AID: American Red Cross:** Bldg 210, C-904-882-5848, After hours C-904-882-2485. **Chaplain:** Bldg 868, C-904-882-2111. **Emergency Relief:** Bldg 210, C-904-882-4395. **Lost/Found:** Bldg 60, C-904-882-5732. **Security Police:** Bldg 272, C-904-882-2502.

**OTHER SERVICES: Exchange:** Bldg 1757, C-904-651-2512. **Bank/Exchange:** Memorial Lake, C-904-651-1112. **Hair Styles:** Bldg 1757: Barber: C-904-651-5122; Beauty: C-904-651-5224. **Laundry/Dry Cleaning:** Bldg 12, C-904-651-4924. **Medical:** Bldg 2825, C-904-885-3337, D-312-872-3337. **Postal:** Bldg 10, C-904-882-3311.

**ATTRACTIONS:** Beaches, sport fishing, dog races.

| IN ROUTE SCHEDULES | |
|---|---|
| **Keesler AFB** | BIX/MEDEVAC-1 BIX/MEDEVAC-2 |

**UNSCHEDULED FLIGHTS**

Frequent flights to CONUS and OCONUS locations. Call for destinations, routing and schedules.

## HOMESTEAD AIR RESERVE BASE (HST)

360 Coral Sea Boulevard
Homestead ARB, FL 33039-1299

**LOCATION:** Exit 6 off Florida Turnpike, left at bottom of the ramp, approximately 1/2 mile to traffic light (SW 288th St.), then left to main gate. *USMRA: page 39, I-14*. NMC: Miami, 40 miles NE. Main installation numbers: C-305-224-7000, D-312-791-7000.

**PAX TERM INFO:** Pax Terminal/lounge Bldg 701, **C-305-224-7518, D-312-791-7518.**

**UNSCHEDULED FLIGHTS**

Frequent flights to CONUS and OCONUS locations via HC-130H and other aircraft.

## HURLBURT FIELD (HRT)

Passenger Service Personnel
Base Operations
Hurlburt Field, FL 32544-5844

**LOCATION:** Off US-98, 5 miles west of Fort Walton Beach. Clearly marked. *USMRA: Page 39 (C-13); Page 53 (H-4).* NMC: Pensacola, 40 miles west. Main Installation Numbers: C-904-882-1110 (Eglin AFB info), D-312-579-1110.

**PAX TERM INFO: C-904-884-5783 (recording), D-312-579-5783.** Bldg 90708, Hrs: Daily: 0730-1630. Also see Eglin AFB listing.

**OTHER SERVICES:** Exchange: C-904-581-0030. Medical: C-904-884-7882, D-312-579-7882. Chaplain: C-904-884-7795.

**TML:** Lodging Office (Bldg 90509), Hrs: 24 hours daily, C-904-884-6245 or 904-581-1627, D-312-579-6245/7115, FAX C-904-884-5043. All ranks. DV/VIP: C-904-884-2308, D-312-579-2308.

**UNSCHEDULED FLIGHTS**

Occasional flights to Central America. Call for destinations, routings and schedules

## JACKSONVILLE NAVAL AIR STATION (NIP)

Box 7, AIRODS
Jacksonville NAS, FL 32212-5000

**LOCATION:** Access from US-17 south (Roosevelt Blvd). On the St Johns River. *USMRA: Page 38 (G-3); Page 50 (B-7).* NMC: Jacksonville, 9 miles northeast. Main installation numbers: C-904-772-2345/2346, D-312-942-2345/2346.

**PAX TERM INFO: C-904-772-3956/3825, D-312-942-3956/3825. FAX: C-904-942-2514.** Bldg 118, Hrs: 24 hours daily. Directions: From main gate, straight on Yorktown Ave to a left on Wasp St to a right on Albemarle Ave. The terminal is on the left. **Pax Service Office:** Same as Pax Terminal. **Pax Paging:** Same as Pax Terminal.

**OTHER SERVICES: Exchange:** C-904-777-7200. **SATO** Ticket Office: C-904-772-3703. **O'Club:** C-904-772-3041. **Medical:** C-904-777-7300. **Security Police:** C-904-772-2661.

***FLORIDA***
***Jackonville Naval Air Station, continued***

**TML:** Lodging Office (Bldg 11), C-904-772-3138/39(EM); C-904-772-3537/4052(Officer), FAX C-904-772-5002. DV/VIP: 904-772-3147/3427. Navy Lodge: C-904-772-6000, D-312-942-6000 or 1-800-NAVY-INN.

**ATTRACTIONS:** Golfing, Beaches, fishing, St. Augustine, Orlando.

| IN ROUTE SCHEDULES | |
|---|---|
| **Norfolk NAS** | APP/NGU-2 |

**UNSCHEDULED FLIGHTS**

Frequent flights to: Charleston AFB/IAP, SC (**CHS**); Guantanamo NS, CU (**GAO**); MacDill AFB, FL (**MCF**); Norfolk NAS, VA (**NGU**); and Roosevelt Roads NAS, PR (**NRR**). - Note: 3 days prior notice on flights. Schedules subject to change. Most flights to East Coast destinations and some to OCONUS and foreign countries.

# KEY WEST NAVAL AIR STATION (NQX)

Operations Dept, Field Services Division
Key West NAS, FL 33040-5000

**LOCATION:** Take Florida Turnpike, US-1 south to exit signs for Key West NAS on Boca Chica Key, 7 miles north of Key West. *USMRA: Page 39 (G-16).* NMC: Miami, 150 miles north. Main installation numbers: C-305-293-3700, D-312-483-3700.

**PAX TERM INFO: C-305-293-2769/2751, D-312-483-2769/2751. REC: C-305-293-2751, D-312-483-2751.** Bldg NAS ATC tower, Hrs: daily 0800-1600. Directions: On Boca Chica Key, easily visible. **Pax Service Office:** Same as Pax terminal, C-305-292-2770 (NCO on duty).

**PAX LOUNGES:** No Pax Term. All Pax processing handled at ATC/Ops, C-305-296-3561/2735. A/C, restrooms, TV, O/S & P/C seats.

**FOOD SERVICE: Cafeteria:** Boca Chica Key, C-305-292-2687. **Dining Hall:** Hrs: daily 0530-1735, C-305-292-2687. **Enlisted Club:** NAS, C-305-292-2495. **NCO/CPO Club:** C-305-292-2407. **O'Club:** NAS, C-305-295-5571.

**TRANSPORTATION: Bus Shuttle:** ATC/Ops, Hrs: Mon-Fri 0800-1600, C-305-292-2342 (on Base). **Car Rentals:** Key West IAP, Avis C-305-296-8744, Hertz C-305-294-1039. **Taxi (Comm):** ATC/Ops, C-305-292-2342/2268. **Parking:** ATC/Ops, (no restrictions).

**TML:** Lodging Office (Bldg 2076), Hrs: 24 hours daily, C-305-293-4100, D-312-483-2112/5571. All ranks. **Navy Lodge:** C-305-292-7556. DV/VIP: C-305-292-2178.

**TRAVELERS AID: American Red Cross:** 600 White St, Key West, Tue and Thu, C-305-296-3651. **Chaplain:** Base Chapel NAS, C-305-292-2318. **Emergency Relief:** Bldg

**OTHER SERVICES: Exchange:** NAS/BX, C-305-294-7262. **Bank/Exchange:** NAS/BX, C-305-294-1796 (US currency only). **Hair Styles:** NAS/BX, C-305-292-7221. **Medical:** NAS, Hrs: 24 hours daily, C-305-292-2335, C-305-294-3500. **Postal:** Bldg 409, C-305-292-2406.

**ATTRACTIONS:** Water sports, Ernest Hemingway Home.

| IN ROUTE SCHEDULES | |
|---|---|
| **Scott AFB** | BLV/MEDEVAC-2 |

**UNSCHEDULED FLIGHTS**

Occasional flights to Cecil Field, FL (**NZC**); Keesler AFB, MS (**BIX**); MacDill AFB, FL (**MCF**) and Orlando IAP, FL (**MCO**). Call for destinations, routings and schedules.

711-A, Hrs: Mon-Fri 0900-1500, C-305-294-3561 (Navy Relief). **Security Police:** Main gate, C-305-292-2455.

# MacDILL AIR FORCE BASE (MCF)

6th Transportation Squadron, Passenger Terminal
2909 Night Hawk Place
MacDill AFB, FL 33621-5501

**LOCATION:** Take I-75 South to I-275 South, exit at Dale Mabry Hwy (US-92) South, 5 miles south to MacDill AFB main gate. *USMRA: Page 38 (E,F-8).* NMC: Tampa, 5 miles north. Main installation numbers: C-813-828-1110, D-312-968-1110.

**PAX TERM INFO: C-813-828-2310/2485, D-312-968-2310/2485, REC: C-813-828-2310, D-312-968-2310, FAX: C-813-828-3202, D-312-968-3202.** Bldg Hangar #4, Hrs: Mon-Fri 0730-1630, weekends as required. Directions: Enter Dale Mabry gate. Turn left on North Boundary Rd to right on Hangar Loop Road, 5th Hangar on right. Hangar #5 Army Aviation, C-813-828-2808, D-312-968-2808. Flights on C-12 aircraft to CONUS destinations. **Pax Service Office:** Same as Pax terminal. No Paging. **Pax Info (Other Services):** Hangar #3, Hrs: Mon-Fri 0730-1630, C-813-828-2808, D-312-968-2808 (Army Aviation).

**PAX LOUNGES:** General lounge is also family lounge. **General:** Hangar #5, Room 101, Hrs: Mon-Fri 0730-1630, C-813-828-2310/2485. A/C, bag check, telephones (local, long distance and defense), TV, restrooms, P/C seats. **DV/VIP:** Hangar #3, Hrs: daily 0730-1630, C-813-828-2485/2350. A/C, coffee/tea served, read/write rooms, telephones (local, long distance and defense), TV, restrooms, showers, O/S seats (06+). **Protocol Service:** Bldg 9, Hrs: Mon-Fri 0730-1630, C-813-828-2056.

**FOOD SERVICE: Burger King:** C-813-840-2992. **Cafeteria:** Bldg 259, C-813-828-0511. **Enlisted Club:** Bldg 499, C-813-828-3357. **In-flight Meals:** Hangar #2, Hrs: Mon-Fri 1030-1500 and 1800-2100, C-813-828-4403/4493. **O'Club:** Bldg 397, C-813-837-1031.

*FLORIDA*
**MacDill Air Force Base, continued**

**TRANSPORTATION: Air Tickets:** SATO: Bldg 528, C-813-828-4327. **Bus (Comm):** Bldg 926, C-813-254-HART. **Car Rentals:** Bldg 17, C-813-840-2303 (Dayton Andrews). **Taxi (Comm):** Gates, United: C-813-253-0121, Yellow: C-813-253-2424. **Taxi (Gov):** Bldg 176, C-813-828-5281 (duty Pax only). **Parking:** Short term-Hangar #2, 5 day limit, C-813-828-2485; long term-across from Hangar #3 by water tower, 2 month limit, C-813-828-3322. Call Security Police for info, C-813-828-3322.

**TML:** Lodging Office (Bldg 411), Hrs: 24 hours daily, C-813-828-4259, D-312-968-4259, FAX C-813-828-2660. All ranks. DV/VIP: C-813-828-2056, O6+.

**TRAVELERS AID: American Red Cross:** Hospital, Bldg 7011, C-813-828-3156. If no answer, call C-813-832-2507. **Chaplain:** Bldg 355, C-813-828-3621. **Emergency Relief:** Bldg 373, C-813-828-3311. **Lost/Found:** Bldg P-26, C-813-828-3322. **Security Police:** Bldg P-26, C-813-828-3322. **USO:** 318 Madison, Tampa, C-813-229-9401.

**OTHER SERVICES: Exchange:** Bldg 926, C-813-828-0511. **Bank/Exchange:** Bldg 102, C-813-837-2451. **Hair Styles:** Bldg 926, Barber: C-813-840-2154/3978; Beauty: C-813-840-0525. **Laundry/Dry Cleaning:** Bldg 17, C-813-840-2329. **Medical:** Bldg 711, Hrs: 24 hours daily, C-813-839-3344, D-312-968-3344. **Postal:** Bldg 344, C-813-828-4438.

| IN ROUTE SCHEDULES | |
|---|---|
| **Scott AFB** | BLV/MEDEVAC-2 |

**UNSCHEDULED FLIGHTS**

Frequent flights to: Andrews AFB, MD (**ADW**); Dover AFB, DE (**DOV**); Eglin AFB, FL (**VPS**); Jacksonville NAS, FL (**NIP**); March AFB, CA (**RIV**); McGuire AFB, NJ (**WRI**); Oceana NAS, VA (**NTU**); Pease ANGB, NH (**PSM**); and Peterson AFB, CO (**COS**). Flight information available one day in advance.

## ORLANDO INTERNATIONAL AIRPORT (MCO)

Pax Service Personnel,
Orlando Naval Training Center
P.O. Box 149472, Orlando, FL 32814-9472
**Scheduled to close 12/31/98**

**LOCATION:** From I-4 in Orlando take FL-50 (Colonial Dr) east about 3 miles, then north on Bennet Rd for .5 miles to Naval Training Center. *USMRA: Page 38 (H-7).* NMC: Orlando, in city limits. Main installation numbers: C-407-646-4111, D-312-791-4111.

**PAX TERM INFO: C-407-643-2360, D-312-791-2360 ask for passenger service.** Bldg AMC Counter, Hrs: During flight processing. Many facilities at the Naval Training Center. Full support of IAP available. **USO:** C-407-647-2241. For full details, see Military Living's *U.S. Forces Travel & Transfer Guide USA and Caribbean Areas.*

**TML:** Lodging Office (Orlando Naval Training Center, Bldg 375), C-407-646-5614, D-312-791-5614, FAX C-407-646-4855.

**ATTRACTIONS:** Disney World, Epcot Center, MGM Studio, Sea World, Cypress Gardens, Universal Studio, Church Street Station, Friday Recruit Review (free).

| IN ROUTE SCHEDULES | |
|---|---|
| **Scott AFB** | BLV/MEDEVAC-2 |

**ATTRACTIONS:** Tampa Bay, Citrus Belt, Busch Gardens.

## PATRICK AIR FORCE BASE (COF)

45th TRNS/LGA, 930 South Patrick Drive,
Patrick AFB, FL 32925-3223

**LOCATION:** I-95 exit 73 (marked Patrick AFB/Wickham Rd), approximately 5 miles south on Wickham Rd, take Hwy 404 east to Patrick AFB exit. Base on Hwy A1A, approximately 5 miles south of Cocoa Beach. *USMRA: Page 38 (I-8).* NMC: Orlando, 60 miles northwest. Melbourne, Cocoa, and Merritt Island - all within 20 miles of Base. Main installation numbers: C-407-494-1110, D-312-854-1110.

**PAX TERM INFO: C-407-494-5631/5632/5633, D-312-854-5631/5632/5633, FAX: C-407-494-7991, D-312-854-7991.** Bldg 800, Hrs: Mon-Fri 0730-1600, Sat 0800-1600. Directions: 1 mile north of South Gate on South Patrick Dr. Pax Svc entrance faces south Patrick Dr. Same Bldg as Base Ops and control tower. **Pax Service Office:** Same as Pax terminal.

**PAX LOUNGES:** No separate family lounge. **General:** Bldg 800, 1st floor, Hrs: Mon-Fri: 0730-1630, Sa: 0800-1600, C-407-494-5631, D-312-854-5631. A/C, TV, O/S seats, restrooms, telephones (commercial and defense), bag check. **DV/VIP:** Bldg 800, Hrs: daily 0730-1630, C-407-494-5631, D-312-854-5631 (06+). A/C, TV, O/S seats, restrooms, telephones (commercial and defense), bag check. **Protocol Services:** Bldg 423, C-407-494-4506, 07+.

**FOOD SERVICE: Cafeteria:** Bldg 546, 2nd floor, Hrs: Mon-Sat 1030-1500, C-407-494-5523 ("Comet Club"). **Enlisted Club:** Bldg 546, Hrs: Mon-Sat 1030-1500, C-407-494-7491. **NCO/CPO Club:** Bldg 967, Hrs: Mon-Fri 0630-2200, Sat-Sun 0800-2000, C-407-494-7491. **O'Club:** Bldg 250, Hrs: Mon-Fri 0630-1930, Sat-Sun 0800-1930, C-407-494-4001. **Restaurant:** Bldg 600, daily 0800-2000, C-407-494-2042 ("Boat House"). **Snack Bars:** Bldg 732, Hrs: Mon-Sat 0800-2300, C-407-494-2598. Snack bars also at bowling alley, golf course C-407-494-6510. **Vending:** Bldg 800, Hrs: Daily: 0730-2300.

*FLORIDA*
*Patrick Air Force Base, continued*

routing). **Car Rentals**: Bldg 400, Hrs: Mon-Fri 0800-1630, C-407-783-2424, **Taxi (Comm):** In Cocoa Beach, Hrs: 24 hours daily, C-407-783-7200/2500. **Taxi (Gov):** Bldg 329, Hrs: Mon-Fri 0730-2300, Sat-Sun 0730-1500, C-407-494-7247 (for military personnel on orders only). Parking: Short term-north of Bldg 800 (Pax Term) Hrs: daily 0730-2300 (no overnight); long term-150 yards south of Bldg 800 (unlimited hours).

**TML:** Lodging Office (Bldg 720, 820 Falcon Ave), Hrs: 24 hours daily, C-407-783-8511, D-312-854-2075. All ranks. Coral Lodge (on C St). DV/VIP: C-407-494-4511.

**TRAVELERS AID: American Red Cross:** Bldg 425, Hrs: Mon-Fri 0730-1630, C-407-494-2402. **Chaplain:** Serving all faiths. Duty hours C-407-494-4073. **Lost/Found:** Bldg 800, Hrs: daily 0730 -1630, C-407-494-5631. **Security Police:** Bldg 405, Hrs: daily 24 hrs, C-407-494-7777.

**OTHER SERVICES: Exchange:** Off Base. Hrs: Mon-Fri 0930-1800, Sat-Sun 0930-1630, C-407-494-7457. **Bank/Exchange:** Bldg 720, Hrs: Mon-Fri 0900-1700, C-407-783-3411. **Hair Styles:** Bldg 415, Barber: C-407-784-2781; Beauty: C-407-784-1241. **Laundry/Dry Cleaning:** Bldg 415, Hrs: Mon-Fri 0930-1800, Sat-Sun 0930-1630, C-407-783-3625. **Postal:** Bldg 424. **Medical:** Bldg 1380, Hrs: 24 hours daily, C-407-494-2333, D-312-854-2333. **Wire:** Western Union available in Cocoa Beach.

**ATTRACTIONS:** NASA Space Flight Center, Daytona Beach, Orlando-Disney World.

| | IN ROUTE SCHEDULES |
|---|---|
| **Charleston AFB** | ACM/CHS-19 |
| **McGuire AFB** | ACM/WRI-21 |
| **Scott AFB** | BLV/MEDEVAC-2 |

**UNSCHEDULED FLIGHTS**

Frequent flights to CONUS and OCONUS locations. Call for destinations, routings and schedules.

# PENSACOLA NAVAL AIR STATION (NPA)

Air Operations, Bldg 1852
Sky Hawk Drive
Pensacola NAS, FL 32508-5000

**LOCATION:** Off US-98, 4 miles south, and 12 miles south of I-10. Take Navy Blve from US-98 or US-29 directly to NAS. *USMRA: Page 39 (A,B-13); Page 53 (A,B-4,5).* NMC: Pensacola, 8 miles north. Main installatio numbers: C-904-452-0111, D-312-922-0111.

**PAX TERM INFO: C-904-452-3311/2431, D-312-922-3311/2431, FAX: C-904-452-8105, REC: C-904-452-3311.** Bldg 1852, Hrs: 24 hours daily. Directions: From main gate, straight on Duncan Rd to right on Taylor Rd to a right onto Radford Rd to Air Ops on the right. Pax Service Office: Same as Pax Terminal. Pax Paging: Same as Pax Terminal.

**PAX LOUNGES:** No separate family lounge. **General/Family Lounge:** Bldg 1852, Room 105, Hrs: 24 hours daily, C-904-452-2431. A/C, bag check, restrooms, TV. **DV/VIP:** Bldg 1852, Hrs: 24 hours daily, C-904-452-2431. A/C, coffee/tea service.

**FOOD SERVICE: Cafeteria:** Bldg 634, C-904-455-0932 EX-222. **Enlisted Club:** "Ducks", Bldg 667, C-904-452-2443; Lighthouse Point, Bldg 3558, C-904-452-3251. **O'Club:** Bldg 253, C-904-455-2276, (Mustin beach). **Snack Bars:** Bowling Center, C-904-452-3899; Golf Course,, C-904-452-3859. **Vending:** Bldg 1852, C-904-452-3311.

**TRANSPORTATION: Air Tickets:** Leisure Travel Service, Bldg 632, C-904-453-8422; SATO, Bldg 680, C-904-452-2589. Bus (Comm): Fairfield Rd, C-904-436-9383. Car Rentals: Enterprise Rent-A-Car, NAS Bldg 470, C-904-456-7468. **Taxi (Comm):** Bldg 1852, C-904-455-8500 (Warrington). **Parking:** Bldg 3585, C-904-452-3311 (short and long term).

**TML:** Lodging Office (Bldg 3472), C-904-452-3438/4609, FAX 904-452-6483. DV/VIP: Bldg 600 (06+). **Navy Lodge:** C-904-456-8676 or 1-800-NAVY-INN.

**TRAVELERS AID: American Red Cross:** Bldg 25, C-904-452-2492, After hours C-904-452-6601. **Chaplain:** Bldg 634, C-904-452-2341. **Emergency Relief:** Bldg 16, C-904-455-8574 (Navy Relief). **Lost/Found:** Bldg 1852, C-904-452-2432. **Security Police:** Main gate, C-904-452-2453.

**OTHER SERVICES: Exchange:** Bldg 634, C-904-453-0392. **Bank/Exchange:** First Navy Bank: Murray Rd, C-904-453-3411. **Hair Styles:** Barber: Bldg 3248, C-904-456-0138; Beauty: Bldg 634, C-904-455-5224. **Laundry/Dry Cleaning:** Bldg 634, C-904-455-5313. **Medical:** Naval Hospital, Hrs: 24 hours daily, C-904-452-6601, D-312-922-6601. **Postal:** Bldg 223, C-904-452-2726.

**ATTRACTIONS:** Sport fishing, dog races, Naval Aviation Museum, Blue Angels, Sailing Facility, and Marina.

## UNSCHEDULED FLIGHTS

Two to ten flights each month to the following locations: Charleston, SC (**CHS**); Corpus Christi NAS, TX (**NGP**); Fort Worth NAS/Joint Reserve Base, TX (**FWH**); Jacksonville NAS, FL (**NIP**); Memphis NAS, TN (**NQA**); Meridian NAS, MS (**NMM**); Norfolk NAS, VA (**NGU**) and Washington NAF, MD (**NSF**). Flights are by C-009 and C-12 ACF.

# GEORGIA

## AMC AT THE WILLIAM B. HARTSFIELD ATLANTA IAP (ATL)

437 APS/TRG
Charleston IAP
5500 International Blvd, Suite 124
Charleston, SC 29418-0308

**LOCATION:** The AMC counter is located in the North Terminal of the William B. Hartsfield IAP in Atlanta, GA. This is at the Lockheed counter next to United Airlines and across from the USO. *USMRA: Pg 37 (B,C-4), Pg 49 (B-4)* Main installation numbers: (At this time all telephone inquiries should be made to Charleston) C-803-566-5794/5795.

**PAX TERM INFO: C-803-566-5794/5795, D-312-673-5794/5795, FAX: C-803-566-3845.** Bldg Base Ops, Hrs: daily 0700-2300. Directions: **Pax Paging:** Same as Pax terminal.

**PAX LOUNGES: USO Lounge:** Located in Atlanta Hartsfield International, C-404-761-8061. Hrs: Mon-Fri 0930-2100, Sat 1000-1900, Sun 1000-2100.

**FOOD SERVICE:** All terminals have dining facilities.

**TRANSPORTATION: Train:** MARTA train is $1.25 for Atlanta area. **Taxi:** available.

**TML:** Available at surrounding military installations: Ft. Gillam, Ft. McPherson and Dobbins ARB.

**TRAVELERS AID:** Personnel Assitance Point (Army) and USO Lounge, C-404-761-8061.

**OTHER SERVICES:** In the airport: Chapels, Post Office, Foreign Currency Exchange, Duty Free shops, etc.

**ATTRACTIONS:** Six Flags over Georgia and the Atlanta area.

| ORIGINATING SCHEDULES | | | |
|---|---|---|---|
| **APP/ATL-1 MON B757** | | | |
| **Location ID** | **Airport (Station)** | **Country/State** | **Days Out** |
| ATL | The WM B Hartsfield, ATL IAP | GA | +0 |
| PHL | Philadelphia IAP | PA | +0 |
| **MHZ** | **RAF Mildenhall** | **UK** | **+1** |
| JFK | John F. Kennedy IAP | NY | +1 |
| ATL | The WM B Hartsfield, ATL IAP | GA | |
| **APP/ATL-2 1/2/3 WED L1011** | | | |
| ATL | The WM B Hartsfield, ATL IAP | GA | +0 |
| PHL | Philadelphia IAP | PA | +0 |
| **FRF** | **Rhein-Main AB** | **GE** | **+1** |

| PHL | Philadelphia IAP | PA | +1 |
|---|---|---|---|
| ATL | The WM B Hartsfield, ATL IAP | GA | |
| | **IN ROUTE SCHEDULES** | | |
| **Charleston AFB/IAP** | APP/CHS-22 | APP/CHS-23 | APP/CHS-24 |

# DOBBINS AIR RESERVE BASE/ATLANTA NAS (MGE)

Base Operations, Bldg 737
1477 Mimosa Drive
Dobbins ARB, GA 30069-4821

**LOCATION:** From I-75 North exit to GA-280 West to ARB. Clearly marked. *USMRA: Page 37 (B-3); Page 49 (A-1).* NMC: Atlanta, 16 miles southeast. Main installation numbers: C-404-919-5000, D-312-925-1110.

**PAX TERM INFO: C-404-919-4903/5359, D-312-925-4903/5359, FAX: C-404-919-5105.** Bldg 737, Base Ops, Hrs: daily 0700-2300. Directions: From main gate, straight on Mimosa Dr to dead end at Pax Term. NAS Ops: Hrs: daily 0700-2300, C-404-919-5359, D-312-925-5359. **Pax Paging:** Same as Pax terminal.

**PAX LOUNGES:** Limited lounge facilities. **General:** Bldg 737, Hrs: daily 0700-2300, C-404-919-4903 (capacity 20). A/C, pay telephones, restrooms, P/C seats. **DV/VIP:** Bldg 737, Hrs: daily 0700-2300. Commercial telephone in Pax Term (capacity 8). Key from dispatcher. A/C, telephones (commercial and defense), restrooms, O/S seats. **Protocol Service:** Bldg 729, Hrs: Mon-Fri 0730-1630, C-404-919-4520 , 06+.

**FOOD SERVICE:** Limited services on Base. **Dining Hall:** Bldg 60 NAS, C-404-919-5469. **Consolidated Club:** Atlantic Ave, C-404-427-5551, C-404-919-4594, C-404-919-5040. **O'Club:** (Take Two Club): Bldg 53 NAS, C-404-919-5393.

**TRANSPORTATION: Air Tickets:** SATO: MAG 42, Marine Corp. Hangar 1, Room 226, NAS, Hrs: Mon-Fri 0730-1615, C-404-919-4848 & C-404-425-2113. Commercial Ticket Office, Omega Travel: Bldg 812, C-404-919-5788, D-312-925-5788. **Bus (Comm):** Hwy 41 North, Greyhound C-404-427-3011, Tradewinds C-404-429-0092. **Car Rentals:** The William B. Hartsfield IAP, Avis: C-404-530-2700, Hertz: C-404-530-2900. **Taxi (Gov):** Motor Pool, Hrs: Mon-Fri 0800-1600, C-404-919-4853 (duty Pax only). **Parking:** Bldg 827, long and short term.

**TML:** Lodging Office (Dobbins Inn, Bldg 800, 1295 Barracks Ct), C-404-919-4745, D-312-925-4745, FAX 404-919-5185. DV/VIP: PAO, C-404-919-4520. 06+. Navy: Bldg 54. C-404-919-5393, D-312-925-5393

*GEORGIA*
*Dobbins Air Reserve Base/Atlanta NAS, continued*

**TRAVELERS AID: Chaplain:** Bldg 32 NAS, Hrs: Wed-Sun 0730-1600, C-404-919-4955/6. **Security Police:** Main gate, C-404-919-4910. **USO:** The William B. Hartsfield IAP, C-404-761-8061 (North Term).

**OTHER SERVICES: Exchange:** Bldg 530, C-404-428-3054. **Hair Styles:** Bldg 530, C-404-425-3092. **Medical:** NAS Clinic, Hrs: 24 hours daily, C-404-919-5302, D-312-925-5302. **Postal:** Bldg 709, C-404-919-5049.

**ATTRACTIONS:** Stone Mountain, Six Flags.

| IN ROUTE SCHEDULES | |
|---|---|
| **Keesler AFB** | BIX/MEDEVAC-2 |

# LAWSON ARMY AIRFIELD (LSF)

DOT Aviation Branch, Base Ops, Bldg 2485
Fort Benning, GA 31905-5593

**LOCATION:** Off I-185 and US-27/280. *USMRA: Page 37 (B-6).* NMC. Columbus, 5 miles NW. Main installation numbers: C-706-545-2011, D-312-784-2011.

**PAX TERM INFO: C-706-545-3524, D-312-835-3524.** Base Ops, Hrs: During flight processing. Ask Security Police for directions. No lounge, Pax wait in base ops. Full Large Base support available. See Military Living's ***US Forces Travel and Transfer Guide USA & Caribbean Areas*** for details.

**TML:** Lodging Office, (Fort Benning, Bldg. 399), C-706-689-0067, D-312-835-3146/7, FAX 706-682-9842.

| IN ROUTE SCHEDULES | |
|---|---|
| **Andrews AFB** | ADW/MEDEVAC-2 |
| **Scott AFB** | BLV/MEDEVAC-1 |

# MOODY AIR FORCE BASE (VAD)

347th TFW/Air Ops
Moody AFB, GA 31699-1511

**LOCATION:** On GA-125, 10 miles north of Valdosta. Also, can be reached from I-75, via GA-122. *USMRA: Page 37 (D,E-9).* NMC: Valdosta, 10 miles south. Main installation numbers: C-912-333-4211, D-312-460-4211.

**PAX TERM INFO: C-912-333-3305, D-312-460-3305.** Bldg 622, Hrs: Mon-Fri 0700-2300, Sat-Sun and Hol: 0900-1700. Directions: From main gate, straight on Mitchell Blvd to Austin Ellipse to Bradley Circle. Right to Dexter St to right on Savannah St. Pax Term at flight apron. All Pax processed by Base Ops. No lounges. Pax wait in Base Ops. **Pax Service Office:** Same as Pax Terminal (NCO on duty).

**FOOD SERVICE: Dining Hall:** C-912-333-3031. **Bowling Alley:** C-912-333-3872. **NCO Club:** C-912-333-3792. **O'Club:** C-912-333-3258.

**TRANSPORTATION: Commercial Travel:** C-912-333-4278. **Taxi:** C-912-333-3461. **Parking:** ATC tower, same as Pax Term. No restrictions.

**TML:** Lodging Office (Bldg. 3131), Hrs: 24 hours daily, C-912-333-3893, D-312-460-3893, FAX 912-333-4971, DSN FAX 312-466-4771. All ranks. DV/VIP: C-912-333-4144, O6+, E-9.

**TRAVELERS AID: American Red Cross:** C-912-333-3542. **Chaplain:** C-912-333-3211. **Security Police:** Bldg 617, Hrs: 24 hours daily, C-912-333-3108.

**OTHER SERVICES: Exchange:** C-912-333-3431. **Hair Styles:** C-912-244-8541. **Medical:** Bldg 900, Hrs: 24 hours daily, C-912-333-3232, D-312-460-3232.

**ATTRACTIONS:** Historic homes in Valdosta, Okefenokee Swamp—50 miles east.

| **ORIGINATING SCHEDULES** | | | |
|---|---|---|---|
| **ACC/VAD-1 4 WED C-130E** | | | |
| **Location ID** | **Airport (Station)** | **Country/State** | **Days Out** |
| VAD | Moody AFB | GA | +0 |
| NGU | Norfolk NAS | VA | +1 |
| NRR | Roosevelt Roads NAS | PR | +1 |
| **STX** | **Alexander Hamilton APT** | **VI** | **+2** |
| NRR | Roosevelt Roads NAS | PR | +2 |
| NGU | Norfolk NAS | VA | +3 |
| VAD | Moody AFB | GA | |
| **IN ROUTE SCHEDULES** | | | |
| **Keesler AFB** | BIX/MEDEVAC-1 | BIX/MEDEVAC-2 | |

## ROBINS AIR FORCE BASE (WRB)

78th Air Base Wing (AFMC)
455 Byron Street, Suite 425
Robins AFB, GA 31098-1860

*GEORGIA*
*Robins Air Force Base, continued*

**LOCATION:** Off US-129 on GA-247 at Warner Robins. Access from I-75 South. *USMRA: Page 37 (D-6).* NMC: Macon, 18 miles northwest. Main installation numbers: C-912-926-1001, D-312-468-1001.

**PAX TERM INFO: C-912-926-3166, D-312-468-4915, FAX: C-912-926-4355, D FAX 468-4355.** Bldg 127, Hrs: Mon-Fri 0800-1600. Directions: From Gate 2 (Visitor Center), straight on 2nd St to a left onto Robins Parkway. Continue to Gate 31. **Pax Service Office:** Same as Pax terminal.

**PAX LOUNGES:** No separate family lounge. **General:** Bldg 127, Hrs: Mon-Fri 0800-1600, C-912-926-3166. A/C, telephones, TV, restrooms. **DV/VIP:** Bldg 110, Hrs: 24 hours daily. A/C, showers, telephones, TV, read/write rooms, O/S seats. **Protocol Service:** Bldg 215, Hrs: 24 hours daily, C-912-926-2761.

**FOOD SERVICE: Cafeteria:** Bldg 166, C-912-922-8635. **Dining Hall:** Bldg 757, C-912-328-3037. **Smith Community Center:** Bldg 767, C-912-922-2105. **NCO Club:** Bldg 956, C-912-923-5581. **O'Club:** Bldg 542, C-912-922-3011. **Vending:** Bldg 110, Hrs: 24 hours daily, C-912-926-2114.

**TRANSPORTATION: Air Tickets:** SATO: Bldg 301, Hrs: Mon-Fri 0800-1600, C-912-926-5363. **Bus (Comm):** Warner Robins, Greyhound C-912-923-8885. **Bus (Gov):** Bldg 245, Hrs: 24 hours daily, C-912-926-3493. **Bus (Shuttle):** Bldg 245, Hrs: daily 0700-1700, C-912-926-3493. **Taxi (Comm):** Warner Robins, Hrs: 24 hours daily, C-912-923-6414. **Taxi (Gov):** Bldg 245, Hrs: 24 hours daily, C-912-926-3493. **Parking:** Any unmarked space outside the controlled area (near gate 31).

**TML:** Lodging Office, (Pine Oaks Lodge, Bldg 557), Hrs: 24 hours daily, C-912-926-2100, D-312-468-2100, FAX C-912-926-0977. All ranks. DV/VIP: C-912-926-2761, O6+.

**TRAVELERS AID: American Red Cross:** Bldg 794, Hrs: Mon-Fri 0900-1300, C-912-926-5493. **Chaplain:** Bldg 769, C-912-926-2821. **Security Police:** Bldg 263, C-912-926-2187. **USO:** Bldg 767, C-912-926-2105. Mon 0900-1200, Thu 1800-2200, Fri 0900-1600.

**OTHER SERVICES: Exchange:** Bldg 914, Hrs: Mon-Sat 0900-2100, Sun: 0900-1700, C-912-923-5537. **Bank/Exchange:** Bldg 911, Hrs: M-F: 0900-1700, C-912-922-7786. **Barber, Beauty:** Bldg 914, C-912-923-7027. **Laundry/Dry Cleaning:** Bldg 914, C-912-922-2332. **Medical:** Bldg 700, Hrs: 24 hours daily, C-912-926-3845, D-312-468-3845. **Postal:** Bldg 910, C-912-926-3078.

**ATTRACTIONS:** Andersonville Trail, RAFB Museum.

| ORIGINATING SCHEDULES | | | |
|---|---|---|---|
| **ACC/WRB-1 2nd/3rd MON, 1st/2nd WED KC135R** | | | |
| **Location ID** | **Airport (Station)** | **Country/State** | **Days Out** |
| WRB | Robins AFB | GA | +0 |
| DOV | Dover AFB | DE | +1 |
| **MHZ** | **RAF Mildenhall** | **UK** | **+2** |
| DOV | Dover AFB | DE | +3 |
| WRB | Robins AFB | GA | |
| **PCC/WRB-2 2nd THU KC13R** | | | |
| WRB | Robins AFB | GA | +0 |
| SUU | Travis AFB | CA | +1 |
| EDF | Elmendorf AFB | AK | +2 |
| **OKO** | **Yokota AB** | **JA** | **+3** |
| SUU | Travis AFB | CA | +4 |
| WRB | Robins AFB | GA | |
| **IN ROUTE SCHEDULES** | | | |
| **Keesler AFB** | BIX/MEDEVAC-1 | | |

**UNSCHEDULED FLIGHTS**

Frequent flights via C-12 and C-21 Administrative Aircraft to Andrews AFB, MD (**ADW**), Wright-Patterson AFB, OH (**FFO**), Eglin AFB, FL (**VPS**). Conus flights on Reserve C-130 aircraft on cargo and training missions. Infrequent flights to RAF Mildenhall, UK (**MHZ**) and Howard AFB, PN (**HOW**) on K-135/EC-137. NOTE: Missions are posted 24 hours in advance when possible.

## SAVANNAH INTERNATIONAL AIRPORT (SAV)

165th TAG (ANG) / PO Box 7568
Garden City, GA 31402-5000

**LOCATION:** From I-95 north or south, Exit 18 to US-80 east to left (north) on GA-307 for 3 miles to IAP. *USMRA: Page 37 (H-7).* NMC: Savannah, 4 miles southeast. Main installation numbers: C-912-966-8201/1941, D-312-860-8201.

**PAX TERM INFO: C-912-964-1941, D-312-860-8201,** ANG area during flight processing.

**TML:** Lodging Office, Hunter AAF, (Bldg 6010), C-912-352-5910/5834 or C-912-355-1060. DV/VIP: C-912-767-8610, D-312-971-8610. 05+.

**OTHER SERVICES:** Services and facilities of an IAP available.

*GEORGIA*
*Savannah International Airport, continued*

**UNSCHEDULED FLIGHTS**

Most flights on weekends via C-130H aircraft to CONUS & OCONUS locations. Also check for Space-A at nearby Hunter AAF, (**SVN**) Army Ops C-912-352-5500, D-312-971-5500. CGAS (**SVN**)

**—— NOTES ——**

# IDAHO

## MOUNTAIN HOME AIR FORCE BASE (MUO)

366th OSS/OSAA
665 Thunderbolt Ave, Bldg. 262
Mountain Home AFB, ID 83648-3401

**LOCATION:** From Boise, take I-84 SE, 39 miles to Mountain Home exit. Follow road through town to Airbase Rd, 10 miles to main gate. *USMRA: Page 98 (C-9)*. NMC: Boise ID, 51 miles northwest. Main installation numbers: C-208-828-2111, D-312-728-1110.

**PAX TERM INFO: C-208-828-2222/2304, D-312-728-2222/2304, FAX 208-828-4128, D FAX 728-4128.** Base Operations: Bldg 262, Hrs: Mon-Fri 0630-2330, Sat-Sun 0800-1600.

**PAX LOUNGES:** No separate family lounge. **General:** Bldg 262, Hrs: Mon-Fri 0630-2330, C-208-828-2304. A/C, bag check, telephones (local and defense), restrooms, P/C seats. **DV/VIP:** Bldg 262, Hrs: daily 0630-2330, C-208-828-2304 (06+). A/C, bag check, read/write rooms, telephones (local and defense), TV, restrooms, O/S seats. **Protocol Service:** Bldg 512, Hrs: Mon-Fri 0730-1630, C-208-828-4536.

**FOOD SERVICE: Dining Hall:** Bldg 2316, C-208-832-2313. **Enlisted Club:** Bldg 195, C-208-828-2106. **NCO/CPO Club:** Bldg 195, C-208-828-2105. **O'Club:** Bldg 2605, C-208-828-2597. **Restaurants:** Rec Center: Bldg 2618, C-208-828-6546. **Snack Bars:** Bldg 2207, C-208-832-4424. **Vending:** Bldg 262, C-208-832-2304.

**TRANSPORTATION: Air Tickets:** SATO: Bldg 512, Hrs: Mon-Fri 0730-1630, C-208-832-2276. **Bus (Shuttle):** Bldg 1126, Hrs: daily 0630-1720, C-208-828-2339. Main Base points. **Taxi (Gov):** Bldg 1126, Hrs: daily 24hrs, C-208-343-2215/2239.

**TML:** Lodging Office (Sagebrush Hotel, Bldg 2604, 455 Falcon St), 24hrs daily, C-208-832-4661, D-312-728-6451. FAX 208-828-4797. All ranks. DV/VIP: C-208-828-4536, O6+.

**TRAVELERS AID: American Red Cross:** Bldg 516, Hrs: Mon-Fri 0800-1700, C-208-828-6622/3. **Chaplain:** Bldg 2606, Hrs: Mon-Fri 0730-1630, C-208-828-6417, after hours C-208-828-2111. **Emergency Relief:** Bldg 278, Hrs: Mon-Fri 0900-1700, C-208-828-2503/6148. **Security Police:** Bldg 1013, Hrs: 24 hours daily, C-208-828-2256.

**OTHER SERVICES: Exchange:** Bldg 2607, C-208-832-4353. **Bank/Exchange:** Bldg 2620, C-208-832-4202; Federal Credit Union: C-208-832-46757. **Hair Styles:** Bldg 2607, Barber: C-208-832-7191; Beauty: C-208-832-4090. **Laundry:** Bldg 2607, C-208-832-7465. **Medical:** Bldg 6000, Hrs: 24 hours daily, C-208-828-6274, D-312-728-6274 (Ambulance) C-208-828-2233. **Postal:** Bldg 2413, C-208-832-7008.

*IDAHO*
***Mountain Home Air Force Base, continued***

**ATTRACTIONS:** Snow skiing, hunting and fishing.

| IN ROUTE SCHEDULES | |
|---|---|
| **Scott AFB** | BLV/MEDEVAC-3 |

**UNSCHEDULED FLIGHTS**

Limited unscheduled flights to CONUS and OCONUS locations, via KC-135E aircraft. Call for flight schedule information.

**—— NOTES ——**

# ILLINOIS

## O'HARE IAP/AIR RESERVE STATION (ORD)

928th OG/OTM
O'Hare IAP ARS, IL 60666-5023
**Scheduled to close under the 1993 BCRL, no final date for closure has been established.**

**LOCATION:** Northeast corner of O'Hare IAP. Main gate 500 feet west of intersection of US-45 (Mannheim Rd) & IL-72 (Higgins Rd). *USMRA: Page 69 (C,D-3,4).* NMC: Chicago, 15 miles southeast. Main installation numbers: C-312-694-6917, D-312-930-6917.

**PAX TERM INFO: Non-Air National Guard: C-312-825-6623, D-312-930-6623, REC: C-312-825-6623, D-312-930-6623.** Base Ops, Hrs: Mon-Fri 0700-1530, **Air National Guard: C-312-825-6983, D-312-930-6983, REC: C-312-825-6983, D-312-930-6983.** Bldg 19, Hrs: Mon-Fri 0730-1600.

**FOOD SERVICE:** O'Hare IAP and O'Hare area. **Consolidated Club:** C-312-825-5448. **Vending:** Buildings 30 & 19.

**TRANSPORTATION:** No Gov transportation to or from O'Hare IAP Civilian Terminal. **Parking:** O'Hare ARFF (short term).

**TRAVELERS AID: Chaplain:** C-312-686-2636. **USO:** O'Hare IAP, C-312-686-7396.

**ATTRACTIONS:** City of Chicago, Art Institute of Chicago, major sports.

| PCC/ORD-1 1st SAT KC135R | | | |
|---|---|---|---|
| **Location ID** | **Airport (Station)** | **Country/State** | **Days Out** |
| ORD | O'Hare IAP/ARS | IL | +0 |
| SUU | Travis AFB | CA | +1 |
| EDF | Elmendorf AFB | AK | +2 |
| **OKO** | **Yokota AB** | **JA** | **+3** |
| SUU | Travis AFB | CA | +4 |
| ORD | O'Hare IAP/ARS | IL | |

### UNSCHEDULED FLIGHTS

Limited flights to CONUS, OCONUS and foreign country destinations via Air National Guard KC-135E and Reserve C-130H aircraft on cargo or training missions. C-130H missions CONUS only. Call before you go for destinations, routings and schedules.

# GREATER PEORIA REGIONAL AIRPORT (PIA)

182nd Airlift Group (ANG)
Peoria, IL 61607-1498

**LOCATION:** In the Southwest section of Peoria, IL. Take I-474 North or South and exit at #5 SW to airport. Follow signs to ANG area. *USMRA: Page 64, (D-4)*. NMC: Peoria 7 miles northeast. Main installation numbers: C-309-791-2282, D-312-724-2282.

**PAX TERM INFO: C-309-791-2282, D-312-724-2282.** Military Diuspensary at the Airport. No other military support available. TML: Rock Island Arsenal, 65 miles northwest, Lodging Office Bldg 110, C-309-782-2376, D-312-793-2376, FAX C-309-782-0133, D-312-793-0133.

**UNSCHEDULED FLIGHTS**

Frequent flights via ANG C-130 aircraft to CONUS and OCONUS locations. Call for destinations, routings and schedules.

# SCOTT AIR FORCE BASE (BLV)

375th TRANS/TROP
801 Hangar Rd. Suite 203
Scott AFB, IL 62225-5045

**LOCATION:** Off I-64 East or West, 19A West on IL-158, south 2 miles and watch for signs to AFB entry. *USMRA: Page 64 (D-8)*. NMC: St Louis MO, 25 miles west. Main installation numbers: C-618-256-1110, D-312-576-1110.

**PAX TERM INFO: C-618-256-1854/4042, D-576-1854/4042, FAX 618-256-1958, D FAX 576-1946.** Bldg P-8, Hrs: daily 0445-2200 (closed Xmas & New Years). Directions: Main gate, Scott Dr straight to 4-way stop, go left on Heritage Dr, 2.5 blocks to Pax Terminal on the right. **Pax Service Office:** Bldg P-8, Hrs: Mon-Fri 0730-1630, C-618-256-4042 (NCO on duty). **Pax Paging:** Same as Pax terminal.

**PAX LOUNGES:** No family lounge. **General:** Bldg P-8, Hrs: daily 0445-2200, C-618-256-1854. A/C, game room, telephones (commercial and defense), TV, restrooms. **Protocol Service:** Bldg 1600, duty hours, C-618-256-5555.

**FOOD SERVICE: Cafeteria:** Bldg P-8, Hrs: Mon-Fri 0430-1500, Sat 0500-0800, Sun closed, C-618-746-4199 (closed major holidays). **Dining Hall:** Bldg 1800, Hrs: daily 0600-1800, C-618-256-4215 ("Gateway Inn"). **Enlisted Club:** Bldg 1948, Hrs: Mon-Fri 0630-2030, Sat 0800-2100, Sun closed, C-618-744-0300. **O'Club:** Bldg 1500, Hrs: daily 1000-2100, C-618-744-1333. **Snack Bars:** Bldg 1650, Hrs: daily 0830-2100, C-618-746-2841 ("Dog House").

*ILLINOIS*
*Scott Air Force Base, continued*

**TRANSPORTATION: Air Tickets:** Rodgers Travel: Bldg P-8, Mon-Fri 0730-1600, C-618-256-5397. **Bus (Gov):** (Duty Pax only) Bldg 548, C-618-256-3201/3066 . **Car Rentals:** Enterprise: C-618-277-8000. **Limo Service:** Bldg P-8, Hrs: Mon-Fri 0615-2000, Sat 0845-1445, Sun & Hol 1000-1600, C-618-256-3201/3066 (BLV to STL). **Taxi (Comm):** Bldg P-8, Professional: C-618-397-4334; Magic Carpet: C-618-744-1300; Tri County: C-618-277-1515. **Parking:** Bldg P-8, short term-west of Pax Term-8 hr limit; long term located south of Post Office. Notify Security Police.

**TML:** Lodging Office (Bldg 1510, F St), 24hrs daily, C-618-744-1200, D-312-576-1844, DSN FAX 312-576-6638. All ranks. DV/VIP: C-618-256-5555, D-312-576-5555.

**TRAVELERS AID: American Red Cross:** Bldg 21, C-618-256-1855, After hours: C-314-658-2000. **Chaplain:** Bldg 1620, Hrs: Mon-Fri 0730-1600, C-618-256-3303, After hours: C-618-256-1110. **Emergency Relief:** Bldg 10, C-618-256-4210. **Lost/Found:** Bldg P-8, C-618-256-3017. **Security Police:** Bldg 1970, C-618-256-2223. **USO:** STL, C-314-429-1234 (airport west end arrival area).

**OTHER SERVICES: Exchange:** Bldg 1650, Hrs: daily 1000-1800, C-618-744-0888. **Bank/Exchange:** Bldg 1644, Hrs: Mon-Fri 0900-1500, Sat 0900-1200, C-618-744-1144. **Hair Styles:** Bldg 1650, Barber: C-618-746-2899; Beauty: C-618-744-1544. **Laundry/Dry Cleaning:** Bldg 1650, C-618-746-2417. **Medical:** Bldg 1530, Hrs: 24 hours daily, C-618-256-7595, D-312-576-7595. **Postal:** Bldg 1900, C-618-256-5942. **Wire:** Bldg 1650, Hrs: daily 1000-1800, C-618-744-0877.

**ATTRACTIONS:** St. Louis nearby, Mississippi River.

| ORIGINATING SCHEDULES | | |
|---|---|---|
| | **BLV/MEDEVAC-1 SUN, WED** | **C-9A** |
| BLV | Scott AFB | IL |
| BIX | Keesler AFB | MS |
| LSF | Lawson AAF | GA |
| AGS | Bush Field | GA |
| CHS | Charleston AFB | SC |
| POB | Pope AFB | NC |
| NKT | Cherry Point MCAS | NC |
| NGU | Norfolk NAS | VA |
| **ADW** | **Andrews AFB** | *MD* |
| | **BLV/MEDEVAC-2 TUE, FRI** | **C-9A** |
| BLV | Scott AFB | IL |
| BIX | Keesler AFB | MS |
| MCO | Orlando IAP | FL |
| MCF | MacDill AFB | FL |
| NQX | Key West NAS | FL |
| COF | Patrick AFB | FL |
| **BIX** | **Keesler AFB** | **MS** |

*ILLINOIS*
*Scott Air Force Base, continued*

| | **BLV/MEDEVAC-3 WED, SAT C-9A** | |
|---|---|---|
| BLV | Scott AFB | IL |
| BKF | Buckley ANGB | CO |
| HIF | Hill AFB | UT |
| MUO | Mountain Home AFB | ID |
| GFA | Malmstrom AFB | MT |
| SKA | Fairchild AFB | WA |
| TCM | McChord AFB | WA |
| **SUU** | **Travis AFB** | *CA* |
| | **BLV/MEDEVAC-4 WED C-9A** | |
| BLV | Scott AFB | IL |
| HOP | Campbell AAF | KY |
| FFO | Wright Patterson AFB | OH |
| **NBU** | **Glenview NAS** | **IL** |
| SZL | Whiteman AFB | MO |
| BLV | Scott AFB | IL |
| | **BLV/MEDEVAC-5 THU, SAT C-9A** | |
| BLV | Scott AFB | IL |
| ADW | Andrews AFB | MD |
| SKF | Kelly AFB | TX |
| **SUU** | **Travis AFB** | **CA** |
| | **BLV/MEDEVAC-6 FRI C-9A** | |
| BLV | Scott AFB | IL |
| HOP | Campbell AAF | KY |
| SDF | Standiford Field ANGB | KY |
| FFO | Wright Patterson AFB | OH |
| **NBU** | **Glenview NAS** | **IL** |
| SAW | K I Sawyer AFB | MI |
| OFF | Offutt AFB | NE |
| IAB | McConnell AFB | KS |
| BLV | Scott AFB | IL |
| | **BLV/MEDEVAC-7 SAT C-9A** | |
| BLV | Scott AFB | IL |
| RDR | Grand Forks AFB | ND |
| **MIB** | **Minot AFB** | **ND** |
| RCA | Ellsworth AFB | SD |
| BKF | Buckley ANGB | CO |
| BLV | Scott AFB | IL |

| | **BLV/MEDEVAC-8 MON, WED C-9A** | |
|---|---|---|
| BLV | Scott AFB | IL |
| SKF | Kelly AFB | TX |
| CVS | Cannon AFB | NM |
| IKR | Kirtland AFB | NM |
| BIF | Biggs AAF | TX |
| DMA | Davis-Monthan AFB | AZ |
| LUF | Luke AFB | AZ |
| **SUU** | **Travis AFB** | **CA** |
| | **BLV/MEDEVAC-9 MON C-9A** | |
| BLV | Scott AFB | IL |
| NBU | Glenview NAS | IL |
| SAW | K I Sawyer AFB | MI |
| FFO | Wright Patterson AFB | OH |
| **SDF** | **Standiford Field ANGB** | **KY** |
| HOP | Campbell AAF | KY |
| BLV | Scott AFB | IL |
| BKF | Buckley ANGB | CO |
| | **BLV/MEDEVAC-10 MON, THU C-9A** | |
| BLV | Scott AFB | IL |
| LRF | Little Rock AFB | AR |
| BAD | Barksdale AFB | LA |
| AEX | Alexandria APT | LA |
| SKF | Kelly AFB | TX |
| TIK | Tinker AFB | OK |
| LAW | Lawton Municipal APT | OK |
| **SKF** | **Kelly AFB** | **TX** |
| | **BLV/MEDEVAC-11 TUE, FRI C-9A** | |
| BLV | Scott AFB | IL |
| TBN | Forney AAF | MO |
| MCI | Kansas City IAP | MO |
| MHK | Manhattan Municipal APT | KS |
| **BKF** | **Buckley ANGB** | **CO** |
| MHK | Manhattan Municipal APT | KS |
| MCI | Kansas City IAP | MO |
| TBN | Forney AAF | MO |
| BLV | Scott AFB | IL |

*ILLINOIS*
*Scott Air Force Base, continued*

| | | | |
|---|---|---|---|
| | **BLV/MEDEVAC-12** | **TUE** | **C-9A** |
| BLV | Scott AFB | | IL |
| **ADW** | **Andrews AFB** | | **MD** |
| BLV | Scott AFB | | IL |
| | **BLV/MEDEVAC-13** | **SAT** | **C-9A** |
| BLV | Scott AFB | | IL |
| ADW | Andrews AFB | | MD |
| WRI | McGuire AFB | | NJ |
| PVD | Providence APT | | RI |
| SWF | Stewart ANGB | | NY |
| RME | Griffiss AFB | | NY |
| **ADW** | **Andrews AFB** | | **MD** |

**—— NOTES ——**

# KANSAS

## FORBES FIELD AIR NATIONAL GUARD BASE (FOE)

190th Air Refueling Group (ANG)
Forbes Field, KS 66619-5370

**LOCATION:** Off US-75 South. Also accessible from I-470/70 East/West. *USMRA: Page 78 (I-4).* NMC: Topeka, 4 miles north. Main installation numbers: C-913-231-4210, D-312-720-4210.

**PAX TERM INFO: C-913-231-4210, D-312-720-4210, FAX 913-861-4555.** Bldg 679 Base Ops, Hrs: During flight processing. Directions: From main gate straight on South Street to dead end at Base Ops. Small BX is the only US military Base support facility.

**TML:** Lodging Office (Ft Riley, Bldg 45, Barry Ave), C-913-239-2830/8073, 1-800-643-8991, FAX C-913-239-8882. DV/VIP: lodging office.

**UNSCHEDULED FLIGHTS**

Air National Guard Unit Flying Training Missions to CONUS and OCONUS locations via KC-135E aircraft. Call for flight schedule information.

## MARSHALL ARMY AIRFIELD (FRI)/ MANHATTAN MUNICIPAL AIRPORT (MHK)

AOD/ Building 743
Fort Riley, KS 66442-5000

**LOCATION:** On KS-18 and off I-70 in the central part of the state. Junction City, 5 miles southwest and Manhattan, 10 miles northeast. *USMRA: Page 78 (G,H-3,4).* NMC: Topeka, 50 miles east. Main installation numbers: C-913-239-3911, D-312-856-1110.

**PAX TERM INFO: C-913-239-2530, D-312-856-2530.** Bldg 743, Hrs: 24 hours daily. Ask for directions and map at main gate. Located at base of Old Tower on AAF. NCO on duty.

**TML:** Lodging Office (Ft Riley, Bldg 45, Barry Ave,) C-913-239-2830/8073, 1-800-643-8991, FAX C-913-239-8882. DV/VIP: see lodging office.

**OTHER SERVICES:** Limited facilities. **DV/VIP** between Hangars 1 and 2 (06+) on request from Pax Service NCO. Full Base facilities available. See Military Living's *US Forces Travel & Transfer Guide USA & Caribbean Areas* for details.

| IN ROUTE SCHEDULES | |
|---|---|
| **Scott AFB** | BLV/MEDEVAC-11 |

*KANSAS*

# McCONNELL AIR FORCE BASE (IAB)

McConnell AFB Passenger Terminal, 53435 Kansas Court, Suite 112
McConnell AFB, KS 67221-3720

**LOCATION:** Take I-35 to Wichita, exit at Kellogg St (US-54) west to Rock Rd south and McConnell AFB. *USMRA: Page 78 (G-6).* NMC: Wichita, 6 miles northwest. Main installation numbers: C-316-652-6100, D-312-743-1110.

**PAX TERM INFO: C-316-652-3701/3840, D-312-743-3840/3701, REC: C-316-652-3897, FAX 316-652-3843.** Bldg 1112, Hrs: 24 hours daily. Directions: From east gate straight on Kansas St for 1.5 miles to Base Ops on the right.

**PAX LOUNGES: General:** Bldg 1112, Hrs: Same as Pax Term. **DV/VIP:** Bldg 1112, Hrs: 24 hours daily, C-316-652-3701. **Protocol Service:** Bldg 1112, Hrs: 24 hours daily, C-316-652-3110.

**FOOD SERVICE: Dining Hall:** Bldg 408, C-316-652-4183; Bldg 421, C-316-652-4186 (In-flight). **O'Club:** Bldg 197, C-316-685-2288.

**TRANSPORTATION:** Very limited transportation on Base. **Air Tickets:** SATO: Bldg 334, Hrs: Mon-Sat 1100-2200, C-316-652-5263. **Taxi (Gov):** Bldg 710, C-316-652-4051 ($15 to Wichita).

**TML:** Lodging Office (Bldg 193, 53030 Glen Elder Suite 1), 24hrs daily, C-316-683-7711, D-312-743-6500. All ranks. DV/VIP: C-316-652-3110, D-312-743-3110.

**TRAVELERS AID: American Red Cross:** Bldg 331, C-316-652-5202. **Chaplain:** Bldg 510, C-316-652-3562. **Emergency Relief:** Bldg 1218, C-316-681-3739 (Air Force Aid). **Security Police:** Bldg 1115, C-316-652-4658 (Desk Sgt).

**OTHER SERVICES: Exchange:** Bldg 352, C-316-685-0231. **Bank/Exchange:** Freedom 1st Federal Credit Union: Bldg 490, C-316-652-5457. **Hair Styles:** Bldg 352, Barber: C-316-686-9971; Beauty: C-316-689-8716. **Laundry/Dry Cleaning:** Bldg 352/357, C-316-685-2434. **Medical:** C-316-652-5164, D-312-743-5164. **Postal:** Bldg 327, C-316-652-4878.

**ATTRACTIONS:** Sedgewick County Zoo, Museum of Art and History.

| ORIGINATING SCHEDULES | | | |
|---|---|---|---|
| **PCC/IAB-1** | **4th/5th THU, 4th SAT** | **KC-135R** | |
| **Location ID** | **Airport (Station)** | **Country/State** | **Days Out** |
| IAB | McConnell AFB | KS | +0 |
| SUU | Travis AFB | CA | +1 |
| EDF | Elmendorf AFB | AK | +2 |
| **OKO** | **Yokota AB** | **JA** | **+3** |
| SUU | Travis AFB | CA | +4 |
| IAB | McConnell AFB | KS | |

| IN ROUTE SCHEDULES | |
|---|---|
| **Buckely ANGB** | BKF/MEDEVAC-1 |
| **Scott AFB** | BLV/MEDEVAC-6 |

# KENTUCKY

## CAMPBELL ARMY AIRFIELD (HOP)

Base Air Operations
Fort Campbell, KY 42223-5030

**LOCATION:** In the southwest part of KY, 4 miles south of intersection US-41A and I-24. Ten miles northwest of Clarksville, TN. *USMRA: Page 40 (E,F-7).* NMC: Hopkinsville, 15 miles north. Main installation numbers: C-502-798-2151, D-312-635-1110.

**PAX TERM INFO: C-502-798-7146, D-312-635-7146, FAX: C-502-798-9288**, D-312-635-9288. Zone H/I, Bldg 7163, Hrs: 24 hours daily. Directions: From Gate 6 on US Alt 41 straight on Morgan Road to AAF on right.

**TML:** Lodging Office (Bldg 1581, Lee Rd), C-502-798-5618, D-312-635-5618. DV/VIP: Protocol Office, C-502-798-9913, 06+.

**OTHER SERVICES:** Full Large Base support facilities available. See Military Living's *US Forces Travel & Transfer Guide USA & Caribbean Areas* for complete details.

| IN ROUTE SCHEDULES | |
|---|---|
| **Scott AFB** | BLV/MEDEVAC-4 BLV/MEDEVAC-6 BLV/MEDEVAC-9 |

## GODMAN ARMY AIRFIELD (FTK)

**Base Air Operations**
**ATTN: G-3/DPTM, AVN Div**
**Fort Knox, KY 40121-5000**

**LOCATION:** From I-65 North in Louisville, exit Jefferson Freeway 841 West to 31 West, go south to Fort Knox. From I-64, exit I-264 West (Waterson) to I-65 South, to Jefferson/Fort Knox to US-31 West, north to Fort Knox. From I-71, exit I-65 South to exit Jefferson Freeway 841 West, to 31 West then south to Fort Knox. *USMRA: Page 40-41 (H,I-3,4).* NMC: Louisville, 25 miles north. Main installation numbers: C-502-624-1181, D-312-464-0111.

**PAX TERM INFO: C-502-624-5545, D-312-464-5545, FAX C-502-624-2421.** Bldg 5220, Hrs: 24 hours daily. Directions: From US-31 West enter Fort on Chaffee Ave to left on Park Road, to left on Pilot Street. Air Ops on left.

**TML:** Lodging Office (Bldg 4770), C-502-943-1000, D-312-464-3491, FAX-502-942-8752. DV/VIP: C-502-624-6951, D-312-464-6951.

**OTHER SERVICES:** Full Large Base support facilities available. See Military Living's *US Forces Travel & Transfer Guide USA & Caribbean Areas* for complete details.

**UNSCHEDULED FLIGHTS**

Flights via Army executive aircraft, C-12A and C-21A to CONUS East Coast and Midwest locations. Call for destinations, routings and schedules.

*KENTUCKY*

# STANDIFORD FIELD/ AIR NATIONAL GUARD BASE (SDF)

123rd TAW
Louisville, KY 40213-2678

**LOCATION:** Take I-65 South to exit 130 to Grade Lane. Turn right for 1 mile. Take another right which runs into main gate of Air National Guard base. Take I-65 North to exit 130 to Preston Street. Turn left at the light and drive 1 block. Turn left at the 2nd light to Grade Lane. Follow Grade to the base. *USMRA: Page 41 (I-3).* NMC: Louisville, Standiford Field in city. Main installation numbers: C-502-364-9400, D-312-989-4400.

**PAX TERM INFO: C-502-364-9459, D-312-989-4459, FAX C-503-364-9664.** Air National Guard Base Ops, Hrs: Tue-Fri 0630-1630, No Pax Terminal. All Space-A managed by Air National Guard Air Operations. NOTE: MEDEVAC scheduled flights are scheduled through the MEDEVAC section at Ireland Army Hospital, Ft Knox, KY, C-502-624-9273.

**TML:** Lodging Office (Fort Knox Bldg 4770, Newgarden Tower), C-502-943-1000, D-312-464-3491. DV/VIP: C-502-624-6951, D-312-464-6951.

**OTHER SERVICES:** Full support of a metropolitan airport available.

| IN ROUTE SCHEDULES | | |
|---|---|---|
| **Scott AFB** | BLV/MEDEVAC-6 | BLV/MEDEVAC-9 |

## UNSCHEDULED FLIGHTS

Flights to CONUS, OCONUS and foreign countries via Air National Guard C-130-E aircraft. Call for destinations, routings and schedules.

# LOUISIANA

## BARKSDALE AIR FORCE BASE (BAD)

2nd TRNSS/LGTT, Air Operations
841 Fairchild Ave, Suite 103
Barksdale AFB, LA 71110-2270

**LOCATION:** Exit I-20 at Airline Drive, go south to Old Minden Road (.25 miles), left on Old Minden Road (1 block), then right on Gate Drive (1 mile) to North Gate of AFB. *USMRA: Page 79 (B-2).* NMC: Shreveport, 1 mile west. Co-located with Bossier City in Shreveport. Main installation numbers: C-318-456-2252, D-312-781-1110.

**PAX TERM INFO: C-318-456-3738, D-312-781-3738, FAX: D-312-781-3800.** Bldg 6448, Hrs: Mon-Fri: 0630-1630. Directions: From West Gate straight on Barksdale Boulevard, Pax Term right at Hangar Line Road. **Pax Service Office:** Bldg 6448, Hrs: Mon-Fri 0630-1630, C-318-456-3738, NCO on duty. Many facilities on and off base. For full details see *U.S. Forces Travel & Transfer Guide U.S.A. and Caribbean Areas.*

**TML:** Lodging Office: Bldg 5155, Hangarline Rd. C-318-747-4708, D-312-781-3091. DV/VIP: PAO, C-318-456-4447, 06+. Retirees Space-A.

| IN ROUTE SCHEDULES | |
|---|---|
| **Scott AFB** | BLV/MEDEVAC-10 |

**UNSCHEDULED FLIGHTS**

Occasional flights to March AFB, CA (**RIV**), McGuire AFB, NJ (**WRI**), Norfolk NAS, VA (**NGU**), & Travis AFB, CA (**SUU**). Other unscheduled flights to CONUS, OCONUS, and foreign countries via KC-135/10 aircraft. Call for destinations, routings, and schedules.

## NEW ORLEANS NAVAL AIR STATION/ JOINT RESERVE BASE (NBG)

Operations Department, Bldg 40, 4th St
New Orleans NAS, LA 70143-7001

**LOCATION:** Off LA-23 in Belle Chasse. Clearly marked. *USMRA: Page 79 (H-7); Page 90 (F-6).* NMC: New Orleans, 10 miles north. Main installation numbers: C-504-393-3011, D-312-363-3011.

**PAX TERM INFO: C-504-393-3213, D-312-363-3213, REC: C-504-393-3103, D-312-363-3103 also 1-800-222-7549 updated daily, FAX: C-504-393-3734.** Bldg 1, Hrs: daily 0700-2300. Directions: From main gate on Russell Ave to a left on RADM Fowler Drive to a right on Coast Guard Road to Air Ops. **Pax Service Office:** Bldg 1, Hrs: daily 0700-2300, C-504-393-3213. **Pax Paging:** Bldg 1, Hrs: daily 0700-2300, C-504-393-3213.

*LOUISIANA*
*New Orleans Naval Air Station, continued*

**PAX LOUNGES:** No separate family lounge. **General:** Bldg 1, Hrs: daily 0700-2300, C-504-393-3213. A/C, telephones (local and defense), TV, restrooms, P/C seats. **DV/VIP:** Bldg 1, Hrs: daily 0700-2300, C-504-393-3100. A/C, coffee, read/write room, telephones (local and defense), TV, restrooms, O/S seats. **Protocol Service:** Bldg PAO, Hrs: Tue-Sat 0730-1000, C-504-393-3260 (06+).

**FOOD SERVICE: Dining Hall:** Bldg 23, C-504-393-3421. **Enlisted Club:** Bldg 410, Hrs: daily 1000-2100, C-504-393-3508. **NCO/CPO Club:** Bldg 300, Tue-Sun 1100-2300, C-504-393-3512. **O'Club:** Bldg 40, Hrs: Wed-Sun 1100-0100, C-504-393-3841. **Vending:** Bldg 1, Hrs: daily 0700-2300.

**TRANSPORTATION: Air Tickets:** SATO: C-504-367-3625. **Car Rentals:** Bldg 1, Hrs: daily 0700-2300, C-504-393-3213. **Taxi (Comm):** Bldg 1, Hrs: 24 hours daily (various cab companies service Base). **Parking:** Bldg 1, Hrs: daily 0800-1600 (short term-no overnight; long term-Fowler Drive).

**TML:** Lodging Office (Bldg 40), 24hrs daily, C-504-393-3841, FAX C-504-392-1959. All ranks. DV/VIP: C-504-393-3202, O6+. **NAVY LODGE:** At New Orleans Naval Support Activity, Bldg 702, Gen. Meyer Ave. C-504-366-3266 OR 1-800-NAVY INN.

**TRAVELERS AID:** Many agencies at NAS and NSA. **Chaplain:** Bldg 403, Hrs: Tue-Sun 0730-1600, C-504-393-3525. **Lost/Found:** Bldg 1, Hrs: daily 0700-2300, C-504-393-3213. **Security Police:** Bldg 70, Hrs:24 hours daily, C-504-393-3461.

**OTHER SERVICES: Exchange:** Bldg 300, Hrs: Tue-Sun 1000-1700, C-504-393-3527. **Bank/Exchange:** Bldg 300, Hrs: Tue-Sat 0900-1300, C-504-393-3527. **Hair Styles:** Barber: Bldg 300, Hrs: Tue-Sun 1000-1700, C-504-393-3510; Beauty: Bldg 300, Hrs: Tue-Sun 0730-1600, C-504-393-3511. **Laundry/Dry Cleaning:** Bldg 300, Hrs: Tue-Sun 1000-1700, C-504-393-3510. **Medical:** Bldg 41, Hrs: 24 hours daily, C-504-393-3660, D-312-363-3660. **Postal:** Bldg 46, Hrs: Tue-Sat 1000-1300, C-504-393-3204. **Wire:** Bldg 300, Hrs: Tue-Sun 1000-1730, C-504-393-3580.

## UNSCHEDULED FLIGHTS

Ten to fifteen flights daily to CONUS. Alameda NAS CA (**NGZ**) (1 per month); Atlanta NAS GA (**NCQ**) (2/3 per month); Corpus Christi NAS, TX (**NGP**) (5 per month); Dallas NAS TX (**NBE**) (5 per month); Houston CGAS Apt, TX (**EFD**) (3 per month); Jacksonville NAS, FL (**NIP**) (1/2 per month); Memphis NAS TN (**NQA**) (1/2 per month); Meridian NAS MS (**NMM**); Norfolk NAS VA (**NGU**) (1 per week); North Island NAS, CA (**NZY**) (1 per month); Pensacola NAS FL (**NPA**) (1/2 per month). Passenger, cargo, and mixed missions via T-39, C-12A, P-3, C-9 and C-130H aircraft.

# POLK ARMY AIRFIELD (POE)

Base Air Operations
Fort Polk, LA 71459-5000

**LOCATION:** Off US-171, at LA-10, 9 miles south of Leesville. *USMRA: Page 79 (C-4).* NMC: Alexandria, 45 miles northeast. Main installation numbers: C-318-531-2911, D-312-863-1110, F: 528-1110.

**PAX TERM INFO: C-318-531-4831/7328, D-312-863-4831/7328**. Army Airfield Base Ops, Hrs: Mon-Fri: 0700-2200, Sat-Sun & Hol: Closed.

**TML:** Lodging Office (Magnolia House, Bldg 522, Utah Ave), C-318-531-2941 or 318-537-9591, D-312-863-2941/4822. DV/VIP: C-318-531-2941 or 537-9591, D-312-863-2941/4822.

**OTHER SERVICES:** Full Large Base support facilities available. See Military Living's *US Forces Travel & Transfer Guide USA & Caribbean Areas.*

| IN ROUTE SCHEDULES | |
|---|---|
| **Kelly AFB** | SKF/MEDEVAC-1 |

**UNSCHEDULED FLIGHTS**

Limited flights via U-21 and C-12 aircraft. Call for destinations, routing and schedules.

**—— NOTES ——**

# MAINE

## BANGOR AIR NATIONAL GUARD BASE (BGR)

101st OPS/CC,
102 Glenn Ave, Suite 491
Bangor IAP (ANG), ME 04401-3099

**LOCATION:** North from I-95 exit on Ohio St, drive two blocks turn left, go one block turn right on Union St (State Rte 222), pass Bangor IAP, turn left on Griffin Rd, entrance 300 yards on right. *USMRA: Page 18 (E-6,7).* NMC: Bangor, Air National Guard Base in city limits. Main installation numbers: C-207-990-7700, D-312-698-7700.

**PAX TERM INFO: C-207-990-7212/7247, D-312-698-7212/7247, FAX: C-207-990-7216, D FAX 312-698-7216.** Bldg 491, Hrs: Mon-Fri 0730-1600, Ask Security Police for directions.

**TRANSPORTATION:** Taxi to Bangor ($4) 5-10 min. City bus: Hrs: daily 0730-1740 every 30 minutes. Car rental at IAP. **Parking:** Building 489, Security Police, Hrs: 24 hours daily, C-207-990-7311.

**TML:** Lodging Office (Pine Tree Inn, Bldg 346, 22 Cleveland Avenue), Hrs: 24 hours daily, C-207-942-2081, D-312-698-7700.

**TRAVELERS AID:** Bldg 489, 24hrs daily, D-312-698-7311 (Security Police).

**OTHER SERVICES:** Facilities of an IAP available. Other facilities off Base. **Exchange:** C-207-990-7233; **Commissary**: C-207-990-7751.

**ATTRACTIONS:** Lobster and other seafood, Bar Harbor, beaches and boating.

| ORIGINATING SCHEDULES | | | |
|---|---|---|---|
| | **ACC/BGR-1 4th TUE KC-135R** | | |
| **Location ID** | **Airport (Station)** | **Country/State** | **Days Out** |
| BGR | Bangor IAP | ME | +0 |
| WRI | McGuire AFB | NJ | +0 |
| **LGS** | **Lajes AB** | **PO** | **+2** |
| WRI | McGuire AFB | NJ | +2 |
| BGR | Bangor IAP | ME | |
| | **PCC/BGR-2 3rd THU KC-135R** | | |
| BGR | Bangor IAP | ME | +0 |
| SUU | Travis AFB | CA | +1 |
| EDF | Elmendorf AFB | AK | +2 |
| **OKO** | **Yokota AB** | **JA** | **+3** |
| SUU | Travis AFB | CA | +4 |
| BGR | Bangor IAP | ME | |

| IN ROUTE SCHEDULES | |
|---|---|
| **Andrews AFB** | ADW/MEDEVAC-1 |

**UNSCHEDULED FLIGHTS**

Flights to: CONUS (ACC Bases), OCONUS (Europe & Pacific areas), & foreign countries via KC-135E Air National Guard aircraft. Call for destinations, routings and schedules.

# BRUNSWICK NAVAL AIR STATION (NHZ)

Air Operations
Brunswick NAS, ME 04011-5000

**LOCATION:** From I-95 North exit US-1 North to Brunswick, Old Bath Rd (RT-24) to main gate of Brunswick NAS. *USMRA: Page 18 (C-9).* NMC: Portland, 30 miles southwest. Main installation numbers: C-207-921-1110, D-312-476-1110.

**PAX TERM INFO: C-207-921-2689/2682, D-312-476-2689/2682.** Bldg 200, Hrs: 24 hours daily. Directions: From Security straight on Fitch Ave, right on Orion St, Air Operations is on the left. **Pax Service Office:** Same as Pax terminal, C-207-921-2689/2682/2256 (NCO on duty).

**PAX LOUNGES:** Limited lounge facilities. DV/VIP lounge. **General:** Bldg 200, main lobby, Hrs: 24 hours daily. Restrooms, telephones (Comm/DSN), vending machines. **Protocol Service:** Bldg 4, Hrs: Mon-Fri 0800-1700, C-207-921-2214.

**FOOD SERVICE:** Dining Hall Bldg 201, C-207-921-2293/2881. Nite Flight/Sportzone Bldg 516, Deli/Pizza, 1100-1300/1600-2200 Tue-Fri, C-207-921-2121. O'Club Bldg 38, lounge open 1500-2100 Fri only. No meals, C-207-729-9594.

**TRANSPORTATION:** Very limited transportation on base. Off base bus service, C-207-725-5573, various taxi service. Parking Bldg 41, C-207-921-2457 (short/long term).

**TML:** Lodging Office: (Bldg 220), C-207-931-2245, FAX (BEQ) 207-729-0232, (BOQ) 207-929-2492. Enlisted, (Bldg 220), C-207-921-2245. DV/VIP: Bldg 512, C-207-921-2214, O5+, Retirees Space-A. Navy Lodge Bldg 364 Topsham Annex, off base, call lodge for directions, C-207-921-2206/1-800-NAVY-INN.

**TRAVELERS AID: Chaplain:** Bldg 585, C-207-921-2231/32. **Emergency Relief:** Bldg 27, C-207-921-2273 (Navy Relief). **Security Police:** Bldg 37, C-207-921-2457.

**OTHER SERVICES: Exchange:** Bldg 11, C-207-921-2378. Credit Union: Bldg 20, C-207-729-1831. **Hair Styles:** Bldg 11, Barber: C-207-921-2346; Beauty: C-207-921-2248. **Laundry/Dry Cleaning:** Bldg 11, C-207-729-9253. **Medical:** Bldg 645, Emergency Service 24 hours daily, C-207-921-2922/2222. Postal Bldg 20, C-207-921-2518.

*MAINE*
***Brunswick Naval Air Station, continued***

**ATTRACTIONS:** Snow skiing area, lobster/seafood, Maine Maritime Museum.

| IN ROUTE SCHEDULES | |
|---|---|
| **Andrews AFB** | ADW/MEDEVAC-1 |

**UNSCHEDULED FLIGHTS**

Frequent flights via P-3A and C009A to: Andrews AFB, MD (**ADW**); Jacksonville NAS, FL (**NIP**); Norfolk NAS, VA (**NGU**); and other CONUS, OCONUS and foreign locations. Call for destinations, routings and schedules.

# MARYLAND

## ANDREWS AIR FORCE BASE (ADW)

89th APS/TROP, 1245 Arnold Ave
Andrews AFB, MD 20331-6320

**LOCATION:** From I-95 (east part of Capital Beltway, I-495) N or S, Exit 9. First traffic light after leaving exit ramp, turn right into main gate of AFB. Also, from I-395 North, exit South Capital St, cross Anacostia River on South Capital St, bear left to Suitland Parkway East. Exit Parkway at Morningside on Suitland Rd East to main gate of AFB. Clearly marked. *USMRA: Page 42 (E-5); Page 55 (I,J-6,7).* NMC: Washington, 6 miles northwest. Main installation number: C-301-981-1110, D-312-858-1110.

**PAX TERM INFO: C-301-981-1854/3526/3604, D-312-858-1854/3526/3604, REC: (updated: 1330, 1800, 0600 daily) Same Day: C-301-981-3527, D-312-858-3527 , Next Day: C-301-981-5851, D-312-858-5851, FAX/Remote Sign-up: C-301-981-4241, D-312-858-4241.** Bldg 1245, Hrs: daily 0600-2200, Directions: Right of Base Ops and ATC tower. Main gate, left on Perimeter Rd. Continue .25 mile, right on Arnold Ave to lst stop. Left to Pax Term. Term open after hrs for later flights. **Navy Ops:** C-301-981-2740/4, D-312-858-2740/4, Bldg 3198, 24hrs daily, (east side of AAFB). No ground transportation provided to Navy Ops. See Washington Naval Air Facility MD (NSF) listing in this book. Also, **D.C. National Guard,** C-301-981-5004. **Pax Service Office:** Bldg 1245, Hrs: Mon-Fri: 0730-1630. **Pax Paging:** Bldg 1245, Hrs: daily: 0600-2200, C-301-981-3604, D-312-858-3604.

**PAX LOUNGES: General:** Bldg 1245, Hrs: daily 0600-2200, C-301-981-3526, D-312-858-3526. A/C, bag check, game room, telephones (commercial, long distance and defense), TV, restrooms, P/C seats. **DV/VIP:** Bldg 1245, 24hrs daily, C-301-981-2100, D-312-858-2100. A/C, coffee/tea served, telephones (commercial, long distance and defense), TV, restrooms, O/S seats. Hostess (06+). Active & retired. **Protocol Service:** Bldg 1245, Hrs: Mon-Fri: 0800-1700, C-301-981-2100, D-312-858-2100 (06+). Active & retired. AMC sponsored.

**FOOD SERVICE: Dining Hall:** Bldg: Arnold Ave #l, 24hrs daily, C-301-981-6516. **Enlisted Club:** Bldg 1889, Hrs: Mon-Thu: 0900-2200, Fri-Sat: 1000-2300, 568-3100. **In-flight Meals:** Bldg: 1201, 24hrs daily, C-301-981-3543. **NCO/CPO Club:** Bldg 1889, Hrs: Mon-Thu: 0900-2200, Fri-Sat: 1000-2300, Sun: 0900-2200, C-301-568-3100. **O'Club:** Bldg 1352, Mon-Thu: 0700-2300, Fri-Sat: 0700-0130, C-301-420-4744. **Snack Bars:** Bldg: 1672, Hrs: Mon, Thu, and Fri: 0700-2300, Sat-Sun: 1000-2300, C-301-981-6152. **Vending:** Bldg: 1245, Hrs: daily 0600-2200.

**TRANSPORTATION: Air Tickets:** SATO: Bldg 1442, Hrs: Mon-Fri: 0800-1630, C-202-433-8320, Official Travel: Bldg 1535, C-301-981-5362. **Bus (Comm):** Departs North Gate to Washington D.C., Hrs: daily 0600-2100, C-301-637-7000. **Bus (Shuttle):** Bldg 1245, Hrs: Mon-Fri: 0600-0900, 1100-1300, 1500-1700, C-301-981-2867. **Car Rentals:**

*MARYLAND*
*Andrews Air Force Base, continued*

Bldg 1245, Hrs: Mon-Fri: 0730-2000, Sat: 0900-1700, Sun: 1200-2000, Thrifty: C-301-568-7900. **Limo Service:** Bldg 1245, Hrs: daily 0730-1400, C-800-441-8775 (Dover Limo). **Taxi (Comm):** Bldg 1245, Hrs: daily 0600-2200, C-301-864-7700 (at Pax Term). **Taxi (Gov):** Bldg 1568, 24hrs daily, C-301-981-2689/5458 (for official duty). **Trains:** AMTRAK: 24hrs daily, C-301-484-7540 (call for schedule). **Parking:** Bldg 1245, 24hrs daily, C-301-981-3528 (short term has 24 hour limit; long term at Bldg 1413 has 30 day limit).

**TML:** Lodging Office (Gateway Inn, Bldg 1375, Arkansas Rd.), 24 hours daily, C-301-423-1412, D-312-858-4614, FAX 301-981-7997. All ranks. DV/VIP: C-301-981-4525, D-312-858-4525 (06+).

**TRAVELERS AID: American Red Cross:** Bldg 1610, Hrs: Mon-Fri: 0800-1600, C-301-981-6008, (hospital). **Chaplain:** Bldg 1345, 24hrs daily C-301-981-2111 (Chapel #l). **Lost/Found:** Bldg 1245, Hrs: daily 0600-2200, C-301-981-3526 (Pax Term, NCO). **Security Police:** Bldg 1845, 24hrs daily, C-301-981-2001 (main gate). **USO:** Bldg 1245, Hrs: Mon-Fri: 0600-1800, C-301-981-2525.

**OTHER SERVICES: Exchange** Bldg: 1683, Hrs: daily 1000-2100, C-301-568-1500. **Bank/Exchange:** Bldg 1677, Hrs: Mon-Fri: 0900-1700, C-301-735-8100. **Hair Styles:** Barber: Bldg 1245, Hrs: Mon-Fri: 0800-1630, C-301-420-9383; Beauty: Bldg 1683, Hrs: Mon-Fri: 0800-1800, Sat: 0800-1700, C-301-735-1988. **Laundry/Dry Cleaning:** Bldg 1668, Hrs: Mon-Sat: 0830-2030, Sun: 0900-1700, C-301-568-2546. **Medical:** Bldg 1050, 24hrs, daily, C-301-981-2333 (hospital emergency). **Postal:** Bldg 1668, Hrs: Mon-Fri: 0800-1615, Sat: 0830-1230, C-301-981-3539 (no wire service). **Valet/Dry Cleaning:** Bldg 1642, Hrs: Mon-Sat: 0900-1800, C-301-736-3246 (no porter service).

**ATTRACTIONS:** Aerial gateway to Wash D.C., home of "Air Force One" (the President's aircraft), monuments, White House, parks & more.

| ORIGINATING SCHEDULES | | | |
|---|---|---|---|
| | **ACC/ADW-1 2nd/4th TUE C-141B** | | |
| **Location ID** | **Airport (Station)** | **Country/State** | **Days Out** |
| ADW | Andrews AFB | MD | +0 |
| DOV | Dover AFB | DE | +1 |
| **MHZ** | **RAF Mildenhall** | **UK** | **+2** |
| DOV | Dover AFB | DE | +3 |
| ADW | Andrews AFB | MD | |
| | **ACC/ADW-2 2nd SUN C-141B** | | |
| ADW | Andrews AFB | MD | +0 |
| DOV | Dover AFB | DE | +0 |
| RMS | Ramstein AB | GE | +2 |
| **AMM** | **King Abdullah AB** | **JR** | **+2** |
| RMS | Ramstein AB | GE | +3 |
| MHZ | RAF Mildenhall | UK | +3 |

| | | | |
|---|---|---|---|
| AVB | Aviano AB | IT | +4 |
| RMS | Ramstein AB | GE | +4 |
| LGS | Lajes AB | PO | +4 |
| DOV | Dover AFB | DE | +5 |
| ADW | Andrews AFB | MD | |
| | **ACC/ADW-3 2nd THU C-141B** | | |
| ADW | Andrews AFB | MD | +0 |
| NGU | Norfolk NAS | VA | +0 |
| KEF | Keflavik APT | IC | +1 |
| **RMS** | **Ramstein AB** | **GE** | **+2** |
| ADW | Andrews AFB | MD | |
| | **ACC/ADW-4 1st/3rd MON C-141B** | | |
| ADW | Andrews AFB | MD | +0 |
| NGU | Norfolk NAS | VA | +0 |
| NRR | Roosevelt Roads NAS | PR | +1 |
| **NBW** | **Guantanamo Bay NAS** | **CU** | **+1** |
| NGU | Norfolk NAS | VA | +1 |
| ADW | Andrews AFB | MD | |
| | **ADW/MEDEVAC-1 SUN C-9A** | | |
| ADW | Andrews AFB | MD | |
| BED | Hanscomb AFB | MA | |
| NHZ | Brunswick NAS | ME | |
| BGR | Bangor ANGB | ME | |
| PBG | Plattsburg AFB | NY | |
| ADW | Andrews AFB | MD | |
| **BLV** | **Scott AFB** | **IL** | |
| | **ADW/MEDEVAC-2 MON, THU C-9A** | | |
| ADW | Andrews AFB | MD | |
| NGU | Norfolf NAS | VA | |
| NKT | Cherry Point MCAS | NC | |
| POB | Pope AFB | NC | |
| CHS | Charleston AFB | SC | |
| AGS | Bush Field AAF | GA | |
| LSF | Lawson AAF | GA | |
| BIX | Keesler AFB | MS | |
| **BLV** | **Scott AFB** | **IL** | |

*MARYLAND*
*Andrews Air Force Base, continued*

| IN ROUTE SCHEDULES | | | |
|---|---|---|---|
| **Allen C Thompson Field** | ACC/JAN-3 | | |
| **Charleston AFB/IAP** | ACC/CHS-16 | | |
| **McGuire AFB** | ACC/WRI-1 | ACC/WRI-2 | ACC/WRI-7 |
| | ACC/WRI-17 | | |
| **Scott AFB** | BLV/MEDEVAC-1 | BLV/MEDEVAC-5 | BLV/MEDEVAC-12 |
| | BLV/MEDEVAC-13 | SUU/MEDEVAC-2 | |

**UNSCHEDULED FLIGHTS**

All unscheduled flights operate with 24 hour notice. Infrequent flights to: Eglin AFB, FL (**VPS**); Guantanamo Bay NS, CU (**GAO**); Hanscom AFB, MA (**BED**); Kelly AFB, TX (**SKF**); Langley AFB, VA (**LFI**); Maxwell AFB, AL (**MXF**); Norfolk NAS, VA (**NGU**); Randolph AFB, TX (**RND**); Roosevelt Roads NAS, PR (**NRR**); Scott AFB, IL (**BLV**); Wright-Patterson AFB, OH (**FFO**). Other destinations vary widely. Equipment is C-12, C-21 or C-9 in most cases. Baggage on these aircraft limited to two pieces, not more than 30 lbs combined except C-009 MEDEVAC which is 45 lbs.

## MARTIN STATE AIRPORT (MTN)

135th TAG (ANG), 2701 Eastern Blvd
Baltimore, MD 21220-2899

**LOCATION:** From US 40E exit to MD-702 East and continue east to MD-150. Enter Air National Guard Base at airport. *USMRA: Page 42 (F,G-3).* NMC: Baltimore, 8 miles southwest. Main installation numbers: C-410-780-8270, D-312-243-6210.

**PAX TERM INFO: C-410-780-8308, D-312-243-6308,** Ops Building, Hrs: During Guard weekends only. Note: Pax Service personnel will not provide flight info over the telephone, only in person. **Parking:** Check with security Police lot short term only.

**TML:** Lodging Office, Aberdeen Proving Ground, 18 miles NE, (Bldg 2207), C-410-278-5148/5149, D-312-298-4373/5148, FAX 410-273-6500-EX-7740. DV/VIP: C-410-278-5156.

**UNSCHEDULED FLIGHTS**

Flights via C-130 aircraft to CONUS, OCONUS and foreign country locations. Note: This organization is not staffed to process requests for Space-A travel on a regular basis.

## PATUXENT RIVER NAVAL AIR WARFARE CENTER (NHK)

Aircraft Division,
Air Operations Department
Patuxent River NAWC, MD 20670-5409

**LOCATION:** From I-95 (east portion of Capital Beltway, I-495) exit 7A to Branch Ave (MD-5) South. Follow MD-5 until it turns into MD-235 near Oraville, on to Lexington Park, and the NAWC. Main gate is on MD-235 and MD-246 (Cedar Point Rd). *USMRA: Page 42 (F,G-6,7).* NMC: Washington DC, 65 miles northwest. Main installation numbers: C-301-826-3000, D-312-326-3000.

**PAX TERM INFO: C-301-826-3836/7, D-312-326-3836/7.** Bldg 103, Hrs: daily 0700-2300. Directions: From main gate straight on Cedar Pt Rd for 2.5 miles. Air Ops sign on the right. **Pax Service Office:** Same as Pax Term, NCO on duty. **Pax Paging:** Same as Pax Term, (P/A System).

**TML:** Lodging Office (Bldg 406), C-301-826-3601, D-312-326-3601, FAX 301-326-1015. Navy Lodge. Bldg 2119, C-301-737-2400 or 1-800-NAVY-INN. DV/VIP: PAO. C-301-826-3601, 06+.

**OTHER SERVICES:** Exchange: C-301-826-8814. CPO Club: C-301-826-3685. SDO/NCO: C-301-826-1097. EM Club: C-301-826-7800. SATO: C-301-826-1873/4. Chaplain: C-301-826-3812. Medical: C-301-826-1506. Many facilities available on base. For full details, see *U.S. Forces Travel & Transfer Guide U.S.A. & Caribbean Areas.*

**ATTRACTIONS:** Calvert Cliffs Nuclear Power Plant Museum, Calvert Marine Museum, Naval Air Test & Evaluation Museum, Potomac River-St Clement's Island Museum, St Mary's City, Sotterley Plantation, Cecil's Mill, Point Lookout State Park, Seafood Festivals.

### UNSCHEDULED FLIGHTS

Occasional flights via C-009A and administrative aircraft to: Jacksonville NAS, FL (**NIP**); Roosevelt Roads NAS, PR (**NRR**). Other CONUS destinations. Call for destinations, routings and schedules.

## WASHINGTON NAVAL AIR FACILITY (NSF)

Operations ATC
Washington, DC 20396-5130

**LOCATION:** From I-95 (east part of Capital Beltway, I-495) North or South, Exit 9. At first traffic light after leaving exit ramp, turn right into main gate of Andrews AFB. Also, from I-395 North, exit south Capital St, cross Anacostia River on South Capital St, bear left to Suitland Parkway East, exit Parkway at Morningside on Suitland Rd East to main gate of Andrews AFB. Follow signs to East side of Andrews AFB, Bldg: 3198, north of Hangar #12. Clearly marked. *USMRA: Page 42 (E-5); Page 55 (I,J-6,7).* NMC: Washington DC, 6 miles northwest. Main installation numbers: C-301-981-9111, D-312-858-9111.

*MARYLAND*
*Washington Naval Air Facility*

**PAX TERM INFO: C-301-981-2740/2744, D-312-858-2740/2744, FAX: C-301-981-3806.** Bldg 3198, Hrs: daily 0600-2200, closed Thanksgiving, Christmas & New Year's Day. Report to ATC desk, 1st floor south end of building. No recording. NOTE: Space-A seats not used by Washington NAF are offered to Andrews AFB and vice versa.

**PAX LOUNGES:** Bldg 3198, Hrs: Same as Pax Term, C-301-981-2740, D-312-858-2744. No overnight use by Pax. Lounge in building lobby. A/C, telephones (commercial), restrooms, P/C seats, TV. **DV/VIP:** Same as Pax Term, C-301-981-2740, D-312-858-2740 (06+). Off lobby. A/C, telephones (commercial and defense), restrooms, O/S seats. **Protocol Service:** Bldg 3198, Hrs: Same as ATC, C-301-981-2740, D-312-858-2740.

**FOOD SERVICE:** Bldg 3198, vending. See Andrews AFB for complete services.

**TRANSPORTATION:** Bldg 3198. See Andrews AFB listing for complete services. **Parking:** Bldg 3198, 24hrs daily. Short & long term available. Contact ATC, C-301-981-2740/2744. No parking in lot next to Bldg 3198.

**TML:** Lodging Office (Gateway Inn, Andrews AFB, Bldg: 1375), C-301-423-1412, D-312-858-4614, FAX 301-981-7997. DV/VIP: C-301-981-4525, D-312-858-4525, O7+.

**OTHER SERVICES: NAF Security Police:** C-301-981-2695/4627. See Andrews AFB listing for other services.

**UNSCHEDULED FLIGHTS**

There are no scheduled flights from the Washington NAF. Most flights are planned 24 hours prior to departure. Call for information. There are frequent unscheduled flights to the following locations: Brunswick NAS, ME (**NHZ**); Cherry Point MCAS, NC (**NKT**); Dallas NAS, TX (**NBE**); Jacksonville NAS, FL (**NIP**); Memphis NAS, TN (**NQA**); New Orleans NAS, LA (**NBG**); Norfolk NAS, VA (**NGU**); Pensacola NAS, FL (**NPA**); South Weymouth NAS, MA (**NZW**). Equipment flown varies with flights and distances. Most aircraft are C-9A, C-12, C-130, P-3C and T-39.

# MASSACHUSETTS

## HANSCOM AIR FORCE BASE (BED)

70 Chennault Street,
Hanscom AFB, MA 01731-5000

**LOCATION:** From I-95 north take Exit 30 to MA-2A west for 2 miles to a right on Hartwell Rd which bisects the AFB. *USMRA: Page 17 (J-3); Page 24 (A-2)*. NMC: Boston, 17 miles southeast. Main installation numbers: C-617-377-4441, D-312-478-4441/5980.

**PAX TERM INFO: C-617-377-3333, D-312-478-3333, FAX 617-377-2383, D FAX 312-478-2383.** Recording after hours. Bldg 1721, Hrs: Mon-Fri: 0800-1200, for Space-A sign up. Terminal will open 2 hrs prior to all advertised flight departures for Space-A pax.

**PAX LOUNGES:** General and DV/VIP lounges available. A/C, restrooms, telephones, TV and vending machines. No inflight meals available. **Protocol Service:** POC D-312-478-5151.

**FOOD SERVICE: Enlisted Club:** C-617-377-2123. **NCO Club:** C-617-377-2123. **O'Club:** C-617-377-3799. **Restaurant:** C-617-274-0133. **Vending:** Pax Term, Hrs: Mon-Fri: 0700-2300.

**TRANSPORTATION: Air Tickets:** C-617-274-6050. **Car Rentals:** On Base, Avis: C-617-274-7488. **Taxi (Gov):** Hrs: Mon-Fri: 0630-1930, C-617-377-2588. **Parking:** Bldg 1721, D-312-478-3333 (long and short term). For long term, notify Security Police at D-312-478-2314.

**TML:** Lodging Office (Hanscom Inn, Bldg 1427), C-617-377-2112, FAX 617-377-4961. DV/VIP: C-617-377-5151, O7+.

**OTHER SERVICES: Exchange:** C-617-377-5258. **Hair Styles:** Barber: C-617-377-5127; Beauty: C-617-377- 6634. **Laundry:** C-617-377-5139. **Medical:** C-617-377-4988. **Postal:** C-617-377-4069. **Valet/Dry Cleaning:** C-617-377-5139. **Wire:** C-617-377-4441.

| IN ROUTE SCHEDULES | |
|---|---|
| **Andrews AFB** | ADW/MEDEVAC-1 |

### UNSCHEDULED FLIGHTS

Limited flights to Andrews AFB, MD (ADW), Wright Patterson AFB, OH (FFO) and other East Coast locations. Call for destiniations, routings and schedules after 1400 for the 24-48 hr departure schedule.

## OTIS AIR NATIONAL GUARD BASE (CPD)

& Cape Cod Coast Guard Air Station
102 FW/OTM, Bldg 165 Otis ANGB, MA 02542-5028

**LOCATION:** Off Rt 28 at the Massachusetts Military Reservation on Cape Cod (Otis ANGB) on former Otis AFB. *USMRA: Page 17 (M-7)*. NMC: New Bedford, 30 miles southwest. Main installation numbers: C-508-968-1000, D-312-557-1000.

**PAX TERM INFO: C-508-968-4831/4832, D-312-557-4831/4832, F: 829-6352, FAX: C-508-968-6321.** Base Ops/PAX Term Bldg 165, Hrs: Mon-Fri 0730-1600.

**TML:** Lodging Office (Bldg 5204), C-508-968-6461.

**OTHER SERVICES:** Small lounge facility. No commercial or military bus on Base. Commercial taxi and rental car available in Falmouth, MA 10 mi south of base. Call Base Ops for number. Off Base Quarters Quality Inn Falmouth (government rate). 1-800-854-1507 (New England) C-508-540-2000. See Coast Guard Air Station for on base military quarters. No messing facilities on base. Commissary: C-508-968-6662, D-557-6662. Exchange: C-508-968-6648, D-557-6648. Emergency Medical C-508-968-4111, D-557-4111.

### UNSCHEDULED FLIGHTS

Very limited Space-A via C-12 and C-130 aircraft. No advance schedules published. Call for information.

## SOUTH WEYMOUTH NAVAL AIR STATION (NZW)

Air Ops Terminal
South Weymouth, MA 02190-5000

**LOCATION:** From MA-3 (Pilgrims Hwy) Exit 16 to MA-18 (Main St) south to 5th traffic light, turn left and drive to the gate. *USMRA: Page 17 (L-4); Page 24 (G,H-10)*. NMC: Boston, 15 miles northwest. Main installation numbers: C-617-786-2933, D-312-955-2933.

**PAX TERM INFO: C-617-786-2713, D-312-955-2713.** Hangar #1, Hrs: daily 0700-2300. Directions: Follow Shea Memorial Dr to its end. Turn left and follow road for 50 yards to walk through gate, to the first office at the end of the hangar (near taxi ramp). **Pax Service Office:** Same as Pax Term.

**PAX LOUNGES:** No separate family lounge. **General:** Hangar #1, Hrs: daily 0700-2300, C-617-786-2713. Bag check, telephones (local, long distance and defense), TV, restrooms, O/S seats. **DV/VIP:** Hangar #1, Hrs: Daily: 0700-2300, C-617-786-2713.

A/C, telephones (local, long distance and defense), TV, restrooms, O/S seats. **Protocol Service:** Bldg: 17, 24hrs daily, C-617-786-2500 (06+).

**FOOD SERVICE: Dining Hall:** C-617-786-2653. **The Commons Restaurant:** C-617-786-2591. **Snack Bars:** C-617-786-2921.

**TRANSPORTATION:** VERC Car Rental: C-617-331-7000. **Taxi:** Green: C-617-335-1933. **Trains:** Braintree MBTA Station. To Boston. **Parking:** C-617-786-2713, All parking-NE of Terminal (East MAT).

**TML:** Lodging Office (Bldg 31, Shea Memorial Dr), C-617-786-2738, 1-800-248-8805, D-312-955-2738. DV/VIP: C-617-786-2600. (06+).

**TRAVELERS AID: Chaplain:** C-617-786-2604. **Security Police:** C-617-786-2610.

**OTHER SERVICES: Exchange:** C-617-786-2952. **Hair Styles:** C-617-786-2809. **Medical:** Bldg 24, 24hrs daily, C-617-786-2674, D-312-955-2674.

**ATTRACTIONS:** Historic Quincy, Boston, Massachusetts Bay.

**UNSCHEDULED FLIGHTS**

Flights are to various CONUS locations including: Brunswick NAS, ME (**NHZ**); Jacksonville NAS, FL (**NIP**); Norfolk NAS, VA (**NGU**); Washington NAF, MD (**NSF**); and Willow Grove NAS, PA (**NXX**) via C-009B, C-12A, P-3C & C-130 aircraft. Call for destinations, routings and schedules.

## WESTOVER AIR RESERVE BASE (CEF)

337th AF Squad
Chicopee, MA 01022-1309

**LOCATION:** Take exit 5 off I-90 (MA Turnpike) in Chicopee. Westover is on Rt 33 north of I-90; signs mark way to base. *USMRA: Page 16 (F-4).* NMC: Springfield, 8 miles south. Main Installation Numbers: C-413-557-1110, D-312-589-1110.

**PAX TERM INFO: C-413-557-2917/2951, D-312-589-2917/2951**. The RAO will provide flight schedules daily by calling 413-557-2549. The actual signing up for a flight will be done only on Wed & Fri, 1000-1200 & 1300-1500. This may be accomplished by calling 413-557-2622. Many facilities available on base. For full details see *US Forces Travel & Transfer Guide USA & Caribbean Areas.*

**TML:** Lodging Office (Flyers Inn, 650 Bldg 2201, Airlift Dr.), C-413-557-2700, D-312-589-2700, FAX: C-413-557-2835, D-312-589-2835. DV/VIP: Bldg: 2200. C-413-557-5421, 05+.

***MASSACHUSETTS***
***Westover Air Reserve Base, continued***

| ORIGINATING SCHEDULES | | | |
|---|---|---|---|
| | **ACC/CEF-1 1st FRI C-5A** | | |
| **Location ID** | **Airport (Station)** | **Country/State** | **Days Out** |
| CEF | Westover ARB | MA | +0 |
| DOV | Dover AFB | DE | +1 |
| CHS | Charleston AFB/IAP | SC | +1 |
| **HOW** | **Howard AB** | **PN** | **+2** |
| CHS | Charleston AFB/IAP | SC | +3 |
| CEF | Westover ARB | MA | |
| | **APM/CEF-2 2nd/4th MON C-5A** | | |
| CEF | Westover ARB | MA | +0 |
| DOV | Dover AFB | DE | +1 |
| RMS | Ramstein AB | GE | +2 |
| **ADA** | **Incirlik APT** | **TU** | **+3** |
| RMS | Ramstein AB | GE | +4 |
| KEF | Keflavik APT | IC | +4 |
| DOV | Dover AFB | DE | +5 |
| CEF | Westover ARB | MA | |
| | **ACC/CEF-3 1st MON C-5A** | | |
| CEF | Westover ARB | MA | +0 |
| DOV | Dover AFB | DE | +1 |
| **RMS** | **Ramstein AB** | **GE** | **+2** |
| LGS | Lajes AB | PO | +3 |
| DOV | Dover AFB | DE | +3 |
| CEF | Westover ARB | MA | |

# MICHIGAN

## SELFRIDGE AIR NATIONAL GUARD BASE (MTC)

127th FW/OTM
Selfridge ANGB, MI 48045-5004

**LOCATION:** Take I-94 North from Detroit, to Selfridge exit, then east on MI-59 to main gate of Base. *USMRA: Page 66 (G-9); Page 70 (G-1)*. NMC: Detroit, 25 miles southwest. Main installation numbers: C-810-307-4011, D-312-273-0111.

**PAX TERM INFO: C-810-307-5884/4011, D-312-273-5884 (Recording).** At this time there is no PAX Terminal.

**PAX LOUNGES:** No lounges. Flights are processed by ANG & USCG Ops.

**FOOD SERVICE:** Limited services on Base. **NCO/CPO Club:** Bldg 300, C-810-307-466-4786. **O'Club:** Bldg 400, C-810-307-4785. **Snack Bars:** Bldg 700, C-810-307-466-5322.

**TRANSPORTATION: Air Tickets:** SATO: Bldg B-128, C-810-307-4931. **Bus (Comm):** Bldg B-50, C-810-307-5322, C-313-466-4628. **Parking:** Across from Base Ops, C-810-307-5322. **Taxi (Comm):** C-1-800-458-9401 (call for schedules).

**TML:** Lodging Office (Bldg 410, George Ave), C-810-307-4062. DV/VIP: C-810-307-5444.

**TRAVELERS AID: Emergency Relief:** Bldg 945 (Army), C-810-307-5903/4514, C-810-739-6558 (AF Aid), C-810-307-4761/3 (Navy Relief). **Chaplain:** Bldg 168, C-313-466-4761/3. **Security Police:** Bldg 305, C-810-307-4222.

**OTHER SERVICES: Exchange:** Bldg 700, C-810-307-4614/4120. **Bank/Exchange:** Bldg 717, C-810-307-2400. **Hair Styles:** Bldg 700, C-810-307-468-8009. **Laundry/Dry Cleaning:** Bldg 700, C-810-307-0610. **Medical:** Bldg 310, Hrs: Mon-Fri: 0715-1600, C-810-307-4650. **Postal:** Bldg 178, C-810-307-4123.

**ATTRACTIONS:** City of Detroit, Lake St Clair, Canada approx 40 minutes.

### UNSCHEDULED FLIGHTS

Several flights each week via C-130 and C-135 to East coast and Southeast CONUS. Flights are processed by ANG and AFRES. NOTE: No regularly scheduled flights. Call recording number for appropriate telephone number of unit flying each mission.

# MINNESOTA

## MINNEAPOLIS-ST PAUL INTERNATIONAL AIRPORT/ AIR RESERVE STATION (MSP)

133rd AW (ANG), 934th AG (AFRES)
684 General Miller Dr
St Paul, MN 55450-2000

**LOCATION:** From I-35 East to crosstown MN-62, exit at 34th Ave and entrance to IAP. Also, MN-55 South to crosstown MN-62, exit to 34th Ave and entrance to IAP. *USMRA: Page 89 (C-3)*. NMC: Minneapolis-St Paul, in city limits. Main installation numbers: C-612-725-5011, ANG: D-312-825-5681, AFRES: D-312-825-5100.

**PAX TERM INFO: AFRES: C-612-725-8018/5552, D-312-825-8018/5552, ANG: C-612-725-5149/5681, D-312-825-5149/5681.** Bldg 821, Base Ops, Hrs: daily 0730-1600. Directions: From main gate straight on main road to Base Ops. Separate facilities maintained by ANG and AFRES.

**PAX LOUNGES:** No lounges. All Pax wait in and are processed by Base Ops.

**TML:** Lodging Office (The North Country Inn, AFRES, Bldg 711-ANG), Hrs: Mon-Thu: 0700-1800, Fri: 0700-2100, Sat-Sun: 0700-1300, C-612-725-5320, D-312-825-5320, FAX 612-725-8158. All ranks. DV/VIP: C-612-725-5320.

**TRAVELERS AID: Security Police:** Main gate, C-612-725-5400.

**OTHER SERVICES:** Limited support facilities available. **Exchange:** Bldg 751, C-612-726-9023. **NCO Club:** C-612-726-5390. **O'Club:** C-612-726-5402.

**ATTRACTIONS:** On the Mississippi and Minnesota Rivers. Mall of America.

### UNSCHEDULED FLIGHTS

Flights to CONUS locations via ANG and AFRES C-130E aircraft. Most flights on weekends. Call for destinations, routings and schedules.

# MISSISSIPPI

## ALLEN C. THOMPSON FIELD (JAN)

172nd AG (ANG), 141 Military Drive
Jackson, MS 39208-8881

**LOCATION:** Off I-20 East or West & US-49 North or South. *USMRA: Page 43 (D-6).* NMC: Jackson, 5 miles west. Main installation numbers: C-601-939-3633, D-312-731-9210.

**PAX TERM INFO: C-601-936-8372, D-312-731-9372, FAX: C-601-936-8605.** Base Ops, Hrs: Mon-Fri: 0730-1600, No separate Pax Term. **No military support facilities.** All the support of a commercial airport provided.

**ATTRACTIONS:** Historic homes.

| ORIGINATING SCHEDULES | | | |
|---|---|---|---|
| | **ACC/JAN-1 1st/2nd THU C-141B** | | |
| **Location ID** | **Airport (Station)** | **Country/State** | **Days Out** |
| JAN | Allen C Thompson Field | MS | +0 |
| DOV | Dover AFB | DE | +1 |
| **MHZ** | **RAF Mildenhall** | **UK** | **+2** |
| DOV | Dover AFB | DE | +3 |
| JAN | Allen C Thompson Field | MS | |
| | **ACC/JAN-2 2nd TUE C-141B** | | |
| JAN | Allen C Thompson Field | MS | +0 |
| SKF | Kelly AFB | TX | +0 |
| **HOW** | **Howard AB** | **PN** | **+1** |
| SKF | Kelly AFB | TX | +1 |
| JAN | Allen C Thompson Field | MS | |
| | **ACC/JAN-3 4th THU C-141B** | | |
| JAN | Allen C Thompson Field | MS | +0 |
| NGU | Norfolk NAS | VA | +0 |
| KEF | Keflavik APT | IC | +1 |
| **RMS** | **Ramstein AB** | **GE** | **+2** |
| ADW | Andrews AFB | MD | +3 |
| JAN | Allen C Thompson Field | MS | |

### UNSCHEDULED FLIGHTS

Flights to: Charleston AFB, SC (**CHS**); RAF Mildenhall, UK (**MHZ**); Rhein Main AB, GE (**FRF**); Lajes Field, Azores PO (**LGS**) and other overseas & CONUS locations via C-141/B aircraft. Call for destinations, routings and schedules. Most flights on training weekends.

*MISSISSIPPI*

# KEESLER AIR FORCE BASE (BIX)

45 AS/OSFAM
817 H St. Suite 102
Keesler AFB, MS 39534-2452

**LOCATION:** From I-10 Exit 46, follow signs to Base. From US-90, north on White Ave to main gate. *USMRA: Page 43 (F-10)*. NMC: Biloxi, in the city. Main installation numbers: C-601-377-1110, D-312-597-1110.

**PAX PROCESSING INFO: C-601-377-4538, D-312-597-4538, REC: C-601-377-4538,** (Updated daily 0800). Bldg 0233, Hrs: daily 0700-2300. Directions: From main gate straight on Larcher Blvd, left on Meadows Dr, right on Hangar Rd to H Street, Terminal faces H Street. Closed all Federal Holidays.

**BASE OPS LOUNGE:** Located on H Street & Hangar Rd. **General:** Bldg 0233, Hrs: Mon-Fri: 0700-2300, C-601-377-2120. A/C, read/write rooms, telephone (local and defense), TV, restrooms, P/C & O/S seats. **DV/VIP:** Bldg 0233, Hrs: Mon-Fri: 0700-2300, C-601-377-2215. Coffee/tea, telephones (long distance). **Protocol Service:** Bldg 2816, Hrs: Mon-Fri: 0700-1630, (07+), C-601-377-3359 (Air Education and Training Command).

**FOOD SERVICE: Cafeteria:** Bldg 2001, Hrs: daily 0415-0730, 1030-1315, 1645-1930, C-601-377-3854 ("Gulf Breeze"). **Enlisted Club:** Bldg 7503, Hrs: Mon-Thu: 0800-2200, Fri: 0800-2400, Sat: 1100-2400, C-601-377-2424. **NCO/CPO Club:** Bldg 2221, Hrs: Daily: 0630-1030, 1100-1330, 1700-2100, C-601-377-3439. **O'Club:** Bldg 3208, Hrs: Mon-Thu: 1730-2030, Fri: 1800-2130, Sat: 1100-2400, C-601-377-2791. **Snack Bars:** Bldg 4328, Hrs: Mon-Fri: 0630-1300, C-601-432-7488. **Vending:** Bldg 3216, 24hrs daily, C-601-435-5130.

**TRANSPORTATION: Air Tickets:** SATO: Bldg 2303, Hrs: Mon-Fri: 0730-1600, C-601-432-2230. **Bus (Comm):** Biloxi, 24hrs daily, 432-2649 (Coastliner). **Bus (Gov):** Bldg 4430, Hrs: daily 0600-2300 upon request, C-601-377-2430. **Bus (Shuttle):** Bldg 4430, Hrs: Mon-Fri: 0630-2200, Sat-Sun: 0630-1940, C-601-377-2430. **Car Rentals:** Biloxi/Gulfport Municipal Airport, 24hrs daily, C-601-864-5181 (military rates). **Limo Service:** Bldg 7303, Hrs: Mon-Fri: 0800-1700, C-601-432-2649 (Coastliner). **Taxi (Comm):** Biloxi, 24hrs daily, C-601-436-3788. **Taxi (Gov):** Bldg 4430, 24hrs daily, C-601-377-2430. avail to AD on PCS/TDY orders only. **Parking:** Bldg 4205, 24hrs daily, C-601-377-3040 (short & long term with no restrictions - notify Security Police).

**TML:** Lodging Office (Consolidated Front Desk for the Inns of Keesler, Bldg 2101. Billeting not available on Reserves Weekends), C-601-377-2631/3663, D-312-597-2631/3663, FAX 601-597-3588. DV/VIP: C-601-377-3359, E9+ & 06+

**TRAVELERS AID: American Red Cross:** Bldg 0701, Hrs: Mon-Fri: 0800-1600, C-601-377-3030 (other hours C-601-377-1110). **Chaplain:** Bldg 1901, Hrs: daily 0730-1600, C-601-377-4410. **Lost/Found:** see Security Police. **Security Police:** Bldg 4703, 24hrs daily, C-601-377-3040.

**OTHER SERVICES: Exchange:** Bldg 2303, Hrs: Mon-Fri: 0900-2100, Sat: 0900-2100, Sun: 1200-1700, C-601-435-2216. **Bank/Exchange:** Bldg 1550, Hrs: Mon-Fri: 0830-1500, C-601-374-1740 (1st Mississippi). **Hair Styles:** Bldg 2303, Hrs: Mon-Sat: 0900-1700, C-601-436-4181 (Barber and Beauty Shop). **Laundry/Dry Cleaning:** Bldg 2303, Hrs: Mon-Fri: 0900-1800, Sat: 0900-1700, C-601-432-0772. **Medical:** Bldg 0468, 24hrs daily, C-601-377-6555/6556. **Postal:** Bldg 3913, Hrs: Mon-Fri: 0800-1630, Sat: 0800-1200, C-601-377-1110.

**ATTRACTIONS:** Beaches, seafood, casinos, New Orleans and Mobile easy drives.

| ORIGINATING SCHEDULES | | |
|---|---|---|
| | **BIX/MEDEVAC-1 WED C-9A** | |
| BIX | Keesler AFB | MS |
| MXF | Maxwell AFB | AL |
| BHM | Birmingham Municipal APT | AL |
| WRB | Robins AFB | GA |
| VAD | Moody AFB | GA |
| VPS | Eglin AFB | FL |
| BIX | Keesler AFB | MS |
| SKF | Kelly AFB | TX |
| **BLV** | **Scott AFB** | **IL** |
| | **BIX/MEDEVAC-2 SAT C-9A** | |
| BIX | Keesler AFB | MS |
| MXF | Maxwell AFB | AL |
| HUA | Huntsville APT | AL |
| MGE | Dobbins ARB | GA |
| VAD | Moody AFB | GA |
| VPS | Eglin AFB | FL |
| BIX | Keesler AFB | MS |
| SKF | Kelly AFB | TX |
| **BLV** | **Scott AFB** | **IL** |

| IN ROUTE SCHEDULES | | |
|---|---|---|
| **Andrews AFB** | ADW/MEDEVAC-2 | |
| **Kelly AFB** | SKF/MEDEVAC-1 | |
| **Scott AFB** | BLV/MEDEVAC-1 | BLV/MEDEVAC-2 |
| **Travis AFB** | SUU/MEDEVAC-2 | |

## KEY FIELD AIRPORT (MEI)

186th Air Refueling Group (ANG)
Meridian, MS 39302-1825

**LOCATION:** From I-20/59 East or West, take exit #150 or US 11 South to airport. USMRA: Page 43 (F, G-6). NMC: Meridian 3 mi NE. Main installation numbers: C-601-484-9000, D-312-778-9210.

**PAX TERM INFO: C-601-484-9000, D-312-778-9210.** No military support at Key Field Airport. **TML**: See Meridian NAS, 18 miles NE. Lodging Office: Bldg 218 (CBQ), Fuller Road, C-601-679-2186/2386, FAX: C-601-679-2745.

### UNSCHEDULED FLIGHTS

Frequent flights via ANG KC-135 aircraft to CONUS and OCONUS locations. Call for destinations, routings and schedules.

## MERIDIAN NAVAL AIR STATION (NMM)

Flight Planning, Box 2, 100 Fuller Rd, Suite 100
Meridian NAS, MS 39309-5000

**LOCATION:** Take MS-39 North from Meridian for 12 miles to 4-lane access road. Clearly marked. Right for 3 miles to NAS main gate. *USMRA: Page 43 (G-6)*. NMC: Meridian, 15 miles southwest. Main installation numbers: C-601-679-2211, D-312-637-2211.

**PAX TERM INFO: C-601-679-2505, D-312-637-2505.** Bldg 1, Hrs: Mon-Fri: 1300-0300, closed Sat & Sun, FAX 1400-2200. Directions: From main gate straight on Whitaker Blvd to a right on Fuller Rd for 2.5 miles to Base Ops on the left. **Pax Service Office:** Base Ops, Hrs: Mon-Thu: 1300-0300, Fri: 1300-2200, C-601-679-2505 (NCO on duty).

**PAX LOUNGES:** Limited lounge facilities. **General:** Base Ops, Hrs: Mon-Fri: 1300-0300, C-601-679-2505. A/C, bag check, restrooms, P/C seats. **DV/VIP:** Base Ops, Hrs: Mon-Thu: 1300-0300, Fri: 1300-2200, C-601-679-2505 (06+ - on request). **Protocol Service:** Bldg 200, Hrs: Mon-Fri: 1300-1800, D-312-446-2318.

**FOOD SERVICE: Cafeteria:** Bldg 1, Hrs: Mon-Fri: 1230-0100, C-601-679-2681. **Enlisted Club:** Bldg 216, Hrs: daily 1600-0400, C-601-679-2640. **NCO/CPO/O' Club:** Bldg 365, Hrs: Mon-Sat: 1600-0400, C-601-679-2650. **Restaurant:** Bldg 1, Hrs: Mon-Fri: 1400-2300, C-601-679-2505. **Snack Bars:** Bldg 1, Hrs: Mon-Fri: 1400-2300, C-601-679-2505. **Vending:** Bldg 1, Hrs: Mon-Fri: 1400-0400, C-601-679-2505.

**TRANSPORTATION: Bus (Shuttle):** Base Ops, Hrs: Fri: 1700-2400, Sat-Sun: 0900-2400, (to Meridian). **Taxi (Gov):** Base Ops, Hrs: Mon-Fri: 0730-1600, C-601-

679-2645. **Parking:** Base Ops, Hrs: Mon-Thu: 1400-0300, Fri-Sun: 1400-2200, C-601-679-2454 (across street - 1 week limit).

**TML:** Lodging Office (Bldg 218, Fuller Rd), C-601-679-2186/2386, FAX 601-679-2745. All ranks. DV/VIP: C-601-679-2186.

**TRAVELERS AID: American Red Cross:** Bldg 362, Hrs: Mon-Fri: 1000-1400, C-601-679-2679. **Chaplain:** Bldg 211, Hrs: Mon-Fri: 0800-1700, C-601-679-2475. **Emergency Relief:** Bldg 362, Hrs: Mon-Fri: 0900-1300, C-601-679-2504 (Navy Relief). **Security Police:** Main gate, 24hrs daily, C-601-679-2361.

**OTHER SERVICES: Exchange:** NEX Mall, Hrs: Mon-Sat: 1000-1800, C-601-679-2725. **Bank/Exchange:** NEX Mall, Hrs: Mon-Fri: 0900-1500, C-601-679-2501 (NFCU). **Hair Styles:** NEX Mall, Hrs: Mon-Sat: 1000-1800, Barber: C-601-679-2569; Beauty: C-601-679-8411. **Laundry:** NEX Mall, Hrs: Mon-Sat: 1000-1800, C-601-679-2632. **Medical:** Map #50, 24hrs daily, C-601-679-2444. **Postal:** Map #30, Hrs: Mon-Fri: 0800-1600, C-601-679-2211.

### UNSCHEDULED FLIGHTS

Flights to CONUS destinations. Call for destinations, routings and schedules.

## VICKSBURG MUNICIPAL AIRPORT (VKS)

5867 Hwy 615
Vicksburg, MS 39180-5000

**LOCATION:** Take US-61 South from I-20 East or West for 6 miles, exit west (right) to airport. *USMRA: Page 43 (C-6)*. NMC: Vicksburg, 6 miles north. Main installation numbers: C-601-638-6550, D- None.

**PAX TERM INFO: C-601-638-6550, FAX 601-636-3958.** ARMY RESERVE, Hrs: daily 0730-1600. ARMY RESERVE Hangar is the largest hangar on south end of field. No Pax Terminal. All Pax processed through Base Ops. Commercial facilities available at Commercial Pax Terminal.

### UNSCHEDULED FLIGHTS

Flights via UH-IH aircraft to: Birmingham Municipal Airport, AL (**BHM**); Cairns AAF, AL (**OZR**); Lawson AAF, GA (**LSF**); Monroe County Airport, AL (**MVC**); and Tuscaloosa Municipal Airport, AL (**TCL**). Call for other destinations, routings and schedules.

# MISSOURI

## FORNEY ARMY AIRFIELD (TBN)

Air Operations
Fort Leonard Wood, MO 65473-5000

**LOCATION:** Two miles south of I-44, adjacent to St Robert & Waynesville, at Ft Leonard Wood exit. *USMRA: Page 81 (E-6)*. NMC: Springfield, 85 miles southwest. Main installation numbers: C-314-596-0131, D-312-581-0110, F-270-0110.

**PAX TERM INFO: C-314-596-0165/4819, D-312-581-0165/4819, FAX: C-314-596-0166.** Base Ops, Hrs: Mon-Fri: 0630-1630, Closed Sat, Sun & Holidays. Directions: From south gate straight on Iowa Ave to left exit to AAF. Commercial Pax Term and commercial flights at the AAF. Commercial number is 314-329-3400. All the support of a large fort available at nearby Fort Leonard Wood. See *Military Living's US Forces Travel Guide USA & Caribbean Areas* for details.

**TML:** Lodging Office (Fort Leonard Wood, Bldg 315, Room 126, Missouri Ave), 24 hrs daily, C-1-800-677-8356, DV/VIP: C-314-596-6183, O6/G5-15.

| IN ROUTE SCHEDULES | |
|---|---|
| **Scott AFB** | BLV/MEDEVAC-11 |

**UNSCHEDULED FLIGHTS**

Flights to east and southeast CONUS via U-21, C-12A and C-21A aircraft. Call for destinations, routings, and schedules. Baggage limit 30 lbs.

## LAMBERT-ST LOUIS INTERNATIONAL AIRPORT (STL)

Det 1, 375th TRNSPS, PO Box 10305
St Louis, MO 63145-0305

**LOCATION:** Twelve mi NW of St Louis, on I-70. Airport is also accessible from I-170. *USMRA: Page 81 (G-5); Page 91 (A-1,2)*. NMC: St Louis, 12 miles southeast. Main installation numbers: C-314-263-6269, D-312-693-6270/6269.

**PAX TERM INFO: C-314-263-6269/6270, D-312-693-6269/6270, REC: C-314-263-6262, D-312-693-6262, FAX: D-312-693-6247.** AMC counter is on the upper level near exit 5. Hrs: as required by flight operations. Daily: 0700-2200. **Pax Paging:** AMC counter, Hrs: as required by flight operations, C-314-263-6262.

*MISSOURI*
*Lambert-St. Louis International Airport, continued*

**PAX LOUNGES:** Lambert IAP Pax Service. **General:** A/C, O/S seats, restrooms, coffee/tea served (USO),nursery (USO). **DV/VIP:** Lambert IAP, limited hours, C-314-263-6269. (Check with Pax Service). **Protocol Service:** Scott AFB, IL, C-618-744-1200, D-312-638-4313 (from STL). **Family Service:** Nursery available at USO, west end of arrival level, C-314-429-1234.

**FOOD SERVICE: Cafeteria:** Located in west end, upper level, of Lambert IAP, 24hrs daily. **Restaurants:** Burger King: Located at east end, upper level, of main Term. **Snack Bars:** Located on all levels of the main Term.

**TRANSPORTATION: Air Tickets: throughout the airport with commercial carriers. Bus (Comm):** Service counter on arrival level, Exit 13. **Bus (Shuttle):** To & from Scott AFB, $15 each way (from STL). **Car Rentals:** Arrival level, near Exit 11, 24hrs daily. **Limo Service:** Lower level, near Exit 6. Departs approximately every 15 minutes for hotels and downtown. **Taxi (Comm):** Lower level, 24hrs daily, C-314-427-9348. **Parking:** Short term across from Term, 24hrs daily; long term-marked, 1.5 miles west (bus to Term). Valet parking upper level, C-314-426-8070.

**TML:** Lodging Office (Scott Inn, Bldg 1510, thirty-eight miles east of airport. Shuttle available to Scott AFB, IL: $15.00), Hrs: daily 0800-2200, C-618-744-1200, D-312-576-1844, DSN FAX 312-576-6638. All ranks. DV/VIP: C-618-256-5555, D-312-576-5555, O6+.

**TRAVELERS AID: American Red Cross:** C-314-658-2061 (STL); C-314-256-3291, D-312-576-3291 (Scott AFB). **Lost/Found:** AMC counter, Hrs: daily 0800-2200, C-314-263-6404, 1-800-851-5761. **USO:** Arrival level, west end, main Term, 24hrs daily, C-314-429-1234. (Retirees are permitted to use the USO lounge up to four times per month.)

**OTHER SERVICES: Hair Styles:** Arrival level, Hrs: daily 0800-1700, C-314-423-3222 (near Concourse B). **Medical:** Lower level, west end (First Aid). **Postal:** Lower level, west end, near Exit 6. **Wire:** Western Union available on "will-call" basis, C-314-429-4999.

**ATTRACTIONS:** St. Louis (nearby), Gateway Arch, Knotts Berry Farm, Six Flags Over Mid America, casino river boats and Mississippi River.

| **ORIGINATING SCHEDULES** | | | |
|---|---|---|---|
| **PPP/STL-1 SUN B-747** | | | |
| **Location ID** | **Airport (Station)** | **Country/State** | **Days Out** |
| STL | Lambert St. Louis IAP | MO | +0 |
| LAX | Los Angeles AIP | CA | +0 |
| **OKO** | **Yokota AB** | **JA** | **+0** |
| DNA | Kadena AB | JA | +1 |
| LAX | Los Angeles IAP | CA | +1 |
| STL | Lambert St. Louis IAP | MO | |

*MISSOURI*
*Lambert-St. Louis International Airport, continued*

| PPP/STL-2 WED B-747 | | | |
|---|---|---|---|
| STL | Lambert St. Louis IAP | MO | +0 |
| LAX | Los Angeles IAP | CA | +0 |
| OKO | Yokota AB | JA | +0 |
| **OSN** | **Osan AB** | **RK** | **+1** |
| OKO | Yokota AB | JA | +1 |
| LAX | Los Angeles IAP | CA | +1 |
| STL | Lambert St. Louis IAP | MO | |
| **IN ROUTE SCHEDULES** | | | |
| **Dallas-Fort Worth** APP/DFW-1 | | | |

# ROSECRANS MEMORIAL AIRPORT (STJ)

139th AG, 705 Memorial Dr.,
St Joseph, MO 64503-9307

**LOCATION:** From US-36 East or West exit N on MO-238. Straight 1.5 miles to airport entrance. *USMRA: Page 81 (B-3)*. NMC: St Joseph, 4 miles southeast. Main installation numbers: C-816-271-3299, D-312-720-9299. (Note: Limit airport services due to flood of 1993. Commercial taxi to Kansas City IAP is only available transportation.)

**PAX TERM INFO: C-816-236-3260, D-312-956-3260, FAX: C-816-236-3239, D FAX 312-956-3239**. No PAX terminal. Base Operations handles pax terminal duties on time available basis. Bldg 17, Squadron Operations, Hrs: daily 0730-1600. Ask Security Police for ANG facility. All support facilities of a regional airport. Main gate open 24 hours daily.

**TML:** Lodging Office, Fort Leavenworth, KS 28 miles south, (Bldg 695, 115 Grant Ave), C-913-651-9522 or 1-800-854-8627, FAX 913-684-4397. DV/VIP: C-913-684-4064, O6+.

**UNSCHEDULED FLIGHTS**

Flights via C-130 aircraft to CONUS Stations. Call for destinations, routings and schedules.

# WHITEMAN AIR FORCE BASE (SZL)

745 Arnold Ave, Suite 2A
Whiteman AFB, MO 65305-5026

**LOCATION:** From I-70 E, exit to US-13 S to US-50 E for 10 miles, then right on Route 132 which leads to AFB. *USMRA: Page 81 (C-5)*. NMC: Kansas City, 60 miles NW. Main installation numbers: C-816-687-1110, D-312-975-1110.

**PAX TERM INFO:** C-816-687-3101, D-312-975-3101, Bldg 35. Full base support available, see Military Living's ***US Forces Travel and Transfer Guide USA & Caribbean Areas*** for more information on the base.

**TML:** Lodging Office (The Whiteman Inn, Bldg 325, Mitchell Ave), C-816-687-1844, FAX 816-687-3052. DV/VIP: C-816-687-6543, O6+.

## UNSCHEDULED FLIGHTS

Occasional MEDEVAC flights to Scott AFB, IL (**BLV**) and limited other CONUS locations. Call for destinations, routing and schedules.

# MONTANA

## MALMSTROM AIR FORCE BASE (GFA)

43rd OSS/DOB, 7224 Flightline Dr., Rm 107
Malmstrom AFB, MT 59402-7526

**LOCATION:** From I-15 North or South take 10th Ave South exit to AFB. From the east take Malmstrom exit off US-87/89 to AFB. Clearly marked. *USMRA: Page 99 (D,E-4).* NMC: Great Falls, 1 mile west. Main installation numbers: C-406-731-1110, D-312-632-1110.

**PAX TERM INFO: C-406-731-2861, D-312-632-2861, REC: C-406-731-2222.** 7224 Flight Line Dr. Base Ops, 24hrs daily. Directions: From main gate straight on Goddard Ave to a right on Ave D to Base Operations. Right at flight line. **Pax Service Office:** Same as Pax terminal.

**PAX LOUNGES:** Limited lounge facilities in Base Operations. **General:** Pax Terminal, 24hrs daily, C-406-731-2861. Bag check, telephones, restrooms. **Protocol Service:** Bldg 160, duty hours, C-406-731-2026.

**FOOD SERVICE: Dining Hall:** C-406-731-4607. **NCO/CPO Club:** Bldg 1305, C-406-452-6421. **O'Club:** C-406-761-6431. **Restaurant:** Burger King: Bldg 695, C-406-727-7480. **Snack Bar:** C-406-727-3081, C-406-731-2494. **Vending:** Pax Terminal, C-406-731-2861 (Base Ops).

**TRANSPORTATION: Air Tickets:** C-406-731-2934. **Bus (Comm):** C-406-727-0382. **Car Rental:** C-406-761-7610. **Taxi (Comm):** C-406-453-3241. **Taxi (Gov):** C-406-731-2843. **Parking:** Pax Terminal (Base Ops), C-406-731-2861 (limited to 24 hours).

**TML:** Lodging Office (Malmstrom Inn, Bldg 1680, 7028 Fourth Ave), 24hrs daily, C-406-727-8600/731-3394, D-312-632-3394, FAX 406-731-3848. All ranks. DV/VIP: C-406-731-3086, O6+.

**TRAVELERS AID: American Red Cross:** C-406-727-2212. **Chaplain:** C-406-731-3721/22. **Emergency Relief:** C-406-731-4881. **Security Police:** C-406-731-3895.

**OTHER SERVICES: Exchange:** C-406-454-1301. **Barber:** C-406-761-8131. **Beauty:** C-406-452-2552. **Laundry/Dry Cleaning:** C-406-453-1031. **Medical:** C-406-731-3483, D-312-632-3483. **Postal:** C-406-454-0716.

**ATTRACTIONS:** Yellowstone and Glacier National Parks

| ORIGINATING SCHEDULES | | | |
|---|---|---|---|
| | **PCC/GFA-1 3rd MON KC-135R** | | |
| **Location ID** | **Airport (Station)** | **Country/State** | **Days Out** |
| GFA | Malmstrom AFB | MT | +0 |
| SUU | Travis AFB | CA | +1 |
| EDF | Elmendorf AFB | AK | +2 |
| **OKO** | **Yokota AB** | **JA** | **+3** |
| SUU | Travis AFB | CA | +4 |
| GFA | Malmstrom AFB | MT | |
| | **IN ROUTE SCHEDULES** | | |
| **Scott AFB** | BLV/MEDEVAC-3 | | |
| **Travis AFB** | SUU/MEDEVAC-4 | | |

**UNSCHEDULED FLIGHTS**

Flights via KC-135 aircraft to CONUS and overseas station. Call for destinations, routings and schedules.

# NEBRASKA

## LINCOLN MUNICIPAL AIRPORT (LNK)

2420 West Butler Avenue
Lincoln, NE 68524-1897

**LOCATION:** Adjucent to Lincoln Municipal Airport, right on I-80. *USMRA: Page 82 (I-5),* NMC: Lincoln, 2 miles east. Main installation numbers: C-402-473-1210, D-312-946-1210.

**PAX TERM INFO: C-402-473-1233, D-312-926-1210.** 155th Air Refueling Group (ANG). BX-474-3454, EM/NCO Club-473-1360, O'Club-473-1361, Police-473-1348.

**TML:** Offutt AFB, 40 miles northeast. Lodging Office: Bldg 44, (Grants Pass Street), C-402-291-9000, D-312-271-3671, FAX: C-402-294-3199.

**UNSCHEDULED FLIGHTS**

Frequent flights via ANG KC-135 aircraft to CONUS and OCONUS locations. Call for destinations, routing and schedules.

| ORIGINATING SCHEDULES | | | |
|---|---|---|---|
| | **PCC/LNK-1 1 MON KC135R** | | |
| **Location ID** | **Airport (Station)** | **Country/State** | **Days Out** |
| LNK | Lincoln MAP | NE | +0 |
| SUU | Travis AFB | CA | +1 |
| EDF | Elmendorf AFB | AK | +2 |
| **OKO** | **Yokota AB** | **JA** | **+3** |
| SUU | Travis AFB | CA | +4 |
| LNK | Lincoln MAP | NE | |

## OFFUTT AIR FORCE BASE (OFF)

55th TRANS/TRTAP
Offutt AFB, NE 68113-2084

**LOCATION:** From I-80 exit to US-73/75 South to AFB exit, 6.5 miles south of I-80/US-73/75 interchange. *USMRA: Page 82 (I, J-5)*. NMC: Omaha, 8 miles north. Main installation numbers: C-402-294-1110, D-312-271-1110.

**PAX TERM INFO: C-402-294-6235 (24 hr recording)/7111, FAX 402-294-6715, D-312-271-6235 (24 hr recording)/7111, D FAX 271-6715.** Bldg: T-47, Hrs: Mon-Fri: 0500-1700, Sat-Sun, closed Holidays. There are 5 gates. Ask SP for directions. From SAC gate, straight on Lincoln Highway to Pax Term on right. **Pax Service Office:** Same as Pax terminal (NCO on duty).

**PAX LOUNGES:** No separate family lounge. **General:** Bldg T-47, see Pax Term for hours, C-402-294-7111. A/C, telephones (local and long distance), TV, read/write rooms, restrooms, P/C seats. **DV/VIP:** Base Ops, see Pax Term, C-402-294-3207. **Protocol Service:** Bldg 500, Hrs: Mon-Fri: 0730-1630, C-402-294-4212/6411 (07+).

**FOOD SERVICE: Cafeteria:** Bldg 165, C-402-291-9596. **Dining Hall:** Bldg 404, C-402-294-3980 (will serve retirees). **Enlisted Club:** Bldg 418, C-402-291-6785. **NCO/CPO Club:** Bldg 132, C-402-292-1600. **O'Club:** Bldg 462, C-402-292-1560. **Snack Bars:** Bldg 64, C-402-291-9596. **Vending:** Bldg T-47, C-402-294-6235.

**TRANSPORTATION: Air Tickets:** SATO: Bldg 500, Room 188, C-402-294-3333; Bldg T-47, C-402-294-5045. **Bus (Shuttle):** Bldg T-47, C-402-294-4375 (every 30 minutes). **Car Rentals:** Bldg 165, C-402-292-9676 (BX). **Limo Service:** Bldg T-47, C-402-342-8000 (airport limo). **Taxi (Comm):** Bldg T-47, Checker: C-402-342-8000, Yellow: C-402-341-9000. **Taxi (Gov):** Bldg T-47, C-402-294-4375/6 (duty Pax only). **Parking:** Bldg T-47, (short term-30 minutes at Term; long term- 24hrs daily). **Security Police:** C-402-294-6110.

**TML:** Lodging Office (Guest Reception Center, Bldg 44), 24hrs daily, C-402-291-9000, D-312-271-3671, FAX 402-294-3199. All ranks. DV/VIP: C-402-294-4212, D-312-271-4212, O7+.

**TRAVELERS AID: American Red Cross:** Bldg C, C-402-294-3600. **Chaplain:** ACC chapel, C-402-294-6244, After hours C-402-294-1110. **Emergency Relief:** Bldg C, C-402-294-4329 (Air Force Aid). **Lost/Found:** Bldg T-47, C-402-294-6235. **Security Police:** Main gate, C-402-294-6110.

**OTHER SERVICES: Exchange:** Bldg: 165, C-402-291-9100. **Bank/Exchange:** BX area, Bellevue: C-402-291-1400. **Hair Styles:** Bldg: 165, Barber: C-402-291-8521; Beauty: C-402-292-1520. **Laundry/Dry Cleaning:** Bldg: 162, C-402-292-1232. **Medical:** Bldg: 4000, Hrs: Daily: 24hrs, C-402-294-3000, D-312-271-3000. **Postal:** Bldg: 137, C-402-294-3523.

**ATTRACTIONS:** City of Omaha, steaks, zoo, art and music.

| IN ROUTE SCHEDULES | |
|---|---|
| **Scott AFB** | BLV/MEDEVAC-6 |

**UNSCHEDULED FLIGHTS**

Frequent Flights to: Andrews AFB, MD (**ADW**); Barksdale AFB, LA (**BAD**); Kelly AFB, TX (**SKF**); RAF Mildenhall, UK (**MHZ**); Peterson AFB, CO (**COS**); Randolph AFB, TX (**RND**); Scott AFB, IL (**BLV**); Wright-Patterson AFB, OH (**FFO**) utilizing C-21 & C-135 aircraft. Note: New flight schedules received daily. Flights confirmed 24 hours in advance. Flights to other CONUS & OCONUS destinations. Call for destinations, routings and schedules.

# NEVADA

## FALLON NAVAL AIR STATION (NFL)

Air Field Services
4755 Pasture Rd.
Fallon NAS, NV 89496-5000

**LOCATION:** From US-50 exit to US-95 South at Fallon, for 5 miles to a left on Union St to NAS. *USMRA: Page 113 (C-4)*. NMC: Reno, 72 miles west. Main installation numbers: Base Operator: C-702-426-5161, D-312-830-2110.

**PAX TERM INFO: C-702-426-3415, D-312-830-3415.** Bldg Hangar 5, Hrs: Mon-Fri: 0630-2245, Sat: 0745-1815, Sun: 1000-1800. Directions: From main gate to 4-way stop, right for 2 miles to a left at the stop sign. **Pax Service Office:** Same as Pax Terminal. **Pax Paging:** Same as Pax Terminal.

**PAX LOUNGES: General:** Bldg Hangar 5, see Pax Term for hours, C-702-426-3415. A/C, coffee served, telephones (local, long distance and defense), TV, restrooms.

**FOOD SERVICE: Cafeteria:** C-702-426-2501. **21 Club:** C-702-426-2519. **O'Club:** C-702-426-2454. **Galley:** C-702-426-2520. **Vending:** C-702-426-3415.

**TRANSPORTATION:** Limited on and off Base. **Car Rentals:** C-702-426-2592. **Taxi (Comm):** C-702-423-5173. **Taxi(on base):** C-702-426-2792. **K-T Bus Lines:** C-702-423-6622. **Parking:** C-702-426-3415.

**TML:** Lodging Office, 24 hrs daily: BEQ: C-702-426-2521/2515, D-312-830-2521-2515, BOQ: C-702-423-6671, FAX 702-426-2908, DSN FAX 312-830-2908, Navy Lodge: C-702-426-2489. DV/VIP: C-702-423-6671 (no DSN available at BOQ). BEQ DSN 830-2515.

**TRAVELERS AID: Chaplain:** C-702-426-2813. **Emergency Relief:** C-702-426-2739. **Lost/Found:** C-702-426-3415. **Security Police:** C-702-426-2803.

**OTHER SERVICES: Exchange:** C-702-426-2670. **Bank/Exchange:** C-702-426-2500. **Hair Styles:** C-702-426-2547. **Laundry/Dry Cleaning:** C-702-426-2674. **Medical:** C-702-426-3100. **Postal:** C-702-426-2738.

**ATTRACTIONS:** Reno and Lake Tahoe nearby.

### UNSCHEDULED FLIGHTS

Frequent flights to: Alameda NAS, CA (**NGZ**); Cecil Field NAS, FL (**NZC**); China Lake NWC, CA (**NID**); El Toro MCAS, CA (**NZJ**); Jacksonville NAS, FL (**NIP**); Lemoore NAS, CA (**NLC**); Miramar NAS, CA (**NKX**); Norfolk NAS, VA (**NGU**); North Island NAS, CA (**NZY**); Oceana NAS, VA (**NTU**); Point Mugu NAWC, CA (**NTD**); Whidbey NAS, WA (**NUW**). Flights are via C-9B, C-12A and T-39. Call for destinations, routings and schedules.

# NELLIS AIR FORCE BASE (LSV)

554th TRANS/TRTA
6255 Depot Rd, Bldg 809
Nellis AFB, NV 89191-7224

**LOCATION:** Off I-15. Also accessible from US-91/93. Clearly marked. *USMRA: Page 113 (G-9)*. NMC: Las Vegas, 8 miles southwest. Main installation numbers: C-702-652-1110, D-312-682-1110.

**PAX TERM INFO: C-702-652-1854/2562, FAX 702-652-2561, D FAX 312-682-2561, D-312-682-1854/2562.** Bldg 809, Hrs: daily 0800-1600. Directions: From main gate straight on Fitzgerald Blvd to a left on "D" St, right on Depot Rd to Base Operations on the left. **Pax Service Office:** Same as Pax Terminal (NCO on duty). **Pax Paging:** Same as Pax Terminal.

**PAX LOUNGES:** Limited lounge facilities. No separate family lounge. **General:** Bldg 809, Hrs: daily 0700-1600, C-702-652-1854. A/C, bag check, restrooms, telephones, TV, wood seats. **DV/VIP:** Bldg 805, 24hrs daily, C-702-652-4600. A/C, lockers, restrooms, telephones, TV. **Protocol Service:** Bldg 620, Hrs: Mon-Fri: 0800-1700, C-702-652-2987.

**FOOD SERVICE: Dining Hall:** Bldg 705, C-702-652-2880. **Enlisted Club:** Bldg 555, C-702-652-5014. **In-flight Meals:** Bldg 567, 24hrs daily, C-702-652-5112. **NCO/CPO Club:** Bldg 324, C-702-652-9732. **O'Club:** Bldg 541, C-702-644-2582. **Restaurants:** Burger King: Bldg 350, C-702-644-3374. **Snack Bars:** Bldg 1619, C-702-652-8571; Bldg 300, C-702-652-8823. **Vending:** Bldg 340, C-702-644-4425.

**TRANSPORTATION: Air Tickets:** SATO: Bldg 282, C-702-644-5400. **Bus (Comm):** Across from Main Gate, Hrs: daily: 0600-2100. **Bus (Gov):** Bldg 837, C-702-652-8305 (Duty Pax only). **Car Rentals:** Bldg 340, C-702-644-5567. **Limo Service:** C-702-739-8414. **Taxi (Comm):** North Las Vegas, C-702-643-1041. **Taxi (Gov):** Bldg 837, C-702-652-1843. **Parking:** Bldg 809, (7 day limit).

**TML:** Lodging Office (Bldg 780, 5990 Fitzgerald Blvd), 24hrs daily, C-702-643-2710, D-312-682-2711, FAX 702-652-9172, D FAX 312-682-9172 (for official orders). Additional lodging Indian Springs AAF, C-702-652-0401, D-312-682-0401. DV/VIP: C-702-652-2987.

**TRAVELERS AID: American Red Cross:** Bldg 115, C-702-652-2106. **Chaplain:** Bldg 615, C-702-652-2950. **Emergency Relief:** Bldg 20, C-702-652-3327 (Air Force Aid). **Lost/Found:** Bldg 2, C-702-652-2311. **Security Police:** Bldg 2, C-702-652-2311.

**OTHER SERVICES: Exchange:** Bldg 340, C-702-644-2044. **Bank/Exchange:** Bldg 374, C-702-385-8040. **Medical:** Bldg 625, 24hrs daily, C-702-652-2333, D-312-682-2333. **Postal:** Bldg 320, C-702-652-4679.

*NEVADA*
***Nellis Air Force Base, continued***

**ATTRACTIONS:** Las Vegas, Lake Mead, Thunderbirds.

| IN ROUTE SCHEDULES | |
|---|---|
| **Travis AFB** | SUU/MEDEVAC-3 |

**UNSCHEDULED FLIGHTS**

Many unscheduled flights, especially during exercise weekends, to various locations throughout CONUS. Call for destinations, routings and schedules.

# NEW HAMPSHIRE

## PEASE AIR NATIONAL GUARD BASE (PSM)

157th ARG/DOTK
302 Newmarket St
Pease ANGB, NH 03803-6505

**LOCATION:** From I-95 North to Spaulding Turnpike (exit #4). North on Spaulding Turnpike to Exit #1. Left to ANGB. *USMRA: Page 23 (H-9)*. NMC: Portsmouth, 3 miles northeast. Main installation numbers: C-603-430-2453, D-312-852-2453.

**PAX TERM INFO: C-603-430-3323, D-312-852-3323.** Bldg: 257, **Pax Service Office:** Comm: **NOTE:** Pease AFB was redesignated as Pease Air National Guard Base. Most support facilities have closed; however, Space-A flights are still available.

**PAX LOUNGES:** Operations lounge: Coffee/vending machine. C-603-430-3323, D-312-852-3323

**TRANSPORTATION: Bus (Comm):** Portsmouth NH. Greyhound & Trailways to all locations & from Park Square Bus Terminal in Boston MA. **Car Rentals:** Portsmouth, Manchester, and Boston. **Limo Service:** Main Gate, C-608-431-2424 (local service to Logan IAP, Boston, $17 one way, $31 round trip). **Taxi (Gov):** C-603-430-3588, off Base, C-603-436-7500/0008/7111/7777. **Parking:** Short term-in front of Pax Term; long term-main gate parking lot. Pick up parking form at main gate.

**TML:** none. See Portsmouth Naval Shipyard Lodging Office, Bldg H-23, C-207-438-1513/2015, FAX 207-438-3580.

**OTHER SERVICES: Exchange:** C-608-436-0302. **Bank/Exchange:** C-608-436-0537/7592. **Hair Styles:** Barber: C-608-436-2903.

**ATTRACTIONS:** Portsmouth, sea coast, snow skiing, camping, fishing.

**UNSCHEDULED FLIGHTS**

Most flights leaving Pease travel to CONUS locations via AFRES aircraft. The ANG has some flights to U.S. and overseas destinations, via KC-135. Call information.

# NEW JERSEY

## LAKEHURST NAVAL AIR WARFARE CENTER (NEL)

ATC Facility
Naval Air Engineering Station
Highway 547
Lakehurst, NJ 08733-5085

**LOCATION:** From Garden State Parkway take NJ-70 West to junction of NJ-547. Turn right and go 1 mile to Base. *USMRA: Page 19 (F-6).* NMC: Trenton, 30 miles northwest. Main installation numbers: C-908-323-2011, D-312-624-1110.

**PAX TERM INFO: C-908-323-2438, D-312-624-2438, FAX: C-908-323-7802.** Bldg 307, Hrs: Mon-Fri: 0700-1630. Directions: From main gate straight to first stop sign, turn right then left on next street to stop sign, left to Pax Term. Limited Base support.

**PAX LOUNGES:** Limited lounge facilities. **General:** Bldg: 307, 1st deck Vending machines. Hrs: Mon-Fri: 0700-1630, 2nd deck: Flight planning room Mon-Fri: 0700-1630.

**FOOD SERVICE: Galley:** C-908-323-2554/2291. **Consolidated Mess:** C-908-323-2340. **Dining Hall:** C-908-323-2554. **In-flight Meals:** C-908-323-2554.

**TRANSPORTATION: Air Tickets:** C-908-323-2035. **Bus/Train(NJ Transit (Comm):** C-800-772-2222. **Taxi (Gov):** C-908-323-2322. **Parking:** Bldg 307, right side of hangar, short and long term.

**TML:** Lodging Office (Enlisted: Bldg 481), C-908-323-2266, D-312-624-2266, FAX 908-323-2269, (Officers: Bldg 33), C-908-323-2266. DV/VIP: C-908-323-2369, O6+.

**TRAVELERS AID: Chaplain:** C-908-323-2272/2539. **Emergency Relief:** C-908-323-2308. **Security Police:** Bldg 8, 24hrs daily, C-908-323-2332.

**OTHER SERVICES: Commissary/Minimart:** C-908-323-7680. **Bank:** Base Credit Union, C-908-323-2496. Berkley Bank, Bldg 38 (ATM only). **Medical/Dental:** Bldg: 39, C-908-323-2204, D-312-624-2204. **Post Office:** C-908-323-2534.

### UNSCHEDULED FLIGHTS

Infrequent flights via Army and Navy administrative aircraft to CONUS East Coast locations. Call for destinations, routings and schedules.

# McGUIRE AIR FORCE BASE (WRI)

438th APS/TROP
McGuire AFB, NJ 08641-5002

**LOCATION:** From NJ Turnpike, Exit 7 to NJ-68 Southeast to AFB. Adjacent to Fort Dix. Clearly marked. *USMRA: Page 19 (E-6)*. NMC: Trenton, 18 miles northwest. Main installation numbers: C-609-724-1110, D-312-440-1110.

**PAX TERM INFO: (Recording) C-609-724-3078, D-312-440-3078, FAX: C-609-724-4621.** Bldg 1706, Hrs: daily: 0500-2300. Directions: From main gate straight through lst & 2nd circle. Pax Term in front of 2nd circle. Space-A desk, lst floor. **Pax Service Office:** Bldg 1706, Hrs: daily: 0630-2300, C-609-724-3078, D-312-440-3078 (Space-A desk). **Pax Paging:** Bldg 1706, 24hrs daily, C-609-724-3655, D-312-440-3655 (Space-A desk). *(NOTE: Sign-up at McGuire also gives you sign up at Philadelphia IAP, PA (PHL)).*

**PAX LOUNGES: General:** Bldg 1706, lst floor, Hrs: daily: 0630-2300, C-609-724-3078. A/C, telephones (commercial and defense), TV, restrooms, showers, P/C seats. **DV/VIP:** Bldg 1706, lst floor, Hrs: daily: 0630-2300, C-609-724-2812, D-312-440-2812. A/C, telephones (commercial and defense), TV, restrooms, O/S seats. Check with counter #l for access to lounge/Protocol Service. **Family:** Bldg 1706, lst floor, Hrs: daily: 0630-2300, C-609-724-3078 (unmanned). A/C, telephones (commercial and defense), restrooms, P/C seats, playroom.

**FOOD SERVICE: Dining Hall:** Bldg 2501, 24hrs daily, C-609-724-2450 (active duty only). **Open Mess:** Bldg 2508, C-609-724-3737. **Golf Course:** Bldg 2003, C-609-724-2169.

**TRANSPORTATION: Auto Shipping:** Wrightstown, C-609-723-3632 (Bell Transportation). **Air Tickets:** SATO: Bldg 1706, Hrs: Mon-Fri: 0800-1700, C-609-723-1323. **Bus (Comm):** Bldg 1706, C-609-723-3833 (to PHL, NY, NJ). **Car Rentals:** Bldg 1706, 0800-1700 daily (some agencies on Base). **Limo Service:** Bldg 1706, 24hrs daily, C-609-723-3220. **Taxi (Comm):** Bldg 1706, Hrs: daily: 0600-2400, C-609-723-2000 (at Pax Term). **Trains:** AMTRAK: Newark NJ, C-800-523-5700. **Parking:** Bldg 1706, 24hrs daily, C-609-724-2001 (short and long term).

**TML:** Lodging Office (All-American Inn, Bldg 2717), C-609-724-3974, D-312-440-2035, FAX 609-724-2035. DV/VIP: Protocol Office, C-609-724-2405, 06+.

**TRAVELERS AID: American Red Cross:** Ft Dix: C-609-562-2258. **Chaplain:** Bldg 2503, duty hours, C-609-724-3811 (after duty hours C-609-724-2000). **Emergency Relief:** Bldg 2916, Hrs: Mon-Fri: 0800-1700, C-609-724-4353. **Lost/Found:** Bldg 1706, Hrs: daily: 0500-2300, C-609-724-2526. **Retired Affairs:** Bldg 2916, duty hours, C-609-724-2450. **Security Police:** Bldg 1814, 24 hrs daily, C-609-724-2001.

**OTHER SERVICES: Exchange:** Bldg: 3452, Hrs: Mon-Sat: 1000-2100, Sun: 1000-1730, C-609-723-6100. **Bank/Exchange:** Bldg: 2605, Hrs: Mon-Fri: 0900-1500, C-609-723-7770. **Hair Styles:** Barber: Bldg: 1706/3453, Hrs: Mon-Fri: 0900-1700, C-609-723-4449. **Medical:** Bldg: 5201, Hrs: Daily: 0730-1630, C-609-724-5509. **Postal:** Bldg: 2603, Hrs: Mon-Fri: 0900-1700, Sat: 0900-1100, C-609-724-4687.

*NEW JERSEY*
*McGuire Air Force Base, continued*

**Wire:** On Fort Dix. **Valet/Dry Cleaning:** Bldg: 3453, Hrs: M-Sa: 1000-1700, C-609-723-6446.

**ATTRACTIONS:** Philadelphia, Liberty Bell, Atlantic City.

| ORIGINATING SCHEDULES | | | |
|---|---|---|---|
| | **ACC/WRI-1 2nd/4th FRI C-141B** | | |
| **Location ID** | **Airport (Station)** | **Country/State** | **Days Out** |
| WRI | McGuire AFB | NJ | +0 |
| ADW | Andrews AFB | MD | +1 |
| KEF | Keflavik APT | IC | +1 |
| **LGS** | **Lajes AB** | **PO** | **+2** |
| ADW | Andrews AFB | MD | +2 |
| WRI | McGuire AFB | NJ | |
| | **ACC/WRI-2 1st/3rd MON C-141B** | | |
| WRI | McGuire AFB | NJ | +0 |
| ADW | Andrews AFB | MD | +0 |
| LGS | Lajes AB | PO | +1 |
| **RMS** | **Ramstein AB** | **GE** | **+2** |
| ADW | Andrews AFB | MD | +3 |
| WRI | McGuire AFB | NJ | |
| | **APM/WRI-3 1st TUE C-141B** | | |
| WRI | McGuire AFB | NJ | +0 |
| CHS | Charleston AFB/IAP | SC | +0 |
| BSB | Brasilia APT | BR | +1 |
| RIO | Rio De Janeiro IAP | BR | +1 |
| **ASU** | **Pres Stroessner APT** | **PG** | **+2** |
| BSB | Brasilia APT | BR | +2 |
| CHS | Charleston AFB/IAP | SC | +3 |
| WRI | McGuire AFB | NJ | |
| | **ACC/WRI-4 4th TUE C-141B** | | |
| WRI | McGuire AFB | NJ | +0 |
| CHS | Charleston AFB/IAP | SC | +0 |
| LIM | Jorge Chavez IAP | PE | +0 |
| SCL | Arturo Merinobenitez APT | CH | +1 |
| **LPB** | **JF Kennedy IAP** | **BO** | **+1** |
| HOW | Howard AB | PN | +2 |
| CHS | Charleston AFB/IAP | SC | +3 |
| WRI | McGuire AFB | NJ | |

| | **APM/WRI-5 4th TUE C-141B** | | |
|---|---|---|---|
| WRI | McGuire AFB | NJ | +0 |
| CHS | Charleston AFB/IAP | SC | +0 |
| LIM | Jorge Chavez IAP | PE | +0 |
| **SCL** | **Arturo Merinobenitez APT** | **CH** | **+1** |
| LPB | JF Kennedy IAP | BO | +1 |
| PTY | Tocumen/Torrijos IAP | PM | +2 |
| CHS | Charleston AFB/IAP | SC | +3 |
| WRI | McGuire AFB | NJ | |
| | **ACC/WRI-6 2nd/4th SUN, 5th THU, 2nd SAT C-141B** | | |
| WRI | McGuire AFB | NJ | +0 |
| DOV | Dover AFB | DE | +1 |
| **MHZ** | **RAF Mildenhall** | **UK** | **+2** |
| DOV | Dover AFB | DE | +3 |
| WRI | McGuire AFB | NJ | |
| | **ACC/WRI-7 2nd/4th MON C-141B** | | |
| WRI | Mcguire AFB | NJ | +0 |
| DOV | Dover AFB | DE | +0 |
| **RMS** | **Ramstein AB** | **GE** | **+2** |
| ADW | Andrews AFB | MD | +2 |
| WRI | McGuire AFB | NJ | |
| | **ACC/WRI-8 2 MON, 4th TUE C-141B** | | |
| WRI | McGuire AFB | NJ | +0 |
| DOV | Dover AFB | DE | +0 |
| RMS | Ramstein AB | GE | +2 |
| **CAI** | **Cairo IAP** | **EG** | **+2** |
| RMS | Ramstein AB | GE | +3 |
| LGS | Lajes AB | PO | +3 |
| DOV | Dover AFB | DE | +4 |
| WRI | McGuire AFB | NJ | |
| | **APM/WRI-9 1st/2nd SAT C-141B** | | |
| WRI | McGuire AFB | NJ | +0 |
| DOV | Dover AFB | DE | +1 |
| RMS | Ramstein AB | GE | +2 |
| **ADA** | **Incirlik APT** | **TU** | **+3** |
| AKT | Akrotiri APT | CY | +3 |
| ADA | Incirlik APT | TU | +4 |
| IGL | Cigli TAFB | TU | +4 |

***NEW JERSEY***
***McGuire Air Force Base, continued***

| | | | |
|---|---|---|---|
| YES | Ataturk/Yesilkoy IAP | TU | +4 |
| ADA | Incirlik APT | TU | +5 |
| DIY | Diyarbakir APT | TU | +5 |
| ESB | Esenboga APT | TU | +5 |
| **ADA** | **Incirlik APT** | **TU** | **+6** |
| RMS | Ramstein AB | GE | +7 |
| KEF | Keflavik APT | IC | +7 |
| DOV | Dover AFB | DE | +8 |
| WRI | McGuire AFB | NJ | |
| | **ACC/WRI-10 4th SUN C-141B** | | |
| WRI | McGuire AFB | NJ | +0 |
| DOV | Dover AFB | DE | +1 |
| RMS | Ramstein AB | GE | +2 |
| **AMM** | **King Abdullah AB** | **JR** | **+2** |
| RMS | Ramstein AB | GE | +3 |
| MHZ | RAF Mildenhall | UK | +3 |
| AVB | Aviano AB | IT | +4 |
| RMS | Ramstein AB | GE | +4 |
| LGS | Lajes AB | PO | +4 |
| DOV | Dover AFB | DE | +5 |
| WRI | McGuire AFB | NJ | |
| | **ACC/WRI-11 1st/4th TUE C-141B** | | |
| WRI | McGuire AFB | NJ | +0 |
| DOV | Dover AFB | DE | +0 |
| RMS | Ramstein AB | GE | +1 |
| KWI | Kuwait IAP | KW | +1 |
| **DHA** | **Dhahran IAP** | **SA** | **+2** |
| SIZ | Sigonella NAS | IT | +2 |
| RTA | Rota NAS | SP | +3 |
| NGU | Norfolk NAS | VA | +4 |
| WRI | McGuire AFB | NJ | |
| | **APM/WRI-12 WED, THU DC862** | | |
| WRI | McGuire AFB | NJ | +0 |
| **LGS** | **Lajes AB** | **PO** | **+0** |
| WRI | McGuire AFB | NJ | |
| | **ACM/WRI-13 3rd MON C-141B** | | |
| WRI | McGuire AFB | NJ | +0 |
| DOV | Dover AFB | DE | +1 |

| | | | |
|---|---|---|---|
| RMS | Ramstein AB | GE | +2 |
| MHZ | RAF Mildenhall | UK | +2 |
| RMS | Ramstein AB | GE | +2 |
| AVB | Aviano AB | IT | +3 |
| MHZ | RAF Mildenhall | UK | +3 |
| RMS | Ramstein AB | GE | +4 |
| AVB | Aviano AB | IT | +4 |
| RMS | Ramstein AB | GE | +5 |
| **ADA** | **Incirlik APT** | **TU** | **+6** |
| RMS | Ramstein AB | GE | +7 |
| MHZ | RAF Mildenhall | UK | +7 |
| AVB | Aviano AB | IT | +8 |
| RMS | Ramstein AB | GE | +8 |
| RTA | Rota NAS | SP | +9 |
| SIZ | Sigonella NAS | IT | +9 |
| RMS | Ramstein AB | GE | +10 |
| LGS | Lajes AB | PO | +10 |
| DOV | Dover AFB | DE | +11 |
| WRI | McGuire AFB | NJ | |
| | **ACC/WRI-14 3rd/5th THU C-141B** | | |
| WRI | McGuire AFB | NJ | +0 |
| DOV | Dover AFB | DE | +1 |
| RMS | Ramstein AB | GE | +2 |
| SIZ | Sigonella NAS | IT | +3 |
| **TTH** | **Thumrait OAFB** | **OM** | **+4** |
| RMS | Ramstein AB | GE | +5 |
| CAI | Cairo IAP | EG | +5 |
| RMS | Ramstein AB | GE | +6 |
| LGS | Lajes AB | PO | +6 |
| DOV | Dover AFB | DE | +7 |
| WRI | McGuire AFB | NJ | |
| | **ACC/WRI-15 2nd THU, 1st/5th FRI C-141B** | | |
| WRI | McGuire AFB | NJ | +0 |
| LGS | Lajes AB | PO | +1 |
| **RMS** | **Ramstein AB** | **GE** | **+9** |
| LGS | Lajes AB | PO | +10 |
| DOV | Dover AFB | DE | +10 |
| WRI | McGuire AFB | NJ | |

***NEW JERSEY***
***McGuire Air Force Base, continued***

| | **ACC/WRI-16 2nd TUE C-141B** | | |
|---|---|---|---|
| WRI | McGuire AFB | NJ | +0 |
| NGU | Norfolk NAS | VA | +0 |
| **KEF** | **Keflavik APT** | **IC** | **+2** |
| NGU | Norfolk NAS | VA | +3 |
| **NBW** | **Guantanamo Bay NAS** | **CU** | **+3** |
| NGU | Norfolk NAS | VA | +4 |
| WRI | McGuire AFB | NJ | |
| | **ACC/WRI-17 3rd/5th THU C-141B** | | |
| WRI | McGuire AFB | NJ | +0 |
| NGU | Norfolk NAS | VA | +0 |
| KEF | Keflavik APT | IC | +1 |
| **RMS** | **Ramstein AB** | **GE** | **+2** |
| ADW | Andrews AFB | MD | +3 |
| WRI | McGuire AFB | NJ | |
| | **ACC/WRI-18 2nd/4th MON C-141B** | | |
| WRI | McGuire AFB | NJ | +0 |
| NGU | Norfolk NAS | VA | +0 |
| NRR | Roosevelt Roads NAS | PR | +1 |
| **NBW** | **Guantanamo Bay NAS** | **CU** | **+1** |
| NGU | Norfolk NAS | VA | +1 |
| WRI | McGuire AFB | NJ | |
| | **ACC/WRI-19 4th SUN C-141B** | | |
| WRI | McGuire AFB | NJ | +0 |
| NGU | Norfolk NAS | VA | +0 |
| RTA | Rota NAS | SP | +2 |
| NAP | Capodichino APT | IT | +2 |
| SIZ | Sigonella NAS | IT | +3 |
| BAH | Bahrain IAP | BA | +3 |
| **FUJ** | **Fujairah IAP** | **UA** | **+4** |
| BAH | Bahrain IAP | BA | +4 |
| SIZ | Sigonella NAS | IT | +5 |
| SOC | Souda Bay NAF | CR | +5 |
| SIZ | Sigonella NAS | IT | +6 |
| NAP | Capodichino APT | IT | +6 |
| RTA | Rota NAS | SP | +7 |
| NGU | Norfolk NAS | VA | +7 |
| WRI | McGuire AFB | NJ | |

| | **ACM/WRI-20 2nd/4th THU KC-10A** | | |
|---|---|---|---|
| WRI | McGuire AFB | NJ | +0 |
| NGU | Norfolkk NAS | VA | +1 |
| RTA | Rota NAS | SP | +2 |
| SIZ | Sigonella NAS | IT | +2 |
| BAH | Bahrain IAP | BA | +3 |
| **FUJ** | **Fujairah IAP** | **UA** | **+4** |
| BAH | Bahrain IAP | BA | +4 |
| SIZ | Sigonella NAS | IT | +4 |
| RTA | Rota NAS | SP | +5 |
| NGU | Norfolk NAS | VA | +6 |
| WRI | McGuire AFB | NJ | |
| | **ACM/WRI-21 2nd/3rd TUE C-141B** | | |
| WRI | McGuire AFB | NJ | +0 |
| COF | Patrick AFB | FL | +1 |
| SJH | V C Bird IAP | AN | +1 |
| **ASI** | **Ascension Aux. Airfield** | **UK** | **+3** |
| SJH | V C Bird IAP | AN | +3 |
| COF | Patrick AFB | FL | +3 |
| WRI | McGuire AFB | NJ | |
| | **APM/WRI-22 MON, TUE, THU, FRI DC862** | | |
| WRI | McGuire AFB | NJ | +0 |
| **THU** | **Thule AB** | **GL** | **+0** |
| WRI | McGuire AFB | NJ | |
| | **PCC/WRI-23 3rd WED KC-10A** | | |
| WRI | McGuire AFB | NJ | +0 |
| SUU | Travis AFB | CA | +1 |
| EDF | Elmendorf AFB | AK | +2 |
| **OKO** | **Yokota AB** | **JA** | **+3** |
| SUU | Travis AFB | CA | +4 |
| WRI | McGuire AFB | NJ | |
| | **PCC/WRI-24 1st SAT KC-10A** | | |
| WRI | McGuire AFB | NJ | +0 |
| SUU | Travis AFB | CA | +0 |
| HIK | Hikam AFB | HI | +2 |
| **OKO** | **Yokota AB** | **JA** | |

| **IN ROUTE SCHEDULES** | |
|---|---|
| **Bangor IAP** | ACC/BGR-1 |

*NEW JERSEY*
***McGuire Air Force Base, continued***

| | |
|---|---|
| **Charleston AFB/IAP** | ACC/CHS-15 |
| **General Mitchell IAP/ARS** | ACC/GMF-1 |
| **McGhee Tyson APT** | ACC/TYS-1 |
| **Scott AFB** | BLV/MEDEVAC-13 |

**UNSCHEDULED FLIGHTS**

Unscheduled flights via C-141 aircraft to: Andrews AFB, MD (**ADW**); Charleston AFB, SC (**CHS**); Coolidge Apt (St. Johns), Antigua (**SJH**); Dover AFB, DE (**DOV**); Guantanamo NAS, CU (**GAO**); Pope AFB, NC (**POB**); and Roosevelt Roads NAS, PR (**NRR**).

# NEW MEXICO

## CANNON AIR FORCE BASE (CVS)

27th TRANS/TRTM, 110E Sextant Avenue, Suite 2025
Cannon AFB, NM 88103-5328

**LOCATION:** From Clovis, West on US-60/84 to AFB. From NM-467 enter the Portales gate. *USMRA: Page 114 (H-5)*. NMC. Clovis, 7 miles east. Main installation numbers: C-505-784-3311, D-312-681-1110.

**PAX TERM INFO: C-505-784-2935, D-312-681-2935.** Bldg 135, Hrs: Mon-Fri: 0700-2300, Sat-Sun: 0700-2100. Ask SP for directions.

**PAX LOUNGE:** Limited, General: Bldg 135, Hrs: Mon-Fri: 0700-2300, Sat-Sun: 0700-2100, C-505-784-2935, D-312-681-2935.

**TML:** Lodging Office (Caprock Inn, Bldg 1801B, 401 S. Olympic Blvd), C-505-784-2918/2919, D-213-681-2918/2919, FAX 505-784-4833. DV/VIP: Protocol Office, Bldg 1, C-505-784-2727, O6+.

**OTHER SERVICES: Exchange:** C-505-784-3387, **Cafeteria:** C-505-784-3621, **Snack Bar:** C-505-784-2280, **O'Club:** C-505-784-2477, **SATO:** C-505-784-2304, **Chaplain:** C-505-784-2507. Full Base support available. See *Military Living's US Forces Travel and Tranfer Guide USA and Caribbean Areas.*

**ATTRACTIONS:** Carlsbad Caverns, Sierre Blanca Ski Resort.

| IN ROUTE SCHEDULES | |
|---|---|
| **Scott AFB** | BLV/MEDEVAC-8 |
| **Travis AFB** | SUU/MEDEVAC-1 |

## KIRTLAND AIR FORCE BASE (ABQ)

377 TRANS/LGTTL
Kirtland AFB, NM 87117-5270

**LOCATION:** From I-40 East, exit on Wyoming Blvd, drive south for 2 miles to Wyoming gate to AFB. *USMRA: Page 114 (D-4)*. NMC: Albuquerque, 1 mile northeast. Main installation numbers: C-505-846-0011, D-312-244-0011.

**PAX TERM INFO: C-505-846-0889, D-312-244-0889.** Bldg 333, Hrs: Mon-Fri: 0600-1800, Sat-Sun: 0800-1700. Directions: From Carlisle gate straight on Carlisle Ave to a right on Clark Ave to Pax Term on right. Carlisle gate 0600-1700. Truman gate after 1700. Ask for directions. **Pax Service Office:** Same as Pax terminal (NCO on duty). **Pax Paging:** Bldg 333, see Pax Term, C-505-846-9070 (Base Ops).

*NEW MEXICO*
***Kirtland Air Force Base, continued***

**PAX LOUNGES:** Adequate lounge facilities. General lounge available. **DV/VIP:** Bldg 333, Hrs: daily 0600-2200, C-505-846-9070 (next to Base Ops desk). A/C, coffee/tea served, separate read/write rooms, restrooms, TV, O/S seats. **Protocol Service:** Bldg 333, Hrs: daily 0600-2200, C-505-846-9070 (06+).

**FOOD SERVICE: Cafeteria:** Bldg 20206, C-505-265-4304. **Dining Hall:** Bldg 923W, C-505-846-0011. **Enlisted Club:** Bldg 20255, C-505-846-5611. **NCO/CPO Club:** Bldg 20255, C-505-846-7512; Bldg 201, C-505-846-3488. **O'Club:** Bldg 20200, C-505-846-7512; Bldg 1900, C-505-846-3488. **Snack Bars:** Bldg 20170, C-505-265-3679/7301. **Vending:** Bldg 333, C-505-265-3679/7301.

**TRANSPORTATION: Air Tickets:** SATO: Bldg 333, C-505-846-0511. **Bus (Comm):** Albuquerque-Greyhound. **Trains:** Albuquerque is a major AMTRAK stop. **Parking:** Bldg 333, C-505-846-4618 (west side of Term).

**TML:** Lodging Office (Kirtland Inn, Bldg 22016, Club Dr), C-505-846-9652, D-312-246-9652. DV/VIP: Protocol Office, C-505-846-4119, D-312-246-4119, O6+.

**TRAVELERS AID: Chaplain:** Bldg 589, C-505-846-2011. **Emergency Relief:** Bldg 20201, Room 112, C-505-846-0011 (AF Aid). **Security Police:** Bldg 20219, C-505-846-4618.

**OTHER SERVICES: Exchange:** Bldg 20170, C-505-265-3679. **Bank/Exchange:** KFCU: Bldg 426, C-505-846-0011. **Hair Styles:** Bldg 20170, C-505-265-3679. **Laundry/Dry Cleaning:** Bldg 20170, C-505-265-3679. **Medical:** Bldg 20140, 24hrs daily, C-505-846-4611, D-312-244-4611. **Postal:** Bldg 926, C-505-846-6688.

**ATTRACTIONS:** National Atomic Museum, Albuquerque.

**UNSCHEDULED FLIGHTS**

Frequent flights to: Andrews AFB, MD (**ADW**); Davis-Monthan AFB, AZ (**DMA**); Hill AFB, UT (**HIF**); Kelly AFB, TX (**SKF**); Offutt AFB, NE (**OFF**); Randolph AFB, TX (**RND**); Scott AFB, IL (**BLV**); Travis AFB, CA (**SUU**), Wright-Patterson AFB, OH (**FFO**). Several flights weekly to each location. Other flights to CONUS locations. An AMC training base. Call for destinations, routings and schedules.

# NEW YORK

## GRIFFISS AIR FORCE BASE (RME)

Base Operations
592 Hangar Road, Suite 202
Griffiss AFB, NY 13441-5000

*NOTE: Griffisss AFB is drawing down, and is anticipated to operate in a standby capacity effective 1 October 1995.*

**LOCATION:** Off NY-49 in Rome. Entrance off NY-49 and from Chestnut St, Floyd St, and East Dominick St. *USMRA: Page 21 (J,K-5,6)*. NMC: Utica, 17 miles southeast. Main installation numbers: C-315-330-1110, D-312-587-1110.

**PAX TERM INFO: C-315-330-7400/7450, D-312-587-7400/7450, REC: C-315-330-2089, FAX: C-312-330-7961.** Base Ops, Bldg 100, 24hrs daily. Ask for directions at main gate. **Pax Service Office:** Same as Pax Term.

**PAX LOUNGES:** Pax lounge. All Pax processed by Base Ops.

**FOOD SERVICE: Cafeteria:** Bldg 1, C-315-339-0700. **Dining Hall:** Bldg 400, C-315-330-7097. **O'Club/NCO Club:** Bldg 890, C-315-330-7034. **Restaurants:** C-315-330-7945.

**TRANSPORTATION: Air Tickets:** SATO: Depot 1, C-315-330-7183. **Taxi (Comm):** IAP & Oneida County Airport, C-315-330-1110. **Taxi (Gov):** Bldg T-9, C-315-330-3541. **Parking:** Bldg 100, 24hrs daily, requires parking sticker.

**TML:** Lodging Office (Bldg 704), Hrs: 24 daily, C-315-330-4391, D-312-587-4391. All ranks. DV/VIP: C-315-330-7415.

**TRAVELERS AID: American Red Cross:** Bldg 14, C-315-330-2942. **Chaplain:** Chapel Center, C-315-330-3017. **Emergency Relief:** Bldg 14, C-315-330-4488 (AF Aid). **Security Police:** Bldg 308, C-315-330-7174.

**OTHER SERVICES: Exchange:** Bldg 1, C-315-339-0700. **Bank/Exchange:** Bldg 311, C-315-339-0300. **Hair Styles:** Bldg 1, C-315-330-0700. **Laundry/Dry Cleaning:** Bldg 1, C-315-339-2259. **Medical:** USAF Hospital, 24hrs daily, C-315-330-5872, D-312-587-5872. **Postal:** Bldg 310, C-315 330-1110

**ATTRACTIONS:** Erie Canal Village, Ft Stannix National Monument, Turning Stone casino, lake Delta State Park, and Oriskany Battlefield.

| IN ROUTE SCHEDULES | |
|---|---|
| **Scott AFB** | BLV/MEDEVAC-13 |

*NEW YORK*

## NIAGARA FALLS INTERNATIONAL AIRPORT (IAG)

914th AG/OGA
Niagara Falls Air Force Reserve Station
Niagara Falls IAP, NY 14304-5010

**LOCATION:** From I-90 North or South, Exit 50, take I-290 to I-190N; I-190 to Exit 23, Right on Packard Road, which merges into Lockport Rd to USAF gate (5 miles east of Exit 23). *USMRA: Page 20 (D-6)*. NMC: Niagara Falls, 5 miles west. Main installation numbers: C-716-236-2000, D-312-238-3011.

**PAX TERM INFO: C-716-236-2174/2371, D-312-238-2174/2371, FAX: C-716-236-2380, D-312-238-2380**. Bldg 807 (SQ OPS), Hrs: Mon-Fri: 0800-1600. Ask guard at gate for directions.

**PAX LOUNGES:** No Pax lounges. Minimum essentials. Restrooms. **Protocol Service:** Bldg 800, Hrs: Mon-Fri: 0800-1600, C-716-236-2138.

**FOOD SERVICE: Consolidated Open Mess:** C-716-297-6604. **Snack Bars:** Rec Center: C-716-236-2329. **Vending:** Bldg 807, Hrs: Mon-Fri: 0800-1600.

**TRANSPORTATION:** Limited. No commercial bus service to/from base. Taxi service is available. Car rental available at commercial side of IAP. **Parking:** Limited. Overnight and long term by arrangement with Security Police.

**TML:** Lodging Office (Bldg 312), Hrs: daily 0730-2300, C-1-800-456-4990, C-716-236-2014, D-312-238-2014, FAX 716-236-6348. DV/VIP: C-716-236-2014, O6+.

**TRAVELERS AID: Security Police:** Main gate, C-716-236-2279.

**OTHER SERVICES: Exchange:** Bldg 805, C-716-236-2100.

**ATTRACTIONS:** Beautiful Niagara Falls, Lake Erie, Lake Ontario, Canada.

### UNSCHEDULED FLIGHTS

Frequent flights via C-130 aircraft to Griffiss AFB, NY (**RME**) also other CONUS locations and less frequent flights to OCONUS locations. Call for destinations, routings and schedules.

## SCHENECTADY COUNTY AIRPORT (SCH)

109th AG/CP, Stratton ANGB
1 Air National Guard Road
Scotia, NY 12302-9752

**LOCATION:** From I-87 North exit to NY-146 West. Continue on Glenridge Rd to Maple Ave. Left to ANG Rd. *USMRA: Page 21 (M,N-6)*. NMC: Schenectady, 3 miles south. Main installation numbers: C-518-381-7300, D-312-974-9221.

**PAX TERM INFO: C-518-381-7420, D-312-974-9420, FAX: C-518-381-7304, D-312-974-9304.** ANG Operations, Hrs: Mon-Fri: 0700-1500, Ask gate guard for directions. All the support facilities of a regional airport. Commissary: C-518-370-5935. NEX: C-518-377-6640.

**UNSCHEDULED FLIGHTS**

Flights to CONUS locations via C-130H aircraft. Also limited flights to Europe and South America. Come in person or FAX for information and sign-up.

# STEWART AIR NATIONAL GUARD BASE (SWF)

105th AG (ANG), 203 Militia Way
Newburgh, NY 12550-0031

**LOCATION:** From I-84 or I-87 take Exit 17 Union Ave South to Rt 17-K West for 3 miles. Follow signs to Stewart ANG Base. *USMRA: Page 21 (M-10)*. NMC: New York City, 60 miles south. Main installation numbers: C-914-563-2001, D-312-636-2001.

**PAX TERM INFO: USMC OPS: C-914-563-2965, D-312-636-2965. ARMY OPS: C-914-563-3298/3359/3478, D-312-220-3298.** Full Base support at US Military Academy (West Point) 15 miles south at the adjacent Stewart Army Sub-post. Limited Pax facilities. Is a United States port of entry. Because of a lack of ground handling equipment and facilities, Space-A seats on board C-005A flights are not available at this time. See Military Living's *US Forces Travel & Transfer Guide USA & Caribbean Areas* for complete support details.

**TML:** Lodging Office (Five Star Inn, The West Point and STAS Guest House, Bldg 2605), Srewart Army Subpost, New Windsor, NY, C-914-563-3311, D-312-688-3009, FAX 914-564-6328.

| **ORIGINATING SCHEDULES** | | | |
|---|---|---|---|
| **ACC/SWF-1 3rd WED C-5A** | | | |
| **Location ID** | **Airport (Station)** | **Country/State** | **Days Out** |
| SWF | Stewart ANGB | NY | +0 |
| DOV | Dover AFB | DE | +1 |
| RMS | Ramstein AB | GE | +2 |
| KWI | Kuwait IAP | KW | +2 |
| **DHA** | **Dhahran IAP** | **SA** | **+3** |
| RMS | Ramstein AB | GE | +4 |
| DOV | Dover AFB | DE | +5 |
| SWF | Stewart ANGB | NY | |

*NEW YORK*
*Stewart Air National Guard Base, continued*

| | **ACC/SWF-2** | **2ND/4TH FRI** | **C-5A** | |
|---|---|---|---|---|
| SWF | Stewart ANGB | | NY | +0 |
| DOV | Dover AFB | | DE | +1 |
| **RMS** | **Ramstein AB** | | **GE** | **+2** |
| LGS | Lajes AB | | PO | +3 |
| DOV | Dover AFB | | DE | +3 |
| SWF | Stewart ANGB | | NY | |
| | **IN ROUTE SCHEDULES** | | | |
| **Scott AFB** | BLV/MEDEVAC-13 | | | |

**UNSCHEDULED FLIGHTS**

Some flights via USMC KC130T or Army C-12A aircraft. Call for destinations, routings and schedules.

## SUFFOLK COUNTY AIR NATIONAL GUARD BASE (FOK)

106th ARRG/Suffolk County Airport (ANG)
Westhampton Beach, NY 11978-1294

**LOCATION:** On Long Island. One mile south of NY-27 (Sunrise Hwy), Exit 63 onto Old Riverhead Rd. *USMRA: Page 20 (F-2)*. NMC: Southhampton, 12 miles east. Main installation numbers: C-516-288-7300, D-312-456-7300.

**PAX TERM INFO: C-516-288-7416, D-312-456-7416.** Bldg 369, Hrs: Mon-Fri: 0730-1600. Directions: Between large hangars, 1/8 mile from main gate. All facilities of a regional airport. Limited military support facilities. CGX: C-516-288-7557, Consolidated Club: C-516-288-7481.

**UNSCHEDULED FLIGHTS**

Flights via HC-130 aircraft to CONUS locations. Call for destinations, routings and schedules.

# NORTH CAROLINA

## CHARLOTTE/DOUGLAS INTERNATIONAL AIRPORT (CLT)

145th TAG (ANG), 5225 Morris Field Drive
Charlotte, NC 28208-5797

**LOCATION:** From I-77 North or South exit 6 A/B to Graham Parkway (US-521) north to Morris Field Drive (3.5 miles), turn left, Base on right. *USMRA: Page 44 (G-4)*. NMC: Charlotte, 3 miles east. Main installation numbers: C-704-391-4100, D-312-583-9210.

**PAX TERM INFO: C-704-391-4177, D-312-583-9177, FAX: C-704-391-4322.** ANG, Hrs: Mon-Fri: 0730-1600. No Pax facilities. All Pax processed by Base Ops. Full support of an IAP available. Limited military base support.

**UNSCHEDULED FLIGHTS**

Flights via C-130B aircraft to CONUS and OCONUS locations on training missions. Call for destinations, routings and schedules.

## CHERRY POINT MARINE CORPS AIR STATION (NKT)

Transient Services Division, Building 199
Cherry Point, NC 28533-5079

**LOCATION:** On NC-101 between New Bern and Moorehead City. US-70 connects with NC-101 at Havelock. *USMRA: Page 45 (M,N-4)*. NMC: Jacksonville, NC 30 miles SW. Main installation numbers: C-919-466-2811, D-312-582-2811.

**PAX TERM INFO: C-919-466-2379/3232/2312, D-312-582-2379/3232/2312, REC: C-919-466-3225, D-312-582-3225.** Bldg 199, 24hrs daily. Directions: From main gate take Roosevelt Blvd to a right on "A" St to end. Pax Service in ATC tower building. Also, **New River MCAS C-919-451-6197.** Helicopters only-very limited Space-A. **Pax Service Office:** Bldg 199, Hrs: daily 0730-1630, C-919-466-2379, D-312-582-2379. **Pax Paging:** Same as Pax Term, (NCO on duty).

**PAX LOUNGES:** No family lounge. **General:** Bldg 199, 24hrs daily, C-919-466-2379. A/C, bag check, restrooms, O/S seats, telephones (local and long distance). **DV/VIP:** Bldg 199, 24hrs daily, C-919-466-2379. A/C, bag check, coffee/tea served, restrooms, O/S seats, separate reading/writing rooms, telephones (local, long distance and defense), TV.

**FOOD SERVICE: Cafeteria:** C-919-466-4381. **Officers Club:** C-919-447-2395. **Snack Bar:** C-919-447-7041. **SNCO Club**: C-919-466-3087.

**TRANSPORTATION: Air tickets:** SATO: C-919-466-2016. **Bus (Comm):** C-919-447-2391. **Bus(Shuttle):** C-919-466-2787. **Taxi (Comm):** Several on station. **Taxi (Gov):** C-919-466-2808 (Duty Pax only).

*NORTH CAROLINA*
***Cherry Point Marine Corps Air Station, continued***

**TML:** Lodging Office (Officer: Bldg 487, Enlisted E1-E9: Bldg 3673), C-919-466-5169/3060, D-312-582-3060/5169, FAX 919-466-5221. DV/VIP: C-919-582-2848, D-312-466-2848.

**TRAVELERS AID: American Red Cross:** C-919-466-3613. **Emergency Relief:** C-919-447-2074. **Chaplain:** C-919-466-4001. **Lost & Found:** C-919-466-3445. **Security Police:** C-919-466-3615.

**OTHER SERVICES: Exchange:** C-919-447-7041. **Bank/Exchange:** C-919-447-2077. **Hairstyles:** Barber: C-919-447-7041; Beauty: C-919-447-1857. **Laundry/Dry Cleaning:** C-919-447-2603. **Medical:** C-919-466-0266, D-312-582-4419. **Postal:** C-919-466-2496.

**ATTRACTIONS:** Outer Banks, Kitty Hawk.

| IN ROUTE SCHEDULES | |
|---|---|
| **Andrews AFB** | ADW/MEDEVAC-2 |
| **Scott AFB** | BLV/MEDEVAC-1 |

**UNSCHEDULED FLIGHTS**

Frequent CONUS flights to: Beaufort MCAS, SC (**NBC**); Norfolk NAS, VA (**NGU**); and Washington NAF (Andrews AFB), MD (**NSF**) via C-9A, T-39, and C-12 aircraft on passenger missions. Occasional OCONUS and foreign flights. Call for destinations, routings and schedules, usually available one week in advance.

# ELIZABETH CITY COAST GUARD AIR STATION (ECG)

Commander/Base Operations
Elizabeth City CGAS, NC 27909-5006

**LOCATION:** Take I-64 East to VA-104S to US-17 South to Elizabeth City, left on Halstead Blvd, 3 miles to main gate of station. *USMRA: Page 45 (O-1)*. NMC: Elizabeth City, 4 miles north. Main installation numbers: C-919-338-3941, D-312-935-1520.

**PAX TERM INFO: C-919-335-6332, D-312-935-1520.** Bldg 49, base of ATC tower, Hrs: Mon-Fri: 0800-1600. Ask gate guard for directions. **Pax Service Office:** Same as Pax Term, (Duty Officer).

**PAX LOUNGES:** No Pax lounges. Pax assemble at Air Ops Center located at base of ATC tower for processing.

**FOOD SERVICE: Dining Hall:** C-919-335-6281. **All Ranks Club:** C-919-335-6301. **Vending Machines:** Bldg 55, 24hrs daily.

**TRANSPORTATION: Air Tickets:** AAA Travel: C-919-335-6321. **Bus (Comm):** Elizabeth City, Trailways: C-919-335-5183. **Car Rentals:** Elizabeth City, National: C-919-335-1860. **Taxi (Comm):** In Elizabeth City. **Parking:** ATC tower, 24hrs daily, (limited/some reserved spaces).

**TML:** Lodging Office (Bldg 7), C-919-335-6548, all ranks.

**TRAVELERS AID: American Red Cross:** C-919-335-2185. **Chaplain:** C-919-335-6202. **Security Police:** Main gate, 24hrs daily, C-919-335-6379.

**OTHER SERVICES: Exchange:** C-919-335-6269. **Bank/Exchange:** C-919-335-6237. **Barber:** C-919-335-6403. **Beauty:** C-919-335-6382. **Medical:** Bldg: 41, 24hrs daily, C-919-338-6460. **Laundry:** C-919-335-2797. **Postal:** (Off base) C-919-338-3869.

**ATTRACTIONS:** North Carolina's Outer Banks, fresh seafood, beaches, deep-sea fishing, hang gliding at Jockey's Ridge, Wright Brothers Memorial.

### UNSCHEDULED FLIGHTS

Infrequent flights via C-130H aircraft to: Borinquen CGAS, PR (**BQN**); Clearwater/St Petersburg Apt, FL (**CLW**). Call for destinations, routings and schedules.

## POPE AIR FORCE BASE (POB)

3APS/TRP, 3393 Surveyor Street
Pope AFB, NC 28308-2087

**LOCATION:** Take I-95, exit to NC-87/24 West. Signs point the direction to AFB and Fort Bragg. *USMRA: Page 45 (J-4)*. NMC: Fayetteville, 12 miles southeast. Main installation numbers: C-910-394-0001, D-312-486-1110.

**PAX TERM INFO: C-910-394-4429/2803, D-312-486-4429, REC: C-910-394-2803, D-312-486-2803, FAX: C-910-394-2474.** Bldg 708, Hrs: Mon-Fri, 0715-1615. Directions: From gate 3, straight on Manchester Rd to a right on Surveyor St to Pax Term on left. Signs at all gates give directions to Pax Term. **Pax Service Office:** Bldg 708, Hrs: Mon-Fri: 0715-1615.

**PAX LOUNGES:** No separate family lounge. **General:** Bldg 708, Hrs: daily 0715-1615, C-910-394-4429. A/C, baggage check, restrooms, TV, P/C seats. **Protocol Service:** Bldg: 309, Hrs: Mon-Fri: 0715-1615, C-910-394-4739, D-312-486-4739.

**FOOD SERVICE: Cafeteria:** Bldg 350, C-910-394-2196. **Pope Club:** Bldg 236, C-910-497-2154. **In-flight Meals:** Bldg 717, 24hrs daily, C-910-394-2534. **Vending:** Bldg 708, 24hrs daily.

*NORTH CAROLINA*
*Pope Air Force Base, continued*

**TRANSPORTATION:** No base shuttle. No on base transportation. **Car Rentals:** Ft Bragg, Hrs: Mon-Sat: 0800-1800, Sun: 1200-1800. SATO Pope AFB.

**TML:** Lodging Office (Caolina Inn, Bldg 302, Ethridge St), C-910-394-4131, D-312-486-4131, FAX 910-394-2572. DV/VIP: Protocol Office, C-910-394-2374/4739. 06+.

**TRAVELERS AID: American Red Cross:** Bldg 1-1139, Hrs: Mon-Fri: 0800-1630, C-910-396-1234, After hours C-910-394-0111. **Chaplain:** Bldg 317, Hrs: Mon-Fri: 0800-1700, C-910-394-2677, After hours C-910-394-0111. **Emergency Relief:** Bldg 308, Hrs: Mon-Fri: 0715-1615, C-910-394-2470 (AF Aid). C-910-394-2800. **Security Police:** Bldg 378, 24hrs daily, C-910-394-2808. **USO:** 333 Ray Ave, Fayetteville.

**OTHER SERVICES:** Also nearby Fort Bragg. **Exchange:** Bldg 355, Hrs: Mon-Fri: 1030-1730, Sat: 1030-1300, C-910-497-2111. **Bank/Exchange:** Bldg 346, Hrs: Mon-Fri: 0900-1700, C-910-497-6161. **Hair Styles:** Bldg 355, Hrs: Mon-Fri: 0700-1700, C-910-497-5119. **Laundry/Dry Cleaning:** Bldg 355, Hrs: Mon-Fri: 0900-1700, Sa: 0900-1500, C-910-497-2111. **Medical:** Bldg 307, 24hrs daily, C-910-394-2232/4421. **Postal:** Bldg 381, Hrs: Mon-Fri: 0715-1630, Sat: 0715-1000, C-910-394-2828.

**ATTRACTIONS:** Raleigh, Durham, Chapel Hill Triangle, 1.5 hours from Atlantic Ocean.

| ORIGINATING SCHEDULES | | | |
|---|---|---|---|
| | **ACC/POB-1 1st/3rd/4th TUE C-130E** | | |
| **Location ID** | **Airport (Station)** | **Country/State** | **Days Out** |
| POB | Pope AFB | NC | +0 |
| NGU | Norfolk NAS | VA | +1 |
| **NRR** | **Roosevelt Roads NAS** | **PR** | **+2** |
| NGU | Norfolk NAS | VA | +3 |
| POB | Pope AFB | NC | |
| | **APM/POB-2 3rd SUN, 3rd WED C-130E** | | |
| POB | Pope AFB | NC | +0 |
| NGU | Norfolk NAS | VA | +1 |
| NRR | Roosevelt Roads NAS | PR | +1 |
| **SJH** | **V C Bird IAP** | **AN** | **+2** |
| NRR | Roosevelt Roads NAS | PR | +2 |
| NGU | Norfolk NAS | VA | +3 |
| POB | Pope AFB | NC | |

| IN ROUTE SCHEDULES | |
|---|---|
| **Andrews AFB** | ADW/MEDEVAC-2 |
| **Scott AFB** | BLV/MEDEVAC-1 |

# SEYMOUR JOHNSON AIR FORCE BASE (GSB)

4th TFW/LGTT
Seymour Johnson AFB, NC 27531-5270

**LOCATION:** From US-70 take Seymour Johnson AFB exit onto Berkeley Blvd which leads to main gate. Clearly marked. *USMRA: Page 45 (L-3)*. NMC: Raleigh, 50 miles west. Main installation numbers: C-919-736-5400, D-312-488-1110.

**PAX TERM INFO: C-919-736-6729, D-312-488-6729, REC: C-919-736-5269.** Bldg Address: 1280 Flightline Road, Hrs: Mon-Fri: 0800-1600, Directions: From gate 1 straight on Wright Ave to a left on Tinker St to a right on Arnold Ave, to a left on Tower Rd to a right on Flightline Rd. Pax Term on right at end of Flightline Road. **Pax Service Office:** Same as Pax Term, (NCO on duty).

**PAX LOUNGES:** Limited, no separate family lounge. **General/DV/VIP:** Bldg 4741, Hrs: daily 0800-1600, C-919-736-6729. A/C, bag check, telephones (local), P/C seats, restrooms, TV. **Protocol Service:** Bldg 2902, Hrs: Mon-Fri: 0730-1630, C-919-736-5411.

**FOOD SERVICE: Dining Hall:** C-919-736-6403. **In-flight Meals:** C-919-736-5258. **NCO/CPO Club:** C-919-734-2757. **O'Club:** C-919-735-8546. **Snack Bars:** Bldg 4741. **Vending Machine:** Bldg 4741, C-919-736-6729.

**TRANSPORTATION: Air Tickets:** C-919-736-6559. **Bus (Comm):** Goldsboro, C-919-734-3811. **Bus (Gov):** C-919-736-6630. **Limo:** Goldsboro, C-919-751-0525. **Taxi (Gov):** C-919-736-6630 (duty Pax only). **Parking:** Bldg 4210, 24hrs daily (no restrictions).

**TML:** Lodging Office (Southern Pines Inn, Bldg 3804, 1235 Wright Ave), 24hrs daily, C-919-736-6705, D-312-488-6705, FAX: C-919-736-5643. DV/VIP: C-919-736-6473.

**TRAVELERS AID: American Red Cross:** C-919-736-6423. **Chaplain:** C-919-736-5211. **Security Police:** C-919-736-6473.

**OTHER SERVICES: Exchange:** C-919-735-9786. **Bank/Exchange:** C-919-735-4680. **Hair Styles:** Barber: C-919-735-9442; Beauty: C-919-734-7504. **Laundry/Dry Cleaning:** C-919-734-7436. **Medical:** Bldg 2800, Hrs: daily 0600-2200, C-919-736-2778, D-312-488-2778. **Postal:** C-919-736-6283.

**ATTRACTIONS:** NC research triangle of Raleigh, Durham, and Chapel Hill.

## UNSCHEDULED FLIGHTS

Unscheduled flights via KC-10A aircraft to various CONUS and foreign locations. Call for destinations, routings and schedules.

# NORTH DAKOTA

## GRAND FORKS AIR FORCE BASE (RDR)

319th OSS/OSAA,
695 Steen Ave
Grand Forks AFB, ND 58205-6245

**LOCATION:** From I-29 take US-2 West for 14 miles to Grand Forks, County Rd B-3 (Emerado/Air Base) 1 mile to AFB. *USMRA: Page 83 (I-3)*. NMC: Grand Forks, 15 miles east. Main installation numbers: C-701-747-3000, D-312-362-3000.

**PAX TERM INFO: C-701-747-4409/4410, D-312-362-4409/4410, REC: C-701-747-4376, FAX 701-747-6540, D FAX 312-362-6540.** Bldg 528, 24hrs daily. Directions: From main gate straight on Steen Blvd for 1 mile to Base Ops on the left under old ATC Tower. **Pax Service Office:** Same as Pax Terminal, (NCO on duty).

**PAX LOUNGES:** General and family lounge combined. **General:** Bldg 528, 24hrs daily, C-701-747-4409. A/C, read/write rooms, telephones (local and defense), restrooms, P/C seats. **DV/VIP:** Bldg 528, 24hrs daily, C-701-747-4409. A/C, bag check, coffee/tea served, TV, O/S seats. **Protocol Service:** Hrs: Mon-Fri: 0730-1630, C-701-747-5055.

**FOOD SERVICE: Dining Hall:** Bldg 220, C-701-747-3276. **Enlisted Club:** Bldg 309, C-701-747-3392. **In-Flight Meals:** Bldg 697, 24hrs daily, C-701-747-4439. **NCO/CPO Club:** Bldg 309, C-701-747-3392. **O'Club:** Bldg 118, C-701-747-3054. **Burger King:** C-701-594-8581. **Snack Bars:** Bowling Alley: Bldg 202, 24hrs daily, C-701-594-2695. **Vending:** Bldg 528, 24hrs daily, C-701-747-4409.

**TRANSPORTATION: Air Tickets:** Bldg 409, C-701-594-5507. **Bus (Gov):** Bldg 459, C-701-747-3976. **Car Rentals:** Grand Forks IAP, 9 miles east of Base. **Taxi (Comm):** Grand Forks IAP, C-701-746-7433. **Taxi (Gov):** Bldg 459, C-701-747-3976 (duty Pax only). **Parking:** Bldg 528, C-701-747-4283. Short term-no restrictions; long term-3 week limit. Leave keys with Base Ops dispatch desk.

**TML:** Lodging Office (Warrior Inn, Bldg 117, Holzapple & 6th Ave), 24hrs daily, C-701-747-3070/6188, D-312-362-3070, FAX 701-747-3069. All ranks. DV/VIP: C-701-747-4513, D-312-362-5055, E-9/O6+.

**TRAVELERS AID: American Red Cross:** Bldg 101, C-701-594-2941; after hours, C-701-747-3000. **Chaplain:** Bldg 109, C-701-747-3076. **Emergency Relief:** Bldg 101, C-701-747-4904 (AF Aid). **Lost/Found:** Bldg 103, C-701-747-5351. **Security Police:** Bldg 103, C-701-747-5351.

**OTHER SERVICES: Exchange:** Bldg 105, C-701-594-5542. **Bank/Exchange:** Bldg 207, C-701-795-3355. **Hair Styles:** Bldg 105, Barber: C-701-594-2124; Beauty: C-701-594-4531. **Laundry/Dry Cleaning:** Bldg 211, C-701-594-2331. **Medical:** Bldg 109,

24hrs daily, C-701-747-5601, D-312-362-5601. **Postal:** Bldg 230, C-701-747-3339. **Valet/Dry Cleaning:** Bldg 211, C-701-594-2331.

**ATTRACTIONS:** Outdoor sports and recreation, Canada easy drive north via I-29.

| IN ROUTE SCHEDULES | |
|---|---|
| **Buckley ANGB** | BKF/MEDEVAC-1 |
| **Scott AFB** | BLV/MEDEVAC-7 |

**UNSCHEDULED FLIGHTS**

Frequent KC-135R flights to CONUS and foreign country locations. Call for destinations, routings and schedules.

## MINOT AIR FORCE BASE (MIB)

5th OSS/OSAA,
221 Flightline Dr.
Minot AFB, ND 58705-5049

**LOCATION:** On US-83, north of Minot. *USMRA: Page 83 (D-2)*. NMC: Minot, 15 miles south. Main installation numbers: C-701-723-1110, D-312-453-1110.

**PAX TERM INFO: C-701-723-1854/2347/2348, D-312-453-1854/2347/2348,** Bldg 746, Base Ops, Hrs: Mon-Thu 24 hrs, Fri closed 2200, Sat-Sun 0800-1700. Directions: From main gate straight on Missile Ave to a left on Peacekeeper Place to Base Ops on the left. **Pax Service Office:** C-701-723-2348, D-312-453-2348.

**PAX LOUNGES:** Limited lounge facilities. **General:** Bldg 746, Hrs: Mon-Thu 24 hrs, Fri closed 2200, Sat-Sun 0800-1700, C-701-723-2347. TV, restrooms, P/C seats. **Protocol Service:** Bldg: 167, Hrs: Mon-Fri: 0730-1630, C-701-723-3474 (06+).

**FOOD SERVICE: Cafeteria:** Bldg 587, C-701-727-4462. **Dining Hall:** Bldg 213, C-701-723-3550. **In-flight Meals:** Bldg 846, Hrs: Mon-Fri: 0001-2200, C-701-723-3079, after hours C-701-723-3503. **NCO/CPO Club:** Bldg 292, C-701-727-6156. **O'Club:** Bldg 174, C-701-727-3731. **Restaurant:** Bldg 202, C-701-727-4377. **Snack Bars:** Bldg 746, C-701-727-4625. **Vending:** Bldg 746, C-701-727-4627. **Burger King:** Hrs: 0900-2100.

**TRANSPORTATION: Air Tickets:** SATO: Bldg 475, C-701-723-2108, Bldg 202, Rec Center, C-701-727-6575. **Taxi (Gov):** C-701-723-3121. **Parking:** Bldg 746.

**TML:** Lodging Office (Sakakawea Inn, Bldg 14, 201 Summit Drive), C-701-723-2184, D-312-453-2184, FAX 701-723-1844. DV/VIP: Protocol Office, Bldg 167, 201 Summit Dr. C-701-723-3474, D-312-453-3474, 06+.

**TRAVELERS AID: American Red Cross:** C-701-727-2477. **Chaplain:** C-701-723-3633. **Security Police:** C-701-723-3096 (Desk Sgt).

*NORTH DAKOTA*
*Minot Air Force Base, continued*

**OTHER SERVICES: Exchange:** Bldg 437, C-701-727-4717. **Bank/Exchange:** Bomber Blvd, C-701-727-6228. **Hair Styles:** Bldg 437, Barber: C-701-727-4868; Beauty: C-701-727-9799. **Laundry/Dry Cleaning:** Bldg 437, C-701-727-6800. **Medical:** Bldg 194, 24hrs daily, C-701-727-5304, D-312-453-5304 (clinic). **Postal:** Bldg 135, C-701-727-4887.

**ATTRACTIONS:** Trestle Valley Ski Area

| IN ROUTE SCHEDULES | |
|---|---|
| **Buckley ANGB** | BKF/MEDEVAC-1 |
| **Scott AFB** | BLV/MEDEVAC-7 |
| **Travis AFB** | SUU/MEDEVAC-4 |

**UNSCHEDULED FLIGHTS**

Infrequent flights to CONUS and OCONUS destinations. Call for destinations, routings and schedules.

# OHIO

## MANSFIELD LAHM AIRPORT (MFD)

179th AG (Air National Guard)
Mansfield Lahm Airport, OH 44901-5000

**LOCATION:** From US-30 East or West exit to OH-13 North for 1 mile on left. *USMRA: Page 67 (D,E-4,5)*. NMC: Mansfield, 3 miles south. Main installation numbers: C-419-521-0100, D-312-696-6210.

**PAX TERM INFO: C-419-521-0124, D-312-696-6124.** Bldg 101, Hrs: Mon-Fri: 0745-1630. Directions: Main gate straight, on right. Limited military support. **Pax Service Office:** Same as Pax terminal. (NCO on duty).

**PAX LOUNGES:** General lounge only. **General:** Bldg 101, Hrs: Mon-Fri: 0745-1630, C-419-521-0124. A/C, coffee/tea served, telephones (commercial, long distance and defense), TV, restrooms, O/S seats.

**TML:** Lodging Office at Defense Construction Supply Center, Columbus, OH (Bldg 1/1, 3990 E Broad St), C-614-692-4758, D-314-850-4758, FAX 614-692-3656, DV/VIP: C-614-692-2167, D-314-850-2167, O6+.

### UNSCHEDULED FLIGHTS

Flights via C-130H aircraft to CONUS, OCONUS and foreign country locations. Frequent destinations in AK, HI, PR, VI, PN, GE, and UK. Call for destinations, routings and schedules up to 30 days in advance.

## RICKENBACKER AIR NATIONAL GUARD BASE (LCK)

121st OSS/OM
7556 South Perimeter Road
Rickenbacker ANGB, OH 43217-5887

**LOCATION:** From I-270 take Alum Creek exit south to Rickenbacker IAP. Also accessible off US-23 onto OH-317. Clearly marked. *USMRA: Page 67 (D-7)*. NMC: Columbus, 13 miles southeast. Main installation numbers: C-614-492-4223, D-312-950-8211.

**PAX TERM INFO: C-614-492-4595, D-312-950-4595, FAX: C-614-492-4578.** Bldg 887, Base Ops, Hrs: Sun-Mon: 0800-1600, Tue-Fri: 0730-2330, Sat: 0730-1930, C-614-492-4595. Directions: Exit I270, 4 miles south on Almm Creek Drive to a left on Fred Haise Ave to Pax Term on right. **Pax Service Office:** Same as Pax Term. **Pax Paging:** Same as Pax Term. Facilities available off base, on base BX only.

*OHIO*
*Rickenbacker Air National Guard Base, continued*

**TML:** Lodging Office at Defense Construction Supply Center, Columbus, OH (Bldg 1/1, 3990 E Broad St), C-614-692-4758, D-314-850-4758, FAX 614-692-3656, DV/VIP: C-614-692-2167, D-314-850-2167, O6+.

**UNSCHEDULED FLIGHTS**

Flights to CONUS, OCONUS and foreign country locations via KC-135 aircraft. Call for destinations, routings and schedules.

## WRIGHT-PATTERSON AIR FORCE BASE (FFO)

88th TRANS/LGTTM
Passenger Terminal, Building 206, Skeel Avenue
Wright-Patterson AFB, OH 45433-5519

**LOCATION:** South of I-70, off I-675 at Fairborn. Also access from OH-4. AFB clearly marked. *USMRA: Page 67 (B-7)*. NMC: Dayton, 10 miles southwest. Main installation numbers: C-513-257-1110, D-312-787-1110 (Area A&C), C-513-785-1110 (Area B).

**PAX TERM INFO: C-513-257-7741, D-312-787-7741, REC: C-513-257-6235, D-312-787-6235, FAX: C-513-476-1580, D-312-986-1580.** Bldg 206, Area C, Hrs: Mon-Fri: 0630-1630, weekends & holidays check in with Base Ops. Directions: Enter Gate 8C, right on Skeel Avenue, Pax Terminal on left. **Pax Service Office:** Bldg 206, Hrs: Mon-Fri: 0730-1630, C-513-257-7741 (NCO on duty). **Pax Paging:** Same as Pax terminal.

**PAX LOUNGES:** No separate family lounge. **General:** Bldg 206, Hrs: Mon-Fri: 0630-1630, C-513-257-7741. A/C, restrooms, TV, card tables, plush seating. **DV/VIP:** Bldg 206, 24hrs daily, C-513-257-6202 (07+). A/C, coffee/tea served, read/write rooms, telephones (commercial, long distance and defense), TV, restrooms, showers, O/S seats. **Protocol Service:** Arnold House, Hrs: Mon-Fri: 0800-1600, C-513-257-3118.

**FOOD SERVICE: Dining Hall:** Bldg 1214, Hrs: daily 0530-0100, C-513-257-2117 (In-Flight Kitchen: 24hrs daily). **Enlisted Club:** Bldg 1226, Hrs: daily 1100-2300, C-513-257-2001. **NCO/CPO Club:** Bldg 1214, Hrs: daily 0630-0100, C-513-257-7292. **O'Club:** Bldg: 800, Hrs: daily 0700-0100, C-513-257-2216. **Restaurants:** Bldg 1, Hrs: daily 0630-1315, C-513-257-4902. **Snack Bars:** Bldg 22, Hrs: daily 0530-1400, C-513-879-4317. **Vending:** C-513-257-4616.

**TRANSPORTATION: Air Tickets:** Bldg 11A & 262, Hrs: daily 0800-1630, C-513-257-6611. **Bus (Gov):** Bldg 262, Hrs: Mon-Fri: 0800-1630, C-513-257-3755 (on Base). **Car Rentals:** Dayton Apt: 24hrs daily (all major companies). **Limo Service:** Bldg 146, Hrs: Mon-Fri: 0605-2005, C-513-898-7171. **Taxi (Gov):** Bldg 262, 24hrs daily, C-513-257-3755 (area not covered by bus). **Parking:** Bldg 206, 24hrs daily (short term-front of Term; long term-overnight parking at north end of building).

**TML:** Lodging Office (Bldg 825, 2439 Schlatter Dr), 24hrs daily, C-513-257-3451, D-312-787-3451, FAX: C-513-257-2787, D-312-787-2787. All ranks. DV/VIP: C-513-257-3118, O7/GS16+.

**TRAVELERS AID: American Red Cross:** Bldg 830, 24hrs daily, C-513-257-7062 or C-513-222-6711. **Chaplain:** Bldg 150, Hrs: Mon-Fri: 0800-1700, C-513-257-7941. **Emergency Relief:** Bldg 2, Hrs: 0800-1700, C-513-257-6405 (AF Aid). **Security Police:** Gate 8C, 24hrs daily, C-513-257-6226. **USO:** Port Columbus IAP, Room 102, C-513-231-7300.

**OTHER SERVICES: Exchange:** Bldg 1250, Hrs: Mon-Sat: 1000-2100, Sun: 1100-1700, C-513-879-5730. **Bank/Exchange:** Bldg 1250, Hrs: Mon-Fri: 0900-1600, Sat: 0900-1230, C-513-449-8990. **Hair Styles:** Bldg 1250, Barber: C-513-879-5171; Beauty: C-513-879-5281. **Laundry/Dry Cleaning:** Bldg 1250, Hrs: Mon-Sat: 1000-1800, C-513-879-5790. **Medical:** Bldg 830, 24hrs daily, C-513-257-2968/2969, D-312-787-2968. **Postal:** Bldg 1044, C-513-257-6523.

**ATTRACTIONS:** Air Force Museum, Wright Brothers Memorial in Dayton.

| **ORIGINATING SCHEDULES** | | | |
|---|---|---|---|
| **ACC/FFO-1 1st TUE, 4th THU C-141B** | | | |
| **Location ID** | **Airport (Station)** | **Country/State** | **Days Out** |
| FFO | Wright-Patterson AFB | OH | +0 |
| DOV | Dover AFB | DE | +1 |
| **MHZ** | **RAF Mildenhall** | **UK** | **+2** |
| DOV | Dover AFB | DE | +3 |
| FFO | Wright-Patterson AFB | OH | |
| **ACC/FFO-2 1st THU C-141B** | | | |
| FFO | Wright-Patterson AFB | OH | +0 |
| DOV | Dover AFB | DE | +1 |
| RMS | Ramstein AB | GE | +2 |
| SIZ | Sigonella NAS | IT | +3 |
| **TTH** | **Thumrait OAFB** | **OM** | **+4** |
| RMS | Ramstein AB | GE | +5 |
| CAI | Cairo IAP | EG | +5 |
| RMS | Ramstein AB | GE | +6 |
| LGS | Lajes AB | PO | +6 |
| DOV | Dover AFB | DE | +7 |
| FFO | Wright-Patterson AFB | OH | |

*OHIO*
*Wright-Patterson Air Force Base, continued*

| | **PCC/FFO-3 2nd/3rd FRI** | **C-141B** | |
|---|---|---|---|
| FFO | Wright-Patterson AFB | OH | +0 |
| SUU | Travis AFB | CA | +1 |
| EDF | Elmendorf AFB | AK | +2 |
| **OKO** | **Yokota AB** | **JA** | **+3** |
| EDF | Elmendorf AFB | AK | +3 |
| SUU | Travis AFB | CA | +4 |
| FFO | Wright-Patterson AFB | OH | |
| | **IN ROUTE SCHEDULES** | | |
| **Scott AFB** | BLV/MEDEVAC-4 | BLV/MEDEVAC-6 | BLV/MEDEVAC-9 |

**UNSCHEDULED FLIGHTS**

Frequent flights to: Barksdale AFB, LA (**BAD**) (weekly); Eglin AFB, FL (**VPS**) (2/weekly); Kelly AFB, TX (**SKF**) (1/2weekly); Langley AFB, VA (**LFI**) (1/2weekly); Maxwell AFB, AL (**MXF**) (weekly); Norfolk NAS, VA (**NGU**) (1/2weekly); Offutt AFB, NE (**OFF**) (2/weekly); Peterson AFB, CO (**COS**) (monthly); Randolph AFB, TX (**RND**) (1/2weekly); Robbins AFB, GA (**WRB**) (weekly); Tinker AFB, OK (**TIK**) (3/monthly) and other CONUS locations utilizing C-21 and similar aircraft. Call for destinations, routings and schedules.

## YOUNGSTOWN/ WARREN/REGIONAL AIRPORT AIR RESERVE STATION (ARS) (YNG)

910th AG (AFRES)
Vienna, OH 44473-0910

**LOCATION:** From OH-193 North or South, exit to King Graves Rd West at signs pointing to U.S Air Force Base, Main Gate 1 mile on left. *USMRA: Page 67 (H-3)*. NMC: Youngstown, 8 miles south. Main installation numbers: C-216-392-1000, D-312-346-1000.

**PAX TERM INFO: C-216-392-1236, D-312-346-1236, FAX: C-216-392-1097, D-312-346-1097.** Ask Security Police for directions. No PAX terminal. No PAX lounge, or comfort facilities. Base operations and command post. After duty hours call the Security Police Law Enforcement Desk: C-216-392-1277. Provides service to neighboring Youngstown Municipal Airport and support to transient U.S. government aircraft. Military support available for transient aircrews and government/military personnel on orders to Youngstown Air Reserve Base. BX: C-216-392-1393, Consol Club: C-216-392-1295.

**TML:** C-216-392-1268.

**UNSCHEDULED FLIGHTS**

Flights via C-130H aircraft to CONUS and OCONUS locations. Space-A opportunities infrequent. Connecting flight opportunities virtually non-existent. Call for destinations, routings and schedules.

# OKLAHOMA

## ALTUS AIR FORCE BASE (LTS)

97th Transportation Sq/ LGTTAP Bldg #178, 509 "E" Ave.
Altus AFB, OK 73523-5270

**LOCATION:** Off US-62 south of I-40 and west of I-44. From US-62 traveling west from Lawton, turn right at 1st traffic light in Altus and follow road to main gate northeast of Falcon Rd. *USMRA: Page 84 (E-5)*. NMC: Lawton, 56 miles east. Main installation numbers: C-405-481-8100, D-312-866-1110.

**PAX TERM INFO: C-405-481-6350, D-312-866-6350, REC: C-405-481-6350, FAX: C-405-481-5065, D-312-866-5065.** Bldg 178, Hrs: Mon-Fri: 0730-1630, Directions: From main gate left on 1st St, right on East Ave to Pax Term on the left. **Pax Service Office:** Same as Pax Term.

**PAX LOUNGES:** Limited. No separate DV/VIP or family lounges. **General:** Bldg 178, Hrs: Mon-Fri: 0730-1630, C-405-481-6350. A/C, bag check, telephone (commercial and defense), TV, restrooms, O/S seats. **Protocol Service:** Bldg 1, Hrs: Mon-Fri: 0800-1700, C-405-481-7554.

**FOOD SERVICE: Dining Hall:** C-405-481-7781. **Enlisted Club:** C-405-481-6295. **Rec Center:** C-405-481-6600. **O'Club:** C-405-481-6224. **Snack Bars:** Bowling Alley: C-405-481-6300.

**TRANSPORTATION: Air Tickets:** Altus: C-405-477-4554, SATO: C-405-481-6466. **Bus (Comm):** Altus: C-405-482-0639, $7-28 (Altus to Lawton-3 times a week MON-WED-FRI) C-405-482-5043. **Taxi (Comm):** C-405-482-0383/1091 ($3-Altus, $40-Lawton). **Taxi (Gov):** C-405-481-6272 (duty Pax only). **Parking:** Bldg 178, 24hrs daily. Long term designated areas, 24+ hours.

**TML:** Lodging Office (Bldg 82), 24hrs daily, C-405-481-7356, D-312-866-7356, FAX 405-481-5704. All ranks. DV/VIP: C-405-481-7554, O6+.

**TRAVELERS AID: American Red Cross:** C-405-481-6526. **Chaplain:** C-405-481-7485. **Lost/Found:** C-405-481-6350/6428. **Security Police:** Bldg 130, 24hrs daily, C-405-481-7444.

**OTHER SERVICES: Exchange:** C-405-482-8733. **Hair Styles:** Barber: C-405-482-8221; Beauty: C-405-482-4051. **Laundry/Dry Cleaning:** C-405-482-7344. **Medical:** Bldg 46, Hrs: Mon-Fri: 0700-1800, C-405-481-5222, D-312-866-5222. **Postal:** C-405-481-6403.

**ATTRACTIONS:** Western prairie country, outdoor sports.

*OKLAHOMA*
*Altus Air Force Base, continued*

| ORIGINATING SCHEDULES | | | |
|---|---|---|---|
| | **ACC/LTS-1 4th WED KC-135R** | | |
| **Location ID** | **Airport (Station)** | **Country/State** | **Days Out** |
| LTS | Altus AFB | OK | +0 |
| DOV | Dover AFB | DE | +1 |
| **MHZ** | **RAF Mildenhall** | **UK** | **+2** |
| DOV | Dover AFB | DE | +3 |
| LTS | Altus AFB | OK | |
| | **PCC/LTS-2 2nd SUN C-5A/B** | | |
| LTS | Altus AFB | OK | +0 |
| SUU | Travis AFB | CA | +0 |
| HIK | Hickam AFB | HI | +1 |
| UAM | Andersen AFB | GU | +3 |
| **DNA** | **Kadena AB** | **JA** | **+3** |
| UAM | Andersen AFB | GU | +4 |
| HIK | Hickam AFB | HI | +5 |
| SUU | Travis AFB | CA | +6 |
| LTS | Altus AFB | OK | |
| | **PCC/LTS-3 2nd/4th SUN C-141B** | | |
| LTS | Altus AFB | OK | +0 |
| SUU | Travis AFB | CA | +0 |
| HIK | Hickam AFB | HI | +2 |
| UAM | Andersen AFB | GU | +3 |
| DNA | Kadena AB | JA | +3 |
| **OSN** | **Osan AB** | **RK** | **+4** |
| OKO | Yokota AB | JA | +4 |
| EDF | Elmendorf AFB | AK | +5 |
| SUU | Travis AFB | CA | +6 |
| LTS | Altus AFB | OK | |

**UNSCHEDULED FLIGHTS**

Infrequent flights to: Dover AFB, DE (**DOV**); Elmendorf AFB, AK (**EDF**); Hickam AFB, HI (**HIK**); Little Rock AFB, AR (**LRF**); McChord AFB, WA (**TCM**); Osan AB, RK (**OSN**); RAF Mildenhall, UK (**MHZ**); Scott AFB, IL (**BLV**); Travis AFB, CA (**SUU**) and Yokota AB, JA (**OKO**). Note: Flight schedules are received on a weekly basis. Call for destinations, routings and schedules.

# HENRY POST ARMY AIRFIELD (FSI)

HPAA, ATTN: Afld Opns, bldg 4907
Fort Sill, OK 73503-5000

**LOCATION:** From I-44 at Lawton, take US-62/277, 4 miles northwest to Post. Clearly marked. *USMRA: Page 84 (E, F-5).* NMC: Wichita Falls, TX, 50 miles south. Main installation numbers: C-405-442-8111, D-312-639-7090.

**PAX TERM INFO: C-405-442-5808/3385, D-312-639-5808/3385, FAX: C-405-442-5643.** Bldg 4907, Hrs: Mon-Fri: 0700-2200, Directions: I-44 north to Gate 2 exit. In the ATC building.

**TML:** Lodging Office (Bldg 5676, Fergusson Rd), C-405-442-5077, D-312-639-5000, FAX 405-442-6908. DV/VIP: Protocol Office, Bldg 460, C-405-442-4825, 06/GS-15+.

**OTHER SERVICES:** Full Base support available. **Snack Bar:** Bldg 5045, Hrs: daily 0630-1400.

### UNSCHEDULED FLIGHTS

Flights via U-21-F/P aircraft to Midwest and East Coast locations. Call for destinations, routings and schedules.

# TINKER AIR FORCE BASE (TIK)

72 ABW/LGTRM, 7701 2nd Street, Suite 217
Tinker AFB, OK 73145-5000

**LOCATION**: Southeast of Oklahoma City, off I-40. Use Gate 1 off Air Depot Blvd. *USMRA: Page 84 (G-4).* NMC: Oklahoma City, 12 miles northwest. Main installation numbers: C-405-732-7321, D-312-884-1110.

**PAX TERM INFO: C-405-739-4339/4360, D-312-339-4339/4360, FAX: C-405-739-4317 DSN FAX 339-4317.** Bldg 268, Hrs: Mon-Fri: 0715-1600. Directions: Gate 1 to a left at 1st light, 1 more light to a right on "H" St then to Sentry Blvd and turn right. Going east on Sentry Blvd go thru stop sign and turn right past Bldg 224. Park in parking lot North Bldg 268. 24 hours notice on flights. **PAX SERVICE OFFICE:** Bldg 1, Hrs: Mon-Fri 0715-1600, C-405-739-5682 (NCO on duty). **PAX PAGING:** Same as Pax terminal.

**PAX LOUNGES:** Family and General lounge combined. **General:** Bldg 268, Hrs: Mon-Fri: 0715-1600, C-405-739-4339/4360, D 312-339-4339/4360. A/C, bag check, read/write rooms, telephones (commercial and defense), TV, restrooms, P/C seats. **DV/VIP:** Bldg 240, 24hrs daily, C-405-734-2191, D 312-884-2191. A/C, bag check, read/write rooms, telephones (commercial and defense), TV, restrooms, O/S seats. **Protocol Service:** Bldg 460, 24hrs daily, C-405-739-3900.

*OKLAHOMA*
*Tinker Air Force Base, continued*

**FOOD SERVICE: Inflight kitchen:** Bldg 240, 24hrs daily, C-405-734-3795, D 312-884-3795. **Dining Hall:** Bldg 5905, Hrs: daily 0530-0100, C-405-734-MENU. **NCO/CPO Club:** Bldg 6001, Hrs: daily 1100-2100, C-405-734-3418. **Vending:** Bldg 268, Hrs: Mon-Fri 0715-1600.

**TRANSPORTATION: Air Tickets:** SATO: Bldg 1, Hrs: Mon-Fri: 0715-1600, C-405-739-5057, D 312-339-5057. **Car Rentals:** OKC Arpt, 24hrs daily, Hertz: C-405-732-0366. **Taxi (Comm):** Gate 1, 24hrs daily, C-405-235-1431 (Safeway). **Taxi (Gov):** Bldg 2101, 24hrs daily, C-405-734-2803 (on Base only). **Parking:** Short term-Bldg 268; long term-Bldg 591, unlimited, C-405-734-3737. Register with Security Police.

**TML:** Lodging Office (Indian Hills Inn, Bldg 5604, 4002 Mitchell St), C-405-734-2822, FAX 405-734-7426. DV/VIP: Bldg 3001, C-405-739-5511, 06/GS-15+.

**TRAVELERS AID: American Red Cross:** Bldg 3067, Hrs: Mon-Fri: 0800-1630, C-405-232-7121. **Chaplain:** Bldg 5701, duty hours, C-405-734-2111. **Security Police:** Bldg 591, 24hrs daily, C-405-734-2000/3737.

**OTHER SERVICES: Exchange:** Bldg 478, Hrs: Mon-Fri: 1000-1800, Sat-Sun: 0900-1600, C-405-734-3035. **Bank/Exchange:** Bldg 478, Hrs: Mon-Fri: 0900-1500, C-405-736-2717. **Hair Styles:** Bldg 478, Hrs: Mon-Fri: 0800-1700, Sat: 0800-1600, Barber: C-405-732-5032; Beauty: C-405-732-6509. **Laundry/Dry Cleaning:** Bldg 478, Hrs: Mon-Fri: 0900-1730, C-405-734-5225. **Medical:** Bldg 581, 24hrs daily, C-405-734-8249, D-405-884-8249; Ambulance, C-405-734-8223. **Postal:** Bldg 758, Hrs: Mon-Fri: 0845-1600, Sat: 0845-1045, C-405-734-3611.

**ATTRACTIONS:** Oklahoma City, National Cowboy Hall of Fame, Oklahoma City Zoo, Remington Park Race Track, Firefighters Museum, Myriad Botanical Gardens, Frontier City Theme Park, Kirkpatrick Center.

| **ORIGINATING SCHEDULES** | | | |
|---|---|---|---|
| | **ACC/TIK-1 3rd WED KC-135R** | | |
| **Location ID** | **Airport (Station)** | **Country/State** | **Days Out** |
| TIK | Tinker AFB | OK | +0 |
| DOV | Dover AFB | DE | +1 |
| **MHZ** | **RAF Mildenhall** | **UK** | **+2** |
| DOV | Dover AFB | DE | +3 |
| TIK | Tinker AFB | OK | |
| | **IN ROUTE SCHEDULES** | | |
| **Scott AFB** | BLV/MEDEVAC-10 | | |

**UNSCHEDULED FLIGHTS**

Flights to Andrews AFB, MD (**ADW**); Kelly AFB, TX (**SKF**); Offutt AFB, NE (**OFF**); Peterson AFB, CO (**COS**); Scott AFB, IL (**BLV**); Wright-Patterson AFB, OH (**FFO**); Plus other conus bases. Flights are scheduled on a 1 day advance notice. Seldom any overseas flights. Only regularly scheduled flight is to Kelly AFB, TX (SKF) on Mon & Thu.

# WILL ROGERS WORLD AIRPORT/ANGB(OKC)

137th TAW/DOO (ANG)
Will Rogers ANGB, OK 73179-1040

**LOCATION:** From I-40 West, exit I44 south to airport. *USMRA: Page 84 (G-4)*. NMC: Oklahoma City, 7 miles northeast. Main installation numbers: C-405-686-5210, D-312-940-8210.

**PAX TERM INFO: C-405-686-5500, D-312-940-5550.** Bldg 1040, Hrs: Mon-Thu: 0630-1700. Directions: From the main gate drive straight for 4 blocks south, then two blocks west. Full services of a regional airport.

**PAX LOUNGES:** No Pax lounge. Canteen and restrooms available.

**OTHER SERVICES: NCO Club:** D-312-940-5550. **Security Police:** 24hrs daily, C-405-685-5300.

**UNSCHEDULED FLIGHTS**

Flights to CONUS and OCONUS via ANG C-130H aircraft. Call for destinations, routings and schedules.

# OREGON

## PORTLAND INTERNATIONAL AIRPORT/ JOINT RESERVE BASE (PDX)

142nd FIG/OTM (Air National Guard)
6801 N.E. Cornfoot Road
Portland, OR 97218-2797

**LOCATION:** From I-205 North or South exit to Airport Way for .5 miles to IAP. *USMRA: Page 100 (C-2); Page 103 (C-1)*. NMC: Portland, 10 miles southwest. Main installation numbers: C-503-335-4000, D-312-638-4000.

**PAX TERM INFO: C-503-335-4390/4421, D-312-638-4390, FAX 503-335-5098, D FAX 312-638-5098.** Air National Guard Ops: 24hrs daily. Ask Security Police for directions( C-503-335-4229). All the support of an IAP. Limited military support facilities. BX:C-503-249-0997; MEDICAL: C-503-335-4757; CONSOLIDATED CLUB: C-503-335-5151. No TML available in immediate vicinity.

### UNSCHEDULED FLIGHTS

Frequent flights via C-9A aircraft to: Whidbey Island NAS, WA (**NUW**). Call for destinations, routings and schedules.

# PENNSYLVANIA

## HARRISBURG INTERNATIONAL AIRPORT (MDT)

193rd Special Ops Grp (Air National Guard)
Middletown, PA 17057-5086

**LOCATION:** From I-76 East or West, exit #19 South on PA-230 (2nd St) South to IAP on the right. *USMRA: Page 22 (G-6)*. NMC: Harrisburg, 5 miles northwest. Main installation numbers: C-717-948-2200, D-312-430-9200.

**PAX TERM INFO: C-717-948-2268, D-312-430-9268, FAX: C-717-948-2599, D FAX 312-430-9599.** Air National Guard Area, Hrs: Mon-Fri: 0730-1600. Ask Security Police for directions. All the support of an IAP. No military facility support.

**TML:** Lodging Office (Defense Distribution Region East, Bldg 268, J Ave), C-717-770-7035. DV/VIP: C-717-770-7192, O6/GS-15+.

**UNSCHEDULED FLIGHTS**

Flights to CONUS and OCONUS locations by ANG EC-130E/H aircraft. Call for destinations, routings and schedules.

## PITTSBURGH INTERNATIONAL AIRPORT/ARS (PIT)

911th AW (AFRES), 316 Defense Ave
Coraopolis, PA 15108-4403

**LOCATION:** Take I-279 West which merges into PA-60 (Airport Parkway) onto exit 3. *USMRA: Page 22 (A-5,6)*. NMC: Pittsburgh, 15 miles southeast. Main installation numbers: C-412-269-8359, D-312-277-8359.

**PAX TERM INFO:** AFRES: **C-412-474-8000, D-312-277-8000.** AFRES Base Ops, Hrs: Mon-Fri: 0730-1600 & flight times. ANGB: **C-412-269-8350, D-312-277-8350**. Air National Guard Base Ops, Hrs: Mon-Fri: 0800-1700, & flight times. All the support of an IAP. Limited military support. BX: C-412-424-8207.

**TML:** C-412-474-8230.

**UNSCHEDULED FLIGHTS**

Frequent flights via AFRES C-130H and ANG KC-135E aircraft to CONUS, OCONUS and foreign country locations. Call for destinations, routings and schedules.

*PENNSYLVANIA*

# PHILADELPHIA INTERNATIONAL AIRPORT (PHL)

DET 1, 365th APS/TRO
Philadelphia IAP, Terminal D
Philadelphia, PA 19153-3701

**LOCATION:** Seven miles southwest of Philadelphia, off I-95 and Rt 291. Clearly marked. *USMRA: Page 22 (I, J-7); Page 27 (C-7).* NMC: Philadelphia, 7 miles northeast. Main installation numbers: C-215-897-5644, D-312-443-5644.

**PAX TERM INFO: C-215-897-5600/5644, D-312-443-5600/5644, FAX: 215-897-5627, DSN FAX 312-443-5627. Telephone Menu D-312-443-5642/5644, REC: C-215-897-5645, D-312-443-5645 (updated 5 times weekly).** Term D, Hrs: Mon-Sat: 0730-2000, Sun: 0730-1500. **Airport Information Center:** C-215-937-6937. **Pax Service Office:** Term D, Hrs: Mon-Fri: 0800-1700, C-215-897-5644, D-312-443-5630. **Pax Paging:** Term D, during flight processing, C-215-897-5640, D-312-897-5640. NOTE: We have a 24 hour self-service SPA sign up available at the Pax Service Center, Term D - upper level. NOTE: Sign-up at Philadelphia gives you sign-up at McGuire AFB, NJ (WRI).

**PAX LOUNGES: General:** Term D, 24hrs daily. A/C, telephones, TV, restrooms, bag check/lockers. **Protocol Service:** Provided by McGuire AFB, C-609-724-2470 (06+). **Family:** USO - Term D, Hrs: daily 0800-2200, C-215-365-8889. A/C, bag check/lockers, TV, refreshments, read/write rooms, restrooms, showers, O/S seats, child care.

**FOOD SERVICE:** Ice cream parlor-Concourse. **Restaurants:** Two restaurants in terminal B with hours from 0600-2200 daily. **Snack Bars:** All Terminals, Hrs: daily 0600-2200. **Vending:** All Terminals, 24hrs daily.

**TRANSPORTATION:** Train-airport line to downtown. **Air Tickets:** Term D, C-215-879-6829 or 1-800-USA-SATO. **Bus (Comm):** Southeast PA Transportation Authority at all Terminals, 24hrs daily. **Bus (Shuttle):** Airport shuttle to Terminals & parking lots, 24hrs daily. **Car Rentals:** Major companies' counters located in baggage claim areas. **Limo Service:** Hrs: Mon-Fri: 0930, 1230, 1530, 1830, 2100; Sat-Sun and Holidays: 0930, 1530, 2100 Eagle Lines to McGuire AFB, C-609-723-2000. J & G Limo scheduled daily to Dover AFB, C-1-800-441-8775. **Taxi (Comm):** Available at all Terminals, 24hrs daily. **Parking:** Short term-Term D arrivals ($6). Garage D ($10 daily). Remote lot approximately $6 daily.

**TML:** Lodging Office: Limited-availability at Philadelphia NB, (Closes Oct 95) C-215-465-9001 or 1-800-NAVY-INN. Willow Grove NAS/JRB Lodging Office (Bldg 6090, C-215-442-5800/5801, FAX 215-442-5817. Hotels/motels in airport area (reduced rates for AMC Pax).

**TRAVELERS AID: American Red Cross:** Term D, 7 days as required, C-215-365-7490. **Chaplain:** Chapel at Philadelphia Naval Base, duty hours, C-215-465-3054/2896. **USO:** Term D, Hrs: daily 0800-2200, C-215-365-8889.

**OTHER SERVICES:** Gift shops, video arcade, bookstore, florist, postal service center. These facilities and services are available within the airport-Concourse C. **Bank/Exchange:** Term C, machine, Hrs: Daily: 24hrs. **Hair Styles:** Term B (barber). **Medical:** Naval Base/Hospital, Hrs: Daily: 24hrs, C-215-897-8057 (emergency).

**ATTRACTIONS:** Liberty Bell historic exhibits and museums in Philadelphia.

| **ORIGINATING SCHEDULES** | | | |
|---|---|---|---|
| | **APP/PHL-1 FRI DC10** | | |
| **Location ID** | **Airport (Station)** | **Country/State** | **Days Out** |
| PHL | Philadelphia IAP | PA | +0 |
| LGS | Lajes AB | PO | +1 |
| AVB | Aviano AB | IT | +1 |
| **ADA** | **Incirlik APT** | **TU** | **+1** |
| AVB | Aviano AB | IT | +1 |
| LGS | Lajes AB | PO | +2 |
| PHL | Philadelphia IAP | PA | |
| | **APP/PHL-2 WED DC10** | | |
| PHL | Philadelphia IAP | PA | +0 |
| FRF | Rhein-Main AB | GE | +0 |
| **DHA** | **Dhahran IAP** | **SA** | **+1** |
| FRF | Rhein-Main AB | GE | +2 |
| PHL | Philadelphia IAP | PA | |
| | **APP/PHL-3 1st THU DC10** | | |
| PHL | Philadelphia IAP | PA | +0 |
| FRF | Rhein-Main AB | GE | +0 |
| **DHA** | **Dhahran IAP** | **SA** | **+0** |
| FRF | Rhein-Main AB | GE | +1 |
| PHL | Philadelphia IAP | PA | |
| | **APP/PHL-4 TUE DC10** | | |
| PHL | Philadelphia IAP | PA | +0 |
| RTA | Rota NAS | SP | +1 |
| NAP | Capodichino APT | IT | +1 |
| SIZ | Sigonella NAS | IT | +1 |
| **BAH** | **Bahrain IAP** | **BA** | **+1** |
| SIZ | Sigonella NAS | IT | +2 |

*PENNSYLVANIA*
*Philadelphia International Airport, continued*

| NAP | Capodichino APT | IT | +2 |
|---|---|---|---|
| RTA | Rota NAS | SP | +2 |
| PHL | Philadelphia IAP | PA | |
| **IN ROUTE SCHEDULES** | | | |
| **The WM B Hartsfield, ATL IAP** | | APP/ATL-1 | APP/ATL-2 |
| **Norfolk NAS** | APP/NGU-3 | APP/NGU-4 | APP/NGU-5 |

# WILLOW GROVE NAVAL AIR STATION/ JOINT RESERVE BASE (NXX)

Air Operations Department
Willow Grove NAS, PA 19090-5010

**LOCATION:** Take PA Turnpike (I-276), exit 27 (Willow Grove), PA-611, 5 miles to NAS. *USMRA: Page 22 (I,J-6)*. NMC: Philadelphia, 23 miles south. Main installation numbers: C-215-443-XXXX, D-312-991-XXXX, operator 1000, OD 6000 24hrs.

**PAX TERM INFO: C-215-443-6217/6215/recording 6216, D-312-991-6216/7, REC: C-215-443-6216, D-312-991-6216, FAX 215-443-6188.** Bldg 780, Hrs: daily 0700-2300. Directions: From main gate circle to the far left, make first right towards control tower. **Pax Service Office:** Same as Pax Terminal.

**PAX LOUNGES:** DV only; no separate family lounge available. Terminal seats 90. **General:** A/C, TV, bag check, telephones (local and defense), restrooms, vending machines, cargo area. Protocol Services: DV/VIP: PAO, Bldg 1, top deck, 1776/77, Hrs Tue-Sat 0800-1600.

**FOOD SERVICE:** Several off base facilities have delivery services to PAX terminal. Navy Galley: 3 meals daily, standard hours, surcharge applies.

**TRANSPORTATION:** Local bus or cab to Greyhound Terminal or local train. Local train to airport (PHL) or AMTRACK. Limo to-from PHL available via local hotels, $20. Car rentals: C&C Ford across from base. Enterprise will p/u - deliver to terminal. Parking: adjacent to main gate (notify Security Department 6067/68).

**TML:** Lodging Office (Bldg 609), C-215-442-5800/5801, FAX 215-442-5817. DV/VIP: PAO. Bldg 1 top deck, C-215-443-1776/1777, Hrs Tue-Sat 0800-1600.

**TRAVELERS AID: Chaplain:** C-215-443-6002/3/4. **Emergency Relief:** C-215-443-6002 (Navy Relief). **Security Police:** Bldg 1, 24hrs daily, C-215-443-6067/68. **USO:** Naval Base PHL, C-215-336-0908.

**OTHER SERVICES:** Bank: NFCU Automated teller. Exchange: Tue-Sun 1000-1700, 6029. Barber: 6030. Postal 6055. Medical: Bldg 37, 6360, Hrs: daily 0800-1600. After hours medical available at local hospitals.

**ATTRACTIONS:** Philadelphia, New Jersey beaches, and Pocono Mountain area.

**UNSCHEDULED FLIGHTS**

Frequent flights via Navy C-9, C-12A and P-3A, and AFRES C-130E aircraft to: Andrews AFB, MD (**ADW**); Brunswick NAS, ME (**NHZ**); Jacksonville NAS, FL (**NIP**); Lajes Fld, PO (**LGS**); New Orleans NAS, LA (**NBG**); Norfolk NAS, VA (**NGU**); and Rota NAS, SP (**RTA**). Call for destinations, routings and schedules.

# RHODE ISLAND

## QUONSET POINT STATE AIRPORT (OQU)

143rd AG/CP (Air National Guard), 7 Flightline,
North Kingston, RI 02852-7548

**LOCATION:** From US-1 North or South exit to RI-RT-4 South. Or Route 95 North or South to RI-4. Follow signs to airport. *USMRA: Page 17 (J-7).* NMC: Providence, 20 miles north. Main installation numbers: C-401-885-3960, D-312-476-3210.

**PAX TERM INFO: C-401-886-1420, D-312-476-3420.** Air National Guard area, Hrs: Tue-Fri: 0700-1730. Ask Security Police for directions. No military support facilities.

### UNSCHEDULED FLIGHTS

Flights via ANG C-130E aircraft to CONUS and OCONUS locations. Call for destinations, routings and schedules.

# SOUTH CAROLINA

## BEAUFORT MARINE CORPS AIR STATION (NBC)

Traffic Management Office, P.O. Box 55010
Beaufort, SC 29904-5010

**LOCATION:** From I-95, exit at Pocataligo to SC-21, 4 miles to MCAS. Clearly marked. *USMRA: Page 44 (G-9)*. NMC: Savannah GA, 40 miles south. Main installation numbers: C-803-522-7100, D-312-832-7100.

**PAX TERM INFO: C-803-522-7143, D-312-832-7143, FAX: C-803-522-7221.** Bldg 860, Hrs: Mon-Fri: 0800-1630. Directions: From main gate straight on Geiger Blvd to a left on Drayton St to Pax Term on the left. **Pax Service Office:** Same as Pax terminal (NCO on Duty). Many facilities on and off base. For full details see: *U.S. Forces Travel & Transfer Guide U.S.A. and Caribbean Areas.*

**TML:** Lodging Office (Bldg 431), C-803-522-7676. de Treville House, Bldg 1108, C-803-522-1633. All ranks. DV/VIP: Contact CO, Bldg 601, C-803-522-7158.

### UNSCHEDULED FLIGHTS

Frequent administrative flights via C-009A and other aircraft to CONUS and OCONUS locations. Call for destinations, routings and schedules.

## CHARLESTON AIR FORCE BASE (CHS)

437th APS/TROP, 105 South Bates St.,
Charleston AFB, SC 29404-5006

**LOCATION:** From I-26 East exit (211A) to West Aviation Ave to 2nd traffic light turn right. Follow road around end of runway to Gate 2 (River Gate). *USMRA: Page 44 (H-8, 9)*. NMC: Charleston, 5 miles southeast. Main installation numbers: C-803-566-6000, D-312-673-6000.

**PAX TERM INFO: C-803-566-3082/3083/3048, D-312-673-3082/3083/3048. FAX: C-803-566-3060, D-312-673-3060.** Bldg 164, Hrs: daily 0500-2300, West side across from commercial airport & ATC tower. Check-in manned 0500-2300 daily. After hours information call C-803-566-3082. **Pax Service Office:** Bldg 164, Hrs: Mon-Fri: 0730-1630, C-803-566-3082, D-312-673-3082. **Pax Paging:** Bldg 164, Hrs: daily 0500-2300, C-803-566-3082, D-312-673-3082. Note: There is dual sign-up between Charleston AFB and Charleston IAP.

**PAX LOUNGES:** Dependents lounge & nursery. See Pax Shift Supervisor. **General:** Bldg 164 (adjacent to check-in scales), Hrs: daily 0500-2300, C-803-566-3082. A/C, bag lockers, telephones (commercial and defense), TV lounge, restrooms, P/C seats. **Dependent Lounge:** Bldg 164 (right of main entrance), Hrs: daily 0500-2300, C-803-

*SOUTH CAROLINA*
*Charleston Air Force Base, continued*

566-3082. **DV/VIP:** Bldg 164, Hrs: daily 0500-2300, C-803-566-3082, D-312-673-3082. Flight line at end of building (unmanned). See Pax Service Shift Supervisor. A/C, telephones (commercial and defense), TV, rest-rooms, O/S seats. **Protocol Service:** Bldg 103, Hrs: Mon-Fri: 0730-1630, C-803-566-5644, D-312-673-5644.

**FOOD SERVICE: Dining Hall:** Bldg 250, 4 meals daily, C-803-566-2395/3590. **In-flight Meals:** Bldg 166, 24hrs daily, C-803-566-3103. **NCO/CPO Club:** Bldg 325, Hrs: daily 0630-2300, C-803-566-2930. **O'Club:** Bldg 355, Hrs: Mon-Sat: 0830-2300, C-803-566-3924 (lunch/dinner). **Burger King:** Hrs: Sat-Thu: 0600-2230, Fri: 0600-2000, C-803-760-1533. **Snack Bars:** Bldg 214, Hrs: Mon-Fri: 0900-2300, Sat: 1000-2400, Sun: 1300-2200, C-803-566-2600 (sandwiches/salad/pizza); Bldg 1990 (BX), Hrs: daily 1000-1800, C-803-552-9415 (snack bar/ice cream). **Golf Course:** Bldg 370, Hrs: daily 0800-1600, C-803-566-4177 (breakfast/sandwiches). **Vending:** Bldg 164, 24 hrs daily, C-803-566-2610.

**TRANSPORTATION: Air Tickets:** SATO: Bldg 164, Hrs: Mon-Fri: 0800-2000, call for weekend hours, C-803-566-3092. **Bus (Comm):** Charleston, Hrs: daily 0630-1000, Greyhound: C-803-744-4245, Trailways: C-803-723-8649. **Car Rentals:** Main Exchange, Hrs: daily 1000-1700, C-803-760-0066. **Taxi (Comm):** Bldg 164, 24hrs daily, C-803-554-7575 (on & off Base). **Taxi (Gov):** Bldg 408, 24hrs daily, C-803-566-3361 (duty only). **Parking:** Long term located at Scott St and Davis Dr. across from child care center.

**TML:** Lodging Office (The Charleston House, Bldg 322, 102 N. Davis Dr), 24hrs daily, C-803-552-9900/803-566-3806, D-312-673-2100 EX-860, FAX: C-803-566-3394. From Pax Term dial 60. DV/VIP: Hrs: daily 0800-1700, C-803-566-5644, O6+. Charleston Naval Base: Navy Lodge: C-803-747-7676 or 1-800-NAVY-INN.

**TRAVELERS AID: American Red Cross:** Bldg 500, Hrs: Mon-Fri: 0800-1700, C-803-566-3377/8, Emergency C-803-566-3552. After hours C-803-744-3552. **Chaplain:** Bldg 217, Hrs: Mon-Fri: 0730-1630, C-803-566-3327 (on call after hours); Bldg 1005, Hrs: Mon-Fri: 0730-1630, C-803-566-2536 (on call after hours). **Emergency Relief:** Bldg 503, Hrs: Mon-Fri: 0730-1630, C-803-566-2457. **Lost/Found:** Bldg 164, Hrs: Mon-Fri: 0730-1630, C-803-566-2369. After hours C-803-566-2348. **Security Police:** Bldg 263, 24hrs daily, C-803-566-3642. **USO:** CHS-IAP, C-803-767-3963 (call for hours).

**OTHER SERVICES: Exchange:** Bldg 1990, Hrs: Mon-Fri: 0900-1800, Thu, Sat: 0900-1900, Sun: 1100-1700, C-803-552-5000. **Bank/Exchange:** SC National: Bldg 306, Hrs: Mon-Fri: 0900-1630, C-803-724-5055, closed 1300-1500. **Hair Styles:** Bldg 1990, Hrs: Mon-Sat: 0800-1800, Sun: 1100-1700, Barber: C-803-552-4880; Beauty: C-803-552-0812; Barber/Beauty: Bldg 237, Hrs: daily 1000-1800, C-803-760-2315. **Laundry/Dry Cleaning:** Bldg 1990, Hrs: Mon-Sat: 1000-1800, C-803-767-3412. **Medical:** Bldg 1000, 24hrs daily, (Emergency) C-803-566-3821, D-312-673-3821. **Postal/Wire:** Bldg 306, Hrs: Mon-Fri: 0900-1600, C-803-566-2370 (Western Union in town). **Porter:** Commercial Term (during commercial contract mission processing only). **POV Shipment:** Airport Auto Processing: C 803 744-7412, 767-8900, Gibson Auto Processing: C-803-553-8180, Carolina Auto Processing: C-803-554-7253/747-0144, Owner Processing: C-803-743-5470.

**ATTRACTIONS:** Charleston Naval Base, Beaches, period homes.

| **ORIGINATING SCHEDULES** | | | |
|---|---|---|---|
| | **APM/CHS-1 2nd TUE C-141B** | | |
| **Location ID** | **Airport (Station)** | **Country/State** | **Days Out** |
| CHS | Charleston AFB/IAP | SC | +0 |
| BSB | Brasilia APT | BR | +1 |
| **BUE** | **Ezeiza APT** | **AG** | **+1** |
| MVD | Carrasco IAP | UG | +2 |
| BSB | Brasilia APT | BR | +2 |
| CHS | Charleston AFB/IAP | SC | |
| | **APM/CHS-2 3rd TUE C-141B** | | |
| CHS | Charleston AFB/IAP | SC | +0 |
| BSB | Brasilia APT | BR | +1 |
| **ASU** | **Pres Stroessner APT** | **PG** | **+1** |
| RIO | Rio De Janeiro IAP | BR | +2 |
| BSB | Brasilia APT | BR | +2 |
| CHS | Charleston AFB/IAP | SC | |
| | **ACC/CHS-3 1st/3rd SUN, 3rd TUE, 4th SAT C-141B** | | |
| CHS | Charleston AFB/IAP | SC | +0 |
| DOV | Dover AFB | DE | +1 |
| **MHZ** | **RAF Mildenhall** | **UK** | **+2** |
| DOV | Dover AFB | DE | +3 |
| CHS | Charleston AFB/IAP | SC | |
| | **ACC/CHS-4 1st/3rd SAT C-17A** | | |
| CHS | Charleston AFB/IAP | SC | +0 |
| DOV | Dover AFB | DE | +1 |
| **MHZ** | **RAF Mildenhall** | **UK** | **+2** |
| DOV | Dover AFB | DE | +3 |
| CHS | Charleston AFB/IAP | SC | |
| | **ACC/CHS-5 3rd TUE C-141B** | | |
| CHS | Charleston AFB/IAP | SC | +0 |
| DOV | Dover AFB | DE | +0 |
| RMS | Ramstein AB | GE | +2 |

*SOUTH CAROLINA*
*Charleston Air Force Base, continued*

| | | | |
|---|---|---|---|
| **CAI** | **Cairo IAP** | **EG** | **+2** |
| RMS | Ramstein AB | GE | +3 |
| LGS | Lajes AB | PO | +3 |
| DOV | Dover AFB | DE | +4 |
| CHS | Charleston AFB/IAP | SC | |
| | **APM/CHS-6 3rd/4th SAT C-141B** | | |
| CHS | Charleston AFB/IAP | SC | +0 |
| DOV | Dover AFB | DE | +1 |
| RMS | Ramstein AB | GE | +2 |
| ADA | Incirlik APT | TU | +3 |
| AKT | Akrotiri APT | CY | +3 |
| ADA | Incirlik APT | TU | +4 |
| IGL | Cigli TAFB | TU | +4 |
| YES | Ataturk/Yesilkoy IAP | TU | +4 |
| **ADA** | **Incirlik APT** | **TU** | **+5** |
| DIY | Diyarbakir APT | TU | +5 |
| ESB | Esenboga APT | TU | +5 |
| ADA | Incirlik APT | TU | +6 |
| RMS | Ramstein AB | GE | +7 |
| KEF | Keflavik APT | IC | +7 |
| DOV | Dover AFB | DE | +8 |
| CHS | Charleston AFB/IAP | SC | |
| | **ACC/CHS-7 3rd TUE C-141B** | | |
| CHS | Charleston AFB/IAP | SC | +0 |
| DOV | Dover AFB | DE | +0 |
| RMS | Ramstein AB | GE | +1 |
| KWI | Kuwait IAP | KW | +1 |
| **DHA** | **Dhahran IAP** | **SA** | **+2** |
| SIZ | Sigonella NAS | IT | +2 |
| RTA | Rota NAS | SP | +3 |
| NGU | Norfolk NAS | VA | +4 |
| CHS | Charleston AFB/IAP | SC | |
| | **ACM/CHS-8 1st/2nd/4th MON C-141B** | | |
| CHS | Charleston AFB/IAP | SC | +0 |
| DOV | Dover AFB | DE | +1 |
| RMS | Ramstein AB | GE | +2 |
| MHZ | RAF Mildenhall | UK | +2 |
| RMS | Ramstein AB | GE | +2 |

| | | | |
|---|---|---|---|
| AVB | Aviano AB | IT | +3 |
| MHZ | RAF Mildenhall | UK | +3 |
| RMS | Ramstein AB | GE | +4 |
| AVB | Aviano AB | IT | +4 |
| RMS | Ramstein AB | GE | +5 |
| **ADA** | **Incirlik APT** | **TU** | **+6** |
| RMS | Ramstein AB | GE | +7 |
| MHZ | RAF Mildenhall | UK | +7 |
| AVB | Aviano AB | IT | +8 |
| RMS | Ramstein AB | GE | +8 |
| RTA | Rota NAS | SP | +9 |
| SIZ | Sigonella NAS | IT | +9 |
| RMS | Ramstein AB | GE | +10 |
| LGS | Lajes AB | PO | +10 |
| DOV | Dover AFB | DE | +11 |
| CHS | Charleston AFB/IAP | SC | |
| | **APP/CHS-9 2nd/4th MON L1011** | | |
| CHS | Charleston AFB/IAP | SC | +0 |
| IAD | Dulles IAP | VA | +0 |
| **FRF** | **Rhein-Main AB** | **GE** | **+1** |
| IAD | Dulles IAP | VA | +1 |
| CHS | Charleston AFB/IAP | SC | |
| | **ACM/CHS-10 TUE C-141B** | | |
| CHS | Charleston AFB/IAP | SC | +0 |
| **PAP** | **Francois Duvalier IAP** | **HA** | **+0** |
| CHS | Charleston AFB/IAP | SC | |
| | **ACC/CHS-11 2nd/3rd TUE, 2nd/3rd WED, 3rd SAT C-17A** | | |
| CHS | Charleston AFB/IAP | SC | +0 |
| **HOW** | **Howard AFB** | **PN** | **+1** |
| CHS | Charleston AFB/IAP | SC | |
| | **ACC/CHS-12 4th TUE C-141B** | | |
| CHS | Charleston AFB/IAP | SC | +0 |
| SKF | Kelly AFB | TX | +0 |
| **HOW** | **Howard AB** | **PN** | **+1** |
| SKF | Kelly AFB | TX | +1 |
| CHS | Charleston AFB/IAP | SC | |
| | **ACC/CHS-13 4th THU C-141B** | | |
| CHS | Charleston AFB/IAP | SC | +0 |

*SOUTH CAROLINA*
*Charleston Air Force Base, continued*

| | | | |
|---|---|---|---|
| LGS | Lajes AB | PO | +0 |
| DKR | Dakar Yoff APT | SE | +1 |
| **FIH** | **Kinshasa Ndjiu APT** | **ZA** | **+1** |
| DKR | Dakar Yoff APT | SE | +2 |
| LGS | Lajes AB | PO | +3 |
| CHS | Charleston AFB/IAP | SC | |
| | **ACC/CHS-14 2nd THU C-141B** | | |
| CHS | Charleston AFB/IAP | SC | +0 |
| LGS | Lajes AB | PO | +1 |
| DKR | Dakar Yoff APT | SE | +2 |
| NDJ | N Djamena IAP | CD | +3 |
| **FIH** | **Kinshasa Ndjiu IAP** | **ZA** | **+3** |
| DKR | Dakar Yoff APT | SE | +4 |
| LGS | Lajes AB | PO | +5 |
| CHS | Charleston AFB/IAP | SC | |
| | **ACC/CHS-15 3rd/4th FRI C-141B** | | |
| CHS | Charleston AFB/IAP | SC | +0 |
| WRI | McGuire AFB | NJ | +0 |
| LGS | Lajes AB | PO | +1 |
| **RMS** | **Ramstein AB** | **GE** | **+9** |
| LGS | Lajes AB | PO | +10 |
| DOV | Dover AFB | DE | +10 |
| CHS | Charleston AFB/IAP | SC | |
| | **ACC/CHS-16 1st THU C-141B** | | |
| CHS | Charleston AFB/IAP | SC | +0 |
| NGU | Norfolk NAS | VA | +0 |
| KEF | Keflavik APT | IC | +1 |
| **RMS** | **Ramstein AB** | **GE** | **+2** |
| ADW | Andrews AFB | MD | +3 |
| CHS | Charleston AFB/IAP | SC | |
| | **ACC/CHS-17 1st/2nd/3rd SUN C-141B** | | |
| CHS | Charleston AFB/IAP | SC | +0 |
| NGU | Norfolk NAS | VA | +0 |
| RTA | Rota NAS | SP | +2 |
| NAP | Capodichino APT | IT | +2 |
| SIZ | Sigonella NAS | IT | +3 |
| BAH | Bahrain IAP | BA | +3 |
| **FUJ** | **Fujairah IAP** | **UA** | **+4** |

| | | | |
|---|---|---|---|
| BAH | Bahrain IAP | BA | +4 |
| SIZ | Sigonella NAS | IT | +5 |
| SOC | Souda Bay NAF | CR | +5 |
| SIZ | Sigonella NAS | IT | +6 |
| NAP | Capodichino APT | IT | +6 |
| RTA | Rota NAS | SP | +7 |
| NGU | Norfolk NAS | VA | +7 |
| CHS | Charleston AFB/IAP | SC | |
| | **ACC/CHS-18 3rd SAT C-141B** | | |
| CHS | Charleston AFB/IAP | SC | +0 |
| NGU | Norfolk NAS | VA | +1 |
| RTA | Rota NAS | SP | +2 |
| SIZ | Sigonella NAS | IT | +3 |
| KRT | Khartoum APT | SU | +3 |
| **NBO** | **Jomo Kenyatta IAP** | **KE** | **+4** |
| SIZ | Sigonella NAS | IT | +5 |
| LGS | Lajes AB | PO | +6 |
| NGU | Norfolk NAS | VA | +6 |
| CHS | Charleston AFB/IAP | SC | |
| | **ACM/CHS-19 1st/4th TUE C-141B** | | |
| CHS | Charleston AFB/IAP | SC | +0 |
| COF | Patrick AFB | FL | +1 |
| SJH | V C Bird IAP | AN | +1 |
| **ASI** | **Ascension AUX AFB** | **UK** | **+3** |
| SJH | V C Bird IAP | AN | +3 |
| COF | Patrick AFB | FL | +3 |
| CHS | Charleston AFB/IAP | SC | |
| | **ACC/CHS-20 2nd/3rd/4th WED C-17A** | | |
| CHS | Charleston AFB/IAP | SC | +0 |
| PLA | Soto Cano AB | HO | +0 |
| **HOW** | **Howard AB** | **PN** | **+1** |
| PLA | Soto Cano AB | HO | +1 |
| CHS | Charleston AFB/IAP | SC | |
| | **ACC/CHS-21 4th WED C-141B** | | |
| CHS | Charleston AFB/IAP | SC | +0 |
| PLA | Soto Cano AB | HO | +0 |
| **HOW** | **Howard AB** | **PN** | **+1** |
| PLA | Soto Cano AB | HO | +1 |

***SOUTH CAROLINA***
***Charleston Air Force Base, continued***

| | | | |
|---|---|---|---|
| PLA | Soto Cano AB | HO | +1 |
| CHS | Charleston AFB/IAP | SC | |
| | **APP/CHS-22 2nd/3rd/4th/5th FRI** | **B727** | |
| CHS | Charleston AFB/IAP | SC | +0 |
| ATL | The WM B Hartsfield, ATL IAP | GA | +0 |
| **HOW** | **Howard AB** | **PN** | **+1** |
| ATL | The WM B Hartsfield, ATL IAP | GA | +1 |
| CHS | Charleston AFB/IAP | SC | |
| | **APP/CHS-23 SUN B757** | | |
| CHS | Charleston AFB/IAP | SC | +0 |
| ATL | The WM B Hartsfield, ATL IAP | GA | +0 |
| HOW | Howard AB | PN | +0 |
| PLA | Soto Cano AB | HO | +1 |
| **HOW** | **Howard AB** | **PN** | **+1** |
| ATL | The WM B Hartsfield, ATL IAP | GA | +1 |
| CHS | Charleston AFB/IAP | SC | |
| | **APP/CHS-24 1st FRI B727** | | |
| CHS | Charleston AFB/IAP | SC | +0 |
| ATL | The WM B Hartsfield, ATL IAP | GA | +0 |
| **PTY** | **Tocumen/Torrijos IAP** | **PN** | **+1** |
| ATL | The WM B Hartsfield, ATL IAP | GA | +1 |
| CHS | Charleston AFB/IAP | SC | |

| **IN ROUTE SCHEDULES** | | | |
|---|---|---|---|
| **Andrews AFB** | ADW/MEDEVAC-2 | | |
| **Dover AFB** | ACC/DOV-1 | | |
| **Kelly AFB** | ACC/SKF-1 | | |
| **McGuire AFB** | APM/WRI-3 | ACC/WRI-4 | APM/WRI-5 |
| **Scott AFB** | BLV/MEDEVAC-1 | | |
| **Westover ARB** | ACC/CEF-1 | | |

**UNSCHEDULED FLIGHTS**

Flights to: Dobbins AFB GA (**MGE**); Greenville/Spartanburg Arpt SC (**GSP**); Jacksonville NAS FL (**NIP**); MacDill AFB FL (**MCF**); Pope AFB NC (**POB**); Roosevelt Roads NAS PR (**NRR**); and Scott AFB IL (**BLV**).

# CHARLESTON INTERNATIONAL AIRPORT (CHS)

437th APS, Aerial Port Gateway,
5500 International Blvd, Suite 124
Charleston IAP, SC 29418-0308

**LOCATION:** From I-26 E take I-526 W 1 mi to airport exit. Turn right onto International Blvd, follow signs to Apt. *USMRA: Page 44 (H-8,9)*. NMC: Charleston, 5 miles SE. Main installation numbers: C-803-566-5794/95, D-312-673-5794/95.

**PAX INFO: C-803-566-5795/94, D-312-673-5794/95, REC: C-803-566-5794 (during non-operation hours), FAX: C-803-566-3845, D-312-673-3845.** Main ticket lobby, Hrs: Mon-Fri: 0700-2000, Sat-Sun: 0800-1700, **Pax Service Office:** Main lobby, same as Pax Term, C-803-566-5794/95. **Pax Paging:** Same as Pax Term, C-803-566-5795/94 or Airport Paging: C-803-767-7009. Note: There is dual Space-A sign-up between Charleston AFB and Charleston IAP.

**PAX LOUNGES:** No separate DV/VIP or family lounges. **General:** Commercial facilities in IAP. USO Lounge on ground floor, under domestic baggage claim, C-803-767-3963 See Charleston AFB listing.

**OTHER SERVICES:** See Charleston Air Force Base listing.

# COLUMBIA METROPOLITAN AIRPORT (CAE)

Jimmie Doolittle Flight Facility
2625-B Airport Blvd
West Columbia, SC 29170-2144

**LOCATION:** From I-26, exit 113 south on SC-302 (Airport Blvd) to airport. USMRA: page 44 (F-6). NMC: Columbia, 5 miles northeast. Main installation numbers: C-803-822-5010.

**PAX TERM INFO: C-803-822-5809/5810, FAX 803-822-5808.** Jimmie Doolittle Flight Facility. Ask Security Police for directions. All support of regional airport. Full post support at nearby Fort Jackkson.

**UNSCHEDULED FLIGHTS**

Very limited flights. Call for destinations, routings and schedules.

# McENTIRE AIR NATIONAL GUARD BASE (MMT)

Eastover, SC 29044-5000

**LOCATION:** On SC Highway 378 between Sumter and Columbia, SC. *USMRA: Page 44 (G-6, 7)*. NMC: Columbia, SC, 15 miles west. Main telephone numbers. C-803-776-

5121, D-312-583-8301.

*SOUTH CAROLINA*

*McEntire Air National Guard Base, continued*

**PAX TERM INFO**: C-803-695-6210, D-312-583-8210. EM Club-EX-326, Medical EX-295, NCO Club-EX-326, Police EX-284.

**TML:** Fort Jackson, SC, 18 miles west. Lodging Office: Bldg 2785, C-803-751-6223, D-312-734-6223.

**UNSCHEDULED FLIGHTS**

Infrequent flights via Army National Guard aircraft and transient aircraft to CONUS locations. Call for destinations, routings and schedules.

# SOUTH DAKOTA

## ELLSWORTH AIR FORCE BASE (RCA)

28 OSS/OSAA,
1820 Vandenberg Ct, Suite 2
Ellsworth AFB, SD 57706-4708

**LOCATION:** Off I-90, 10 miles east of Rapid City. Clearly marked. *USMRA: Page 85 (B-5)*. NMC: Rapid City, 10 miles west. Main installation numbers: C-605-385-1000, D-312-675-1110.

**PAX TERM INFO: C-605-385-1052, D-312-675-1052, FAX: C-605-385-1063.** Bldg 7506, 24hrs daily. Directions: From main gate straight on Rushmore Dr to a right on Sixth St. Left on East-West Rd to dead end at Pax Term (Base Ops). **Pax Service Office:** Bldg: 7506, 24hrs daily, C-605-385-1052 (NCO on duty).

**PAX LOUNGES:** No separate family lounge. **General:** Bldg 7506, 24hrs daily, C-605-385-1052. A/C, restrooms, showers, lobby seats. **DV/VIP:** Bldg 7506, 24hrs daily, C-605-385-1052. A/C, coffee/soda available, O/S seats. **Protocol Service:** Bldg 7810, C-605-385-1205.

**FOOD SERVICE: Dining Hall:** Bldg 2106, C-605-385-1625. **NCO/CPO Club:** Bldg 2010, C-605-385-1764. **O'Club:** Bldg 5903, C-605-385-1764. **Snack Bar:** Bldg 4001, C-605-923-1455. **Vending:** Bldg 7506, 24hrs daily.

**TRANSPORTATION:** Very limited on base. Rent-a-car on/off base and taxi in Rapid City. **Taxi (Gov):** Bldg 7510, C-605-385-2910 (duty Pax only). **Parking:** Bldg 7506, C-605-385-1052 (reserved spaces in front).

**TML:** Lodging Office (Pine Tree Inn, Bldg 1103, 2349), 24hrs daily, C-605-385-2844, D-312-675-2844, FAX 605-385-2718. All ranks. DV/VIP: C-605-385-1205, O6+.

**TRAVELERS AID: American Red Cross:** Bldg 1107, C-605-385-1381, after hours C-605-385-1000. **Chaplain:** Bldg 2009, C-605-385-1598. **Lost/Found:** Bldg 7506, C-605-385-1052. **Security Police:** Bldg 4400, C-605-385-4010.

**OTHER SERVICES: Exchange:** Bldg: 4001, C-605-923-5821. Also, hair styles and laundry/dry cleaning. **Bank/Exchange:** Bldg: 4005, C-605-923-1405. **Medical:** Bldg: 6000, Hrs: Daily: 24hrs, C-605-385-7630, D-312-675-7630. **Postal:** Bldg: 3602, C-605-385-6229.

**ATTRACTIONS:** Black Hills and Mt Rushmore nearby, outdoor recreation.

| IN ROUTE SCHEDULES | |
|---|---|
| **Buckley ANGB** | BKF/MEDEVAC-1 |
| **Scott AFB** | BLV/MEDEVAC-7 |

# TENNESSEE

## McGHEE TYSON AIRPORT (TYS)

134th ARFG/OTB
Louisville, TN 37901-5000

**LOCATION:** Exit north or south from US-129 to airport. *USMRA: Page 41 (L-8)*. NMC: Knoxville, 10 miles northeast. Main installation numbers: C-615-985-3200, D-312-266-8200.

**PAX TERM INFO: C-615-985-4403, D-312-266-4403.** Air National Guard area, Hrs: Mon-Fri: 0800-1630. Limited support on base. Dispensary: C-615-985-4277; BX C-615-985-3400.

**TML:** Lodging Office, C-615-985-3330, all ranks.

| ORIGINATING SCHEDULES | | | |
|---|---|---|---|
| **ACC/TYS-1 3rd TUE KC135R** | | | |
| **Location ID** | **Airport (Station)** | **Country/State** | **Days Out** |
| TYS | McGhee Tyson APT | TN | +0 |
| WRI | McGuire AFB | NJ | +0 |
| **LGS** | **Lajes AB** | **PO** | **+2** |
| WRI | McGuire AFB | NJ | +2 |
| TYS | McGhee Tyson APT | TN | |

**UNSCHEDULED FLIGHTS**

Flights to CONUS and OCONUS locations via ANG KC-135A aircraft. Call for destinations, routings and schedules.

## MEMPHIS INTERNATIONAL AIRPORT (MEM)

164th AG (ANG)
2815 Democrat Road
Memphis, TN 38181-0026

**LOCATION:** From I-55 North or South, exit 5A (Brooks Rd) East 2 miles to IAP, left on Airways to Democrat Rd, right to 164th Air National Guard Base (North side of IAP). *USMRA: Page 40 (A-10)*. NMC: Memphis, 3 miles. Main installation numbers: C-901-369-4111, D-312-966-8210.

**PAX TERM INFO: C-901-541-7131, D-312-966-8131, FAX: C-901-541-7230, D-312-966-8230.** Air National Guard area, Hrs: Mon-Fri: 0715-1545. Ask Security Police for directions. All the facilities of an IAP. On base clinic.

***Note: There are no lodging, dining, or transportation facilites available. For Support Services See Memphis Naval Air Station.***

| ORIGINATING SCHEDULES | | | |
|---|---|---|---|
| | **ACM/MEM-1 3rd THU C-141B** | | |
| **Location ID** | **Airport (Station)** | **Country/State** | **Days Out** |
| MEM | Memphis IAP | TN | +0 |
| DOV | Dover AFB | DE | +1 |
| **MHZ** | **RAF Mildenhall** | **UK** | **+2** |
| DOV | Dover AFB | DE | +3 |
| MEM | Memphis IAP | TN | |
| | **ACC/MEM-2 FRI C-141B** | | |
| MEM | Memphis IAP | TN | +0 |
| NGU | Norfolk NAS | VA | +1 |
| **NBW** | **Guantanamo Bay NAS** | **CU** | **+1** |
| NRR | Roosevelt Roads NAS | PR | +2 |
| NGU | Norfolk NAS | VA | +2 |
| MEM | Memphis IAP | TN | |

**UNSCHEDULED FLIGHTS**

Flights to CONUS and OCONUS locations via ANG C-141B aircraft. Call for destinations, routings and schedules.

# MEMPHIS NAVAL AIR STATION (NQA)

Air Operations N2
Millington, TN 38054-5060

**LOCATION:** From US-51 North at Millington, exit to Navy Rd, turn right to first gate on right (main gate). *USMRA: Page 40 (B-9,10)*. NMC: Memphis, 20 miles southwest. Main installation numbers: C-901-873-5111, D-312-966-5111.

**PAX TERM INFO: C-901-873-5331/5332/5726, D-312-966-5331/5332/5726, REC: C-901-873-5332, D-312-966-5332.** Bldg N-2, Hrs: Mon-Fri 0700-2000, Sat-Sun 0800-1700. Directions: From Gate #2, straight on 5th Ave to dead end at Air Term. Duty desk - lst floor. **Pax Service Office:** Bldg N-2, Hrs: Mon-Fri 0700-2000, Sat-Sun 0800-1700, C-901-873-5331 (NCO on duty).

**PAX LOUNGES:** Limited lounge facilities. General lounge seats 26. **General:** Bldg N-2, Hrs: Mon-Fri 0700-2000, Sat-Sun 0800-1700, C-901-873-5331. A/C, telephones (local and long distance), TV, restrooms, P/C seats. **DV/VIP:** Bldg N-2, Hrs: Mon-Fri 0700-2000, Sat-Sun 0800-1700, C-901-873-5331 (07+). A/C, coffee served, telephones (local and defense), O/S seats, TV. **Protocol Service:** Bldg S-1, 24hrs daily, C-901-873-5500.

*TENNESSEE*
*Memphis Naval Air Station, continued*

**FOOD SERVICE: Cafeteria:** C-901-872-1170. **Dining Hall:** Ellison, C-901-873-5111. **Enlisted Club:** C-901-873-5131. **NCO/CPO Club:** C-901-873-5442. **O'Club:** C-901-873-5115. **Snack Bars:** C-901-873-7762. **Vending:** C-901-873-5331.

**TRANSPORTATION: Air Tickets:** SATO: C-901-872-0104. **Bus (Shuttle):** C-901-577-7750 ($8.00 to Memphis). **Car Rentals:** Ryburn: C-901-872-8181. **Taxi (Comm):** C-901-872-3321; C-901-873-5752/5509. **Parking:** C-901-873-5331 (short term-24 hours in front; long term-30 days if approved by Ops Duty Officer).

**TML:** Lodging Office, C-901-873-7082/5348/5459, D-312-966-7082, FAX: C-901-873-7271. Navy Lodge. Bldg N-762, N-931, C-901-872-0121 or 1-800-NAVY-INN, FAX: C-901-873-1695. DV/VIP: Cmdr, C-901-872-5101/2, 06+.

**TRAVELERS AID: American Red Cross:** C-901-873-5607, after hours C-901-873-5509. **Chaplain:** C-901-873-5344. **Emergency Relief:** C-901-873-7266 (Navy Relief). **Security Police:** Bldg: S-2, C-901-873-5533. **USO:** C-901-872-7722.

**OTHER SERVICES: Exchange:** C-901-872-7716/0138. **Hair Styles:** Barber: C-901-872-2191; Beauty: C-901-872-2197. **Laundry/Dry Cleaning:** C-901-872-2427. **Medical:** C-901-873-5801/5444, D-312-966-5921/5444. **Postal:** C-901-873-5577.

**ATTRACTIONS:** Mississippi River, Graceland, Beal Street.

| IN ROUTE SCHEDULES | |
|---|---|
| **Kelly AFB** | SKF/MEDEVAC-1 |

**UNSCHEDULED FLIGHTS**

Frequent flights to the following destinations via Navy C-12A/P, and C9 aircraft. Call for routings and schedules which are updated every 12 hours: Alameda NAS, CA (**NGZ**); Birmingham Municipal Apt, AL (**BHM**); Buckley ANGB, CO (**BKF**); Cecil Field NAS, FL (**NZC**); Cherry Point MCAS, NC (**NKT**); Columbia Metro Apt, SC (**CAE**); Columbus AFB, MS (**CBM**); Dallas NAS, TX (**NBE**); Dobbins AFB/Atlanta NAS, GA (**MGE**); Glenview NAS, IL (**NBU**); Jacksonville, NAS FL (**NIP**); Keesler AFB, MS (**BIX**); Key West NAS, FL (**NQX**); Kingsville NAS, TX (**NQI**); Lemoore NAS, CA (**NLC**); Miramar NAS, CA (**NKX**); New Orleans NAS, LA (**NBG**); Norfolk NAS, VA (**NGU**); North Island NAS, CA (**NZY**); Oceana NAS, VA (**NTU**); Orlando Executive Apt, FL (**ORL**); Patuxent River NAWC, MD (**NHK**); Pensacola NAS, FL (**NPA**); Point Mugu NAS, CA (**NTD**); Richards-Gebaur AFB, MO (**GVW**); Rickenbacker ANGB, OH (**LCK**); Scott AFB, IL (**BLV**); Selfridge ANGB, MI (**MTC**); Washington NAF, MD (**NSF**); and Whidbey Island NAS, WA (**NUW**).

# NASHVILLE METROPOLITAN AIRPORT (BNA)

118th AW, ANG
240 Knapp Boulevard
Nashville, TN 37217-0267

**LOCATION:** From I-40 East to Exit 216B, from I-40 West to Exit 216. South on Donelson Pike 2 miles, right on Knapp Blvd. *USMRA: Page 40 (G,H-8)*. NMC: Nashville, 4 miles northwest. Main installation numbers: C-615-361-4600, D-312-778-6210.

**PAX TERM INFO: C-615-399-6581, D-312-778-6581.** After 1530 hrs C-615-399-5807. Bldg 721, Hrs: Mon-Fri: 0700-1530. Ask Security Police for directions. All the support facilities of a regional airport. Limited military support facilities, BX: C-615-399-5638.

## UNSCHEDULED FLIGHTS

Flights to CONUS and OCONUS locations via ANG C-130E aircraft. Must show I.D. for schedules.

# TEXAS

## BIGGS ARMY AIRFIELD (BIF)

1733 Pleasonton Road
Fort Bliss, TX 79916-6816

**LOCATION:** Accessible from I-10 or US-54 North or South. *USMRA: Page 86 (B-6)*. NMC: El Paso, within northeast section of the city limits. Main installation numbers: C-915-568-2121, D-312-978-0831.

**PAX TERM INFO: C-915-568-8097, D-312-978-8097.** Bldg 11210, Hrs: Mon-Fri: 0600-2200, Sat-Sun: 0800-1600. Northeast of main post off Wilson Rd. Limited facilities.

**PAX LOUNGES: General:** Bldg 11210 near south entrance, same hours and phone as above. A/C, restrooms, P/C and O/S seats. **DV/VIP:** Bldg 11210 opposite dispatch counter, same hours and phone as above. **Protocol Service:** Hrs: Mon-Fri: 0730-1630, C-915-568-5330.

**TML:** Lodging Office (Bldg 251, Club Rd), C-915-568-4888, D-312-978-4888. The Inn at Fort Bliss, C-915-565-7777, FAX: C-915-568-7078, D-312-978-7078, all ranks. DV/VIP: Protocol Office, C-915-568-5319/5225, O7+

**ATTRACTIONS:** Museums, Rio Grande River, Tigua Indian Reservation

| IN ROUTE SCHEDULES | |
|---|---|
| **Scott AFB** | BLV/MEDEVAC-8 |
| **Travis AFB** | SUU/MEDEVAC-1 |

### UNSCHEDULED FLIGHTS

Limited flights via C-12A and C-21A aircraft. Some transient aircraft activity via C-141B and C-005A/B. Call for destinations, routings, and schedules.

## CORPUS CHRISTI NAVAL AIR STATION (NGP)

Air Operations Dept/Flight Clearance
Corpus Christi NAS, TX 78419-5021

**LOCATION:** On TX-358, southeast side of Corpus Christi. The South Gate is on NAS Drive. *USMRA: Page 87 (K-8)*. NMC: Corpus Christi, 10 miles west. Main installation numbers: C-512-939-2811, D-312-861-1110.

**PAX TERM INFO: C-512-939-2505, D-312-861-2505, REC: C-512-939-3385, D-312-861-3385.** Hangar 58, 1st floor, Hrs: Mon-Fri: 0800-1700. Directions: From South Gate straight on Lexington Blvd to a left on 1st St to a left on Ave D to Pax Term on the left. **Pax Service Office:** Same as Pax Term, C-512-939-2505 (POIC on duty).

**PAX LOUNGES:** Limited facilities. No separate DV/VIP or family lounges. **General:** C-512-939-2505. A/C, restrooms, P/C seats. **Protocol Service:** Bldg 1, Hrs: Mon-Fri: 0800-1600, C-512-939-2284.

**FOOD SERVICE: Restaurant:** C-512-937-2249, **Club:** C-512-939-2541.

**TRANSPORTATION: Bus (Comm):** C-512-989-2600. **Taxi:** American Cab: 512-881-8294. **Limo Service:** C-512-989-5466. **Parking:** At Hangar 58 (must have tag from Security Police).

**TML:** Lodging Office (Bldg 101 & 1281, Ocean Drive), Hrs: Mon-Fri: 0800-1700, C-512-939-2388/89, D-312-861-6361. EM: C-512-939-2187, FAX 512-939-3275, 1-800-NAVY-INN, or C-512-937-6361. All ranks. DV/VIP: C-512-939-2380/3285, Cmdr. Direction.

**TRAVELERS AID: American Red Cross:** C-512-939-3751. **Chaplain:** C-512-939-3751. **Navy Relief:** C-512-939-2560. **Security Police:** C-512-939-2480. **USO:** C-512-939-2391.

**OTHER SERVICES: Exchange:** C-512-939-2033. **Bank/Exchange:** C-512-939-3113. **Barber:** C-512-939-8880. **Beauty:** C-512-939-8901. **Laundry/Dry Cleaning:** C-512-937-8942. **Medical:** C-512-939-2688. **Postal:** C-512-939-2984.

**ATTRACTIONS:** Bay and gulf water sports, historic homes, Texas State Aquarium, USS Lexington Museum.

**UNSCHEDULED FLIGHTS**

Various flights to: Pensacola NAS, FL (**NPA**); Dallas NAS, TX (**NBE**); Memphis NAS, TN (**NQA**); New Orleans NAS, LA (**NBG**), and other CONUS, Midwest, West Coast, and OCONUS locations via USN T-44A, USCG HU-25, and transient aircraft. Call for destinations, routings and schedules.

## DALLAS NAVAL AIR STATION (NBE)

Air Operations Dept/Pax Terminal
8100 West Jefferson Boulevard
Dallas, TX 75211-9501

**NOTE: Dallas NAS will move to Fort Worth NAS/Joint Reserve Base in 1996. Dallas NAS will close after the move is complete. Call ahead to ensure that the facility you need is still operating.**

**LOCATION:** Exit from I-30 at loop 12, west of Dallas, go south on loop 12 to Jefferson Ave West exit on the left, NAS on left or south side of Ave. Near Grand Prairie. *USMRA:*

*TEXAS*
***Dallas Naval Air Station, continued***

*Page 88 (E-3)*. NMC: Dallas, 15 miles northeast. Main installation numbers: C-214-266-6111, D-312-874-6111.

**PAX TERM INFO: C-214-266-6651, D-312-874-6651, REC: C-214-266-6376, FAX: C-214-266-6253, D-312-874-6253.** Bldg 20, Hrs: daily 0700-2200. Main hangar is on SW corner of Base building complex.

**PAX LOUNGES:** Ltd lounge facilities. Separate DV/VIP lounge. **General:** Bldg 20, Hrs: daily 0700-2300, C-214-266-6651. A/C, restrooms, P/C seats.

**FOOD SERVICE: Moreland Dinning Hall:** C-214-266-6520. **All Hands Rec Center:** C-214-266-6424. **McDonalds:** Bldg 20. Also vending.

**TRANSPORTATION:** Limited on Base. **Car Rentals:** Economy Rate Rent-A-Car: C-817-640-7368, Enterprize Rent-A-Car: C-214-266-7498, Mid-Cities Auto: C-214-265-1134. **Taxi (Comm):** City C-214-261-7551, State: C-214-823-2161, Yellow: C-214-426-6262. **Parking:** Bldg 20, 24hrs daily, short term. Long term outside Term. **Exchange:** C-214-266-6411. **Hair Styles:** Barber: C-214-266-6400. **Laundry/Dry Cleaning:** C-214-266-6400. **Medical:** Map # 9, 24hrs daily, C-214-266-6283, D-312-874-6283.

**TML:** Lodging Office (Hutchins Hall, Bldg 209, 8100 West Jefferson Blvd), C-214-266-6155, D-312-874-6155, FAX: C-214-266-6608. DV/VIP: C-214-266-6103/6104, Cmdr direction.

**TRAVELERS AID: Chaplain:** C-214-266-6132. **Security Police:** Main gate, 24hrs daily, C-214-266-6139.

**ATTRACTIONS:** Dallas, and Fort Worth nearby. Wet N Wild Water Park, and Six Flags over Texas in Arlington.

**UNSCHEDULED FLIGHTS**

Frequent flights via Navy administrative aircraft, ANG C-130A aircraft, and transient aircraft to: Albuquerque, (also Kirtland AFB) NM (**ABQ**); Buckley ANGB, CO (**BKF**); El Paso Int! Apt, TX (**ELP**); Houston CGAS, TX (**EFD**); Kelly AFB, TX (**SKF**); Kingsville NAS, TX (**NQI**); Miramar NAS, CA (**NKX**); New Orleans NAS, LA (**NBG**); North Island NAS, CA (**NZY**); Pensacola NAS, FL (**NPA**); Tinker AFB, OK (**TIK**); Tulsa Intl Apt, OK (**TUL**); Whidbey Island NAS, WA (**NUW**) and other CONUS locations. Naval Unit VR-59, has 3 C-009A Aircraft which are task with missions in CONUS and some overseas missions.

# DALLAS/FORT WORTH INTERNATIONAL AIRPORT (DFW)

Dallas, TX 75211

**Operated by Lambert St Louis, IAP (STL)**
Det 1, 375th TRANSPS
PO Box 10305
St. Louis, MO 63145-0305

**PAX TERM INFO: C-314-263-6269/6270, D-312-693-6269/6270, REC: 314-263-6262, FAX 314-263-6247, DSN FAX 312-693-6247.** Send Space-A travel request to above FAX.

| ORIGINATING SCHEDULES | | | |
|---|---|---|---|
| | **APP/DFW-1 1st/2nd/4th TUE B747** | | |
| **Location ID** | **Airport (Station)** | **Country/State** | **Days Out** |
| DFW | Dallas-Fort Worth IAP | TX | +0 |
| STL | Lambert ST Louis IAP | MO | +0 |
| **FRF** | **Rhein-Main AB** | **GE** | **+1** |
| STL | Lambert ST Louis IAP | MO | +1 |
| DFW | Dallas-Fort Worth IAP | TX | |

# DYESS AIR FORCE BASE (DYS)

Air Pax Term/96th Trans Sq/LGTTA
Dyess AFB, TX 79607-1244

**LOCATION:** Six miles southwest of Abilene. Main gate is 3 miles east of I-20. Also from I-20 & US-277. *USMRA: Page 87 (I-3)*. NMC: Abilene, 6 miles northeast. Main installation numbers: C-915-696-3113, D-312-461-1110.

**PAX TERM INFO: C-915-696-3108, D-312-461-3108.** Bldg 9001, 24hrs daily. Directions: From North Gate straight on 3rd St to a right on Ave A to Base Ops on the right. **Pax Service Office:** Bldg 7008, Hrs: Mon-Fri: 0730-1630, C-915-696-3108 (NCO on duty).

**PAX LOUNGES:** Limited lounge facilities. DV/VIP: Bldg 9001, see Pax Service NCO. **General:** Bldg 9001, 24hrs daily, C-915-696-3108. A/C, bag check/lockers, restrooms, P/C seats. **DV/VIP:** Bldg 9001, 24hrs daily, C-915-696-3108. **Protocol Service:** Bldg 8030, C-915-696-5610.

**FOOD SERVICE: Dining Hall:** Bldg 7215, C-915-696-3287; Bldg 6142, C-915-696-2421. **Enlisted Club** Bldg: 7106, Hrs: daily 1100-2400, C-915-696-4311. **In-flight Meals:** Bldg 9001, 24hrs daily, C-915-696-2478. **NCO/CPO Club:** Bldg 7106, Hrs: daily 1100-2400, C-915-696-4311. **O'Club:** Bldg 7402, C-915-696-2405. **Vending:** Bldg 9001, 24hrs daily, C-915-696-3108.

*TEXAS*
*Dyess Air Force Base, continued*

**TRANSPORTATION: Air Tickets:** Bldg 7113, Hrs: Mon-Sat: 0800-1500, C-915-696-7286. **Bus (Gov):** Bldg 9001, 24hrs daily, C-915-696-4728 (limited). **Car Rental:** Budget: C-915-677-7777. **Taxi (Gov):** Bldg 9001, 24hrs daily, C-915-696-4728. **Parking:** Bldg 9001, 24hrs daily, C-915-696-2258 (no restrictions).

**TML:** Lodging Office (Dyess Inn, Bldg 441, Fifth St), C-915-696-8610, D-312-461-2681, FAX: D-312-461-2836. DV/VIP: Protocol Office, C-915-696-5610, 06+.

**TRAVELERS AID: American Red Cross:** Bldg 2409, Hrs: Mon-Fri: 0800-1700, C-915-696-2409. **Bank/Exchange:** Bldg 7206, Hrs: Mon-Fri: 0900-1430, C-915-692-9797. **Chaplain:** Bldg 6219, Hrs: Mon-Fri: 0800-1700, C-915-696-4224 After hours C-915-636-3203. **Emergency Relief:** Ask the Commander, C-915-696-3355. **Security Police:** Bldg 6117, 24hrs daily, C-915-696-2131.

**OTHER SERVICES: Exchange:** Bldg 7338, Hrs: Mon-Sat: 1000-1800, Sun: 1200-1700, C-915-692-8976. **Bank/Exchange:** Bldg 7206, Hrs: Mon-Fri: 0900-1430, C-915-692-9797. **Hair Styles:** Bldg 7338, Barber: C-915-692-9974; Beauty: C-915-692-9257. **Medical:** Bldg 9201, 24hrs daily, C-915-696-4677, D-312-461-4677. **Postal:** Bldg 7332, Hrs: Mon-Fri: 0830-1700, C-915-696-2655. **Valet/Dry Cleaning:** Bldg 7324, C-915-695-0231.

**ATTRACTIONS:** Abilene and outdoor sports.

### UNSCHEDULED FLIGHTS

Limited flights to: Eielson AFB, AK (**EIL**); Elmendorf AFB, AK (**EDF**); Hickam AFB, HI (**HIK**); Pope AFB, NC (**POB**); Tinker AFB, OK (**TIK**); Travis AFB, CA (**SUU**) and other CONUS, OCONUS, and foreign country locations. Flight schedules are posted each Friday for the following week. Call for destinations, routings and schedules.

## ELLINGTON AIR NATIONAL GUARD BASE / HOUSTON COAST GUARD AIR STATION (EFD)

Air Operations, 1178 Ellington Field
Houston, TX 77034-5569

**LOCATION:** From I-45 North or South to Exit 3, east to Ellington Field. *USMRA: Page 89 (D-4,5).* NMC: Houston, 15 miles northwest. Main installation numbers: C-713-481-0025, D-312-954-2316/2637, F: 526-7609/7610.

**PAX TERM INFO: C-713-481-0025, D-312-929-2316, FAX: C-713-481-9628.** Bldg 1178, Hrs: Mon-Fri: 0800-1600. Ask Security Police for directions. No Pax lounge. Base Ops processes all PAX. Barber shop available.

### UNSCHEDULED FLIGHTS

Very limited flights available. Houston CGAS does not report any Space-A flights; however, Southwest Services, a contract carrier, has aircraft that occasionally transit Ellington Field. These aircraft may have empty seats for Space-A pax. Call for destinations, routings and schedules.

## ROBERT GRAY ARMY AIRFIELD (GRK)

Flight Operations
Fort Hood, TX 76544-5000

**LOCATION:** From US-190 take the West Fort HOod exit via Clark Rd for 3 miles to Bldg 90049. *USMRA: Page 87 (K-4,5)*. NMC: Killeen, at main Post entrance. Main installation numbers: C-817-287/288-1110, D-312-737/738-1110.

**PAX TERM INFO: C-817-288-9281, D-312-738-9281, FAX 817-288-1930.** Bldg 90049, Hrs: Mon-Fri: 1800-2400. Pax Service is administered by Flight Operations.

**TML:** Lodging Office (Bldg 36006, Wratten Dr), C-817-287-3815/2700, FAX 817-288-7604. DV/VIP: Executive Service, Bldg 1, C-EX-5001, O6/GS-15+.

**UNSCHEDULED FLIGHTS**

Infrequent flights to CONUS locations via transient Air Force C-141B and C-5A aircraft. Commercial ground transportation only.

## KELLY AIR FORCE BASE (SKF)

San Antonio Air Logistics Center
Kelly AFB, TX 78241-5000

**LOCATION:** All of the following, I-10, I-35, I-37, and I-410 intersect with US-90. From US-90 take either the Gen Hudnell or Gen McMullen exit and go south to AFB. *USMRA: Page 91 (B-3,4)*. NMC: San Antonio, 7 miles northeast. Main installation numbers: C-210-925-1110, D-312-945-1110.

**PAX TERM INFO: C-210-925-8714/5, D-312-945-8714/5, REC C-210-925-1854** (updated 0730 daily). Bldg 1614, Hrs: daily 0700-1900. Directions: From Gate #1 straight on Duncan Dr to a right on Luke Dr to Pax Term on the left. **Pax Service Office:** Bldg 1614, same as Pax Term, C-210-925-8714/5 (NCO on duty). **Pax Paging:** Bldg 1614, same as Pax Term, C-210-925-8714/5.

**PAX LOUNGES:** No separate family lounges. **General:** Bldg 1614, same as Pax Term, C-210-925-8714. A/C, telephones (local and defense), TV, restrooms, P/C seats. **DV/VIP:** Bldg 1610, as needed. See Pax Service NCO, C-210-925-8714/5. **Protocol Service:** Post Commander, 24hrs daily, C-210-925-6906 (SA-Air Logistics Center).

**FOOD SERVICE: Cafeteria:** Bldg 1614, C-210-925-3875. **Dining Hall:** Bldg 1650, C-210-925-5791, C-210-925-8350 (in-flight meals). **NCO/CPO Club:** Bldg 1700, C-210-924-4511. **O'Club:** Bldg 1676, C-210-924-7127.

**TRANSPORTATION: Air Tickets** SATO: Bldg 1614, C-210-925-7371. **Bus (Comm):** San Antonio, Greyhound: C-210-227-8351, Trailways: C-210-226-6136, Bldg 1614, City Bus: (VIA) C-210-227-2020. **Bus (Shuttle):** Bldg 1614, Hrs: daily 0700-0130, C-210-925-6372 (Base area). **Limo Service:** Bldg 1614, C-210-671-3555 (Lackland Taxi). **Taxi**

*TEXAS*
*Kelly Air Force Base, continued*

**(Comm):** Bldg 1614, Yellow: C-210-226-4242, Checker: C-210-222-2151. **Taxi (Gov):** Motor Pool, C-210-925-6372. **Trains:** AMTRAK, C-210-223-3226. **Parking:** Bldg 1614, 24hrs daily. Short term-lot 718, across from Pax Term, 15 days max; long term-lot 105 near main gate.

**TML:** Lodging Office (Bldg 1650, Goodrich Rd), 24hrs daily, C-210-925-1844/924-7201, D-312-945-1844. All ranks. DV/VIP: C-210-925-7678, O7/GS-16.

**TRAVELERS AID: Family Services:** Bldg 147, C-210-925-4181. **American Red Cross:** Bldg 9016, C-210-671-3381; after hours, C-210-671-4225. **Chaplain:** Bldg 1669, C-210-925-7874. **Emergency Relief:** Bldg 1650, C-210-925-7114/6 (AF Aid). **Security Police:** Bldg 105, C-210-925-6811. **USO:** 1410 South Alamo, San Antonio, C-210-227-9373.

**OTHER SERVICES: Exchange:** Bldg 1637, C-210-924-9247. **Medical:** Bldg 1740, 24hrs daily, C-210-925-4544. **Postal:** Bldg 1650, C-210-925-8255. **Weather:** Bldg 1610, C-210-925-1115.

**ATTRACTIONS:** Alamo, River Walk, Tower of the Americas.

| **ORIGINATING SCHEDULES** | | | |
|---|---|---|---|
| | **ACC/SKF-1 1st TUE, 2nd/4th FRI C-5A** | | |
| **Location ID** | **Airport (Station)** | **Country/State** | **Days Out** |
| SKF | Kelly AFB | TX | +0 |
| DOV | Dover AFB | DE | +1 |
| CHS | Charleston AFB/IAP | SC | +1 |
| **HOW** | **Howard AB** | **PN** | **+2** |
| CHS | Charleston AFB/IAP | SC | +3 |
| SKF | Kelly AFB | TX | |
| | **SKF/MEDEVAC-1 TUE, FRI C-9A** | | |
| SKF | Kelly AFB | TX | |
| POE | Polk AAF | LA | |
| BIX | Keesler AFB | MS | |
| SSC | Shaw AFB | SC | |
| NQA | Memphis NAS | TN | |
| **BLV** | **Scott AFB** | **IL** | |

| **IN ROUTE SCHEDULES** | | | |
|---|---|---|---|
| **Allen C Thompson Field** | ACC/JAN-2 | | |
| **Charleston AFB/IAP** | ACC/CHS-12 | | |
| **Keesler AFB** | BIX/MEDEVAC-1 | BIX/MEDEVAC-2 | |
| **Scott AFB** | BLV/MEDEVAC-5 | BLV/MEDEVAC-8 | BLV/MEDEVAC-10 |
| **Travis AFB** | SUU/MEDEVAC-1 | SUU/MEDEVAC-2 | |

**UNSCHEDULED FLIGHTS**

Various flights to CONUS, Pacific and European areas including but not limited to: Dover AFB, DE (**DOV**); Hickam AFB, HI (**HIK**); Ramstein AB, GE (**RMS**); Rhein-Main AB, GE (**FRF**); RAF Mildenhall, UK (**MHZ**); Travis AFB, CA (**SUU**) on C-5 aircraft.

# LAUGHLIN AIR FORCE BASE (DLF)

47th OSS/DOCB, Bldg 306
541 1st Street, Suite 1
Laughlin AFB, TX 78843-5209

**LOCATION:** Take US-90 West from San Antonio, 150 miles or US-277 South from San Angelo, 150 miles to Del Rio area. The AFB is clearly marked off US-90. *USMRA: Page 86 (H-9)*. NMC: Del Rio, 6 miles northwest. Main installation numbers: C-210-298-3511, D-312-732-1110.

**PAX TERM INFO: C-210-298-5308, D-312-732-5308.** Bldg 306, Hrs: Mon-Fri: 0600-1900, Sat-Sun: 0900-1800, closed holidays. Directions: From main gate straight on Liberty Dr to a left on Florida Ave to Base Ops on the left. See Military Living's *US Forces Travel & Transfer Guide USA and Caribbean Areas* for details.

**TML:** Lodging Office (Laughlin Manor, Bldg 470, 416 Liberty Drive), C-210-298-5731, FAX: C-210-298-5272, D-312-732-5272. DV/VIP: Bldg 338, Room 1, C-210-298-5041, O6+.

**UNSCHEDULED FLIGHTS**

Limited flights to CONUS locations via Air Force administrative aircraft.

# RANDOLPH AIR FORCE BASE (RND)

12th Trans Sqdn/LGTT
Randolph AFB, TX 78150-4424

**LOCATION:** Take Exit 172 off I-35, Pat Booker Rd. Off I-10 take Exit 587, TX-FM-1604. *USMRA: Page 91 (E-2)*. NMC: San Antonio, 20 miles southwest. Main installation numbers: C-210-652-1110, D-312-487-1110.

**PAX TERM INFO: C-210-652-1854/3725, D-312-487-1854/3725, FAX: C-210-652-5718, D-312-487-5718.** Bldg 399, Room B36, Hrs: Mon-Fri: 0730-1615, Sat-Sun: as required. Directions: From main gate turn left on 1st Ave East to a right on 5th St East for .75 mile to Pax Term on the right. **Pax Service Office:** Same as Passenger Terminal(NCO on duty).

**PAX LOUNGES:** Limited lounge facilities. No separate family lounge. **General:** Bldg 399, Room B36, Hrs: Mon-Fri: 0730-1645, C-210-652-1854. A/C, telephones (local, long

*TEXAS*
***Randolph Air Force Base, continued***

distance and defense), TV, restrooms, O/S seats. **DV/VIP:** Bldg 8, Hrs: Mon-Fri: 0600-2200, C-210-652-3416. A/C, coffee/tea served, telephones (local, long distance and defense), TV, restrooms, O/S seats. No host. **Protocol Service:** Bldg 100, Hrs: Mon-Fri: 0800-1700, C-210-652-1110.

**FOOD SERVICE: Cafeteria:** Bldg 11, Hrs: Mon-Fri: 0600-2000, Sat-Sun: 0600-1900, C-210-658-1338. **Dining Hall:** Bldg 860, Hrs: daily 0500-1800, C-210-652-1110. **NCO/CPO Club:** Bldg 598, C-210-658-3557. **O'Club:** Bldg 500, C-210-658-7445. **Snack Bars:** Bldg 1071, Hrs: daily 0900-2200, C-210-658-1440. **Vending:** Hangar #7, 24hrs daily, C-210-652-1854.

**TRANSPORTATION: Air Tickets:** Bldg 399, Hrs: Mon-Fri: 0730-1615, C-210-652-2650. **Taxi(Gov):** Bldg 172, 24hrs daily, C-210-652-8294. **Parking:** Hangar #7, 24hrs daily, C-210-652-5700 (See Security Police for long term).

**TML:** Lodging Office (Bldg 118), 24hrs daily, C-210-652-1844, D-312-487-1844, FAX 210-652-2616. All ranks. DV/VIP: C-210-652-4126, O7/SES.

**TRAVELERS AID: American Red Cross:** Bldg 662, Hrs: Mon-Fri: 0830-1600, C-210-652-1855, after hours C-210-652-1859. **Chaplain:** Bldg 103, Hrs: Mon-Fri: 0730-1615, C-210-652-6121. **Security Police:** Bldg 235, 24hrs daily, C-210-652-5700. **USO:** 410 South Alamo, San Antonio, C-210-227-9373.

**OTHER SERVICES: Exchange:** Bldg 1073, Hrs: Mon-Sat: 0930-1730, Sun: 0930-1600, C-210-658-2681. **Bank/Exchange:** Bldg 1074, Hrs: Mon-Fri: 0800-1600, C-210-658-7427. **Hair Styles:** Bldg 1073, Hrs: Mon-Fri: 0800-1730, Sat: 1600, Barber: C-210-658-0581; Beauty: C-512-658-7755. **Laundry:** Bldg 1073, Hrs: Mon-Fri: 0800-1730, C-210-659-4260. **Medical:** Bldg 1040, 24hrs daily, C-210-652-2743, D-312-487-2743. **Postal:** Bldg 220, Hrs: Mon-Fri: 0830-1630, C-210-652-2606.

**ATTRACTIONS:** San Antonio, New Braunfels, Canyon Lake, Sea World, Fiesta Texas.

### UNSCHEDULED FLIGHTS

Frequent flights to: Andrews AFB, MD (**ADW**); Colorado Springs, CO (**COS**); Maxwell AFB, AL (**MXF**); Wright-Patterson AFB, OH (**FFO**); and other CONUS locations utilizing C-21 aircraft. Call for destinations, routing and schedules.

## REESE AIR FORCE BASE (REE)

64th FTW, Base Operations
145 North Davis Drive
Reese AFB, TX 79489-5301

**LOCATION:** From I-289 (Loop) take 4th St, 6 miles west. The road terminates at AFB, main gate is one block north. *USMRA: Page 86 (F-4)*. NMC: Lubbock, 6 miles east. Main installation numbers: C-806-885-4511, D-312-838-1110.

**PAX TERM INFO: C-806-885-3105, D-312-838-3105, FAX: C-806-885-1028, D-312-838-6540.** Bldg 79, Base Ops, Hrs: Mon-Fri: 0700-1700, Sat: 0900-1700, Sun: 1100-1700, closed Holidays. Directions: From main gate straight on Main St, cross Hangar Line Rd, Base Operations on the right. **Pax Service Office:** Same as Pax Terminal (Dispatcher on duty).

**PAX LOUNGES:** Very limited. **General:** Bldg 79, Pax Term hours, C-806-885-3105. A/C, bag check, restrooms, O/S seats. **DV/VIP:** Bldg 79, Pax Term hours, C-806-885-3105. A/C, bag check, coffee/tea served, restrooms, O/S seats.

**TML:** Lodging Office (The Reese Inn, Bldg 155, K St), C-806-885-3155/3185, FAX C-806-885-6510, D-312-838-3155. DV/VIP: Wing Protocol, Bldg 800, C-806-885-6187.

**OTHER SERVICES:** Full Large Base support. For details see Military Living's *U.S. Forces Travel & Transfer Guide USA & Caribbean Areas.*

**UNSCHEDULED FLIGHTS**

To CONUS and OCONUS locations. Call for destinations, routing and schudules.

## SHEPPARD AIR FORCE BASE (SPS)

Hq Sheppard Tech Tng Ctr/Air Ops
Sheppard AFB, TX 76311-5000

**LOCATION:** Take US-281 North from Wichita Falls, exit to TX-325 which leads to main gate. Clearly marked. *USMRA: Page 87 (J-1).* NMC: Wichita Falls, 5 miles southwest. Main installation numbers: C-817-676-2511, D-312-736-1001.

**PAX TERM INFO: C-817-676-6474/2180, D-312-736-6474/2180.** Bldg 1360, Hrs: daily 0800-2000. Main gate right on 1st St to a left on Ave J to Base Ops on the right. **Pax Service Office:** Bldg 1360, Hrs: daily 0800-2000, C-817-676-6474/2180 (NCO on duty).

**PAX LOUNGES:** Limited lounge facilities. No separte family lounge. **General:** Bldg 1360, Hrs: daily 0800-2000, C-817-676-6474. A/C, bag check, telephones (local and defense), restrooms, P/C seats. **DV/VIP:** Bldg 1360, Hrs: daily 0800-2000, C-817-676-6474 (O6+). A/C, bag check, coffee/tea served, read/write rooms, telephones (local and defense), restrooms, O/S seats. **Protocol Service:** Bldg 400, Hrs: Mon-Fri: 0730-1630, C-817-676-2930.

**TML:** Lodging Office (Sheppard Inn, 710 H Ave), C-676-855-7370, D-312-736-6359/4351. DV/VIP: Bldg 400, C-EX-2123, D-EX-2123, O6+.

**OTHER SERVICES:** Full Large Base support facility available. For details see Military Living's *US Forces Travel & Transfer Guide USA & Caribbean Areas.*

**UNSCHEDULED FLIGHTS**

One or two flights per week via C-21A and CT-39 aircraft to CONUS locations. Call for destinations, routings and schedules.

# UTAH

## HILL AIR FORCE BASE (HIF)

2849th Air Base Group/OO+ALC/DPCC
6064 Dogwood Ave., Hill AFB, UT 84056-5816

**LOCATION:** Adjacent to I-15 between Ogden and Salt Lake City. Take Exit 336 East on UT-193 to south gate. *USMRA: Page 112 (D-2,3)*. NMC: Ogden, 8 miles north. Main installation numbers: C-801-777-7221, D-312-458-1110.

**PAX TERM INFO: C-801-777-1854, D-312-458-1854, FAX 801-775-3249.** Bldg 405, Area 1, Hrs: Mon-Fri: 0700-1500. Directions: From west area, east on 2nd Street, to Bldg 405 on South Gate Drive, then west to Bldg 405. **Pax Service Office:** Bldg 405, Hrs: Mon-Fri: 0700-1500, C-801-777-9943/1854.

**PAX LOUNGES:** Good facilities. **General:** Bldg 405, Hrs: Mon-Fri: 0700-1500, C-801-777-1854. A/C, restrooms, TV, P/C seats. **DV/VIP:** Bldg 1, 24hrs daily, C-801-777-5565 (06+). A/C, restrooms, read/write rooms, TV, O/S seats. **Protocol Service:** Bldg 180, Area 2, Hrs: Mon-Fri: 0800-1700, C-801-777-7221.

**FOOD SERVICE: Cafeteria:** C-801-777-7945. **Dining Hall:** C-801-777-3428. **Enlisted Club:** C-801-777-3428. **In-Flight Meals:** C-801-777-1010. **NCO/CPO Club:** C-801-777-3841. **O'Club:** C-801-773-4924. **Restaurant:** C-801-777-4165. **Snack Bars:** C-801-777-7947.

**TRANSPORTATION: Air Tickets:** C-801-777-4677. **Bus (Gov):** C-801-777-1843. **Bus (Shuttle):** C-801-777-1843 (20 min schedule on Base). **Limo Service:** Ogden, Key Limo: C-1-800-678-2360; Salt Lake, Bonneville Limo: C-801-364-6520. **Taxi (Comm):** C-801-777-1843, Yellow: C-801-394-9411. **Parking:** C-801-777-3056. Short term and long term, see Security Police. Pick up and discharge only.

**TML:** Lodging Office (Mountain View Inn, Bldg 146, D. Ave), 24hrs daily, C-801-777-1844/2601, D-312-458-1844/2601, FAX 801-942-2012. All ranks. DV/VIP: C-801-777-5565, O6+.

**TRAVELERS AID: American Red Cross:** C-801-777-1855, after hours C-801-927-3533. **Chaplain:** C-801-777-2107, after hours C-801-777-3007. **Emergency Relief:** C-801-777-4681 (AF Aid), after hours C-801-777-3007. **Security Police:** Bldg 1219, 24hrs daily, C-801-777-3056 (Desk Sgt).

**OTHER SERVICES: Exchange:** C-801-773-1207. **Bank/Exchange:** C-801-773-4602. **Hair Styles:** Barber: C-801-773-4602; Beauty: C-801-773-4076. **Laundry:** C-801-773-3823. **Medical:** Bldg 570, 24hrs daily, C-801-777-5285/1847,D-312-458-5285/1847. **Postal:** C-801-777-2509.

**ATTRACTIONS:** Salt Lake City, snow skiing, Park City, Temple Square.

| IN ROUTE SCHEDULES | |
|---|---|
| **Scott AFB** | BLV/MEDEVAC-3 |
| **Travis AFB** | SUU/MEDEVAC-4 |

### UNSCHEDULED FLIGHTS

Flights via C-141B/M AFRES to McChord AFB, WA (**TCM**); Alameda NAS, CA (**NGZ**) and other CONUS W and SW locations and returning to HIF largely on weekends. Flights via C-21 to CONUS locations. Call for destinations, routings and schedules.

## SALT LAKE CITY INTERNATIONAL AIRPORT (SLC)

51st Air Refueling Group
Utah Air National Guard
Air Operations/DOTA
765 N. 2200 W.
Salt Lake City, UT 84116-2999

**LOCATION:** From I-215 N or S exit 26 west. ANG is on the immediate left. *USMRA: Page 112 (D-3); Page 116 (B-2).* NMC: Salt Lake City, 5 miles southeast. Main installation numbers: C-801-595-2200, D-312-790-9210.

**PAX TERM INFO: C-801-595-2274, D-312-790-9274, REC: C-801-595-2415, D-312-924-9415, FAX: C-801-595-2271, D-312-790-9271.** ANG area, Bldg 40, Room 105, Hrs: Mon-Fri: 0700-1545. Ask Gate Sentry for directions.

**TML**: Lodging Office, C-801-777-1844.

**OTHER SERVICES:** Full support of IAP. Officers/Enlisted Club, Exchange and other services available at Hill AFB. **Base NCO Club**: 801-595-2269. **Base Exchange:** 801-355-1923, **Barber**: 801-595-2500. Base dispensary.

### UNSCHEDULED FLIGHTS

Flights via KC-135E/R ANG aircraft to CONUS and OCONUS locations. Call for destinations, routings and schedules.

# VIRGINIA

## DAVISON ARMY AIRFIELD (DAA)

Air Operations
Fort Belvoir, VA 22060-5726

**LOCATION:** From I-95 North and US-1 North or South take Fort Belvoir exits. Signs clearly mark support facilities. *USMRA: Page 47 (L,M-5)*. NMC: Washington DC, 10 miles northeast. Main installation numbers: C-703-806-7225/7509, D-312-354-7225/7509.

**PAX TERM INFO: C-703-806-7546, D-312-656-7546, FAX: C-703-806-7297.** Bldg 3136, 24hrs daily. Directions: On main road inside Hwy 1, gate sign points to DAAF. **Pax Service Office:** Bldg 3136, 24hrs daily, C-703-806-7792 (NCO on duty).

**PAX LOUNGES:** General Lounge with DV/VIP in separate room. **General:** Bldg 3136, 24hrs daily, C-703-806-7224. A/C, read/write room, telephones (commercial and defense), TV, restrooms, P/C and O/S seats.

**FOOD SERVICE: Snack Bars:** Bldg 3137, Hrs: Mon-Fri: 0600-1400, C-703-781-3609; **Vending:** Bldg 3136.

**TML:** Lodging Office (Bldg 470, 9775 Gaillard Road), C-800-295-9750, FAX 703-805-3566. DV/VIP: O'Club, O6+. Call numbers above.

**OTHER SERVICES:** Full Large Base Support. Enterprise Rent-A-Car: C-703-922-3808; Thrifty Rent-A-Car: C-703-360-3400. See Military Living's *Assignment: Washington II, A Guide to Washington Area Military Installations* for full details on more than 18 military installations in the Washington DC area.

### UNSCHEDULED FLIGHTS

Frequent flights via C-12A/P & U-21A/P aircraft to Langley AFB, VA (**LFI**) and other CONUS East Coast, Southeast and Midwest locations. There is usually no more then a two day advanced notice on flights. Call for destinations, routings, and schedules.

## LANGLEY AIR FORCE BASE (LFI)

1st TRANS/TRT
190E Flightline Road
Langley AFB, VA 23665-5518

**LOCATION:** From I-64 East in Hampton take Armistead Ave exit, right to stop light; right onto LaSalle Ave and enter AFB. *USMRA: Page 47 (N-9); Page 52 (E-3)*. NMC: Hampton, 1 mile west. Main installation numbers: C-804-764-9990, D-312-574-9990.

**PAX TERM INFO: C-804-764-4698/4311, D-312-574-4698/4311, REC: C-804-764-5807, D-312-574-5807, FAX: C-804-764-5941, D-312-574-5941.** Bldg 754B, Hrs: Mon-Fri: 0730-1630. Directions: From LaSalle gate (I-64) right on Nealy Ave to left on Danforth St to Pax Term on left. **Pax Service Office:** TRADOC Army Det, Pax Term, Hrs: Mon-Fri: 0500-1900, C-804-727-3707, D-312-680-3707.

**PAX LOUNGES:** General and family lounges combined. **General:** Bldg 754B, Hrs: Mon-Fri: 0730-1630, C-804-764-4311/4698. A/C, telephones (commercial and defense), TV, restrooms, P/C seats. **DV/VIP:** Bldg 754, as required, C-804-764-2504 (06+). A/C, bag check, read/write rooms, telephones (commercial and defense), TV, restrooms. **Protocol Service:** Bldg 693, Hrs: Mon-Fri: 0645-1900, C-804-764-5044 (07+).

**FOOD SERVICE: Cafeteria:** C-804-766-1255. **Dining Hall:** C-804-764-3694. **NCO/CPO Club:** C-804-766-1220. **O'Club:** C-804-766-1361. **Snack Bar:** C-804-766-1237.

**TRANSPORTATION: Air Tickets:** Bldg 15, C-804-764-5989. **Car Rentals:** Avis: C-804-877-0291, Hertz: C-804-877-9229. **Limo Service:** C-804-877-9477. **Taxi (Comm):** C-804-723-3377. **Taxi (Gov):** C-804-764-8294. **Parking:** Bldg 754B. Short & long term near Pax Term.

**TML:** Lodging Office (Bldg 75, 66 Nealy Ave), C-804-764-4667, D-312-574-4667, FAX 804-764-3038. DV/VIP: Protocol Office, Bldg 703, C-804-764-5044, 06+.

**TRAVELERS AID: American Red Cross:** C-804-764-6161 (After hours C-804-838-7320). **Chaplain:** C-804-764-7847 (After hours C-804-764-9990). **Emergency Relief:** C-804-764-3991 (AF Aid). **Lost/Found:** C-804-764-5092. **Security Police:** C-804-764-5091. **USO:** C-804-827-1063.

**OTHER SERVICES: Exchange:** C-804-766-1253. **Bank/Exchange:** C-804-827-7200. **Barber:** C-804-766-1805. **Beauty:** C-804-766-1283. **Laundry/Dry Cleaning:** C-804-766-1287. **Medical:** C-804-764-6800, D-312-574-6800. **Postal:** C-804-764-3136.

**ATTRACTIONS:** VA tidewater area, Williamsburg, Norfolk, Virginia Beach.

## UNSCHEDULED FLIGHTS

Frequent Air Force flights via C-12A and C-21A aircraft to: Andrews AFB, MD (**ADW**); Davison AAF, VA (**DAA**); Eglin AFB, FL (**VPS**); Hanscom Field Apt, MA (**BED**); Maxwell AFB, AL (**MXF**); Randolph AFB, TX (**RND**), Scott AFB, IL (**BLV**); and Wright-Patterson AFB, OH (**FFO**). Call for destinations, routings and schedules. TRADOC Army Det. Also flights to: Cairns AAF, AL (**OZR**); Columbia Metro Apt, SC (**CAE**); Fulton Co Apt, GA (**FTY**); Godman AAF, KY (**FTK**); Phillips AAF, MD (**APG**); Redstone Arsenal AAF, AL (**HUA**), and Simmons AAF, SC (**FBG**).

*VIRGINIA*

# NORFOLK NAVAL AIR STATION (NGU)

Naval Air Terminal, Code 053
8449 Air Cargo Road
Norfolk Naval Air Station, VA 23511-4497

**LOCATION:** From the north take I-64 West, take Naval Base exit, follow signs. From the south take I-64 exit to I-564 into Gate 3. *USMRA: Page 52 (F-5,6)*. NMC: Norfolk, in city limits. Main installation numbers: C-804-444-0000, D-312-564-0111, FTS: 954-0111.

**PAX TERM INFO: C-804-444-4118/4148/3947, D-312-564-4118/4148/3947, FAX: C-804-445-6563/7501, D-312-565-6563/7501.** Recording after hours: C-804-445-6538, D-312-564-6538. Bldg LP-84, Hrs: daily 0600-2200, Directions: AMC Term 3 miles from Gate 4 off Patrol Rd on A-Term Rd. **Note:** Sign up for additional Navy and Marine Corps Space-A flights at LP-1 (Control Tower), C-804-444-2780. **Pax Service Office:** Bldg LP-84, Hrs: daily 0600-2200, C-804-444-4118/4517, D-312-564-4118/4517 (duty NCO). **Pax Paging:** Bldg LP-84, Hrs: daily 0600-2200, C-804-444-4118, D-312-564-4118 (Space-A desk).

**PAX LOUNGES:** Bldg LP-84. No separate family lounge. **General:** Bldg LP-84, Hrs: daily 0600-2200, C-804-444-4118, D-312-564-4118/4148. A/C, nursery, free TV, O/S & P/C seats, restrooms. **DV/VIP:** Bldg LP-84, Hrs: daily 0600-2200, C-804-444-4118/4148, D-312-564-4118/4148. A/C, showers, TV, restrooms, game room. No hostess. **Protocol Service:** Bldg LP-1, 24hrs daily, C-804-444-2780 (Base Ops), C-804-444-2442 (SDO).

**FOOD SERVICE:** Many clubs, messes, & dining halls on Naval Base complex. **Cafeteria:** Bldg LP-84, Hrs: daily 0600-2200, C-804-444-4118 (AMC Term grill). **Dining Hall:** Bldg 1-AA (NS), Hrs: Mon-Fri: 0600-1730, C-804-444-7024 (call for meal hours); Bldg U-16 (NAS), Hrs: Mon-Fri: 0700-1730, C-804-444-3744 (call for meal hours). **Enlisted Club:** Bldg X-360, Hrs: daily 0600-2400, C-804-444-5438. **NCO/CPO Club:** Bldg U-93, Hrs: daily 0600-2400, C-804-444-2125. **O'Club:** Bldg SP-45 (NAS), Hrs: daily 0600-2400, C-804-423-0773; Bldg SC-400 (AFSC), Hrs: daily 0600-2400, C-804-423-4713. **Snack Bars:** Bldg LP-84, 24hrs daily, C-804-440-2282. **Vending:** Bldg LP-84, 24hrs daily, C-804-440-2282 (also pay telephone).

**TRANSPORTATION:** Facilities and means throughout Naval Base complex. **Air Tickets:** SATO: Bldg A-48, Hrs: Mon-Fri: 0830-1700, C-804-444-0400. **Bus (Comm):** Bldg LP-84, 24hrs daily, C-804-444-3830, Greyhound: C-804-423-8471, Trailways: C-804-622-7181. **Bus (Shuttle):** Bldg LP-84, Hrs: daily 0600-2200, C-804-444-4118/4148 (from Term to major points). **Car Rentals:** Bldg LP-84, 24hrs daily, Avis: C-804-855-1944, Budget: C-804-855-1038, Dollar: C-804-480-1500, Hertz: C-804-855-1961, National: C-804-855-2037. **Limo Service:** Bldg LP-84, Hrs: daily 0600-2200, C-804-857-1231 (to Norfolk IAP-fare $6.25). **Taxi (Comm):** Bldg LP-84, 24hrs daily, Ace: C-804-543-3333, B&W: C-804-489-7777, Norview: C-804-855-3333, Yellow: C-804-622-3232. Front of Bldg LP-84. **Trains:** AMTRAK: Norfolk, 24hrs daily, C-804-

444-0111. **Parking:** Bldg LP-84, 24hrs daily, C-804-444-4118. Short term-2 hours; long term-30 days.

**TML:** Lodging Office (BEQ: Bldg I-A, Pocahontas & Bacon Sts), C-804-444-4294, FAX C-804-444-9888, BOQ: C-804-444-4425. Navy Lodge (Bldg SDA-314, take I-64 to 564 exit to Terminal Blvd, left on Hampton Blvd; lodge on left). C-804-489-2656 or 1-800-NAVY-INN. DV/VIP: Bldg KBB, C-804-444-2788. C-804-444-6323, 07+.

**TRAVELERS AID:** Personal Service Center: 7920 Hampton Blvd, 24hrs daily, C-804-622-3111. **American Red Cross:** Bldg A-67, 24hrs daily, C-804-423-4610; Norfolk: 24hrs daily, C-804-446-7700. **Chaplain:** Bldg U-53/SP-108, 24hrs daily, C-804-444-7361 (all faiths). **Emergency Relief:** 7920 Hampton Blvd, 24hrs daily, C-804-444-6289; Navy Relief, C-804-423-8830. **Lost/Found:** Bldg LP-84, Hrs: daily 0600-2200, C-804-445-6563 and Pax Service office. **Security Police:** Bldg CEP-161, 24hrs daily, C-804-444-2361 (Desk Sgt). **USO:** Coliseum Mall (Entrance-A), Hampton, C-804-838-4182, C-804-827-1063.

**OTHER SERVICES:** Throughout Naval Base complex. **Exchange:** Bldg U-40 (NAS), hours vary, C-804-440-2214, Bldg LP-84, Hrs: daily 0800-1600. **Bank/Exchange:** NASFCU, C-804-497-9631; NFCU, C-804-480-1777. **Medical:** Bldg CD-2, 24hrs daily, C-804-444-1531; Portsmouth Naval Hospital, C-804-398-5413. **Postal:** Bldg U-20. **Wire:** Pier 7 24hrs daily, C-804-440-2254, C-804-622-4311 (Western Union).

**ATTRACTIONS:** MacArthur Memorial, Norfolk NS tour, Colonial Williamsburg, Virginia Beach.

| ORIGINATING SCHEDULES | | | |
|---|---|---|---|
| | **APP/NGU-1 TUE B727** | | |
| **Location ID** | **Airport (Station)** | **Country/State** | **Days Out** |
| NGU | Norfolk NAS | VA | +0 |
| NBW | Guantanamo Bay NAS | CU | +0 |
| **KIN** | **Norman Manley IAP** | **JM** | **+0** |
| NBW | Guantanamo Bay NAS | CU | +0 |
| NGU | Norfolk NAS | VA | |
| | **APP/NGU-2 FRI B727** | | |
| NGU | Norfolk NAS | VA | +0 |
| NIP | Jacksonville NAS | FL | +0 |
| **NBW** | **Guantanamo Bay NAS** | **CU** | **+0** |
| NIP | Jacksonville NAS | FL | +0 |
| NGU | Norfolk NAS | VA | |

*VIRGINIA*
*Norfolk Naval Air Station, continued*

| | APP/NGU-3 SAT B757 | | |
|---|---|---|---|
| NGU | Norfolk NAS | VA | +0 |
| PHL | Philadelphia IAP | PA | +0 |
| **KEF** | **Keflavik APT** | **IC** | **+0** |
| PHL | Philadelphia IAP | PA | +0 |
| NGU | Norfolk NAS | VA | |
| | **APP/NGU-4 1st/2nd/3rd SAT DC862** | | |
| NGU | Norfolk NAS | VA | +0 |
| PHL | Philadelphia IAP | PA | +1 |
| LGS | Lajes AB | PO | +1 |
| SIZ | Sigonella NAS | IT | +1 |
| BAH | Bahrain IAP | BA | +1 |
| **NKW** | **Diego Garcia Atoll** | **UK** | **+2** |
| BAH | Bahrain IAP | BA | +3 |
| SIZ | Sigonella NAS | IT | +3 |
| LGS | Lajes AB | PO | +3 |
| PHL | Philadelphia IAP | PA | +3 |
| NGU | Norfolk NAS | VA | |
| | **APP/NGU-5 4th SAT DC862** | | |
| NGU | Norfolk NAS | VA | +0 |
| PHL | Philadelphia IAP | PA | +1 |
| LGS | Lajes AB | PO | +1 |
| SIZ | Sigonella NAS | IT | +1 |
| BAH | Bahrain IAP | BA | +1 |
| NKW | Diego Garcia Atoll | UK | +2 |
| **MNL** | **Ninoy Aquino IAP** | **RP** | **+3** |
| NKW | Diego Garcia Atoll | UK | +4 |
| BAH | Bahrain IAP | BA | +5 |
| SIZ | Sigonella NAS | IT | +5 |
| LGS | Lajes AB | PO | +5 |
| PHL | Philadelphia IAP | PA | +5 |
| NGU | Norfolk NAS | VA | |

| IN ROUTE SCHEDULES | | | |
|---|---|---|---|
| **Allen C Thompson Field** | ACC/JAN-3 | | |
| **Andrews AFB** | ACC/ADW-3 | ACC/ADW-4 | ADW/MEDEVAC-2 |
| **Charleston AFB/IAP** | ACC/CHS-7 | ACC/CHS-16 | ACC/CHS-17 |
| | ACC/CHS-18 | | |
| **Dover AFB** | APM/DOV-2 | ACM/DOV-3 | |

| | | | |
|---|---|---|---|
| **Little Rock AFB** | ACC/LRF-1 | ACC/LRF-2 | ACC/LRF-3 |
| | ACM/LRF-4 | | |
| **March AFB** | APM/RIV-1 | | |
| **McGuire AFB** | ACC/WRI-11 | ACC/WRI-16 | ACC/WRI-17 |
| | ACC/WRI-18 | ACC/WRI-19 | ACM/WRI-20 |
| **Memphis IAP** | ACC/MEM-2 | | |
| **Moody AFB** | ACC/VAD-1 | | |
| **Pope AFB** | ACC/POB-1 | APM/POB-2 | |
| **Scott AFB** | BLV/MEDEVAC-1 | | |

## OCEANA NAVAL AIR STATION (NTU)

Air Terminal, Bldg 100, NAS Oceana
Virginia Beach, VA 23460-5120

**LOCATION:** From I-64 exit to Norfolk-Virginia Beach Expressway (VA-44E), east on Virginia Beach Blvd. Bordered by Oceana Blvd (VA-615) and London Bridge Rd. Also, bordered by Potters Rd and Harpers Rd. *USMRA: Page 47 (O-9); Page 52 (I,J-7)*. NMC: Virginia Beach, in city limits. Main installation numbers: C-804-433-2000, D-312-433-2000.

**PAX TERM INFO: C-804-433-2903/2260, D-312-433-2903/2260.** Bldg 100, 24hrs daily. Directions: From main gate straight on Princess Anne Rd to a right on London Bridge Rd and Pax Term at circle dead end. **Pax Service Office:** Bldg 100, 24hrs daily, C-804-433-2162/3 (NCO on duty).

**PAX LOUNGES:** No separate family lounge. **General:** Bldg 100, 24hrs daily, C-804-433-2260. A/C, restrooms, P/C seats. **DV/VIP:** Bldg: 100, Room 119 (as required), C-804-433-2260. A/C, restrooms, TV, O/S seats.

**FOOD SERVICE: Enlisted Club:** C-804-433-2122/2453. **NCO/CPO Club:** C-804-433-2637. **O'Club:** C-804-428-0036. **McDonalds**.

**TRANSPORTATION:** Very limited on Base. **Car Rentals:** C-804-855-1921. No Parking at Bldg 100. Long Term: notify Security Police C-804-433-3123.

**TML:** Lodging Office (Bldg 460, G Street across from O'Club), C-804-425-0500-EX-168/171/172, D-312-433-3293. DV/VIP: Bldg 460, C-804-425-3293, 06+.

**TRAVELERS AID: American Red Cross:** C-804-425-8955. **Chaplain:** C-804-433-2871. **Navy Relief:** C-804-425-5789. **Security Police:** C-804-433-3123. **USO:** C-804-838-4182.

*VIRGINIA*
***Oceana Naval Air Station, continued***

**OTHER SERVICES: Exchange:** C-804-491-4260. **Bank/Exchange:** C-804-473-2834. **Hair Styles:** C-804-491-4260. **Laundry/Dry Cleaning:** C-804-491-4260. **Medical:** C-804-433-2221, D-312-433-2221. **Postal:** Bldg 531.

**UNSCHEDULED FLIGHTS**

Frequent flights via Navy UC-12B and other administrative aircraft to: Cecil Field NAS, FL (**NZC**); Charleston AFB/IAP, SC (**CHS**); El Centro NAF, CA (**NJK**); Jacksonville NAS, FL (**NIP**); Key West NAS, FL (**NQX**); Los Angeles IAP, CA (**LAX**); Mayport NAS, FL (**NRB**); North Island NAS, CA (**NZY**); Pensacola NAS, FL (**NPA**) and Roosevelt Roads NAS, PR (**NRR**). Call for destinations, routings and schedules.

# WASHINGTON

## FAIRCHILD AIR FORCE BASE (SKA)

92nd OSS/OSAA, Bldg 1, 901 West Boston Ave.,
Fairchild AFB, WA 99011-5000

**LOCATION:** Take US-2 exit from I-90 West of Spokane. Follow US-2 through Airway Heights, after 2 miles turn left to Base main gate and visitors' control center. *USMRA: Page 101 (I-4)*. NMC: Spokane, 12 miles east. Main installation numbers: C-509-247-1212, D-312-657-1110.

**PAX TERM INFO: C-509-247-5435, D-312-657-5435, REC: C-509-247-5440, D-312-657-5440, FAX 509-247-4909, D FAX 657-4909.** Bldg 1, Base Ops, 24hrs daily. Directions: From main gate straight on Mitchell Ave to a right on Bong St to a left on Seattle Ave to a right on Arnold St to a left on O'Malley Ave to Pax Term on the right. **Pax Service Office:** Bldg 1, 24hrs daily, C-509-247-5481, NCO on duty (days).

**PAX LOUNGES:** Limited Lounge facilities. **General:** Bldg 1, 24hrs daily, C-509-247-5435. Bag check, telephones (commercial and defense), restrooms, O/S seats. **DV/VIP:** Bldg 1, 24hrs daily, C-509-247-5435. Coffee/tea served, telephones (commercial), TV, restrooms, O/S seats. **Protocol Service:** Hq Bldg, Hrs: Mon-Fri: 0730-1630, C-509-247-2127.

**FOOD SERVICE: Dining Hall:** Bldg 2262, Hrs: daily 0530-0100, C-509-247-5348. **In-flight Meals:** Bldg 2262, 24hrs daily, C-509-247-5140. **Enlisted Club:** Bldg 2452, Hrs: Mon-Sat: 1100-2300, C-509-247-3622. **NCO/CPO Club:** Bldg 2452, Hrs: Mon-Sat: 1100-2300, C-509-247-3622. **O'Club:** Bldg 2452, Hrs: Mon-Sat: 1100-2300, C-509-244-3622. **Burger King:** Bldg 2459, Hrs: daily 0630-2100, C-509-244-2680. **Snack Bars:** Bldg 2245, C-509-244-2162. **Vending:** Bldg 1, 24hrs daily, C-509-247-5435.

**TRANSPORTATION: Air Tickets:** SATO: Bldg 2245, Hrs: Mon-Fri: 0730-1630, C-509-247-2211. **Bus (Comm):** Main gate, Spokane Transit System, C-509-328-9336. **Bus (Gov):** Motor Pool, 24hrs daily, C-509-247-2244. **Car Rentals:** Spokane, 24hrs daily, Avis: C-509-747-8081, National: C-509-624-8995, Thrifty: C-509-838-8223. **Taxi (Comm):** Bldg 1, 24hrs daily, Checker: C-509-624-4741, Yellow: C-509-624-4321. **Taxi (Gov):** Motor Pool, 24hrs daily, C-509-247-2244. **Parking:** BX lot facing fence, 24hrs daily, C-509-247-5435 (long and short term).

**TML:** Lodging Office (Bldg 2392, Short St), C-509-247-5519, D-312-657-5519. DV/VIP: Bldg 2392, C-509-247-2127. 06+.

**TRAVELERS AID: American Red Cross:** Bldg 2245, Hrs: Mon-Fri: 0730-1630, C-509-247-5650; After hours, C-509-326-3330. **Chaplain:** Bldg 4200, Hrs: Mon-Fri: 0730-1630, C-509-247-2264. **Emergency Relief:** Bldg 3505, Hrs: Mon-Fri: 0730-1630,

*WASHINGTON*
*Fairchild Air Force Base, continued*

C-509-247-5081 (AF Aid). **Lost/Found:** Bldg 325, 24hrs daily, C-509-247-5496. **Security Police:** Bldg 2525, 24hrs daily, C-509-247-5493.

**OTHER SERVICES: Exchange:** Bldg 2264, Hrs: Mon-Fri: 0900-2100, Sat-Sun: 0900-1600, C-509-244-2832. **Bank/Exchange:** Bldg 2464, 24hrs daily (Money Machine). **Hair Styles:** Bldg 2452, call for hours, Barber: C-509-244-3968; Beauty: C-509-244-2848. **Laundry:** Bldg 644, 24hrs daily. **Medical:** Bldg 9000, 24hrs daily, C-509-247-5661 (emergency room), D-312-657-5661. **Postal:** Bldg 644, Hrs: Mon-Fri: 1000-1630, C-509-244-5879 (civilian); C-509-244-5368 (military). **Valet/Dry Cleaning:** Bldg 2264, Hrs: Mon-Fri: 1000-1630, C-509-244-9786. **Wire:** Bldg 2264, Hrs: Mon-Fri: 0900-2100, Sat-Sun: 0900-1600, C-509-244-2832 (ask for customer service).

**ATTRACTIONS:** Spokane, Expo Site, parks.

| ORIGINATING SCHEDULES | | | |
|---|---|---|---|
| | **ACC/SKA-1 1st/4th MON KC135R** | | |
| **Location ID** | **Airport (Station)** | **Country/State** | **Days Out** |
| SKA | Fairchild AFB | WA | +0 |
| DOV | Dover AFB | DE | +1 |
| **MHZ** | **RAF Mildenhall** | **UK** | **+2** |
| DOV | Dover AFB | DE | +3 |
| SKA | Fairchild AFB | WA | |
| | **PCC/SKA-2 2nd/4th MON, 1st THU, 3rd SAT KC135R** | | |
| SKA | Fairchild AFB | WA | +0 |
| SUU | Travis AFB | CA | +1 |
| EDF | Elmendorf AFB | AK | +2 |
| **OKO** | **Yokota AB** | **JA** | **+3** |
| SUU | Travis AFB | CA | +4 |
| SKA | Fairchild AFB | WA | |
| | **IN ROUTE SCHEDULES** | | |
| **Scott AFB** | BLV/MEDEVAC-3 | | |
| **Travis AFB** | SUU/MEDEVAC-4 | | |

## GRAY ARMY AIRFIELD (GRF)

Air Operations, Bldg 3082
Fort Lewis, WA 98433-0085

**LOCATION:** On I-5 in Puget Sound area, 14 miles north of Olympia. Exits clearly marked. *USMRA: Page 101 (C-5); Page 103 (A,B-7)*. NMC: Tacoma, 12 miles north. Main installation numbers: C-206-967-1110, D-312-357-1110.

**PAX TERM INFO: C-206-967-6628/5998, D-312-357-6628/5998.** Bldg 3082, 24hrs daily. Directions: Enter main gate on 41st Division Dr, go left on Stryker then left on 18th St straight to Bldg 3082. **Pax Service Office:** Same as Passenger terminal, (NCO on duty).

**TML:** Lodging Office (Bldg 2110, between Utah and Pendleton Avenues), Main Post: C-206-967-2815/7862/6754, D-312-357-2815/357-7862, FAX 206-967-2253, DSN FAX 312-357-2253. DV/VIP: Protocol Office, Bldg 2025, C-206-967-5834, D-312-357-5834, 07+.

**OTHER SERVICES:** Full Large Base support. See Military Living's *US Forces Travel & Transfer Guide USA & Caribbean Areas* for full details.

**UNSCHEDULED FLIGHTS**

Flights via Army C-12A, U-21 and CH-47 aircraft to CONUS West Coast and Midwest locations. Call for destinations, routings and schedules.

# McCHORD AIR FORCE BASE (TCM)

62nd APS/TRP
1422 Union Ave
McChord AFB, WA 98438-5000

**LOCATION:** Nine miles south of Tacoma WA. From I-5 Exit 125 onto Bridgeport Way. One mile to main gate. *USMRA: Page 101 (C-5); Page 103 (B-7)*. NMC: Tacoma, 9 miles north. Main installation numbers: C-206-984-1910, D-312-984-1110.

**PAX TERM INFO: C-206-984-5327, REC: C-206-984-2657/2658, (3-day forecast), FAX: C-206-984-5659.** Bldg 1179, Hrs: daily 0500-2200. Directions: From main gate, left on Battery Rd, one block to A St, left at stop sign, one mile to Pax Terminal. **Pax Service Office:** Bldg 1179, duty hours, C-206-984-5658. **Pax Paging:** Same as Pax terminal.

**PAX LOUNGES:** No family lounge. **USO lounge:** Bldg 1183, Hrs: daily 0600-1800 - with cribs and restrooms, C-206-984-2400, D-312-984-2400. **General:** Bldg 1179, Hrs: daily 0500-2200, C-206-984-2400, D-312-976-2400. Free TV, restrooms, bag check/lockers, P/C seats, telephones. **DV/VIP:** Bldg 1179, Hrs: daily 0500-2200, C-206-984-5913, D-312-984-5913. Rear of Terminal behind Pax Service office. A/C, separate reading room, free TV, restrooms, O/S seats. **Protocol Service:** Bldg 100, Hrs: daily 0800-1600, C-206-984-2788, D-312-984-2788.

**FOOD SERVICE: Olympic Dining Hall:** Bldg 548, C-206-984-2525, D-312-984-2525. **Enlisted Club:** Bldg 746, C-206-984-5134. **O'Club:** Bldg 171, C-206-984-5581. **Bowling Snack Bars:** Bldg 737, C-206-984-2892. **Encore Pizzeria:** Bldg 1155, C-206-

*WASHINGTON*
*McChord Air Force Base, continued*

984-5148. **Wrangler Chicken & Ribs:** Bldg 746, C-206-984-5165. **Burger King:** Bldg 510, C-206-582-1188.

**TRANSPORTATION: Air Tickets:** N & N Travel and Tours, Inc: 1179, Hrs: Mon-Fri: 0730-1800, C-206-584-0836. **Bus (Shuttle):** From Pax Term every 30 minutes on the half hour, Hrs: Mon-Fri: 0600-1800. **Car Rentals:** Budget: U-SAVE:, hotline in Terminal Building, Hrs: Mon-Fri: 0700-1800, Sat: 0800-1700, Sun: 0900-1700. **SEA-TAC Airporter:** Leaves at 0520, last run 2320, two-hour intervals, reservations required, C-1-800-562-7948. **Taxi (Comm):** Bldg 1179, 24hrs daily, C-206-984-3331. **Parking:** Short term in front of Pax Terminal (Bldg 1179) 24hr limit; long term in walking distance, modest fee.

**TML:** Lodging Office (Bldg 166, Main Street), C-206-584-1471, D-312-976-1471. DV/VIP: Bldg 100, C-206-584-2621, 06/GS-15+.

**TRAVELERS AID: American Red Cross:** Bldg 521, Hrs: daily 0800-1600, C-206-984-5577, After hours, C-206-967-7686. **Chaplain:** Bldg 180, Hrs: Mon-Fri: 0800-1700, C-206-984-5556/7. **Lost/Found:** Bldg 1179, In Pax Service Office: 24hrs daily, C-206-984-5658. **Security Police:** Main gate, C-206-984-2119. **USO:** SEA-TAC Intl Arpt: 24hrs daily, C-206-433-5438; McChord Terminal: Hrs: daily 0600-2200, C-206-984-2400.

**OTHER SERVICES: Exchange:** Main BX: Bldg 543, C-206-582-9450. Shoppette: Bldg 506, C-206-582-0788. **Bank/Exchange:** Bldg 550, C-206-593-5772. Credit Union: Bldg 530, C-206-584-6413. **Hair Styles:** Bldg 543, Barber: C-206-588-2345; Beauty: C-206-584-1595. **Laundry/Dry Cleaning:** Bldg 506, C-206-584-7038. **Medical:** Bldg 164, 24hrs daily, C-206-984-5601/3. **Postal:** Bldg 735, C-206-984-2093.

**ATTRACTIONS:** Seattle (30 miles north), Cascade Mts (Mt Rainier).

| **ORIGINATING SCHEDULES** | | | |
|---|---|---|---|
| **PPM/TCM-1 FRI C-141B** | | | |
| **Location ID** | **Airport (Station)** | **Country/State** | **Days Out** |
| TCM | McChord AFB | WA | +0 |
| SUU | Travis AFB | CA | +0 |
| **EIL** | **Eielson AFB** | **AK** | **+0** |
| EDF | Elmendorf AFB | AK | +1 |
| TCM | McChord AFB | WA | +1 |
| SUU | Travis AFB | CA | +2 |
| TCM | McChord AFB | WA | |
| **PCC/TCM-2 WED C-141B** | | | |
| TCM | McChord AFB | WA | +0 |
| EDF | Elmendorf AFB | AK | +1 |
| ADK | Adak Island NS | AK | +2 |
| EDF | Elmendorf AFB | AK | +2 |
| **SYA** | **Eareckson AS** | **AK** | **+3** |

*WASHINGTON*
*McChord Air Force Base, continued*

| | | | |
|---|---|---|---|
| EDF | Elmendorf AFB | AK | +3 |
| TCM | McChord AFB | WA | |
| | **PCC/TCM-3 1st/2nd/4th TUE C-141B** | | |
| TCM | McChord AFB | WA | +0 |
| SUU | Travis AFB | CA | +1 |
| EDF | Elmendorf AFB | AK | +2 |
| **OKO** | **Yokota AB** | **JA** | **+3** |
| EDF | Elmendorf AFB | AK | +3 |
| SUU | Travis AFB | CA | +4 |
| TCM | McChord AFB | WA | |
| | **PCC/TCM-4 1st FRI C-141B** | | |
| TCM | McChord AFB | WA | +0 |
| SUU | Travis AFB | CA | +1 |
| EDF | Elmendorf AFB | AK | +2 |
| **OKO** | **Yokota AB** | **JA** | **+24** |
| EDF | Elmendorf AFB | AK | +24 |
| SUU | Travis AFB | CA | +25 |
| TCM | McChord AFB | WA | |
| | **PCC/TCM-5 1st/2nd/4th TUE C-141B** | | |
| TCM | McChord AFB | WA | +0 |
| SUU | Travis AFB | CA | +0 |
| EDF | Elmendorf AFB | AK | +1 |
| OKO | Yokota AB | JA | +2 |
| **OSN** | **Osan AB** | **RK** | **+3** |
| OKO | Yokota AB | JA | +3 |
| EDF | Elmendorf AFB | AK | +4 |
| SUU | Travis AFB | CA | +5 |
| TCM | McChord AFB | WA | |
| | **PPM/TCM-6 2nd/4th TUE C-141B** | | |
| TCM | McChord AFB | WA | +0 |
| SUU | Travis AGB | CA | +0 |
| HIK | Hickam AFB | HI | +1 |
| UAM | Andersen AFB | GU | +2 |
| DNA | Kadena AB | JA | +3 |
| **OSN** | **Osan AB** | **RK** | **+3** |
| OKO | Yokota AB | JA | +4 |
| HIK | Hickam AFB | HI | +4 |
| SUU | Travis AFB | CA | +5 |

*WASHINGTON*
*McChord Air Force Base, continued*

| | | | |
|---|---|---|---|
| TCM | McChord AFB | WA | |
| | **PCC/TCM-7 SUN C-141B** | | |
| TCM | McChord AFB | WA | +0 |
| SUU | Travis AFB | CA | +0 |
| HIK | Hickam AFB | HI | +1 |
| PPG | Pago Pago IAP | AS | +2 |
| CHC | Christchurch IAP | NZ | +3 |
| RCM | Richmond RAAFB | AU | +3 |
| **UMR** | **Woomera AS** | **AU** | **+4** |
| RCM | Richmond RAAFB | AU | +4 |
| CHC | Christchurch IAP | NZ | +5 |
| PPG | Pago Pago IAP | AS | +6 |
| HIK | Hickam AFB | HI | +7 |
| SUU | Travis AFB | CA | +8 |
| TCM | McChord AFB | WA | |
| | **PPM/TCM-8 1st/3rd TUE C-141B** | | |
| TCM | McChord AFB | WA | +0 |
| SUU | Travis AFB | CA | +1 |
| HIK | Hickam AFB | HI | +2 |
| **OKO** | **Yokota AB** | **JA** | **+4** |
| HIK | Hickam AFB | HI | +4 |
| SUU | Travis AFB | CA | +5 |
| TCM | McChord AFB | WA | |
| | **IN ROUTE SCHEDULES** | | |
| **Scott AFB** | BLV/MEDEVAC-3 | | |
| **Travis AFB** | SUU/MEDEVAC-4 | | |

Frequent CONUS flights available but scheduled on a day-to-day basis as needed. Call C-206-206-984-2659 or D-312-976-2659 for status information. Flight schedules change month to month. Call for schedules.

## WHIDBEY ISLAND NAVAL AIR STATION (NUW)

Air Operations Division
Oak Harbor, WA 98278-5200

**LOCATION:** Take WA-20 to Whidbey Island, 3 miles west of WA-20 on Ault Field Road. *USMRA: Page 101 (C-2,3)*. NMC: Seattle, 60 miles southeast. Main installation numbers: C-360-257-2211, D-312-820-0111.

**PAX TERM INFO: C-360-257-2604, D-312-820-2604, REC: C-360-257-2328, D-312-820-2328, after hours, FAX: C-360-257-1942, D-312-820-1942.** Bldg 2734, Hrs: daily 0700-1900. Directions: From main gate straight on Langley Blvd, left on Charles Porter Ave to a right on Lexington St to Pax Term on left.

**PAX LOUNGES:** General lounge only. No family lounge. **General:** Bldg 2734, Hrs: daily 0700-1900, C-360-257-2604. TV, restrooms, O/S seats. **DV/VIP:** Bldg 2734, Hrs: daily 0700-1900, C-360-257-2604. Coffee served, showers (06+). **Base Operator:** Bldg 113, Hrs: Mon-Fri: 0730-1630, C-360-257-2211.

**FOOD SERVICE: Cafeteria:** C-360-657-5981. **Dining Hall:** C-360-257-2211. **Enlisted Club:** C-360-257-3308. **NCO/CPO Club:** C-360-257-2829. **O'Club:** C-360-257-2521. **Admiral Nimitz Hall:** C-360-257-2717. **McDonalds:** C-360-257-8888. **Snack Bar:** C-360-675-8598. **Vending:** C-360-257-2604.

**TRANSPORTATION: Air Tickets:** SATO: C-360-679-4415. **Car Rentals:** C-360-675-1244. **Taxi (Comm):** C-360-675-1244. **Taxi (Gov):** C-360-257-3133. **Parking:** C-360-257-3121 (short/long term, Bldg 117, near base gym).

**TML:** Lodging Office (McCormick Center, Bldg 973, 5th Street), Officer/CPO, Hrs: daily 0730-1630, C-360-257-2529/2076, D-312-820-2529/2076. Enlisted: Bldg 2701, 8th Street, C-360-257-5513, FAX 360-257-5603. DV/VIP: C-360-257-2345, O6+.

**TRAVELERS AID: American Red Cross:** C-360-675-2559 (After hours C-360-257-2631). **Chaplain:** C-360-257-2414. **Navy Relief:** C-360-657-5177/2728. **Security Police:** C-360-257-3121. **YMCA:** C-360-675-2771.

**OTHER SERVICES: Exchange:** C-360-679-5200. **Bank/Exchange:** C-360-675-0763. **Hair Styles:** C-360-679-5200. **Laundry/Dry Cleaning:** C-360-679-5200. **Medical:** C-360-679-9500, D-312-820-9500.

**ATTRACTIONS:** Beautiful island setting. Summer: hiking, mountain biking, fishing; winter: skiing, snowboarding, snowmobiling.

**UNSCHEDULED FLIGHTS**

Frequent flights via Navy C-009B, P-3A and other aircraft to: Alameda NAS, CA (**NGZ**); McChord AFB, WA (**TCM**); Norfolk NAS, VA (**NGU**); and North Island NAS, CA (**NZY**). Call for destinations, routings and schedules.

# WEST VIRGINIA

## EASTERN WEST VIRGINIA REGIONAL AIRPORT (MRB)

167th ANG (Air Nation Guard)
Martinsburg, WV 25401-7720

**LOCATION:** From US-11, 3 miles south of Martinsburg, turn left on Paynes Ford Rd, 1 mile to sign for Air National Guard Base. *USMRA: Page 47 (K-3,4)*. NMC: Martinsburg, 3 miles north. Main installation numbers: C-304-267-5110, D-312-242-9210.

**PAX TERM INFO: C-304-267-5250, D-312-242-9250, FAX: C-304-267-5144, D-312-242-9144.** Bldg 120, 2nd Floor, Hrs: Mon-Fri: 0730-1600. Ask Security Police for directions. **Pax Service Office:** Bldg 120, Hrs: Mon-Fri: 0730-1600, C-304-267-5311 (scheduling NCO).

**PAX LOUNGES:** Limited. **General:** Bldg 120, Hrs: Mon-Fri: 0730-1600, C-304-267-5250. A/C, bag check, restrooms, showers.

**TML**: Lodging Office, very limited, C-304-267-5174.

**OTHER SERVICES:** Located approx 100 miles from Washington National Airport; 60 miles from Dulles International Airport; 20 miles from Hagerstown, MD Airport. No commercial Airlines/Bus service available at Martinsburg WV. AMTRAK has commuter service to Washington DC each AM & PM Mon-Fri. **BX:** C-304-267-5204, **Consol Club:** C-304-267-5298, **Medical:** C-304-267-5244.

### UNSCHEDULED FLIGHTS

Flights to other CONUS & OCONUS locations. Call for destinations, routings and schedules.

## YEAGER AIRPORT (CRW)

130th TAG/OTM (Air National Guard)
Charleston, WV 25311-5000

**LOCATION:** Off I-77 North or South, exit 102, follow signs to airport. *USMRA: Page 46 (E-6)*. NMC: Charleston, 4 miles southwest. Main installation numbers: C-304-357-5100, D-312-366-6210.

**PAX TERM INFO: C-304-357-6185/6240, D-312-366-6185/6240, FAX: C-304-357-6142/6001.** Air National Guard area, Hrs: Mon-Fri: 0730-1600. Ask Security Police for directions. All support of regional airport. **BX**: C-304-341-4957, **Medical**: C-304-341-6252.

**TML**: No US Military Lodging.

**UNSCHEDULED FLIGHTS**

Flights via ANG C-130A aircraft to CONUS and OCONUS locations. Call for destinations, routings and schedules.

# WISCONSIN

## GENERAL MITCHELL INTERNATIONAL AIRPORT/ARS (GMF)

128th ARFG (ANG), Building 113
Milwaukee, WI 53207-6299

**LOCATION:** From I-94 North or South, exit 318 East to airport. *USMRA: Page 68 (G-9)*. NMC: Milwaukce, 3 miles north. Main installation numbers: Air National Guard: C-414-747-4410, D-312-580-8410; AFRES: C-414-482-5000, D-312-950-5000.

**PAX TERM INFO: C-414-747-4132, D-312-580-8132 (recording).** Bldg 113, limited hours of operations (call). Directions: East side of building. Ask at gate. ANG/AFRES Base. Limited military Base support. No TML available.

| ORIGINATING SCHEDULES | | | |
|---|---|---|---|
| | **ACC/GMF-1 1st/2nd TUE KC135R** | | |
| **Location ID** | **Airport (Station)** | **Country/State** | **Days Out** |
| GMF | General Mitchell IAP/ARS | WI | +0 |
| WRI | McGuire AFB | NJ | +0 |
| **LGS** | **Lajes AB** | **PO** | **+2** |
| WRI | McGuire AFB | NJ | +2 |
| GMF | General Mitchell IAP/ARS | WI | |

**UNSCHEDULED FLIGHTS**

Flights via ANG KC-135R and AFRES C-130H aircraft to CONUS, OCONUS, and foreign country locations. Call for destinations, routings and schedules.

## VOLK FIELD AIR NATIONAL GUARD BASE (VOK)

Air Operations, CRTC/OTM
Camp Douglas, WI 54618-5001

**LOCATION:** Take I-90/94 North or South. Take Exit 55 West to Camp Douglas. Clearly marked. *USMRA: Page 68 (D-7)*. NMC: La Crosse, 50 miles west. Main installation numbers: C-608-427-1210, D-312-798-3210.

**PAX TERM INFO: C-608-427-1210, D-312-798-3210, FAX: C-608-427-1266.** Bldg 508, Base Ops, Hrs: Tue-Sat: 0800-1600. **Pax Service Office:** Bldg 508, Hrs: Tue-Sat: 0800-1600, C-608-427-1205 (NCO/Civilian, GS employee on duty).

**PAX LOUNGES:** Limited. **General:** Bldg 508, Hrs: Tue-Sat: 0800-1600. A/C, coffee/tea served, telephones (commercial and defense), restrooms, O/S seats. **Protocol Service:** Bldg 100, Hrs: Mon-Fri: 0800-1600, C-608-427-1210, D-312-798-3210.

**FOOD SERVICE: Restaurants:** Good off base. **Vending:** Bldg 508.

**TRANSPORTATION: Bus (Comm):** Tomah, WI, Greyhound: C-608-372-4466. **Taxi (Comm):** Tomah, WI, C-608-372-2345. **Parking:** Bldg: 511 (no restrictions).

**TRAVELERS AID: Security Police:** C-608-427-1210 (ask for security).

**UNSCHEDULED FLIGHTS**

Air National Guard Training Site. Flights via transient ANG aircraft. Call for destinations, routings and schedules.

# WYOMING

## CHEYENNE MUNICIPAL AIRPORT (CYS)

217 Dell Range Blvd, Bldg 16, Rm 122
Cheyenne, WY 82003-2268

**LOCATION:** From I-25 North or South, exit on Central Ave East to airport. *Turn on to Yellowstone Rd to first light. Turn on to Dell Range Blvd, first right into guard base. USMRA: Page 102 (I-8).* NMC: Cheyenne, 1 mile south. Main installation numbers: C-307-772-6201, D-312-943-6201.

**PAX TERM INFO: C-307-772-6132/6347, D-312-943-/61326347, FAX 307-772-6000, D FAX 943-6000.** Bldg 116, Hrs: Mon-Fri: 0730-1630.

**TML:** Lodging Office (Francis E. Warren AFB, Crow Creek Inn, Bldg 216, Randall St), C-307-775-1844. DV/VIP: PAO. C-307-775-2137/3052, E8+/06+. Historic houses.

**OTHER SERVICES:** Full support of a regional airport. No military facilities.

**UNSCHEDULED FLIGHTS**

Flights to CONUS and OCONUS locations via ANG C-130H aircraft. Call for destinations, routings, and schedules.

# OUTSIDE CONTINENTIAL UNITED STATES (OCONUS)

# ALASKA

## ADAK ISLAND NAVAL STATION (ADK)

PO Box 1242
FPO AP 96506-1202
Will close under the 1993 BRAC. No date established for closure

**LOCATION:** On Adak Island of the Aleutian Island chain, accessible only by air or ship. *USMRA:Page 128 (H-8)*. NMC: Anchorage, 1200 air miles northeast. Main installation numbers: C-907-592-8001, D-317-692-8001.

**PAX TERM INFO: C-907-592-4196, D-317-692-4196, FAX 907-592-8088, DSN FAX 692-4196.** Bldg 30003, Hrs: Mon-Fri: 0800-1700 (other hours as required). On main road at flight line. Isolated and restricted station. *Space-A pax must have island clearance before arriving. Clearance must be applied for by an island resident at least 30 days prior to arrival.* **Pax Service Office:** Same as Pax Term, C-907-592-8026 (NCO on duty). **Pax Paging:** Same as Pax Term.

**PAX LOUNGES:** Bldg 30003. General & DV/VIP lounges. No family lounge. **General:** Hrs: Mon-Fri: 0800-1700, C-907-592-4196. Telephones (commercial and defense), restrooms, P/C seats. **DV/VIP:** Bldg 30003, Hrs: Mon-Fri: 0800-1700, C-907-592-4196. A/C, bag check, TV, restrooms, showers. **Protocol Service:** Bldg 30003, Hrs: Mon-Fri: 0800-1700, C-907-592-4196.

**FOOD SERVICE: Enlisted Club:** C-907-592-8104. **NCO/CPO Club:** C-907-592-8393. **O'Club:** C-907-592-8354. **Restaurant:** C-907-592-8104. No commercial eateries.

**TRANSPORTATION: Air Tickets:** C-907-592-3466. **Bus (Shuttle):** C-907-592-8345. **Car Rentals:** C-907-592-4154.

*ALASKA*
*Adak Island Naval Station, continued*

**TML:** Lodging Office, Hrs: daily 0800-1700, C-907-592-8211/4134, D-317-692-8604, FAX 907-592-4468. DV/VIP: C-907-592-8287.

**TRAVELERS AID: Chaplain:** C-907-592-4169/8203. **Security Police:** C-907-592-8051.

**OTHER SERVICES: Medical:** C-907-592-8382, D-317-692-8382.

**ATTRACTIONS:** Hunting, fishing, and other outdoor sports.

| IN ROUTE SCHEDULES | |
|---|---|
| **McChord AFB** | PCC/TCM-2 |

**UNSCHEDULED FLIGHTS**

Weekly flights to Elmendorf AFB, AK (EDF) and Eareckson AS, AK (SYA) utilizing B-737 aircraft. Please call for destinations, routings and schedules.

## EIELSON AIR FORCE BASE (EIL)

354rd TRNS/LGTTA
Eielson AFB, AK 99702-1870

**LOCATION:** On the Richardson Hwy (AK-2), AFB is clearly marked. *USMRA:Page 128 (F,G-4).* NMC: Fairbanks AK, 26 miles northwest. Main installation numbers: C-907-377-1110, D-317-377-1110.

**PAX TERM INFO: C-907-377-1854, D-317-377-1854, FAX 907-377-2287.** Bldg 1221, Hrs: Mon-Fri: 0730-1630, other hours as required. Directions: From main gate to Flight Line Ave. Pax Term next to Thunder Dome. **Pax Service Office:** Same as Pax terminal.

**PAX LOUNGES:** Bldg 1221. No separate **DV/VIP** or family lounges. **General:** Bldg 1138, Hrs: daily 0730-1630, C-907-377-1854. Telephones (defense), TV, restrooms, P/C seats. **Protocol Service:** Bldg 3112, duty hours, C-907-377-6101 (ask for Wing Executive Officer).

**FOOD SERVICE: Burger King:** Bldg 3315, Hrs: Mon-Thu: 0600-2200, Fri: 0600-2300, Sat: 0800-2300, Sun: 0800-2200. **Cafeteria:** Bldg 2216, Hrs: Mon-Fri: 1100-2100, Sat: 1200-1800, C-907-377-1126. **Dining Hall:** Bldg 2207, Hrs: daily 0600-1800, C-907-377-2563. **In-flight Meals:** Bldg 2207, 24hrs daily, C-907-377-1444. **NCO Club:** Bldg 2225, Hrs: Mon-Sat: 1000-2300, C-907-377-2635. **O'Club:** Bldg 5223, Hrs: Mon-Fri: 0800-2100, C-907-377-1121. **Snack Bars:** Bowling Alley: Bldg 3301, C-907-377-5154. **Vending:** Bldg 1221, Hrs: Mon-Fri: 0730-1600, C-907-377-1854.

**TRANSPORTATION: Air Tickets:** SATO: Bldg 3112, Hrs: Mon-Fri: 0800-1630, C-907-372-2288. **Bus (Gov):** Bldg 3425, 24hrs daily, C-907-377-2197/1843 (duty pax only). **Taxi (Comm):** North Pole Taxi Service, 24hrs daily, C-907-488-7900 (ten miles from base). **Taxi (Gov):** Bldg 3425, 24hrs daily, C-907-377-2197/1843 (duty pax only).

**TML:** Lodging Office (Gold Rush Inn, Bldg 2270, Central Ave), 24hrs daily, C-907-372-4101, D-317-377-1844, FAX 907-777-2559. DV/VIP: C-907-377-6101, E-9/O6+.

**TRAVELERS AID: American Red Cross:** Bldg 3347, C-907-377-1855. **Chaplain:** Bldg 3307, C-907-377-2130. **Emergency Relief:** Bldg 3125, C-907-377-2178 (AF Aid). **Security Police:** Bldg 2222, C-907-377-5130.

**OTHER SERVICES: Exchange:** Bldg 3310, C-907-372-2139. **Hairstyles:** Bldg 3310. Barber: C-907-372-2290; Beauty: C-907-372-3265. **Laundry/Dry Cleaning:** Bldg 2262, C-907-372-2280. **Medical:** Bldg 3349, Hrs: daily 0730-2100, C-907-377-2259, D-317-377-2259. **Postal:** Bldg 2216, C-907-372-1234. **Wire:** Bldg 3310, Hrs: Mon-Fri: 0900-1800, Sat: 0930-1730, Sun: 1100-1700 (Western Union).

**ATTRACTIONS:** Fairbanks, North Pole (Santa Claus House), outdoor sports & recreation.

| IN ROUTE SCHEDULES | |
|---|---|
| **McChord AFB** | PPM/TCM-1 |

## ELMENDORF AIR FORCE BASE (EDF)

632 AMSS/TROP, 7th St, Bldg 32-233
Elmendorf AFB, AK 99506-3565

**LOCATION:** Off Glenn highway (AK-1). Take Muldoon, Boniface, Post Road or Government Hill exits. The AFB is adjacent to Fort Richardson. *USMRA:Page 128 (F-5) & Page 131 (B,C,D,E-1)*. NMC: Anchorage AK, 2 miles southwest. Main installation numbers: C-907-552-1110, D-317-552-1110.

**PAX TERM INFO: C-907-552-3781/5189, D-312-552-3781/5189, FAX 317-552-3996, D FAX 317-552-3996, within DSN FAX 94-552-3996.** Bldg 32-233, 24hrs daily. Directions: From Post Rd gate to a left on 6th St to dead end at Pax Term. **Pax Service Office:** Bldg 32-233, Hrs: daily 0700-1700, **Pax Paging:** Same as Pax terminal.

**PAX LOUNGES: Nursery lounge:** restricted to families with infants. **General:** Bldg 32-233, 24hrs daily, C-907-552-3781. Bag check, game room, rest-rooms, telephone (local and long distance), P/C & O/S seats, TV. **DV/VIP:** Bldg 32-233, 24hrs daily, C-907-552-3781 (06+). Restrooms, telephones (local and ong distance), O/S seats, TV. **Family:** Bldg 32-233, 24hrs daily, C-907-552-3781. TV, O/S seats. Armed Services YMCA Lounge located in inbound section TV/Info area.

**FOOD SERVICE: Cafeteria:** Bldg 32-233, 24hrs daily, C-907-753-6146. Next to Pax Term. **Dining Hall:** Bldg 1-86, Hrs: daily 0530-1830, C-907-552-2253. **Enlisted Club:** Bldg 31-145, C-907-753-5190/6131. **O'Club:** Bldg 9-580, C-907-753-3131. **Snack Bars:** Bldg 31-148, Hrs: Vary with season, C-907-552-3669 (Polar Bowl). **Vending:** Bldg 31-233, C-907-552-3781. Also facilities available at Fort Richardson.

*ALASKA*
*Elemendorf Air Force Base, continued*

**TRANSPORTATION:** Local ground transportation also available at Fort Richardson. **Air Tickets:** Anchorage, C-907-753-3592/0509 (SATO). **Bus (Shuttle):** Bldg 32-233, Hrs: daily 0600-1830, C-907-552-2454 (schedule at billeting). **Car Rentals:** Dollar: Bldg 32-233, Hrs: Mon-Fri: 0700-2000, Sat-Sun: 0800-1700, C-907-753-2178 (other major companies at Anchorage IAP). **Taxi (Gov):** Bldg 32-260, 24hrs daily, C-907-552-2792/3 (duty Pax only). **Parking:** Bldg 32-233, 24hrs daily, C-907-552-3781 Limit 60 days, fill out pass at Pass Counter.

**TML:** Lodging Office (North Star Inn, Bldg 31-0250), 24hrs daily, C-907-753-6110, D-317-552-2454, FAX 907-552-8276. All ranks. DV/VIP: C-907-552-3210, O6+.

**TRAVELERS AID: American Red Cross:** Bldg 2-864, C-907-552-5253. **Chaplain:** Bldg 24-800, duty hours, C-907-552-4422; other hours, C-907-552-5533. **Lost/Found:** Terminal, C-907-552-4616. **Security Police:** Bldg 6-900, C-907-552-3421 (Desk Sgt).

**OTHER SERVICES:** Full range of support available at EDF and Fort Richardson. **Exchange:** Bldg 4-932, C-907-753-4260. **Bank/Exchange** Bldg 3-850, C-907-753-1179 (lst National Bank). **Hair Styles:** Bldg 4-932, C-907-753-1215. **Laundry/Dry Cleaners:** Bldg 31-160, C-907-552-2215, Dry Cleaning: Hrs: Mon-Fri: 0800-1730. **Medical:** Bldg 24-800, 24hrs daily, C-907-552-5555 (emergency), C-907-552-2748 (appointment). **Postal:** Bldg 9-854, C-907-552-1110.

**ATTRACTIONS:** Anchorage and outdoor sports (hunting, fishing, etc.).

| | **IN ROUTE SCHEDULES** | | |
|---|---|---|---|
| **Altus AFB** | PCC/LTS-3 | | |
| **Bangor IAP** | PCC/BGR-2 | | |
| **Fairchild AFB** | PCC/SKA-2 | | |
| **Lincoln MAP** | PCC/LNK-1 | | |
| **Malmstrom AFB** | PCC/GFA-1 | | |
| **March AFB** | PCC/RIV-2 | PCC/RIV-3 | |
| **McChord AFB** | PPM/TCM-1 | PCC/TCM-2 | PCC/TCM-3 |
| | PCC/TCM-4 | PCC/TCM-5 | |
| **McConnell AFB** | PCC/IAB-1 | | |
| **McGuire AFB** | PCC/WRI-23 | | |
| **O'Hare IAP** | PCC/ORD-1 | | |
| **Robins AFB** | PCC/WRB-2 | | |
| **Travis AFB** | PCC/SUU-1 | PCC/SUU-2 | PCC/SUU-3 |
| | PCC/SUU-4 | PCC/SUU-6 | |
| **Wright-Patterson AFB** | PCC/FFO-3 | | |

# KODIAK COAST GUARD AIR STATION (ADQ)

P. O. Box 190033
Kodiak, AK 99619-0033

**LOCATION:** From Kodiak take main road (Rezanof Drive West) southwest for 9 miles. Base is on left side. *USMRA:Page 128 (E-7)*. NMC: Kodiak, 9 miles northeast. Main installation numbers: C-907-487-5267, D-317-487-5267.

**PAX TERM INFO: C-907-487-5149, D-317-487-5149, REC: C-907-487-5158, FAX: C-907-487-5273** (for flight schedule, not for sign-up). Hangar #1, Hrs: Mon, Tue, Thu, Fri: 0900-1200. Directions: From Rezanof Drive West turn left on 6th St. and proceed through the Front Gate. Take the 2nd right onto Albatross Rd. Hangar I is located at the end on the left. **Pax Service Office:** Rm 222. **PAX Lounge:** Rm 120.

**FOOD SERVICE: Cafeteria:** C-907-487-5748. **Enlisted Club:** Kings Inn: C-907-487-5110. **NCO/CPO Club:** Golden Anchor: C-907-487-5440 (E7+).

**TRANSPORTATION: Air Tickets:** Kodiak Apt, (see directory for major airlines). **Bus (Shuttle):** C-907-487-5471 (on Base & $1 to city). **Car Rentals:** Kodiak Apt, see directory (Avis, Hertz). **Taxi (Comm):** Ace Mecca, C-907-486-3211.

**TML:** Lodging Office (Guest House, Bldg N-30), Hrs: daily 0745-1630, C-907-487-5446, D-317-487-5310/5446. All ranks. DV/VIP: C-907-487-5260.

**TRAVELERS AID: American Red Cross:** Support Center, C-907-487-5200. **Chaplain:** Support Center, C-907-487-5730/5731. **Lost/Found:** C-907-487-5267. **Security Police:** Main Gate, C-907-487-5266.

**OTHER SERVICES: Exchange:** Support Center, Provides most support (Hair Styles, Laundry/Dry Cleaning, etc.). **Medical:** Support Center, 24hrs daily, C-907-487-5757, D-317-487-5757.

**ATTRACTIONS:** Hunting and fishing paradise.

## UNSCHEDULED FLIGHTS

*Note: Only military personnel may travel to ATU, KPC, SYA and SNP. Prior permission required for non-assigned personnel to travel to ADK.*

Frequent flights to: Attu CGS, AK (**ATU**); *Cordova CGS, AK (**CDV**); Elmendorf AFB, AK (**EDF**); *Juneau CGS, AK (**JNU**); *Ketchikan IAP, AK (**KTN**); Port Clarence, CGS, AK (**KPC**); St Paul Island CGS, AK (**SNP**); Eareckson, AS, AK (**SYA**); *Sitka CGS, AK (**SIT**); *Valdez Apt, AK (**VDZ**).* Indicates destinations on station's SE Alaska logistical flight. Flight lasts two days, one in and one out. Destinations may vary according to mission.

# KULIS AIR NATIONAL GUARD BASE/ ANCHORAGE INTERNATIONAL AIRPORT (ANC)

176th GP, 5005 Raspberry Rd
Anchorage, AK 99502-5000

**LOCATION:** From Elmendorf AFB south on Post Rd to a left on Minnesota Dr to a right onto IAP Rd to Satellite Dr to terminal. *USMRA:Page 128 (F-5) & Page 131 (A-4).* NMC: Anchorage, 5 miles northeast. Main installation numbers: C-907-249-1444, D-317-626-1659.

**PAX TERM INFO: C-907-249-1225, D-317-626-1225, FAX 907-249-1648, DSN FAX 626-1648.** Base Ops, Bldg 21, Hrs: Mon-Fri: 0700-1600, All facilities of an IAP. NOTE: Space-A passengers are not allowed on flights going overseas. See Elmendorf AFB listing for support, including TML.

UNSCHEDULED FLIGHTS

ANG flights to CONUS and OCONUS destinations including Eielson AFB, AK (**EIL**). Call for destinations, routings and schedules.

# ALASKA ISOLATED STATIONS (AIS)

**(Not listed separately in this book)**

The stations listed below have Space-A air opportunities. Base support facilities are very limited. Lodging is not available except at Fort Greely. Camping, fishing, hiking, hunting and all outdoor recreation are outstanding. Permission of the station Commander is required for all visitors except for Fort Greely.

**ALLEN ARMY AIRFIELD, (BIG)**, USAG AVN Det, Fort Greely, APO AP 96508-5000. *USMRA:Page 128 (F,G-4).* **C-907-873-4170, D-317-873-4170.** See Fort Greely for support, including TML.

**CLEAR AIR STATION, (Z84),** PO Box 40013, Clear AS, AK 99704-5000. *USMRA: Page 128 (F-4).* NMC: Fairbanks, 80 miles NE. **C-907-585-6409, D-317-585-6416.** TML: Fort Wainwright, AK 75 miles NE; Lodging Office, (Bldg 1045), C-907-353-7291.

**EARECKSON AIR STATION, (SYA),** OL-E, 616th ALSS/TRO, Shemya AK, APO AP 96512-5000. *USMRA: Page 128 (F-7).* NMC: Anchorage, 1800 air miles NE. **C-907-392-3000, D-317-392-3000.** PAX TERM INFO: **C-907-392-3471/3064.**

**GALENA AIRPORT (GAL),** 5072nd CSS/DON, APO AP 96510-5000. *USMRA:Page 128 (E-4).* **C-907-446-3440/1, D-312-446-3440/1.**

**SITKA COAST GUARD AIR STATION, (SIT),** 611 Airport Rd, Sitka, AK 99835-6500. *USMRA:Page 128 (I-7).* **C-907-966-5420, D-None,** FAX: C-907-966-5428. CGX: C-907-966-5436, TML: C-907-966-5591.

**UNSCHEDULED FLIGHTS**

Flights to: Adak Island NS, AK (**ADK**); Anchorage IAP, AK (**ANC**); Elmendorf AFB, AK (**EDF**); McChord AFB, WA (**TCM**); and Eareckson, AS, AK (**SYA**).

# AMERICAN SAMOA

## PAGO PAGO INTERNATIONAL AIRPORT (PPG)

PPG/Pago Pago International Airport
P.O. Box 280
Pago Pago, American Samoa 96799

**LOCATION:** On the south coast of the Island of Tutuila in American Samoa. Approximately 3,500 miles southwest of Honolulu HI, and 3,000 miles northeast of Christchurch NZ. *ML-ARM: (172°00'W/14°00'S).* NMC: Village of Utulei, main US Government offices, 9 miles from IAP. Main installation numbers: C-011-684-699-1515, D-None.

**PAX TERM INFO: C-011-684-699-1515, FAX 011-684-699-9991.** Pax Term, Hrs: 24 hours daily. At IAP. One gate for departures. Contact AMC rep, C-011-684-699-1515. Basic refuel station. **Pax Service Office:** Pax Term, Hrs: 24 hours daily, AMC Contractor: Pritchard Airport Service, C-011-684-699-9106, FAX 011-684-699-9991. (AMC control-Air Service Samoa). **Pax Paging:** Same as Pax terminal (P.A. system).

**PAX LOUNGES:** Pax Term, Hrs: 24 hours daily. Commercial IAP lounges available for Space-A Pax. **General:** Pax Term, Hrs: 24 hours daily, C-684-699-1515. Bag check/lockers, restrooms, wood seats. **DV/VIP:** Pax Term, Hrs: 24 hours daily, C-011-684-699-1515. A/C, restrooms, O/S seats. No hostess.

**FOOD SERVICE:** Service at IAP, Rainmaker Hotel & American Samoa Exchange Reservations Center. **Enlisted Club:** 4 blocks from PPG, Vet's Club open to Space-A Pax. **Restaurants:** Pax Term, C-011-684-699-9981 (open for AMC flights). **Snack Bars:** Rainmaker Hotel, C-011-684-633-4241.

**TRANSPORTATION: Air Tickets:** Air Service Samoa: Pax Term, C-011-684-699-4222. **Bus (Comm):** Pax Term, C-011-684-699-1515. **Bus (Gov):** Pax Term, C-011-684-699-1515 (AMC rep). **Car Rentals:** PPG/hotels, C-011-684-633-4323/5520 (Hertz, Morris). **Taxi (Comm):** Pax Term, C-011-684-639-9270 (PPG to hotels $7). **Parking:** Pax Term, (no restrictions). **Medical:** LBJ Medical Center, Hrs: 24 hours daily, C-011-684-633-2222 (emergency).

**TML:** No military or government TML. Rainmaker Hotel, C-011-684-633-4241 ($50-$60).

**TRAVELERS AID: American Red Cross:** LBJ Medical Center, C-011-684-633-5222. **Security Police:** Pax Term, C-011-684-699-9101.

**ATTRACTIONS:** Beautiful tropical islands, beaches, and fishing.

| IN ROUTE SCHEDULES | |
|---|---|
| **McChord AFB** | PCC/TCM-7 |
| **Travis AFB** | PCC/SUU-10 |

# GUAM

**ANDERSEN AIR FORCE BASE (UAM)**
605th MASS/TROP
APO San Francisco 96542-5000

**LOCATION:** On the north end of the island, access from Marine Drive (GU-1) which extends the entire length of the island of Guam. *USMRA:Page 130 (E,F-1,2)*. NMC: Agana GU, 15 miles south. Main installation numbers: C-011-671-351-1110, D-315-322-1110.

**PAX TERM INFO: C-671-366-2095, D-315-366-2095, FAX 671-366-2079.** Bldg 17002, Hrs: daily 0600-2200. Directions: Follow Perimeter Rd from main gate to Term on left. **Pax Service Office:** Bldg 17002, Hrs: Mon-Fri: 0730-1630, C-671-366-2166/5165. **Pax Paging:** Same as Pax terminal (see Pax Service Representative).

**PAX LOUNGES:** Bldg 17002, 24hrs daily (see Pax NCO for services). **General:** Bldg 17002, Hrs: daily 0600-2200, C-671-366-5165. A/C, bag lockers, game room, telephone (defense), restrooms, showers, P/C seats. **DV/VIP:** Bldg 17002, Hrs: daily 0600-2200, C-671-366-4102 (no hostess). A/C, bag lockers, coffee/tea served, restrooms, TV, showers, O/S seats. **Protocol Service:** Bldg 23003, duty hours, C-671-366-4228. **Family:** Bldg 17002, Hrs: daily: 0600-2200, C-671-366-4102 (off Gen Pax lounge). A/C, TV, O/S seats, playroom, cribs, refrigerator.

**FOOD SERVICE: Cafeteria:** Bldg 17002, 24hrs daily, C-671-366-8283. **Dining Hall:** Hall B, Hrs: Mon-Fri: 0530-1800, Sat-Sun: 0600-1730, C-671-366-2195. **NCO Club/O'Club:** Bldg 26006, Hrs: Mon-Fri: 0800-2400, Sat-Sun: 0800-0400, C-671-362-3173/3247. **Snack Bars:** Latte Stone Drive-In: Bldg 27030, Hrs: daily 0600-2200, C-671-362-3149. **Vending:** Bldg 17002, 24hrs daily.

**TRANSPORTATION: Air Tickets:** SATO: Bldg 22002, Hrs: Mon-Fri: 0730-1630, C-671-362-3172. **Bus (Shuttle):** Bldg 17002, Hrs: daily 0600-1800, C-671-366-2239. **Car Rentals:** Bldg 17002, Hrs: daily 0800-1700, C-671-362-2181. **Taxi (Gov):** Bldg 1800, 24hrs daily, C-671-366-2239 (duty Pax only). **Parking:** Bldg 17002, 24hrs daily, short-term available/long term-30 days max.

**TML:** Lodging Office (Bldg 27006, 4th & Caroline Ave), 24hrs daily, C-011-671-366-8201, D-315-366-8144. All ranks. DV/VIP: C-011-671-351-4228, O7+.

**TRAVELERS AID: American Red Cross:** Bldg 21000, C-671-366-6270, after hours call C-671-366-8144. **Chaplain:** Bldg 22024, C-671-366-6139, after hours call C-671-366-8144. **Emergency Relief:** Bldg 21000, C-671-366-4295 (Help Line), after hours call C-671-363-2913. **Lost/Found:** Bldg 17002, 24hrs daily, C-671-366-5135. **Security**

**Police:** Bldg 21000, 24hrs daily, C-671-366-2913. **USO:** Bldg 17002, 24hrs daily, C-671-366-4246.

**OTHER SERVICES: Exchange:** Bldg 22026, Hrs: daily 1000-1800, C-671-362-1136. **Bank/Exchange:** Bldg 21000, Hrs: Mon-Fri: 0900-1500, C-671-363-2984/5 (Pentagon Federal Credit Union); Bldg 17002 Automatic Teller Machine. **Hair Styles:** Bldg 25005, Hrs: Mon-Fri: 0800-1730, Sat: 0800-1600, Barber: C-671-362-2187; Beauty: C-671-362-5164. **Laundry/Dry Cleaning:** Bldg 05005, Hrs: Mon-Fri: 0800-1800, Sat: 0800-1600, C-671-362-3120. **Medical:** Bldg 26000, Hrs: daily 0700-1630, Appointments: C-671-366-2978, D-315-366-2978; Urgent Care: Hrs: daily 1700-2130, C-671-366-4276, D-315-366-4276. **Postal:** Bldg 21001, Hrs: Mon-Fri: 0800-1600, Sat: 0800-1200, C-671-366-3243.

**ATTRACTIONS:** US Naval Base, WWII battle areas, beaches.

| IN ROUTE SCHEDULES | | | |
|---|---|---|---|
| **Altus AFB** | PCC/LTS-2 | PCC/LTS-3 | |
| **McChord AFB** | PPM/TCM-6 | | |
| **Travis AFB** | PCC/SUU-6 | PPM/SUU-7 | PCC/SUU-8 |
| **Yokota AB** | PPM/OKO-1 | PPM/OKO-2 | |

## UNSCHEDULED FLIGHTS

Frequent flights to Hickam AFB, HI (**HIK**); Kadena AB, JA (**DNA**); Osan AB, RK (**OSN**); Travis AFB, CA (**SUU**) and Yokota AB, JA (**OKO**). Call for destinations, routings and schedules.

# HAWAII

## HICKAM AIR FORCE BASE (HIK)

619th APS/TROP
635 O' Malley Blvd
Hickam Air Force Base, HI 96853-5328

**LOCATION:** Adjacent to the Honolulu IAP. Accessible from H-1 or HI-92. Clearly marked. Follow signs to Hickam AFB. *USMRA:Page 129 (D-7) & Page 131 (B,C-3,4)*. NMC: Honolulu HI, 6 miles east. Main installation numbers: C-808-471-7110, D-315-471-7110.

**PAX TERM INFO: C-808-449-1515/1854/6833, D-315-449-1515/1854, FAX 808-448-1503.** Bldg 2028, 24hrs daily. Directions: From main gate on O'Malley Blvd, then left before Base Ops Building to Pax Term. **Pax Service Office:** Bldg 2028, Hrs: daily 0730-1700, C-808-449-1581, D-315-449-1581. **Pax Paging:** Bldg 2028, 24hrs daily, C-808-449-1515, D-315-449-1515. Also manages departures & arrivals at Honolulu IAP (HNL).

**PAX LOUNGES:** Bldg 2028. USO lounge open 24 hrs daily. **General:** Bldg 2028, 24hrs daily, C-808-449-2887. A/C, free TV, restrooms, bag check/lockers, game room, cribs, pay telephones. No food in lounge. **DV/VIP:** Bldg 2028, 24hrs daily, C-808-449-1153. A/C, free TV, restrooms. **Protocol Service:** Bldg 1102, duty hours, C-808-449-1781.

**FOOD SERVICE: Cafeteria:** Bldg 2028, Hrs: Mon, Wed, Thu: 0400-2000; Tue, Fri: 0300-2000; Sat: 0600-1900; Sun: 0600-1300; C-808-422-8000 (Aloha Inn). **Dining Hall:** Bldg 1860, Hrs: daily 0530-1800, C-808-449-1555. **NCO Club:** Tradewinds: Bldg 422, Hrs: daily 0630-2100, C-808-449-1092. **O'Club:** Bldg 901, Hrs: daily 1115-2100, C-808-449-1998. **Restaurants:** Sea Breeze: Hrs: Tue-Sun: 1100-2100, C-808-449-9909. **Snack Bars:** Sub Stop: Bldg 1113, Hrs: daily 0700-2230, C-808-422-5335. **Vending:** Bldg 2028, 24hrs daily, C-808-422-8000 (also, pay-telephone).

**TRANSPORTATION: Air Tickets:** SATO: Bldg 1113, Hrs Mon-Fri: 0800-1700, C-808-422-0548; Terminal: Bldg 2028, Hrs: Mon-Sat: 0800-1600, C-808-422-2729. **Bus (Comm):** Bldg 2028, Hrs: Mon-Fri: 0600-0100 (every 20 minutes), C-808-531-1611, Bus #19-HIK, Term, $.85 (exact amount only); 0635-2315 weekends every 30 minutes). NO LARGE LUGGAGE. **Bus (Shuttle):** Bldg 2028, Hrs: Mon-Fri: 0600-1800 (every 15 minutes), C-808-449-1742 (key Base points). **Car Rentals:** Bldg 2028, Hrs: daily 0700-2000, C-808-422-6915 (EBF/AAFES). **Taxi (Comm):** Bldg 2028, 24hrs daily, C-808-533-4999 (front door of lobby). **Taxi (Gov):** Motor Pool, 24hrs daily, C-808-449-1742 (duty Pax only). **Parking:** NW of Term, 24hrs daily, 30-day long term parking available, check with passenger agents.

**TML:** Lodging Office (Bldg 1153), 24hrs daily, C-808-449-2603, D-315-449-2603, FAX 808-449-3572; Hale Koa, C-808-367-6027, D-315-438-6739, 0800-1600 hours HI local time. DV/VIP: C-808-449-1781 (07+).

**TRAVELERS AID: American Red Cross:** Pearl Harbor Bldg 1514, 24hrs daily C-808-471-3155. **Chaplain:** Bldg 1750, Hrs: daily 0730-1640, C-808-449-1754 (all faiths). **Emergency Relief:** Bldg 1102, 24hrs daily, C-808-449-5987 (Air Force Aid); Bldg 1514, 24hrs daily, C-808-423-1314 (Navy Relief-Pearl Harbor). **Lost/Found:** Bldg 2028, 24hrs daily, C-808-449-1515. **Security Police:** Bldg 1004, 24hrs daily, C-808-449-6372 (Desk Sgt). **USO:** Bldg 2028, 24hrs daily, C-808-449-2887/448-0723.

**OTHER SERVICES: Exchange:** Bldg 2028, Hrs: daily 0700-2200, C-808-422-8400 (Main BX); Bldg 1232, C-808-423-1304. **Bank/Exchange:** First Hawaii Bank: Bldg 1242, Hrs: Mon-Thu: 0800-1500, Fri: 0800-1800, C-808-422-2781. **Hair Styles:** Bldg 1232, Barber: Hrs: Mon-Fri: 0930-1800, C-808-422-4045 Beauty: Hrs: Mon-Sat: 0930-1700, C-808-422-6121. **Laundry/Dry Cleaning:** Bldg 1232, Hrs: Mon-Fri: 0930-1800, Sat: 0930-1700, C-808-422-5821/5555. **Medical:** Bldg 559, 24hrs daily, C-808-449-5248, D-315-471-5248 (Tripler AMC). **Postal:** Bldg 2097, Hrs: Mon-Fri: 0830-1500, C-808-449-9480.

**ATTRACTIONS:** Honolulu, Waikiki beach, and Pearl Harbor.

| **ORIGINATING SCHEDULES** | | | |
|---|---|---|---|
| **PPP/HIK-1 TUE, FRI DC862** | | | |
| **Location ID** | **Airport (Station)** | **Country/State** | **Days Out** |
| HIK | Hikam AFB | HI | +0 |
| JON | Johnston Atoll | JO | +0 |
| **KWA** | **Bucholz AAF KMR** | **KA** | **+1** |
| JON | Johnston Atoll | JO | +1 |
| HIK | Hikam AFB | HI | |

| **IN ROUTE SCHEDULES** | | | |
|---|---|---|---|
| **Altus AFB** | PCC/LTS-2 | PCC/LTS-3 | |
| **March AFB** | PCM/RIV-4 | | |
| **McChord AFB** | PPM/TCM-6 | PCC/TCM-7 | PPM/TCM-8 |
| **McGuire AFB** | PCC/WRI-24 | | |
| **Travis AFB** | PCC/SUU-3 | PCC/SUU-5 | PCC/SUU-6 |
| | PPM/SUU-7 | PCC/SUU-8 | PPM/SUU-9 |
| | PCC/SUU-10 | PCC/SUU-11 | |
| **Yokota AB** | PPM/OKO-2 | | |

# PACIFIC ISLANDS

## WAKE ISLAND AIR FORCE BASE (AWK)

Terminal Building
Wake Island
APO AP 96518-5000

**LOCATION:** A US island in the Mid-Pacific, 2100 air miles west of Hawaii. *ML-ARM (166°45'E/18°30'N).* NMC: Honolulu, 2100 air miles southeast. Main installation numbers: C- Honolulu AT&T Operator - ask for Wake Island + EX D-315-424-2+EXT.

**PAX TERM INFO: C-808-424-2101/2320, FAX 808-424-2165, DSN FAX 315-424-2435.** Base Ops, Hrs: 24 hours daily, EX-101. All arrivals via air. Letter of approval from base commander required for all active duty/non active duty visitor. All Space-A Pax processed by **Pax Service Office:** Base Ops, Hrs: Mon-Sat 0800-1700, EX-2101.

**PAX LOUNGES:** Terminal Building, 1st Floor, Hrs: Mon-Sat 0800-1700, EX-424-2210. A/C, telephones (commercial), restrooms, P/C seats. General lounge only.

**FOOD SERVICE:** Limited, EX-486. **Bar:** Drifters Reef: Bldg 1109, EX-424-2310.

**TRANSPORTATION: Bus (Gov):** Bus (Gov), Base Ops, EX-101. Term to support facilities.

**OTHER SERVICES: BX:** EX-310. Barber, Laundry; **Post Office:** EX-424-2259.

**TML:** Lodging Office, Hrs: Mon-Sat 0800-1700, EX-424-2222 (very limited).

**ATTRACTIONS:** Tropical climate and nice beaches.

| IN ROUTE SCHEDULES | |
|---|---|
| **Travis AFB** | PPM/SUU-9 |

## US PACIFIC ISLANDS

(Not listed separately in this book)

The stations listed below have Space-A air opportunities. Base support facilities are very limited. Billeting and mess arrangements for extended visits should be made and confirmed in advance of your planned visit.

**JOHNSTON ATOLL, JO (JON) (USA),** FCDNA Term Ops JQ/AMC REP, Johnston Atoll, APO AP 96558-5000. *ML-ARM: (160°30'W/16°00'N).* **C-011-808-621-3044-X-2252. D-312-441-2252, FAX 808-621-3044/2343, DSN FAX 312-441-2343.** *NOTE: Permission/official approval required to visit Johnston Atoll (see Appendix B).*

| IN ROUTE SCHEDULES | |
|---|---|
| **Hickam AFB** | PPP/HIK-1 |
| **March AFB** | PCM/RIV-4 |
| **Travis AFB** | PPM/SUU-9 |

**KWAJALEIN ATOLL, U.S. Army, KA (KWA) (USA), Republic of the Marshall Islands,** Kwajalein Missile Range, ATTN: CSSD-KA-P, PO Box 26, APO AP 96555-2526. *ML-ARM: (167°45'E/8°45'N).* **C-011-805-238-7994, EX 2169, D-315-254-1110 (from CONUS), C-480-1110 (from Pacific locations) PAC DSN 480-2169, DSN 254-2169 PAC DSN FAX 480-1215, PAC DSN FAX (TERM) 480-3421.** *Note: Permission/official approval required to visit KWA (see Appendix B).*

| IN ROUTE SCHEDULES | |
|---|---|
| **Hickam AFB** | PPP/HIK-1 |
| **March AFB** | PCM/RIV-4 |
| **Travis AFB** | PPM/SUU-9 |

# PUERTO RICO

## BORINQUEN COAST GUARD AIR STATION (BQN)

CGAS Borinquen
Aquadilla, PR 00604-5000

**LOCATION:** At Rafael Hernandez Airport (the old Ramey AFB), west of Aquadilla, PR. Take PR-2 west from San Juan or north from Mayaguez to PR-110 north to CGAS. *USMRA:Page 130 (B,C-2)*. NMC: San Juan PR, 65 miles east. Main installation numbers: C-FTS 809-882-3500, D-313-831-3385.

**PAX TERM INFO: C-809-890-8423.** CG hangar, Hrs: Mon-Fri: 0800-1600, Station hangar adjacent to main gate. Directions to parking provided by gate guard. Pax gather in training room next to maintenance control in the southeast corner of the hangar. A/C, bag check, restrooms, telephones, TV. **DV/VIP:** Officers' wardroom on second floor in the northeast corner of the hangar. A/C, restrooms, TV. Commuter flights available between San Juan & Mayaguez. Taxi from Mayaguez to Aquadilla. SATO office available.

**TML:** Lodging Office (La Plaza, Rm 26), C-809-890-3127/2581, non-duty hours call SDO C-809-890-3501. Housing area, Hrs: Mon-Fri: 0800-1600. EX-3127/8701. All ranks. Old Lighthouse guest quarters are exceptional.

**OTHER SERVICES: Cafeteria:** C-809-882-7109, in appt terminal. **Exchange:** 809-890-3127 EX-3127. **Medical:** Housing Area, 24hrs daily, EX-8514. Active duty only.

**ATTRACTIONS:** Local beaches (excellent surfing, diving, snorkeling, wind surfing, sailing, flying) & restaurants.

**UNSCHEDULED FLIGHTS**

Various, irregular flights via C-130H aircraft. Space-A at Borinquen is very limited. Space-A pax are advised that aircraft may be diverted at any time to participate in urgent search-and-rescue or law enforcement missions.

## ROOSEVELT ROADS NAVAL AIR STATION (NRR)

Air Term Officer, Box 3008
FPO AA 34051-3001

**LOCATION:** From San Juan, east on PR-3 for 45 miles. Sign on right indicating exit to Naval Station. *USMRA:Page 130 (F-2,3)*. NMC: San Juan, 50 miles northwest. Main installation numbers: C-809-865-2000, D-313-831-2000.

**PAX TERM INFO: C-809-865-4383, D-313-831-4383/3257, REC: C-809-865-3257 FAX 809-865-4208, D FAX 831-4271.** Bldg 426, Hrs: Mon-Fri: 0700-1600.
Directions: From main gate straight to first right to Air Ops on left. **Pax Service Office:** Same as Pax Terminal.

**PAX LOUNGES: General:** Bldg 426, Hrs: daily 0700-1600, C-809-865-4383. A/C, bag check, restrooms, TV, P/C seats. **DV/VIP Lounge:** Bldg 426, Hrs: daily 0700-1600, C-809-865-4383.

**FOOD SERVICE: Cafeteria:** Bldg 426, Same as Pax Term. **Dining Hall:** Anchor Inn: STOP 5, Hrs: daily 0545-0130, C-809-865-4138/9. **Enlisted Club:** STOP 7, Hrs: Mon, Wed, Thu, Sun: 1930-2330, C-809-865-4142. **NCO/CPO Club:** Acey-Deucey: STOP 8, Hrs: daily 1100-2400, C-809-865-5279. **O'Club:** STOP 3, Hrs: daily 1100-2400, C-809-865-7200/5211. **Restaurants:** Seabreeze: Hrs: daily 1800-2400, C-809-865-5641. **Snack Bars:** Bldg 426, Hrs: daily 0800-1600, C-809-865-4263. **Vending:** Bldg 426, Hrs: daily 0800-1600.

**TRANSPORTATION: Air Tickets:** SATO Building, Hrs: Mon-Fri: 0800-1800, C-809-865-3138. **Bus (Shuttle):** Bldg 426, C-809-865-4013 (every half hour - One block from terminal). **Car Rentals:** Hertz: C-809-885-3660 (Drop box at terminal). **Taxi (Comm):** Bldg 426, 24hrs daily, C-809-865-4013. **Parking:** Air Term, 24hrs daily, C-809-865-4011 (see Security Police).

**TML:** Lodging Office (Bldg 729), 24hrs daily. Enlisted: C-809-865-2000-4334/3364, Officer: C-809-865-2000-4145/4147. Navy Lodge: C-809-865-8281/8282, FAX 809-865-8283. All ranks. DV/VIP: C-809-865-3364, O7+.

**TRAVELERS AID: American Red Cross:** STOP 19, Hrs: Mon-Fri: 0800-1600, C-809-865-5134; after hours, C-809-865-2000. **Chaplain:** STOP 17, C-809-865-4326/8. **Emergency Relief:** STOP 12, Hrs: Mon-Fri: 0800-1600, C-809-865-5226 (Navy Relief). **Lost/Found:** Air Ops Bldg, Hrs: Mon-Sat: 0630-1800, C-809-865-4383 (Pax Service NCO). **Security Police:** Gate 1, 24hrs daily, C-809-865-4011 (Desk Sgt). **USO:** STOP 6, Hrs: daily 0800-2300, C-809-865-7350/7275 (near Pier 3).

**OTHER SERVICES: Exchange:** STOP 21, Hrs: Mon-Fri: 1000-1700, Sat: 1000-1600, C-809-865-3252. **Bank/Exchange:** NFCU: STOP 18, Hrs: Tue-Fri: 0900-1700, Sat: 0900-1400, C-809-865-8630. **Hair Styles:** STOP 21, Hrs: Mon-Fri: 0830-1700, Sat: 0830-1630, C-809-865-5531. **Laundry/Dry Cleaning:** STOP 21, Hrs: Mon-Sat: 1000-1700, C-809-865-5202/5243. **Medical:** Naval Hospital, 24hrs daily, C-809-865-4144, D-313-831-4144 (emergency); C-809-865-4133 (appointment). **Postal:** STOP 6, Hrs: Mon-Fri: 0900-1500, C-809-865-4335.

**ATTRACTIONS:** El Yuunque rain forest, waterfalls, hiking, restaurants.

| IN ROUTE SCHEDULES | | | |
|---|---|---|---|
| **Andrews AFB** | ACC/ADW-4 | | |
| **Little Rock AFB** | ACC/LRF-1 | ACC/LRF-2 | ACC/LRF-3 |
| | ACM/LRF-4 | | |
| **McGuire AFB** | ACC/WRI-18 | | |
| **Memphis IAP** | ACC/MEM-2 | | |
| **Moody AFB** | ACC/VAD-1 | | |
| **Pope AFB** | ACC/POB-1 | APM/POB-2 | |

# US VIRGIN ISLANDS

## ALEXANDER HAMILTON AIRPORT (STX)

Army Aviation Operations Facility,
VI National Guard, PO Box 2270, Kingshill
St Croix, VI 00851-2270

**LOCATION:** On the south central coast of the island of St Croix. *USMRA, p. 130, H/4.* NMC: Christiansted, Virgin Island, 8 miles northeast. Main installation numbers: C-809-778-2200/2884, Defense: None.

**PAX TERM INFO: C-809-778-2165/9261.** Virgin Island Army National Guard Hangar, Hrs: Mon-Fri: 0730-1630 (west end ramp).

**PAX LOUNGES:** Commercial Pax Term. All support facilities can be used. No separate military lounges. All flights handled through Ops Division. Emergency, call office of the Adjutant General, C-809-778-2884. There are no US military facilities, including TML, available for Space-A Pax.

| IN ROUTE SCHEDULES | |
|---|---|
| **Moody AFB** | ACC/VAD-1 |

# FOREIGN COUNTRIES

# AFRICA

## AFRICA STATIONS

**(Not listed separately in this book)**

The stations listed below have Space-A air opportunities. Base support facilities are provided by United States Embassies and are very limited. Passenger management is accomplished by US Embassy, military or contractor personnel. Procedures for processing passengers at each station are the result of local conditions and services available. Stations in most cases are located at International Airports which have all essential facilities and services for international travelers. Defense telephone service is not available. **See appendix B for personnel entrance requirements.**

**DAKAR YOFF AIRPORT, SE (DKR),** USDAO Dakar, State Department Pouch Room, Washington, DC 20521-2130. Dakar, SE. *ML-ARM: (17°15'E/14°55'N).* **Location:** On the west coast of central Africa, opposite the Cape Verde Islands. **PaxTerm:** Flights coordinated by USDAO, Hrs: Daily: 0800-1700. **C: 011-221-23-42-96/23-36-81, FAX: C: 011-221-22-29-91. PaxLg:** All facilities of local airport available.

| IN ROUTE SCHEDULES | | |
|---|---|---|
| **Charleston AFB/IAP** | ACC/CHS-13 | ACC/CHS-14 |

**KHARTOUM AIRPORT, SU (KRT)**, US Embassy, PO Box 699, Sharia Ali Abdul Latif, APO AE 09829-5000, Khartoum, Sudan. *ML-ARM: (32°30'E/16°30'N)* **Location:** In northeast Africa on the Nile River, 400 miles west of the Red Sea. **PaxTerm:** Flights coordinated by Embassy, Hrs: During Flight Processing. **C: 011-00-74700 or 74611-EX-273/274, (Thru International Operator). PaxLg:** All facilities of local airport available.

| IN ROUTE SCHEDULES | |
|---|---|
| **Charleston AFB/IAP** | ACC/CHS-18 |

**KINSHASA N'DJILI AIRPORT, ZA (FIH),** Operations Coordinator, USDAO Kinshasa, Unit 31550, APO AE 09828-3900. Kinshasa, Zaire. *ML-ARM: (15°10'E/04°30'S)* **Location:** In central Africa near west coast. Kinshasa is on Zaire river 225 miles northeast of the Atlantic ocean. Airport is 15 miles southeast of Kinshasa, ZA. **PaxTerm:** Pax processed by USDAO/OPSCO. Hrs: Mon-Sat 0700-1600 GMT. **C: 011-243-12-46929/21532/21628, FAX: C: 011-243-12-43467.** No facilities at airport. Valid Zairian Visa required prior to entry or remain at planeside.

| IN ROUTE SCHEDULES | | |
|---|---|---|
| **Charleston AFB/IAP** | ACC/CHS-13 | ACC/CHS-14 |

*AFRICA*

**JOMO KENYATTA INTERNATIONAL AIRPORT, KE (NBO)** Kenya US Liason Office (KUSLO), Unit 64101, APO AE 09831-4101. **PaxTerm: C-011-254-2-334141-EX-215/6/7, FAX 011-254-2-340838**. Essential services of a local airport available. *ML-ARM: (39°30'E/04°00'S).* **Location:** Nairobi, Kenya. NOTE: Ordinary leave travel to Kenya via AMC aircraft is authorized only with permission from KUSLO.

| IN ROUTE SCHEDULES | |
|---|---|
| **Charleston AFB/IAP** | ACC/CHS-18 |

**N'DJAMENA IAP, CD (NDJ),** US Embassy B.P., 413 Rue Felix Eboue, N'Djamena, Chad. *ML-ARM: (15°00'E/12°20'N).* **Location:** in central Africa, 75 miles south of Lake Chad. **PaxTerm:** Pax processed by USDAO personnel. **USDAO N'Djamena, Dept of State, State Pouch Room, Washington, DC 20521-2410. C: 011-235-51-40-09 or 51-47-59/ or 51-62-11. FAX: C: 011-235-51-56-64 or 011-235-51-33-72. PaxLg:** All facilities of local airport are available but limited.

| IN ROUTE SCHEDULES | |
|---|---|
| **Charleston AFB/IAP** | ACC/CHS-14 |

# AUSTRALIA

## ALICE SPRINGS AIRPORT (ASP)

Det 421, AMC Representative
APO AP 96548-0007

**LOCATION:** In the northern territory of AU, 1250 air miles northwest of Sydney, AU and 900 air miles south of Darwin, AU. *ML-ARM: (134°OO'E/23°54'S)*. NMC: Alice Springs, AU, 9.5 miles. Main installation number: C-011-61-89-530-570, D-none.

**PAX TERM INFO: C-011-61-89-530-570/633, FAX: C-011-61-89-530-382**. Direction: At the ASP airport. Pax Term, daylight hours daily. Limited support facility available. **Pax's must sign-up by at least the Friday preceeding the flight.** Contact AMC represenative for all required support.

**PAX LOUNGES:** Very limited lounge facilities, essentials only. Use ASP Airport terminal.

**FOOD SERVICE:** Restaurants, snack bars, coffee houses, and pubs in ASP.

**TRANSPORTATION:** ASP has commercial air, train, and motor coach services. **Taxi (Comm):** Pax Term, 24 hours daily, C-011-89-522-201 (9 miles to ASP).

**TML:** No US government billeting. Hotel rates in ASP are AU $20+, Backpacker accomadations. Three and four star accomadations AU $100.

**ATTRACTIONS:** Royal Flying Doctors Base, Ayers Rock (200 air miles southwest).

| IN ROUTE SCHEDULES | |
|---|---|
| **Travis AFB** | PCC/SUU-10 |

## RICHMOND RAAFB (RCM)

Detachment #l, 615 AMSG, Unit 11028
APO AP 96554-5000

**LOCATION:** Two miles west of Windsor AU and 45 miles northwest of Sydney AU. *ML-ARM: (151°30'E/33°48'S)*. NMC: Sydney, 45 miles southeast. Main installation number: C-011-61-045-70-2340, D-none.

**PAX TERM INFO: C-011-61-45-70-2340/70-2341/78-3309(roll call line)/78-3879(prerecorded infor line), FAX: C-011-61-45-88-5366 (Note: Within Australia you must dial 045 as the area code instead of 45)**. Pax Term, Hrs: Mon-Fri 0900-1500. Direction: One hundred and fifty yards from rear of flight line. $20.00 AUS departure tax (all Pax 12 years +). US Pax Services by AMC Pax rep personnel ONLY, not RAAFB personnel. Telephone for seat availability. Enter Base for sign-up or revalidation only at above hours or during flight processing. **Pax Service Office:** Bldg 308, Mon-Fri

*AUSTRALIA*
*Richmond RAAFB, continued*

0900-1500, C-011-61-45-78-3309 (see NCO for flight info). **Pax Paging:** Pax Term, during flight processing, C-011-61-45-78-3309.

**PAX LOUNGES:** RAAFB Pax Term Building. **General:** Pax Term, lst floor, Daily: 0800-1700, C-011-61-45-78-1300. A/C, restrooms, P/C seats.

**FOOD SERVICE:** In-flight meals $3.00 AU, C-011-61-45-70-2340. **Snack Bars:** Pax Term, as required for RAAF flights, **Vending:** Pax Term, 0800-1900 daily,(RAAFB facility).

**TRANSPORTATION:** Train and commercial taxi only available at RAAFB RCM. **Air Tickets:** Sydney, 24 hours daily, major airlines-Kingsford Smith Apt. **Taxi (Comm):** Pax Term, 24 hours daily, Comm: 001-61-02-622-2200. Serves local area/Sydney. **Trains:** Station, 0500-2400 daily, C-in AU-001-61-02-29-7614. SDY to RCM $8 AU and change trains in Riverstone. Station to RCM via taxi $5 AU. **Parking:** Security Police area, 24 hours daily.

**TML:** No TML on RAAF Base. Several motels in Richmond/Windsor area. Ask at Pax Terminal for list.

**TRAVELERS AID:** Building 308, Sun-Fri 0900-1500, C-011-61-45-70-2340/2341. See AMC Pax NCO.

**OTHER SERVICES:** No service at RAAFB RCM. No US BX or banking. **Money exchange at banks in Richmond or Windsor**. All services available in Sydney.

**ATTRACTIONS:** Sydney (population 4 million), Great Barrier Reef, Ayers Rock, Tasmania Island. Continent geographically as large as USA.

| IN ROUTE SCHEDULES | |
|---|---|
| **McChord AFB** | PCC/TCM-7 |
| **Travis AFB** | PCC/SUU-10 |

# WOOMERA AIR STATION (UMR)

5WS/LGLTC, Woomera AS, AU, Unit 11014
APO AP 96552-5000

**LOCATION:** On the Trans-Australian Railway, 900 air miles west of Sydney in South Australia. *ML-ARM: (136°30'E/31°15'S).* NMC: Port Augusta, 100 air miles southeast. Main installation numbers: C-011-61-86-739-438, D-315-730-1350-EX-438.

**PAX TERM INFO: C-011-61-86-739-438, C-(inside australia)-086-739-438, D-315-730-1350-EX-438, FAX-C-011-61-86-739-439, FAX inside australia 086-739-439,**

**DSN FAX 730-1350 EX 439.** Pax Term, 8 hours daily. Limited support facility available at UMR. Contact AMC representative for support services.

**PAX LOUNGES:** Very limited lounge facility, essentials only.

**FOOD SERVICE:** Restaurant and snack bars in UMR.

**TRANSPORTATION:** Motorcoach nightly (at 2359 hrs) to Adelaide and Alice Springs; train pick-up point 3 miles outside UMR village to Adelaide and Alice Springs (2 per week 0100 hrs). No public transportation to pick-up point. Advanced reservations required. Commercial flights to Adelaide daily Mon-Fri, one flight per day, cost: $100.

**ATTRACTIONS:** Adelaide, AU is 325 air miles southeast, modern city.

| IN ROUTE SCHEDULES | |
|---|---|
| McChord AFB | PCC/TCM-7 |

# BAHRAIN

## BAHRAIN INTERNATIONAL AIRPORT (BAH)

Bahrain Naval Support Unit
Supply Office/PTO
FPO AE 09834-2800

**LOCATION:** An island off the coast of Saudi Arabia in the Persian Gulf. *ML-ARM: (50°50'E/26°45'N)*. NMC: Dhahran, Saudi Arabia, 30 miles northwest. Main installation numbers: C-011-973-243-277, D-318-439-1110.

**PAX TERM INFO: C-011-973-727-347, 011-973-335-250, D 318-439-1110 EX 727-368, FAX 011-973-727-360.** Pax Term, Sat-Wed, during flight processing, closed Thu-Fri. Check with Navy Pax Service desk at Mannai Plaza for assistance.

**TML:** Lodging Office, limited, C-011-973-727-762.

**OTHER SERVICES:** Naval support unit has Shipstore, Officers'/CPO Clubs, and emergency medical. Commercial facilities also available. Taxi service 24 hours daily. A/C taxi to city - $3 US.

| IN ROUTE SCHEDULES | | | |
|---|---|---|---|
| **Charleston AFB/IAP** | ACC/CHS-17 | | |
| **Dover AFB** | APM/DOV-2 | ACM/DOV-3 | APM/DOV-10 |
| **March AFB** | APM/RIV-1 | | |
| **McGuire AFB** | ACC/WRI-19 | ACM/WRI-20 | |
| **Norfolk NAS** | APP/NGU-4 | APP/NGU-5 | |
| **Philadelphia IAP** | APP/PHL-4 | | |

# BELGIUM

## CHIEVRES AIR BASE (CHE)

Det 1, 52nd FW, Unit 21409
APO AE 09705-5000

**LOCATION:** Off BE-56 in village of Chievres. HE: Page 35 (E-3). *ML-ARM: (03°50.4'E/50°34.8'N)*. NMC: Mons, 8 miles southeast. Main installation numbers: C-011-32-68-27-5411, D-314-361-5411.

**PAX TERM INFO: C-011-32-68-27-5411, D-314-361-5501, FAX 011-32-68-27-5573.** Bldg 27, Hrs: Mon-Fri 0900-1700.

**PAX LOUNGES: General:** Bldg 27, Hrs: Mon-Fri 0900-1700, D-314-361-5411. Restrooms, showers, telephone. **DV/VIP:** Hangar #1, northeast of Building 27, Hrs: Mon-Fri 0900-1700, D-314-361-5411 (notify Base Ops before going to Hangar #1). Coffee/tea served, restrooms, showers, telephone.

**FOOD SERVICE:** Limited. Full club service at SHAPE. **Cafeteria:** D-314-423-4434 (breakfast & lunch only).

**TRANSPORTATION: Bus (Gov):** SHAPE Hq, D-314-423-4514.

**TML:** Lodging Office, Hotel Raymond in Mons, diagonally across from the train station. C-011-65-32-7511, FAX 011-32-65-34-6213.

**OTHER SERVICES: Exchange:** D-314-423-3601 (recording of rates).

### UNSCHEDULED FLIGHTS

To Andrews AFB, (**ADW**) MD, Ramstein AB, (**RMS**) GE, Stuttgart IAP, (**STR**) GE and Europe stations during NATO training exercises. Limited seats available.

# CARIBBEAN, CENTRAL & SOUTH AMERICA

The stations listed below have Space-A air opportunities. Base support facilities are provided by United States Embassies in each foreign country and are very limited. Passenger management is accomplished by US Embassy, military or contractor personnel. Procedures for processing passengers at each station are the result of local conditions and services available. Stations in most cases are located at International Airports which have all essential facilities and services for international travelers. Defense telephone service is not available at these stations unless indicated in their listing. Stations are listed in alphabetical order. **See Appendix B for personnel entrance requirements.**

**ASUNCION, PA (ASU),** *ML-ARM: (57°50'W/25°50'S).* USODC Unit 4742, APO AA, 34036-0008. **C-011-595-21-20-8207/1592/8315, FAX 011-595-21-21-0827.**

| | IN ROUTE SCHEDULES |
|---|---|
| **Charleston AFB** | APM/CHS-2 |
| **McGuire AFB** | APM/WRI-3 |

**BOGOTA, CO (BOG),** *ML-ARM: (74°00'W/04°50'N).* AFSRC USMILGP Columbia, APO AA, 34038-0008. **C-011-57-1-413-8692/8359/9000, FAX 011-57-1-413-8692/256-0909.**

**BRASILIA AIRPORT, BR (BSB),** *ML-ARM: (47°40'W/16°00'S).* US Military Liaison Office, US Embassy, Brasilia, Brazil, Unit 3500, APO AA 34030-5000. **C-011-55-61-226-3145, 011-55-61-321-7272 EX 431/432, FAX 011-55-61-321-3615**. A VISA is a must prior to leaving US and cannot be done at an airport. Actual C-141 schedule may not be stable due to world events, etc.

| | IN ROUTE SCHEDULES | |
|---|---|---|
| **Charleston AFB** | APM/CHS-1 | APM/CHS-2 |
| **McGuire AFB** | APM/WRI-3 | |

**BUENOS AIRES, AR (BUE),** *ML-ARM: (58°60'W/34°60'S).* USMILGP/AFSEC , Unit 4334, Argentina, APO AA 340034-0008. **C-011-54-1-480-0332 (office & FAX).**

| | IN ROUTE SCHEDULES |
|---|---|
| **Charleston AFB** | APM/CHS-1 |

**BELIZE IAP, BZ (BZE),** *ML-ARM: (88°70'W/19°08'N).* USMLO Belize Section, Care of Pouch Room, Dept of State, Washington DC 20520, Unit 7401, APO AA 34025-5000. **C-011-501-2-52009/2019, FAX 011-501-2-52553.**

**CARRASCO IAP, UG (MVD),** *ML-ARM: (56°18'W/34°58'S)*. USDAO, US Embassy (Montevideo), APO AA 34035-0008. **C-011-598-2-48-77-77-X-2328/29, FAX 011-598-2-48-86-11.**

| IN ROUTE SCHEDULES | |
|---|---|
| **Charleston AFB/IAP** | APM/CHS-1 |

**EZEIZA APT, AG (BUE),** *ML-ARM: (58°30'W/34°40'N)*. USMILGP, Argentina, Unit 4334, APO AA 34034-0008. **C-011-54-1-777-1207, FAX C-011-54-1-331-5243**.

| IN ROUTE SCHEDULES | |
|---|---|
| **Charleston AFB/IAP** | APM/CHS-1 |

**GUATEMALA CITY AIRPORT (GUA)**, USMILGP/AFSBC Guatemala, APO AA 34024-0008. *ML-ARM: (90°60'W/14°60'S)*. **C-011-31-9245/5747, 011-32-323555 FAX 011-502-34-8472**.

**FRANCOIS DUVALIER IAP, HA (PAP),** *ML-ARM: (72°30'W/18°30'N)*. Small Terminal Operator, USMLO, US Embassy, Port-Au-Prince, Haiti, Department of State Pouch Room, Washington, DC 20521-3400. **C-011-509-22-0200 or 509-22-0363, FAX 011-509-23-1641**.

| IN ROUTE SCHEDULES | |
|---|---|
| **Charleston AFB/IAP** | ACM/CHS-10 |

**J.F. KENNEDY, BO (LPB),** *ML-ARM: (68°20'W/16°45'S)*. USDAO, US Embassy (La Paz), APO AA 34032-5000. **C-011-591-2-350251-X-236, FAX 011-509-2-359875**.

| IN ROUTE SCHEDULES | | |
|---|---|---|
| **McGuire AFB** | ACC/WRI-4 | APM/WRI-5 |

**JORGE CHAVEZ IAP, PE (LIM),** *ML-ARM: (77°15'W/12°00'S)*. USMAAG, US Embassy (Lima), Unit 3700, APO AA 34031-5000. **C-011-51-14-52-3765 (terminal), 011-51-14-33-8000 EX 7292/7138 (MAAG), FAX 011-51-14-33-4540.**

| IN ROUTE SCHEDULES | | |
|---|---|---|
| **McGuire AFB** | ACC/WRI-4 | APM/WRI-5 |

**KINGSTON, JM (KIN),** *ML-ARM: (76°65'W/18°05'N)*. USMLO Kingston, State Dept -Pouch Room, Washington, DC 20520-3210. **C-011-809-929-4850 EX-5127, FAX 011-809-929-4850 EX 5055.**

| IN ROUTE SCHEDULES | |
|---|---|
| **Little Rock AFB** | ACC/LRF-3 |
| **Norfolk NAS** | APP/NGU-1 |

# LA AURORA INTERNATIONAL AIRPORT/AB (GUA)

AMC Station Guatemala
USMILGP, Unit 3301
APO AA 34024-5000

**LOCATION:** Avenue Hincapie, 12th St Guatemalan Air Base Main Entrance. *ML-ARM: (90°45'W/14°45'N)*. NMC: Guatemala City. Main Installation Number: C-011-502-2-32-32-35, D-none.

**PAX TERM INFO: C-011-502-2-31-92-45/2-32-32-35, FAX 011-502-2-32-28-44.** Bldg 2402, Hrs: daily 0500-2200. Directions: AMC Station Manager's office is located in Avenue Hincapie 14-15 Zone 13, across the street from the main entrance to La Aurora Guatemalan Air Base.

**PAX LOUNGES: General:** A small passenger waiting area and cafeteria run by Guatemalans. Located east of military ramp. Operating hrs: 0700-1300. Coffee/tea served, restrooms, P/C seats, telephones. DV/VIP: Located east of military ramp. Run by Guatemalan Air Force. Coffee/tea served, restrooms, P/C seats, telephones. Must have 24 hr advance notice to open lounge. Note: restrooms are not recommended for female use in the General Lounge Cafeteria as they are usually very dirty. They may use the AMC Station Manager's restroom. Wendy's Restaurant also has very clean restrooms.

**FOOD SERVICE: Main Lounge:** Mon-Sat 0700-1300. **Wendy's:** Across the street, daily 1000-2300. In-flight meals: daily, 24 hrs, very expensive.

**TRANSPORTATION:** Taxis are available upon request. Car rentals (Avis, Budget, National, etc.) are also available at various locations. Military transportation only for duty personnel. Short term parking facilities are available 24 hrs, located across the street from the main entrance to the Base. Notify Post 7 (US Marine Guard, US Embassy) 2-31-23-54/69-04.

**TRAVELERS AID: Emergency Relief:** All emergencies are handled by USMILGP military personnel. **Bank/Money Exchange:** US Embassy, Mon-Fri 0900-1100. **Chaplain:** Available upon request.

***Note: No scheduled flights at press time.***

**LA PAZ BO, (LPZ),** *ML-ARM: (67°70'W/16°00'S)*. USMILGP, Section/Station Manager, Unit 3911, APO AA 34032-0008. **C-011-591-2-284-0260, FAX 011-591-2-43-0421.**

**LIMA, PE (LIM),** *ML-ARM: (75°85'W/12°09'S)*. US Embassy/MAAG, APO AA 34031-0008. **C-011-51-14-52-3765, FAX 011-51-14-33-4540/4588.**

| IN ROUTE SCHEDULES | | |
|---|---|---|
| **McGuire AFB** | ACC/WRI-4 | APM/WRI-5 |

**MAIQUETIA, VE (MIQ),** *ML-ARM: (66°85'W/11°11'N)*. American Embassy, Caracas, MILGP Unit 4980, APO AA 34037-5000. **C-011-58-2-62-0344/61-4301, FAX 011-58-2-61-8468.**

**MANAGUA, NU (MGA),** *ML-ARM: (75°85'W/12°09'S)*. US Defense Attach Office, Unit 2701, box 13, APO AA, 34021-2701. **C-011-505-2-66-6039/6010 EX 216/217/251, FAX 011-505-2-66-8022.**

**MONTEVIDEO, UG (MVD),** *ML-ARM: (56°10'W/34°09'S)*. US ODC Uruguay, Unit 4506, APO AA 34035-0008. **C-011-598-2-71-25-28, FAX 011-598-2-41-86-78.**

| **IN ROUTE SCHEDULES** | |
|---|---|
| **Charleston AFB/IAP** | APM/CHS-1 |

**NORMAN MANLEY IAP, JM (KIN),** *ML-ARM: (76°45'W/17°58'N)*. US Military Liaison Office, US Embassy (Kingston), Kingston 5, Jamaica or US State Department Pouch Room, Washington, DC 20521-5000. **C-011-809-929-4850-X-5127, FAX 011-809-926-6743**.

| **IN ROUTE SCHEDULES** | |
|---|---|
| **Little Rock AFB** | ACC/LRF-3 |
| **Norfolk NAS** | APP/NGU-1 |

**PORT AU PRINCE, HA (PAP),** *ML-ARM: (72°65'W/18°85'N)*. USMLO, Port Au Prince, Haiti, State Dept - Pouch Room, Washington, DC 20520-3210. **C-011-509-23-0970/22-0200, FAX 011-509-23-1641.**

| **IN ROUTE SCHEDULES** | |
|---|---|
| **Charleston AFB/IAP** | ACM/CHS-10 |

**PORT OF SPAIN, TRINIDAD & TOBAGO (PAS),** *ML-ARM: (61°60'W/10°75'N)*. USMLO Port of Spain AMEmbassy, PO Box 752, 15 Queen's Park West, Port of Spain, Trinidad West Indies OR USMLO Port of Spain, US Dept of State, Washington, DC 20521-3410. **C-011-809-622-1742, FAX 011-809-628-5462/622-6371.**

**PRESIDENT STROESSNER IAP, PG (ASU),** *ML-ARM: (57°30'W/25°20'S)*. USDAO, Unit 4737, US Embassy (Asuncion), APO AA 34036-0001. **C-011-595-21-213715-X-317, FAX 011-595-21-213-728**.

| **IN ROUTE SCHEDULES** | |
|---|---|
| **Charleston AFB/IAP** | APM/CHS-2 |
| **McGuire AFB** | APM/WRI-3 |

**PUDAHEL APT/ARTURO MERINO BENITEZ IAP, CH (SCL),** *ML-ARM: (70°45'W/33°30'S)*. USDAO, Unit 4115, APO AA 34033-5000. **C-011-56-2-671-0133 or 522-5000, FAX 011-56-2-330-3710.**

| **IN ROUTE SCHEDULES** | | |
|---|---|---|
| **McGuire AFB** | ACC/WRI-4 | APM/WRI-5 |

**QUITO, EC (UIO),** *ML-ARM: (78°25'W/00°09'S).* Chief, USMLO Quito, APO AA 34039-0008. **C-011-593-2-223-2107/256-6890 EX-595/596/597, FAX 011-593-2-504-550.**

**RIO DE JANEIRO IAP, BR (RIO),** *ML-ARM: (43°00'W/23°10'S).* USMLO BRC OFC Rio De Janeiro BR, Unit 3501, APO AA 34030-5000. **C-011-55-21-220-8880 & 262-7117-X-2750, FAX 011-55-21-220-0439/5521.**

| IN ROUTE SCHEDULES | |
|---|---|
| **Charleston AFB/IAP** | APM/CHS-2 |
| **McGuire AFB** | APM/WRI-3 |

**SAN ISIDRO AIR BASE, DR (SDQ),** *ML-ARM: (70°00'W/18°30'N).* USMAAG, US Embassy (Santo Domingo), Unit 5500, APO AA 34041-5000. **C-011-809-682-1953/4807/4835, FAX 011-809-682-3991**.

**SAN JOSE, CS (OCO),** *ML-ARM: (84°20'W/10°02'N).* CHODR American Embassy, Costa Rica, APO AA, 34020-0008. **C-011-506-442-1121, FAX 011-506-231-7094.**

**SAN SALVADOR, ES (SAL),** *ML-ARM: (89°20'W/13°65'N).* USMILGP/AFSEC El Salvador, Unit 3116, APO AA 34023-0008. **C-011-503-95-0240, FAX 011-503-79-0569.**

**SANTIAGO, CI (SCL),** *ML-ARM: (33°85'W/71°85'S).* USDAO Santiago, Chile, Unit 4127, APO AA 34033-0008. **C-011-56-2-522-5000/528-2313, FAX 011-56-2-632-4863.**

| IN ROUTE SCHEDULES | | |
|---|---|---|
| **McGuire AFB** | ACC/WRI-4 | APM/WRI-5 |

**SOTO CANO AIR BASE (PLA), HO,** AMC Station Manager, US Embassy (Tegucigalpa), APO AA 34022-5000. *ML-ARM: (87°12'W/14°08'N).* USMILGP, (Honduras), AMC Station Manager, US Embassy (Tegucigalpa), Unit 2942, APO AA 34022-5000. **C-011-504-33-4618 & 33-6247, FAX C-011-504-36-7776**.

| IN ROUTE SCHEDULES | | | |
|---|---|---|---|
| **Charleston AFB/IAP** | ACC/CHS-20 | ACC/CHS-21 | APP/CHS-23 |

**TEGUCIGALPA, HO (TGU),** *ML-ARM: (87°25'W/14°15'N).* USMILGP/AFSEC, Honduras, Unit 3001, APO AA 34022-0008. **C-011-504-33-4618/6247, FAX 011-504-33-5189/6171.**

**TOCUMEN/TORRIJOS IAP, PN (PTY),** *ML-ARM: (79°50'W/09°20'N).* USDAO, US Embassy, Avenida Balboa y Calle 38, Apartado 6959, RP 5, Panama, Republic of Panama and Unit 0945, APO AA 34002-5000. **C -011-507-27-1777, FAX 011-507-27-1964.**

| IN ROUTE SCHEDULES | |
|---|---|
| **Charleston AFB/IAP** | APP/CHS-24 |
| **McGuire AFB** | APM/WRI-5 |

# CUBA

## GUANTANAMO BAY NAVAL STATION (GAO/NBW)

Transportation Office, PERSUPPDET
PSC 1005, Box 95
FPO AA 09593-0095

**LOCATION:** In the southeast corner of the Republic of Cuba. Accessible only by air. *ML-ARM: (75°10'W/20°10'N)*. NMC: Miami, 525 air miles northwest. Main installation numbers: C-011-53-99-6XXX, D-313-723-3690 or 313-564-4063.

**PAX TERM INFO: C-011-53-99-64204/6408, D-313-564-4063, FAX 011-53-99-5092.** Map B/2, Hours during flight processing. All arrivals and departures via air. Prior approval required for non-AD personnel to visit or transfer through station. See appendix B for personal entry requirements. There is no access to Cuba from the Naval Station. All personnel are restricted to the base at all times. **Pax Service Office:** Base Map E/3, C-011-53-996-8523 (NCO on duty).

**PAX LOUNGES:** Limited, but adequate facilities. Base Map B/2, available during flight processing, C-011-53-996-8850 (see Pax NCO).

**FOOD SERVICE:** Extensive facilities operated by clubs and BX. **Cafeteria:** BX food service, C-011-53-996-4115. **Enlisted Club:** C-011-53-996-2304. **CPO Club:** C-011-53-996-2501. **O'Club:** C-011-53-996-2132.

**TRANSPORTATION: Taxi (Comm):** On Base, Hrs: Sun-Thu 0600-0030, Fri-Sat 0600-0200, C-011-53-996-2517.

**TML:** Lodging Office, 24hrs daily, C-011-53-99-2400/01, D-313-564-4063 EX 2400/01, FAX C-011-53-99-2154. All ranks. Navy Lodge: C-011-53-99-3103 or 1-800-NAVY INN. DV/VIP: C-011-53-99-2400-01.

**TRAVELERS AID: Chaplain:** Bldg 762, C-011-53-996-4550. **Security Police:** Term, Hrs: Daily: 24hrs, C-011-53-996-4105.

**OTHER SERVICES: Exchange:** C-011-53-996-2682 (Marine Corps); C-011-53-996-4461 (Navy). **Medical:** Base Map J/16, Hrs: 24 hours daily, C-011-53-996-7201 (emergency); C-011-53-996-4424 (appointment).

**ATTRACTIONS:** Beaches, fishing, and warm climate.

| IN ROUTE SCHEDULES | | |
|---|---|---|
| **Andrews AFB** | ACC/ADW-4 | |
| **McGuire AFB** | ACC/WRI-16 | ACC/WRI-18 |
| **Memphis IAP** | ACC/MEM-2 | |
| **Norfolk NAS** | APP/NGU-1 | APP/NGU-2 |

# CYPRUS

## AKROTIRI RAFB (AKT)

AMC Rep, USDAO Nicosia
State Department Pouch Room
Washington, DC 20520 or
APO AE 09836-5000

**LOCATION:** On Cape Gata, Southern Coast, Island of Cyprus. At a UK Akrotiri RAF Base. *ML-ARM (32°56'E/35°02'N)*. NMC: Limassol, Cyprus, 5 miles northeast. Main installation numbers: at USDAO C-011-357-21-65151. D- None.

**PAX TERM INFO:** Pax Term, during flight processing, EX-357-51, ask for AMC representative. FAX 011-357-2-465604. Limited access. See Appendix B for personnel entrance requirements. All major support is in Nicosia, Cyprus, 55 miles northeast.

| | IN ROUTE SCHEDULES |
|---|---|
| **Charleston AFB/IAP** | APM/CHS-6 |
| **McGuire AFB** | APM/WRI-9 |

# DENMARK

## THULE AIR BASE (GREENLAND) (THU)

12th SWS/CCF, Unit 82501
APO AE 09704-5000

**LOCATION:** Northwest coast of island of Greenland DN; 800 miles south of North Pole; 800 miles south of Arctic Circle; 2500 miles north of McGuire AFB NJ. Closer to Seattle, WA than New York City, NY by 5 miles. *ML-ARM: (69°50'W/77°35'N)*. Main installation numbers: C-011-299-50-124/636 EX 2155, D-312-834-1211-EX-2155. **Prior written permission from Commander, 12th SWS/CCF, Unit 82501, APO AE 09704-5000 is required to visit Thule AB in a Space-A status.**

**PAX TERM INFO:** Bldg: 623, **FAX 011-299-50-636 EX 2556, D-312-834-1211 EX 2556**. Hrs: Mon-Fri 0800-1700, Sat as needed, EX-2155. Access limited. See Appendix B for personnel entrance requirements.

**PAX LOUNGES:** Limited but adequate lounge facilities.

**FOOD SERVICE:** Good on Base. None off Base. **Dining Hall:** Bldg: 707, EX-2614. **NCO/CPO Club:** Bldg: 236.

**TRANSPORTATION:** Limited on Base. **Bus (Shuttle):** On Base, (bus does not service Pax Term). **Taxi (Gov):** Bldg: 836, EX-2022.

**TML:** Lodging Office (Bldg 97), Hrs: 24 hours daily, EX-2270. No TML June-September.

**OTHER SERVICES: Exchange:** EX-2732. **Bank:** EX-2586. **Hair Styles:** EX-3127. **Laundry:** EX-2249. **Medical:** EX-2696. **Postal:** EX-2615. **Chaplain:** EX-2211. **Security Police:** EX-3234.

| IN ROUTE SCHEDULE | |
|---|---|
| **McGuire AFB** | APM/WRI-22 |

# EGYPT

## CAIRO INTERNATIONAL AIRPORT (CAI)

OL-B 623 AMSG/AMC - Unit 64901, BOX 43
APO AE 09839-4901

**LOCATION:** The Cairo IAP is 9 miles northeast of Cairo on the east side of the Nile River and approximately 75 miles west of the Gulf of Suez. *ML-ARM: 31°25'E/30°10'N).* NMC: Cairo, 9 miles southwest. Main installation numbers: C-011-20-2-357-3212, D-312-725-1456-EX-3212 (Direct Dial from CONUS).

**PAX TERM INFO: C-011-20-2-357-2596, D-314-725-1456-EX-2596, FAX C-011-20-2-357-2273.** Bldg: Pax Term, Hrs: Sat-Thu 0800-1630 Directions: The AMC Terminal is located on the opposite side of the main runway from the IAP side of the airport, and is located on Cairo East Air Base, an Egyptian military installation. All flights are managed by US Embassy Cairo, Office of Military Cooperation. There are no U. S. military installations located in the United Arab Republic of Egypt. See Appendix B for detailed personnel entrance requirements. NOTE: Personnel must have authorization to fly into Cairo IAP/Cairo East Air Base. They must also have a sponsor present when they arrive and when they leave the base. Facilities are extremely limited.

**PAX LOUNGES:** Pax Term, 0800-1630 Sun-Thu, phone as above. Seats 15, A/C.

**TRANSPORTATION:** Limited. **Taxi (Comm):** No transportation available at AMC terminal. Taxis available off base.

**OTHER SERVICES:** This is a small terminal located on an Egyptian AB. There are no provisions for lodging, food service, car rentals, bank or other normal services. Many hotels provide all services.

**ATTRACTIONS:** Pyramids, museums, bazaars, Nile River.

| | IN ROUTE SCHEDULES | |
|---|---|---|
| **Charleston AFB/IAP** | ACC/CHS-5 | |
| **McGuire AFB** | ACC/WRI-8 | ACC/WRI-14 |
| **Wright-Patterson AFB** | ACC/FFO-2 | |

# GERMANY

## RAMSTEIN AIR BASE (RMS)

86th Airlift Wing
APO AE 09094-3295

**LOCATION:** Adjacent to Autobahn 6 (Saarbruken-Mannheim). Take the Flugplatz-Ramstein exit. East and West gates are within 2 miles of exit. From the East gate, follow signs to the south side of the base. From the West gate, follow the main road to Burger King and turn right at the traffic light. The new terminal is located across from the south side billeting office on Maxwell Avenue. *ML-ARM: (07°30'E/49°25'N).* NMC: Kaiserslautern, 12 miles east. Main installation numbers: C-011-49-6371-47-1110, D-314-480-1110.

**PAX TERM INFO: C-011-49-6371-47-2120/2433/5364, D-314-480-2120/5364/2433, REC C-011-49-6371-47-5363, D-314-480-5363, FAX 011-49-6371-47-2364.** Bldg 2402, Hrs: daily 0500-2200. Directions: From East or West gate follow signs to south side of base, behind 316 Air Division Building and across from Base Ops on flight line. **Pax Paging:** C-011-49-6371-47-5364, D-314-480-5364.

**PAX LOUNGES: General:** Bldg 2202, Hrs: daily 0500-2200, EX-5363/5364. TV, restrooms, P/C seats, telephones (commercial, defense and base). **DV/VIP:** Bldg 2402, front area, Hrs: daily 0500-2200, EX-2433/5362. TV, restrooms. **Protocol Service:** Bldg 201, Hrs: Daily: 0500-2200, EX-6854 (06+).

**FOOD SERVICE: Cafeteria:** Bldg 1101, Hrs: daily 0700-2400, EX-6061. **Dining Hall:** Bldg 2107, EX-5750. **Enlisted Club:** Bldg 2411, Hrs: 24 hours daily, EX-5637. **NCO Club:** Bldg 2411, Hrs: 24 hours daily, EX-2333. **O'Club:** Bldg 302, EX-2848. **Restaurants:** Bldg 2411, EX-5637. **Snack Bar:** Bldg 2202. **Vending:** Bldg 2202, EX-5364. **Fred's Lounge:** Bldg. 2113, EX 5777. **Burger King:** Bldg 1135, EX 2555. **Donut Land:** Bldg 2171, EX 3163. **Vesuvio's:** Bldg. 302, EX 6200. **Popeyes:** Bldg. 2163, EX 7000. **Rhineland Inn:** Bldg. 2107. **Jawbone Inn:** Bldg. 2398. **Starlight Inn:** Bldg. 2300.

**TRANSPORTATION: Air Tickets:** SATO: Bldg 2406, C-011-49-6371-44161/42203. **Bus (Comm):** Bldg 2408, EX-2411 (call for schedule). **Bus (Gov):** Bldg 2202, EX-5961 (off base routes). **Bus (Shuttle):** Bldg 2408, (every 40 minutes on base route). Also, government contract bus service from RMS-FRF - from Pax Term, 3 times daily. **Car Rentals:** Budget: C-011-49-6371-47-43978, Hertz: C-011-49-6371-47-44202, Powell's Auto: C-011-49-6371-52169, Landstuhl: C-011-49-6371-2330, Raule: C-011-49-6371 52169. **Taxi (Comm):** Bldg 2113, Hrs: 24 hours daily, C-011-49-6371-50510/12604/hot line in Bldg 2202. **Trains:** Excellent train service throughout or call train station (Bahnhof) C-011-49-631-19419. **Parking:** Three long term parking lots available by permit only (permits available from PAX terminal).

*GERMANY*
***Ramstein Air Base, continued***

**TML:** Lodging Office (Bldg 305), 24 hrs daily, C-011-49-6371-47-7345/7864, D-314-480-7345/7864. All ranks. DV/VIP: C-011-49-6371-47-47-4851 (Protocol Office).

**TRAVELERS AID: American Red Cross:** Bldg 2118, EX-5464. After hours, EX-2171. **Chaplain:** Bldg 2403, EX-5753. **Emergency Relief:** Bldg 2402, EX-5539. **Lost/Found:** Bldg 2202, EX-5364/2364. **Security Police:** Bldg 2409, Hrs: 24 hours daily, EX-2050 (Desk Sgt). **USO:** Bldg 412, EX-6326.

**OTHER SERVICES: Exchange:** Bldg 1101, EX-7110. **Bank/Exchange:** Merchants National: Bldg 2163, EX-2390, foreign money ATM located at the BX complex. **Hair Styles:** Barber: Bldg 2162, EX-5673; Beauty: Bldg 1101, EX-6040. **Laundry/Dry Cleaning:** Bldg 2187, EX-2412. **Medical:** Bldg 2114, EX-5225 (clinic), Emergency EX-5116. **Postal:** Bldg 426, EX-7206. **Wire:** Bldg 1101, EX-7110 (BX).

**ATTRACTIONS:** Frankfurt, 78 miles northeast (fairs and retail centers); Kaiserslautern, 10 miles east (wine strasse); and Mannheim-40 miles east.

| **ORIGINATING SCHEDULES** | | | |
|---|---|---|---|
| | **ACM/RMS-1 2nd/4th MON C-130E** | | |
| **Location ID** | **Airport (Station)** | **Country/State** | **Days Out** |
| RMS | Ramstein AB | GE | +0 |
| AVB | Aviano AB | IT | +0 |
| GRX | Araxos APT | GR | +0 |
| AVB | Aviano AB | IT | +1 |
| SIZ | Sigonella NAS | IT | +1 |
| **SOC** | **Souda Bay NAF** | **GR** | **+2** |
| SIZ | Sigonella NAS | IT | +2 |
| NAP | Capodichino APT | IT | +2 |
| SIZ | Sigonella NAS | IT | +3 |
| OLB | Olbia/Costa Smeralda APT | IT | +3 |
| NAP | Capodichino APT | IT | +4 |
| OLB | Olbia/Costa Smeralda APT | IT | +4 |
| SIZ | Sigonella NAS | IT | +4 |
| RMS | Ramstein AB | GE | |
| | **APM/RMS-2 SUN, TUE, THU DC862** | | |
| RMS | Ramstein AB | GE | +0 |
| **DHA** | **Dhahran IAP** | **SA** | **+1** |
| RMS | Ramstein AB | GE | |
| | **ACM/RMS-3 2nd TUE DC862** | | |
| RMS | Ramstein AB | GE | +0 |
| **DHA** | **Dhahran IAP** | **SA** | **+2** |
| RMS | Ramstein AB | GE | |

| | **ACM/RMS-4 1st/3rd MON C-130E** | | |
|---|---|---|---|
| RMS | Ramstein AB | GE | +0 |
| SIZ | Sigonella NAS | IT | +0 |
| NAP | Capodichino APT | IT | +0 |
| SIZ | Sigonella NAS | IT | +1 |
| **SOC** | **Souda Bay NAF** | **GR** | **+1** |
| SIZ | Sigonella NAS | IT | +2 |
| OLB | Olbia/Costa Smeralda APT | IT | +2 |
| NAP | Capodichino APT | IT | +3 |
| OLB | Olbia/Costa Smeralda APT | IT | +3 |
| SIZ | Sigonella NAS | IT | +3 |
| RMS | Ramstein AB | GE | |
| | **ACM/RMS-5 MON C-141B** | | |
| RMS | Ramstein AB | GE | +0 |
| YSK | Skopje (NO SPACE-A) | MK | +0 |
| YZA | Zagreb (NO SPACE-A) | BK | +0 |
| RMS | Ramstein AB | GE | |

| | **IN ROUTE SCHEDULES** | | |
|---|---|---|---|
| **Allen C Thompson Field** | ACC/JAN-3 | | |
| **Andrews AFB** | ACC/ADW-2 | ACC/ADW-3 | |
| **Charleston AFB/IAP** | ACC/CHS-5 | APM/CHS-6 | ACC/CHS-7 |
| | ACM/CHS-8 | ACC/CHS-15 | ACC/CHS-16 |
| **Dover AFB** | ACC/DOV-4 | APM/DOV-5 | ACM/DOV-6 |
| | APM/DOV-7 | ACC/DOV-8 | ACC/DOV-9 |
| | APM/DOV-10 | | |
| **McGuire AFB** | ACC/WRI-2 | ACC/WRI-7 | ACC/WRI-8 |
| | APM/WRI-9 | ACC/WRI-10 | ACC/WRI-11 |
| | ACM/WRI-13 | ACC/WRI-14 | ACC/WRI-15 |
| | ACC/WRI-17 | | |
| **Stewart ANGB** | ACC/SWF-1 | ACC/SWF-2 | |
| **Westover ARB** | APM/CEF-2 | ACC/CEF-3 | |
| **Wright-Patterson AFB** | ACC/FFO-2 | | |

*GERMANY*

# RHEIN-MAIN AIR BASE (FRF)

626 Air Mobility Support Squadron
APO AE 09057-5000

**LOCATION:** Adjacent to Frankfurt IAP 10 miles south of Frankfurt GE. Take the Rhein-Main exit from Autobahn A-5 which runs north to Frankfurt, and Bremerhaven GE, and south to Darmstadt GE, and the Black Forest GE, area. *ML-ARM: (08°35'E/50°10'N).* NMC: Frankfurt, 10 miles north. Main installation numbers: C-011-49-69-699-1110, D-314-330-1110.

**PAX TERM INFO: C-011-49-69-699-7746, D-314-330-7746, REC: C-011-49-69-699-7015/7016, D-314-330-7015/7016, FAX 011-49-69-699-6309, DSN FAX 314-330-6309.** Bldg 400, Hrs: daily 0500-2100. From main gate go straight to Vaughn Rd, right to Springer Rd, left to Pax Term on right. **Pax Service Office:** Bldg 400, Hrs: daily, 0730-1630.

**PAX LOUNGES: General:** Bldg 400, Hrs: daily 0500-2100. Entire upper level. Enter from front of Term. Go up escalator. AC, bag lockers, game room, telephones (commercial and defense), TV, restrooms, O/S seats, showers. **DV/VIP:** Bldg 400, Hrs: daily 0500-2100, C-011-49-69-699-6345/7475 (Hostess). Center of upper level next to cafeteria (O6+, GS-15+ eligible). AC, coffee/tea service, telephone (defense), TV, restrooms, O/S seats. **Protocol Service:** USAFEUR, C-011-49-69-699-6264.

**FOOD SERVICE: Cafeteria:** Bldg 400, Hrs: daily 0600-1800, C-011-49-69-699-7212. **Enlisted Club:** Bldg 150, Hrs: daily 1100-2200, C-011-49-69-699-7727/7997. **Vending:** Bldg 400, Hrs: daily 0500-2100, C-011-49-69-699-7746.

**TRANSPORTATION: Air Tickets:** SATO: Bldg 400, Hrs: Mon-Sat 0830-1630, C-011-49-69-699-7746. **Bus (Comm):** Bldg 400, schedule available at TMO counter. **Bus (Shuttle):** Bldg 400, Hrs: daily 0730-1900, every hour. On base and to commercial terminal(FRF). Check with Pax Term for bus to RMS & other Army and AF installations. **Limo Service:** Bldg 400, Hrs: daily 0500-2100, C-011-49-69-06374/1805 (Rhein-Main/Ramstein only). **Taxi (Comm):** Bldg 400, 24 hrs daily, C-011-49-69-699-7528. **Taxi (Gov):** Bldg 244, Hrs: 24 hours daily, C-011-49-69-699-7051. **Trains:** Excellent service from Frankfurt to all of Europe. Must have tickets in advance-automatic ticket machines. Schedule available at TMO counter. **Parking:** No short-term parking. If you must leave vehicle on base, long term parking is approximately one mile from terminal.

**TML:** Lodging Office (Gateway Gardens, Bldg 600, 24 hrs daily, C-011-49-69-699-7265/7266, D-314-330-7265/7266. DV/VIP: Bldg 27, C-011-49-69-699-6059, O6+.

**TRAVELERS AID: American Red Cross:** Bldg 400, C-011-49-69-699-4224, after hours EX-7765. **Chaplain:** Bldg 155, C-011-49-69-699-7501/6228. **Lost/Found:** Bldg 400, Hrs: Mon-Fri 0730-1630, C-011-49-69-699-7592.(After normal duty hours contact Passenger Service Shift supervisor for assistance.) **Security Police:** Bldg 343, Crime stop,

C-011-49-699-7171; Emergency C-011-49-69-699-114. **USO:** Bldg 400, 2nd floor, C-011-49-69-699-6424, D-314-330-6424.

**OTHER SERVICES: Exchange:** Mini Exchange: Bldg 400, Hrs: 0830-1500; Main Exchange, Bldg 166, C-011-49-69-699-7456. **Bank/Exchange:** Andrews Federal Credit Union ATM, Bldg 400, Hrs: Mon-Sat 1000-1400, C-011-49-69-699-7235/7139. Money exchange at commercial bank Bldg 168, duty hours, Bldg 353 if AD or Retired with any club membership. **Hair Styles:** Bldg 150, Barber: Hrs: Mon-Fri 0900-1730, Sat 0900-1545, C-011-49-69-699-7214; Beauty: Hrs: Mon-Fri 0830-1730, Sat 0830-1600, C-011-49-69-699-7245. **Laundry/Dry Cleaning:** Bldg 349. **Medical:** Bldg 170, emergency clinic, C-011-49-69-699-6246 (Ambulance-116). **Postal:** Bldg 166,C-011-49-069-699-638417680.

**ATTRACTIONS:** Frankfurt, trade fairs, zoo.

| **IN ROUTE SCHEDULES** | | |
|---|---|---|
| **Charleston AFB/IAP** | APP/CHS-9 | |
| **Dallas-Fort Worth IAP** | APP/DFW-1 | |
| **The WM B Hartsfield, ATL IAP** | | APP/ATL-2 |
| **Philadelphia IAP** | APP/PHL-2 | APP/PHL-3 |

# GREECE

## SOUDA BAY NAVAL SUPPORT ACTIVITY/ AIR FACILITY (CRETE) (SOC)

AMC Liaison Office
OL-A Det 2, 621 AMSG
Souda Bay, Crete, GR
FPO AE 09865-0007

**LOCATION:** On the northwest end of the island of Crete on Souda Bay. The NATO Missile Firing Installation (NAMFI) is 5 miles north of Souda, Greece. *ML-ARM: (24°10'E/35°30'N)*. NMC: Chania, GR, 10 miles west. Main installation numbers: C-011-30-821-63388/63340, D-314-661-2010-X-275.

**PAX TERM INFO: C-011-30-821-63388/63340 EX-296/390, D-314-266-1275/1383, FAX 011-30-821-66200-1297, D FAX 314-266-1297.** During flight processing. Call and ask for Air Terminal (EX-383). Air Terminal processes all Space-A Pax. Chania, Greece Airport co-located with Souda Bay NAF.

**PAX LOUNGES:** Pax Term Lounge located next to the hanger.

**FOOD SERVICE:** Enlisted Dining Facility (Bldg 2) and All Hands Club (Sirocco Winds) available, EX-289. Local food establishments.

**TRANSPORTATION: Air Tickets:** MWR Tours agency, Chania term, Olympic Airlines. **Taxi (Comm):** C-011-30-821-98700/98701. Taxis available outside main gate. No taxis allowed on base. Ten minute walk from terminal to main gate. Base shuttle bus to the downtown area available at regular schedule daily intervals.

**TML:** Lodging Office. C-011-30-821-63388/63340, ask for lodging office.

**OTHER SERVICES:** MWR, NEX (EX-432) and limited medical facilities (EX-290) on base.

**ATTRACTIONS:** Museums, historical sights & great beaches!

| IN ROUTE SCHEDULES | | |
|---|---|---|
| **Charleston AFB/IAP** | ACC/CHS-17 | |
| **McGuire AFB** | ACC/WRI-19 | |
| **Ramstein AB** | ACM/RMS-1 | ACM/RMS-4 |

# ICELAND

## KEFLAVIK AIRPORT (KEF)

Dept. of the Navy, Commanding Officer
Air Operations Dept/ATD, PSC 1003, Box 27
FPO AE 09728-0327

**LOCATION:** In North Atlantic, 2300 miles northeast of NY City and 1000 miles northwest of Oslo, NO. On the southwest coast of the island. *ML-ARM: (22°40'W/64°01'N)*. NMC: Reykjavik, 45 miles northeast. Main installation numbers: C-011-354-25-0111, D-EUR-314-450-0111, D-USA-312-450-0111.

**PAX TERM INFO: C-011-354-25-6139/2280, FAX 011-354-25-4649.** Bldg 782, Hrs: Mon-Fri 0800-1700. Directions: Main gate straight to dead-end at Pax Term, red building to the right of the Navy Lodge. **Pax Service Office:** Same as Pax Term. **Pax Paging:** Same as Pax Term.

**PAX LOUNGES:** Bldg 782, Hrs: 24 hours daily, next to arrival/departure area. **General:** Bldg 782, EX-6139. Restrooms, TV, P/C seats. **DV/VIP:** Bldg 810, Hrs: 24 hours daily, EX-6139. Private area, coffee/tea service, restrooms. Host as required. **Protocol Service:** Bldg 782, duty hours, EX-4494.

**FOOD SERVICE: Dining Hall:** Bldg 743, Hrs: daily 0600-2330, EX-2220/4459 (4th meal 2230-0030). **Marine Enlisted Club:** Bldg 741, Hrs: Sun-Thu 1100-2300, Fri-Sat 1100-0100, EX-7083. **Cactus Cantina/Parcheezi's:** Bldg 749, Hrs: Sun-Thu 1100-2200, Fri-Sat 1100-2300, EX 6126. **Three Flags O'Club:** Bldg. 691. Lunch Tue-Fri 1100-1300, Dinner Tue-Sat 1800-2100, Sun Brunch 1100-1400. EX 7004. **Wendy's:** Bldg. 771, Mon-Fri 0700-2130, Sat 0830-2100, Sun 1200-2100.

**TRANSPORTATION: Tour Office:** Bldg. 771, Mon-Fri 0900-1645.**Air Tickets:** Iceland Air: IAP Term, Hrs: 24 hours daily, EX-9-50200. **Bus (Comm):** Keflavik, Hrs: Mon-Fri 0645-2300 (Keflavik to Reykjavik). Proceed out main gate, left to bus station. Also at IAP Terminal ($4 for 45 minute ride to Reykjavik hotels). **Bus (Shuttle):** Bldg 782 (Stop #34), Hrs: Mon-Fri: 0700-2140 (Bus #1); Mon-Fri: 1400-1700 (Bus #2). All on base locations. **Car Rentals:** Navy Lodge, Bldg 786, Hrs: 24 hours daily, EX-2210/7594. **Taxi Service:** 24 hrs, EX 2525/4141. **Parking:** Bldg. 782, 24 hours daily, EX 2280 (limited spaces, no restrictions). **Taxi:** Adalston: EX-2525, Okuleidir: EX-4141. Any place on base: $5.00.

**TML:** Lodging Office (Bldg 761), 24 hrs daily, C-011 354-25-4333. All ranks. Bldg 786. **Navy Lodge:** 011-354-25-7595/2210, 1-800-NAVY-INN. DV/VIP: 011-354-25-4414.

**TRAVELERS AID: American Red Cross:** Bldg 782, Hrs: Mon-Fri 0800-1630, EX-6210. **Chaplain:** Bldg 775 (Chapel), Hrs: daily 0735-1700, EX-4111. **Emergency Relief:** Bldg 782, Hrs: Mon-Fri 0900-1400, EX-4923. **Lost/Found:** Bldg 782, 24 hrs

*ICELAND*
*Keflavik Airport, continued*

daily, EX-2280. **Security Police:** Bldg 810, Hrs: 24 hours daily, Emergency, EX-110. Police Dispatcher, EX 2211. **USO:** Bldg 758, Hrs: Mon-Thu: 0700-0400, Fri-Sun: 0800-2200. EX-6113/7980/6124. Full service including grill and free coffee.

**OTHER SERVICES: Exchange:** Bldg 869B, Hrs: Mon-Fri 1000-1800, Sat 1000-1600, Sun 1300-1600, EX 2141. **Bank/Exchange:** NFCU: Bldg 771, Hrs: Mon-Fri 0900-1630, EX-6641. **Beauty Salon:** Bldg. 771, Mon-Thu 0900-1900, Fri-Sat 0900-1700 EX 6211; **Barber:** Mon-Fri 0900-1800, Sat 0900-1600, Sun 1300-1800. **Laundry/Dry Cleaning:** Bldg 632, Hrs: Mon-Fri 0800-1700, Sat 1000-1300, EX 4163. **Medical:** Bldg 710, 24 hrs daily, C-011-354-25-0111-X-3301, D-314-450-011-X-3301. **Postal:** Bldg 771, Hrs: Mon-Fri 0900-1600, Sat: 1000-1400, EX-2203.

**ATTRACTIONS:** Wildlife, glaciers, and ice-caps.

| | **IN ROUTE SCHEDULES** | | |
|---|---|---|---|
| **Allen C Thompson Field** | ACC/JAN-3 | | |
| **Andrews AFB** | ACC/ADW-3 | | |
| **Charleston AFB/IAP** | APM/CHS-6 | ACC/CHS-16 | |
| **Dover AFB** | ACM/DOV-6 | APM/DOV-7 | |
| **McGuire AFB** | ACC/WRI-1 | APM/WRI-9 | ACC/WRI-16 |
| | ACC/WRI-17 | | |
| **Norfolk NAS** | APP/NGU-3 | | |
| **Westover ARB** | APM/CEF-2 | | |

# INDIAN OCEAN

## DIEGO GARCIA ATOLL (NKW)

Air Terminal Officer, Box 20
FPO AP 96464-0031

**LOCATION:** In the Chagos Archipelago, approximately 1000 miles off the southern tip of India in the Indian Ocean. *ML-ARM: (72°00'E/07°10'S)*. NMC: Colombo, Sri Lanka, 900 air miles northeast. Main installation numbers: Comm: No commercial phone service, D-315-370-0111.

**PAX TERM INFO: D-315-370-2787, DSN FAX 315-370-2987.** Bldg 360, daily, 0600-2200, Center of island near main pier. **Space-A passengers must be stationed at or employed at Diego Garcia in order to fly into, out of or through Diego Garcia; no families are permitted on the island - No exceptions. See Appendix B for personnel entrance requirements. Pax Service Office:** See Pax Term info.

**PAX LOUNGES:** Pax Term, Hrs: daily 0600-2200. Also, **DV/VIP** lounge. **Protocol Service:** Bldg 136, Hrs: daily 0800-1600, D-315-370-4002, other hours contact Quarter Deck at EX-4120/4121.

**FOOD SERVICE: Dining Hall:** Bldg 140, hours vary, EX-2738. **Enlisted Club:** Bldg 110, EX-2810. **NCO/CPO Club:** Bldg 114, EX-2897. **O'Club:** Bldg 127, EX-4737. **Restaurants:** Peacekeeper Inn, EX-2810; Diego Burger II, EX-2816. **Seaman's Club:** EX-2878.

**TRANSPORTATION:** Official bus & taxi for duty Pax only. EX-2771 for TAXI and EX-2770 for Shuttle. N0 COMMERCIAL TRANSPORTATION.

**TML:** Lodging Office (BEQ #3), very limited space, no commercial facilities, EX-4415. DV/VIP: EX-4415.

**OTHER SERVICES: Exchange:** Bldg 133, Hrs: daily 1100-1900, EX-2995. **Bank/Exchange:** Bldg 132, Tue-Sun, EX-3671/2966. **Hair Styles:** Bldg 132, Hrs: daily 0800-1900, EX-2720 (Barber); BEQ 12, EX-2721 (appointments necessary). **Laundry:** Bldg 157, Hrs: Tue-Sat 0800-2200, EX-2926. **Medical:** Bldg 151, Hrs: 24 hours daily, EX-92. **Post Office:** Bldg 132, Hrs: daily 0800-1700, EX-4114.

**TRAVELERS AID: American Red Cross:** Bldg 141, Hrs: daily 0200-1000, EX-4603. **Chaplain:** Bldg 141, Hrs: daily 0200-1000, EX-4601. **Police:** Bldg 208, Hrs: 24 hours daily, EX-4600.

| IN ROUTE SCHEDULES | | | |
|---|---|---|---|
| **Norfolk NAS** | APP/NGU-4 | APP/NGU-5 | |
| **Yokota AB** | PCM/OKO-24 | PPM/OKO-25 | PPM/OKO-26 |
| | PPM/OKO-27 | PPM/OKO-28 | PCM/OKO-29 |
| | PCM/OKO-30 | | |

# INDONESIA

## HALIM PERDANAKUSUMA IAP (DJK) (JARKARTA AIRPORT)

OMADP, Box 2, Unit 8133
APO AP 96520-8133

**LOCATION:** On northwest end of the island of Java. The airport is 8 miles southeast of Jakarta. *ML-ARM: (107°00'E/06°05'S).* NMC: Jakarta, 8 miles northwest. Main installation Number: C-011-62-21-360-360-X-2629, D- none.

**PAX TERM INFO: C-011-62-21-360-360-X-2629, FAX: C-011-62-21-372-518.** Pax Term, Hrs: Mon-Fri 0730-1600. Enter military gate 500 yards from airport. No US Base support facility. All support facility at local airport. Cab from DJK to Jakarta approximately $8 US.

**PAX LOUNGES:** Base Ops, Hrs: 24 hours daily, C-011-62-21-801-108-EX-352. **General** and **DV/VIP** lounges. A/C, telephones (local), restrooms, wood seats.

**TML:** None.

| IN ROUTE SCHEDULES | | |
|---|---|---|
| **Kadena AB** | PPM/DNA-3 | |
| **Yokota AB** | PCM/OKO-8 | PPM/OKO-9 |

# ISRAEL

## BEN GURION INTERNATIONAL AIRPORT (TEL AVIV) (TLV)

OL-A, 621 AMSG/CH, Unit 7228
APO AE 09830-5000

**LOCATION:** In the Eastern Mediterranean. The airport is 9 miles east of the city. *ML-ARM: (35°55'E/32°01'N).* NMC: Tel Aviv Yafo, 9 miles west. Main installation numbers: C-011-972-3-971-2018.

**PAX TERM INFO: C-011-972-3-517-4338, FAX 011-972-3-510-2444.** Pax Term. Near Gate 3. Pax processed **by contractor, Laufer Aviation**. Full services of IAP. No US military facilities available.

**TRANSPORTATION: Bus Service:** Pax Term, Hrs: daily 0400-2400 (United Tours #222, TLV to city, $3 US). **Taxi:** Pax Term, 24 hours daily (TLV to city, $25.00 US, 15-20 minute ride).

| IN ROUTE SCHEDULES | |
|---|---|
| **Dover AFB** | ACC/DOV-4 |

### UNSCHEDULED FLIGHTS

Flights to: Ramstein AB GE (**RMS**); Rhein-Main AB GE (**FRF**); and Sigonella Arpt IT (**SIZ**). Call for destinations, routings and schedules.

# ITALY

## AVIANO AIR BASE (AVB)

Det 3, 608th ALSG/TROP, Unit 6165, Box 215
APO AE 09601-5215

**LOCATION:** From A-28 North exit Pordenone to IT-159 North for 8 miles to Aviano AB. *ML-ARM (12°35'E/46°05'N)*. NMC: Pordenone, 6 miles south. Main installation numbers: C-011-39-434-66-113, D-314-632-1110.

**PAX TERM INFO: C-011-39-434-66-7680, D-314-632-7680. REC: C-011-39-434-66-7520, D-314-632-7520, FAX 011-39-434-66-7822, DSN FAX 314-632-7782.** Bldg 933, Hrs: Mon-Fri 0600-2100, Sat-Sun 0800-1700. Directions: In area F, south of Aviano on the right of Pordenone. **Pax Service Office:** Same As Pax Term, C-011-39-434-66-7730 (NCO on duty). **Pax Paging:** Same as Pax Term Info.

**PAX LOUNGES:** Bldg 933, family lounges available. **General:** Bldg 933, Hrs: Mon-Fri 0600-2100, Sat-Sun 0800-1700. C-011-39-434-66-7730. A/C, restrooms, TV, O/S seats. **Family Lounge:** Small dependents' lounge located within main louge. Microwave, refrigerator, sink. **Protocol Service:** Hq 40th TACG, Hrs: Mon-Fri 0800-1700, C-011-39-434-66-7604 (ask for Chief of Staff).

**FOOD SERVICE: Cafeteria:** Bldg 914, Hrs: Mon-Fri 0600-1700, C-011-39-434-66-7736. **Consolidated Club:** Bldg 147, Hrs: daily: 1100-0200, C-011-39-434-66-7483. **Dining Hall:** Bldg 244, C-011-39-434-66-7297; Bldg 250, C-011-39-434-66-7463. **Snack Bars:** Food Mall (Area 1), Hrs: daily 0630-2100, Holidays: 0800-1630, C-011-39-434-66-7335. **Vending:** Bldg 933, Hrs: 24 hours daily.

**TRANSPORTATION: Air Tickets:** SATO: Bldg 933, Hrs: Mon-Fri 0800-1700, C-011-39-434-66-7791. **Bus (Comm):** Town Square Aviano. Service to Pordenone. **Car Rentals:** Beside main exchange, C-011-39-434-66-0287 (Europcar). **Taxi (Gov):** Bldg 1004, Hrs: 24 hours daily, C-011-39-434-66-7666. **Trains:** Pordenone, Hrs: 24 hours daily (Venice-50 miles southwest, 1 hour, $7 roundtrip). **Parking:** Bldg 1020, Hrs: 24 hours daily, C-011-39-434-66-7200. Short & long term. Check with Security Police.

**TML:** Lodging Office (Bldg 273), 24 hrs daily, C-011-39-434-65-2306, D-314-632-7262/7722, FAX 011-39-434-66-0598 (area 2-limited). All ranks. DV/VIP: C-011-39-434-66-7604, D-314-632-7604. Ask for 40th TACG. O6+.

**TRAVELERS AID: American Red Cross:** Bldg 150, Hrs: Mon-Fri 0900-1200 and 1300-1500, C-011-39-434-66-7215. **Chaplain:** Bldg 172, Hrs: Mon-Fri 0800-1700, C-011-39-434-66-7211. **Emergency Relief:** Bldg 600, Hrs: Mon-Fri 0800-1700, C-011-39-434-66-7216. **Lost/Found:** Bldg 933, Hrs: Mon-Fri 0600-2100, Weekends: 0800-1700, C-011-39-434-66-7680. **Security Police:** Bldg 1019, Hrs: 24 hours daily, C-011-39-434-66-7200 (Desk Sgt).

**OTHER SERVICES: Exchange:** Bldg 179, Hrs: Mon-Sat 1000-1900, Sun 1100-1600, C-011-39-434-66-7571. **Bank/Exchange:** Bldg 140, Hrs: Mon-Fri 0900-1430, C-011-39-434-66-7637. **Hair Styles:** Bldg 179, Hrs: Mon-Fri 0900-1800, Sat 0900-1600, Barber: C-011-39-434-66-7539; Beauty: C-011-39-434-66-7539. **Laundry:** Bldg 257, Hrs: 24 hours daily (coin operated). **Medical:** Bldg 121, Hrs: Mon-Fri 0730-1900, C-011-39-434-66-7571, D-314-632-7571 (emergency); after hours call C-011-39-434-66-7673. **Postal:** Bldg 142, Hrs: Mon-Fri 1100-1730, Sat 1100-1300, C-011-39-434-66-7735. **Valet/Dry Cleaning:** Bldg 256, Hrs: Mon-Sat 1000-1800.

**ATTRACTIONS:** Excellent snow skiing in nearby Piancavallo.

| IN ROUTE SCHEDULES | | |
|---|---|---|
| **Andrews AFB** | ACC/ADW-2 | |
| **Charleston AFB/IAP** | ACM/CHS-8 | |
| **McGuire AFB** | ACC/WRI-10 | ACC/WRI-13 |
| **Philadelphia IAP** | APP/PHL-1 | |
| **Ramstein AB** | ACM/RMS-1 | |

# CAPODICHINO AIRPORT (NAPLES) (NAP)

PSC #817, Box 57
FPO AE 09622-1200

**LOCATION:** On the Gulf of Naples. Take Capodichino exit off Naples, Tangenziale (local highway by-passing city). Route to airport is marked. *ML-ARM: (14°20'E/40°48'N)*. NMC: Naples, 3 miles southeast. Main installation numbers: C-011-39-81-724-1110, D-314-625-1110.

**PAX TERM INFO: C(USA)-011-39-81-568-5283, C(EUR)-039-81-568-5283, D-314-625-5336, REC-C-011-39-81-568-5336, USA FAX 011-39-81-568-5259, EUR FAX 039-81-568-5259, D FAX 314-625-5259.** Bldg 405, Hrs: Mon-Sat: 0600-2200, closed Sun. **Pax Service Office:** Same as Pax Term, C-011-39-81-724-5266. AMC Liaison, C-011-39-81-724-5240/5266. **Pax Paging:** Same as Pax Term, C-011-39-81-724-5283.

**PAX LOUNGES:** No family lounge. **General:** Bldg 405, Hrs: Mon-Sat 0600-2200, C-011-39-81-724-5283. A/C, nursery, restrooms, TV, P/C seats. **DV/VIP:** Across from Pax Term, Hrs: Mon-Sat 0600-2200, C-011-39-81-724-5283. A/C, restrooms, TV, O/S seats. No host. **Protocol Service:** Map #8, Hrs: Mon-Sat 0700-1900, C-011-39-81-724-5224/6.

**FOOD SERVICE: Cafeteria:** NSA #2, Hrs: daily 0630-2200, C-011-39-81-724-4386 (basement). **Dining Hall:** AFSOUTH Bldg D, Hrs: daily 0615-1800, C-011-39-81-721-2792. Also at NAP Map #13. **Enlisted Club:** AFSOUTH: Flamingo Club: Bldg B,

*ITALY*
*Capodichino Airport, continued*

Hrs: daily 0800-0030, C-011-39-81-721-2240. **NCO/CPO Club:** NSA #12, Hrs: daily 1100-2400, C-011-39-81-721-4673. **O'Club:** AFSOUTH: Allied Club: Bldg T, Hrs: daily 1100-2400, C-011-39-81-721-2801. **Restaurants:** NSA #2, Hrs: daily 1700-2300, C-011-39-81-724-1110 (basement-dinner only). **Snack Bars:** NSA #2, Hrs: daily 1100-1700, C-011-39-81-724-1110 (superdog/pizza-NAP Map #14). **Vending:** Bldg 405, Hrs: daily 0600-2200, C-011-39-81-724-5283.

**TRANSPORTATION: Air Tickets:** SATO: NSA #2, Hrs: Mon-Fri 0800-1600, Sat 0800-1200, C-011-39-81-724-4253. **Bus (Comm):** NAP, Hrs: 24 hours daily. Ask for schedule (500 lire per ride). **Bus (Shuttle):** Bldg 405, Hrs: daily 0600-0105. Every 90 minutes NAP-NSA-HOSP-AFSOUTH to fleet landing. Every 30 minutes when fleet is in. **Car Rentals:** NAP Apt, 24 hrs daily, Avis: C-011-39-81-780-5790, Hertz: C-011-39-81-780-2971, Italy-By-Car: C-011-39-81-780-5702, Eurocar: (BX) C-011-39-81-780-5643. **Taxi (Comm):** Commercial airport, 24 hrs daily. **Taxi (Gov):** GAETA, 24 hrs daily, C-011-39-81-724-4797 (duty Pax only). **Trains:** Naples Central Station, 24 hrs daily. **Parking:** Bldg 405, 24 hrs daily, 100 yards from terminal. Check with Security Police.

**TML:** Lodging Office: BEQ (Bldg 71) Hrs: 24 hours daily, C-011-39-81-724-4842, FAX 011-39-81-724-3512, DSN FAX 314-625-3512. Very limited. TML for E-6 and below. DV/VIP: C-011-39-81-724-4721. Navy Lodge at Pinetamare, C-011-39-81-509-7120/21/22/23. Hotel references given.

**TRAVELERS AID: American Red Cross:** NSA #30, C-011-39-81-724-4788/9; after hours, C-011-39-81-724-4546. **Chaplain:** NSA #30, Hrs: 24 hours daily, C-011-39-81-724-4546/4786. **Emergency Relief:** NSA #30, C-011-39-81-724-4139 (Navy Relief). **Lost/Found:** Bldg 405, Hrs: Mon-Fri 0700-1900, C-011-39-81-724-5214/5283. **Security Police:** NSA #9, Hrs: 24 hours daily, C-011-39-81-724-4109/4530. **USO:** NSA #10, Hrs: Mon-Fri 0800-1630, C-011-39-81-724-4664. Also, near fleet landing, Hrs: daily 0815-2200, C-011-39-81-724-4142.

**OTHER SERVICES:** Services at NSA, AFSOUTH Post, and GAETA. **Exchange:** NSA #2, Hrs: Tue-Fri 1000-1730, Sat 1000-1600, C-011-39-81-724-4386. **Bank/Exchange:** NSA #10, Hrs: Mon-Fri 0800-1600, C-011-39-81-724-4774. **Hair Styles:** NSA #2, Barber: Hrs: Tue-Fri 0900-1700, Sat 0900-1600, C-011-39-81-724-5267; Beauty: Hrs: Tue-Fri 0830-1730, Sat 0830-1530, C-011-39-81-724-4349. **Laundry/Dry Cleaning:** NSA #2, Hrs: Tue-Fri 0800-1800, Sat 0800-1600, C-011-39-81-724-4386. **Medical:** Naval Hospital, Hrs: 24 hours daily, C-011-39-81-724-4110, D-314-625-4110 (ambulance), C-011-39-81-724-3333, D-314-625-3333 (emergency). **Postal:** NSA #4, Hrs: Mon-Fri 0900-1600, C-011-39-81-724-1110.

**ATTRACTIONS:** Flea markets, Pompei, Island of Capri, archeological sites.

| IN ROUTE SCHEDULES | | |
|---|---|---|
| **Charleston AFB/IAP** | ACC/CHS-17 | |
| **McGuire AFB** | ACC/WRI-19 | |
| **Philadelphia IAP** | APP/PHL-4 | |
| **Ramstein AB** | ACM/RMS-1 | ACM/RMS-4 |

## OLBIA/COSTA SMERALDA AIRPORT (OLB)

USNSO, Supply Office, PSC 816
FPO AE 09612-0007

**LOCATION:** The airport is located on the northeastern coast of the Island of Sardinia. To reach the navy support office, from the airport follow highway SS-125 to Palau. At Palau, buy ticket for ferry (Palau Pier) and take ferry to La Maddalena. The installation is located next to the Italian Navy Hq approximately three blocks east of the ferry landing. *ML-ARM: (09°30'E/40°50'N).* NMC: Olbia, 27 miles southeast. Main installation numbers: C-011-39-789-790-541, D-314-726-2541/3331.

**PAX TERM INFO: C-011-39-789-790-319/254 (limited) D-314-623-8254.** UNIMARE/US Navy Office at Airport Terminal, Hrs: daily 0700-2300 hours.

| IN ROUTE SCHEDULES | | |
|---|---|---|
| **Ramstein AB** | ACM/RMS-1 | ACM/RMS-4 |

## SIGONELLA AIRPORT (SICILY) (SIZ)

PSC 812
FPO AE 09627-5000

**LOCATION:** On the island of Sicily. Accessible from A-19 or IT-417. *ML-ARM: (15°00'E/37°20'N).* NMC: Catania, 10 miles northeast. Main installation numbers: C-011-39-95-86-1110 (NAS II), C-011-39-95-56-1113 (NAS I), D-314-624-1113.

**PAX TERM INFO: C-011-39-95-86-5575/5576, D-314-624-5576, FAX 011-39-95-86-5211, D FAX 314-624-5211.** Bldg 436, Hrs: 24 hours daily. Main gate NAS II straight to Pax Term. **Pax Service Office:** Bldg 436, Hrs: daily 0730-1600, C-011-39-95-86-5576 (AMC and Navy on duty). **Pax Paging:** Same as Pax Term, C-011-39-95-86-5576 (see Pax Services).

**PAX LOUNGES:** Bldg 436. **General:** Bldg 436, Hrs: 24 hours daily, C-011-39-95-86-5576. A/C, game room, telephones (commercial and defense), TV, restrooms, P/C

***ITALY***
***Sigonella Airport, continued***

seats. **DV/VIP:** Bldg 436, Hrs: 24 hours daily, C-011-39-95-86-5575/6 (06+). A/C and other facilities in Terminal. **Protocol Service:** Bldg 476, Hrs: daily 0730-1600, C-011-39-95-86-5218. **Family:** Bldg 436, Hrs: 24 hours daily, C-011-39-95-86-5575. A/C, nursery, and other facilities in Terminal.

**FOOD SERVICE: Wendys:** Bldg 436, Hrs: 24 hours daily, C-011-39-95-86-5469. **Dining Hall:** Bldg 564, Hrs: daily 0600-1830, C-011-39-95-86-1110. **Enlisted Club:** Bldg 151, Hrs: Thu-Sun 1100-2330, C-011-39-95-56-4263. **NCO/CPO Club:** NAS II Pavilion, C-011-39-95-86-5245. **O'Club:** City Beat (No hours or phone number furnished). **Restaurants:** NAS I, Hrs: Wed-Sun 1700-2200, C-011-39-95-56-4272. **Snack Bars:** Bowling Alley: NAS I, Hrs: Thu-Sun 1100-2230, Fri-Sat 1100-2330, C-011-39-95-56-4302. **Vending:** Bldg 436, Hrs: 24 hours daily, C-011-39-95-86-5576.

**TRANSPORTATION: Air Tickets:** SATO: Bldg 436, Hrs: Mon-Fri 0900-1500, C-011-39-95-86-5428. **Bus (Comm):** Bldg 200, Hrs: daily 0600-2400, C-011-39-95-56-4201/2. **Bus (Shuttle):** Bldg 436, Hrs: daily 0600-1700, C-011-39-95-86-5576. **Car Rentals:** Bldg 436, Hrs: Mon-Fri 0830-1330, Mon-Sat C-011-39-95-86-5468. **Taxi (Comm):** Bldg 200, 24 hrs daily, C-011-39-95-56-4201/2 (to Catania $20-25). **Parking:** Bldg 436, 24hrs daily, C-011-39-95-56-4201/2 (see Security Police).

**TML:** Lodging Office (Bldg 436), Hrs: 24 hours daily, C-011-39-95-86-5575/5467 (limited availability). DV/VIP: Bldg 545, C-011-39-95-86-5313, O6+.

**TRAVELERS AID: American Red Cross:** NAS I, Hrs: Mon-Fri 0800-1300, C-011-39-95-56-4382; after hours, C-011-39-95-56-1110. **Chaplain:** Bldg 180, C-011-39-95-56-4295/6. **Emergency Relief:** NAS I, Hrs: Mon-Fri 0900-1300, C-011-39-95-56-4490. **Lost/Found:** Bldg 436, C-011-39-95-86-5576 (Pax Service NCO). **Security Police:** Bldg 200, Hrs: 24 hours daily, C-011-39-95-56-4201/2 (Desk Sgt). **USO:** NAS II (MWR), Hrs: Mon-Fri 0730-1600, C-011-39-95-86-5271.

**OTHER SERVICES: Exchange:** Bldg 549, Hrs: daily 0700-1900, C-011-39-95-86-5423/4; Bldg 192, Hrs: daily 0700-1900, C-011-39-95-56-4326/30. **Hair Styles:** Bldg 549, Hrs: Mon-Sat 0700-1900, C-011-39-95-86-5423 and C-011-39-95-56-4268; Bldg 192, Hrs: Tue-Fri 0800-1700, C-011-39-95-56-4337. **Laundry:** Bldg 174, Hrs: 24 hours daily, C-011-39-95-56-4346 (coin operated). **Medical:** Bldg 201, Hrs: 24 hours daily, C-011-39-95-42-5011 and C-011-39-95-56-4333. **Postal:** Bldg 189, Hrs: Mon-Fri 0900-1700, C-011-39-95-86-5242. **Valet/Dry Cleaning:** Bldg 174, Hrs: Mon-Fri 0600-2400, C-011-39-95-86-5423/4.

**ATTRACTIONS:** Mount Etna (popular ski resort) - 20 miles north; Taromina (popular beach) - 40 miles.

| IN ROUTE SCHEDULES | | | |
|---|---|---|---|
| **Charleston AFB/IAP** | ACC/CHS-7 | ACM/CHS-8 | ACC/CHS-17 |
| | ACC/CHS-18 | | |
| **Dover AFB** | APM/DOV-2 | ACM/DOV-3 | APM/DOV-10 |
| **March AFB** | APM/RIV-1 | | |
| **McGuire AFB** | ACC/WRI-11 | ACM/WRI-13 | ACC/WRI-14 |
| | ACC/WRI-19 | ACM/WRI-20 | |
| **Norfolk NAS** | APP/NGU-4 | APP/NGU-5 | |
| **Philadelphia IAP** | APP/PHL-4 | | |
| **Ramstein AB** | ACM/RMS-1 | ACM/RMS-4 | |
| **Wright-Patterson AFB** | ACC/FFO-2 | | |

# JAPAN

## ATSUGI NAVAL AIR FACILITY (NJA)

Air Operations, Box 13, PCS 477
FPO AP 96306-1213

**LOCATION:** In Central Japan off Tokyo Bay. Yokohama is 15 miles east and Tokyo is 28 miles northeast. Camp Zama is 5 miles north. *ML-ARM: (139°20'E/35°25'N)*. NMC: Tokyo, 28 miles northeast. Main installation numbers: C-011-81-3117-64-3334, D-315-264-3334.

**PAX TERM INFO: C-011-81-468-21-1944 EX 3801 after working hours; D-315-228-3803, FAX 011-81-468-21-1944-3149, FAX 315-264-3149**. Bldg 202, Hrs: daily 0600-2200. Directions: Main gate to traffic circle, turn left, 4 blocks turn left 1/4 mile on right, Pax Term on left. No immigration facilities. Persons not assigned in Japan must acquire entry & exit stamps on passports at Yokohama within 24 hours. **Pax Service Office:** Bldg 206, Hrs: daily 0600-2200, C-011-81-468-21-1944 EX 3803. **Pax Paging:** Bldg 206, Hrs: daily 0600-2200, EX-3803.

**PAX LOUNGES: General:** Bldg 202. **DV/VIP:** Bldg 202. **Protocol Service:** Bldg 66, Hrs: 24 hours daily, EX-3111. **Enlisted Club:** Bldg 55, EX-6233/3736. **NCO/CPO Club:** Bldg 75, EX-3658. **O'Club:** Bldg 495, EX-3616. **Vending:** Bldg 202, Hrs: daily 0600-2200, EX-3803.

**TML:** Lodging Office: BOQ (Bldg 482), BEQ (Bldg 989), C-011-81-3117-64-3698, D-315-264-3698, FAX (BOQ) 011-81-467-77-5321, FAX (BEQ) 011-81-3117-64-3256; DV/VIP: C-011-81-467-78-2664, D-315-264-3201. O6+.

**OTHER SERVICES: Air Tickets:** Bldg 77, EX-3786 (tours office). **Exchange:** Bldg 37, EX-3721. **Medical:** Bldg 21, Hrs: 24 hours daily, EX-3311 (hospital at Camp Zama). **Navy Lodge:** Hrs: Daily: 0700-2300, D-315-228-6880.

**ATTRACTIONS:** Tokyo, New Sanno US Forces Center, Tama Hills Rec area.

Note: Atsugi NAF JA (**NJA**) is used as alternate location for Yokota AB, JA (**OKO**) during runway downtime. Flight info 24 hours in advance only. **No scheduled flights at press time.**

## FUKUOKA AIRPORT (FUK)

630 AMSS/OL-B,
Itazuke/TR
PSC Box 12
FPO AP 96322-0006

**LOCATION:** On the northwest corner of Island of Kyushu. *ML-ARM: (130°30'E/33°45'N).* NMC: Fukuoka, in the city. Main installation numbers: C-011-81-92-451-2558, D-315-225-2438.

**PAX TERM INFO: C-011-81-92-451-2558, D-315-225-2438.** Bldg 2518, Hrs: Tue-Fri 0730-1630, Sat 1200-2000 (All hours subject to change depending on flight schedule). Ask at west gate for directions to Pax Term. The terminal is located on what remains of Itazuke AB. The base was closed and returned to the Japanese government in 1971. We maintain only one building and a small parking area for POV's. The terminal has a soda machine only. There are no other facilities here. The nearest military base is U.S. Fleet Activities, Sasebo, about 115 kilometers away (2 hour drive) depending on traffic. Although a small facility, Sasebo offers the usual services available on larger military bases.

| IN ROUTE SCHEDULES | | | |
|---|---|---|---|
| **Kadena AB** | PPM/DNA-2 | PCM/DNA-4 | |
| **Yokota AB** | PPM/OKO-3 | PPM/OKO-4 | PPM/OKO-5 |
| | PCM/OKO-13 | | |

# FUTENMA MARINE CORPS AIR STATION (NFO)

Air Freight & Passenger Terminal
Air Operations Division
FPO AP 96372-0618

**LOCATION:** On southern part of Okinawa Island off JA-58. *ML-ARM: (27°40'E/27°50'S).* NMC: Naha, 10 miles southwest. Main installation numbers: C-011-81-98-892-5111, D-315-640-1110.

**PAX TERM INFO: C-011-81-98-892-3039/3041, D-315-636-3039/3041.** Bldg 541, Hrs: Duty Hrs. From main gate to a right at runway. Follow Perimeter Rd to Building 541 on the left. All flights processed by Pax Terminal.

**PAX LOUNGES:** Each lounge has essential facilities. **General:** Same as Pax Term. **DV/VIP:** Bldg 510, adjacent to Term, C-011-81-98-636-3060.

**FOOD SERVICE: Enlisted Club:** EX-3438. **SNCO Club:** EX-3246/3769, **O'Club:** EX-3091. **Snack Bar:** EX-5176/4149.

**TML:** Lodging Office (Camp S.D. Butler), C-011-81-98892-2459, FAX 011-81-61175-7549, D-315-635-2191.

**OTHER SERVICES: Exchange:** EX-4156. **Laundry/Dry Cleaning:** EX-5153. **Chaplain:** EX-3219. **Barber Shop:** EX-5114. **Car Rental:** EX-5153.

***JAPAN***
***Futenma Marine Corps Air Station, continued***

**UNSCHEDULED FLIGHTS**

Frequent flights to: Iwakuni MCAS, JA (**IWA**); Iwo Jima AB, JA (**IWO**); Misawa AB, JA (**MSJ**); and Osan AB, RK (**OSN**); Yokota AB, JA (**OKO**). Call for destinations, routings, and schedules.

# IWAKUNI MARINE CORPS AIR STATION (IWA)

Logistic Department
ATD, PSC 561, Box 1872
FPO AP 96310-1872

**LOCATION:** Facing the Inland Sea on the south portion of the island of Honshu, 450 miles southwest of Tokyo, .5 mi off JA-188 on JA-189. *ML-ARM: (132°15'E/34°15'N).* NMC: Hiroshima, 25 miles north. Main installation numbers: C-011-81-827-21-4171-EX-5509, D-315-253-5509.

**PAX TERM INFO: C-011-81-827-21-4171-EX-5509/3947, D-315-253-5509/3947, FAX 011-81-6117-53-3301, D FAX 315-253-3301.** Bldg 779, Hrs: daily 0600-2200. Directions: Main gate left to 2nd intersection, right to next intersection, left to flight line and Pax Term. **Pax Service Office:** Same as Pax Term, EX-3818 (NCO on duty). **Pax Paging:** Same as Pax Term, C-011-81-827-21-4171-EX-5509 (see Pax Service NCO).

**PAX LOUNGES:** No family lounge. **General:** Bldg 779, Hrs: daily 0600-2200, C-011-81-827-21-4171-EX-5509. A/C, bag check, telephone (local, long distance and defense), TV, restrooms. **DV/VIP:** Bldg 779, Hrs: daily 0600-2200, C-011-81-827-21-4171-EX-5509 (06+). A/C, bag check, restrooms, TV, O/S seats. **Protocol Service:** Bldg 360, Hrs: Mon-Fri 0800-1630, C-011-81-827-21-4171-EX-4211 (06+).

**FOOD SERVICE: Consolidated Club:** Samurai Club: Bldg 1470, EX-3803. **Enlisted Club:** Bldg 175, EX-3803. **O'Club:** Bldg 601, EX-3327. **Restaurants:** Pizza Inn bldg 401 EX 4444, Eagle's Nest: Bldg 702, EX-3407. **Snack Bars:** Bldg 779, during flight operations, EX-3801. **Vending:** Bldg 779, EX-3570.

**TRANSPORTATION: Air Tickets:** SATO Travel Bureau: Bldg 210, Hrs: Mon-Fri 0800-1630, EX-3572. **Train:** Iwakuni train station: 99-21-3933/3935; Shin Iwakuni Train station: 99-46-0655. **Car Rentals:** Bldg 139, EX-3186 (Special Services). **Taxi (Comm):** Bldg 779, 99-21-1111. **Taxi (Gov):** Bldg 170, EX-3063 (duty Pax only). **Trains:** IWA, See Travel Bureau for schedules. **Parking:** Bldg 779, across from Term. See Security Police.

**TML:** Lodging Office (Bldg 444), Hrs: 24 hours daily, C-011-81-827-21-4171-EX-3181, D-315-253-5409. **Hostess House:** EX-3221. All ranks. DV/VIP: C-011-81-827-21-4171-EX-3063 (06+).

**TRAVELERS AID: American Red Cross:** Bldg 210, EX-3252; after hours, EX-4211. **Chaplain:** Bldg 360, EX-3414. **Emergency Relief:** Bldg 210, EX-5311 (Navy Relief). **Lost/Found:** Bldg 610, EX-4590. **Security Police:** Bldg 610, C-011-81-827-21-4171-EX-3222/119 (Desk Sgt).

**OTHER SERVICES: Exchange:** Bldg 408, EX-5673. **Bank/Exchange:** NFCU: Bldg 201, EX-4794; AMEXCO: Bldg 201, Hrs: Mon-Fri 0900-1500, EX-4777. **Hair Styles:** Barber: Bldg 408, EX-4728; Beauty: Bldg 408, EX-4708. **Laundry/Dry Cleaning:** Bldg 348, EX-4710. **Medical:** Bldg 125, Hrs: 24 hours daily, C-011-81-0827-21-4171-EX-3300, D-315-253-3300. **Postal:** Bldg 405, EX-5435. **Valet/Dry Cleaning:** Bldg 408, EX-4744.

| IN ROUTE SCHEDULES | | | |
|---|---|---|---|
| **Kadena AB** | PPM/DNA-2 | PCM/DNA-4 | |
| **Yokota AB** | PPM/OKO-4 | PPM/OKO-5 | PPM/OKO-6 |

## KADENA AIR BASE (OKINAWA) (DNA)

633 APS/TRP
APO AP 96368-5000

**LOCATION:** On central Okinawa, adjacent to JA-58, 27 and 16. *ML-ARM: (128°00'E/26°00'N)*. NMC: Naha JA, 15 miles south. Main installation numbers: C-011-81-611-938-1111, D-315-630-1110.

**PAX TERM INFO: C-011-81-611-938-634-4462/1281. D-315-630-4462/1281, REC: C-011-81-611-634-4000, FAX 011-81-611-734-4221.** Bldg 3409, Hrs: daily 0600-2300, after hours as needed. Directions: From gate 1 on Douglas Blvd to a left on Schreiber Avenue to Term on the right. **Pax Service Office:** Bldg 3409, Hrs: Mon-Fri 0700-1630, C-011-81-98-634-4495/1273 (Space-A counter). **Pax Paging:** Same as Pax Term, C-011-81-098-634-4462/1281 (see Pax Service NCO). Space-A calls now 2hrs+30

**PAX LOUNGES:** No separate family lounge. **General:** Bldg 3409, Hrs: daily 0600-2300, C-011-81-611-634-4462/1281 (center building). A/C, bag lockers, game room, restrooms, TV, video movies, O/S seats, nursery. No food or sleeping overnight. **DV/VIP:** Bldg 3409, Hrs: daily 0600-2300, C-011-81-611-634-4462 (at Gate 2). A/C, bag check, restrooms, showers, TV, separate read/write rooms, coffee/tea service, O/S seats. Staffed as required (06+). **Protocol Service:** Bldg 3409, Hrs. daily 0600-2300, C-011-81-611-634-3795.

**FOOD SERVICE: Cafeteria:** Bldg 3409, 2nd floor, Hrs: daily 0600-2300, C-011-81-098-633-3183. Breakfast and lunch, burgers and chicken (Flag room). **Dining Hall:** Bldg 3522. Hrs: daily 0600-2300, C-011-81-0611-634-1684. **Enlisted Club:** Banyan Tree:

*JAPAN*
***Kadena Air Base, continued***

Bldg 431, Hrs: daily 0600-2400, C-011-81-611-634-0644. **NCO/CPO Club:** Bldg 621, Hrs: daily 0630-2400, C-011-81-611-634-0740. **O'Club:** Bldg 313, Hrs: daily 0630-2400, C-011-81-611-634-0482. **Restaurants:** Skoshi Room: Bldg 9950, Hrs: Wed-Sun 1700-2200, C-011-81-611-633-3220. **Snack Bars:** Vincent Ave, Hrs: daily 0430-2200, C-011-81-611-633-9150 (drive-in). **Vending:** Bldg 3409, Hrs: 24 hours daily, C-011-81-611-634-4370.

**TRANSPORTATION: Air Tickets:** Bldg 3409, Hrs: daily 0800-1500, C-011-81-611-634-0519 (also AMEXCO service mall). **Bus (Comm):** Bldg 412, Hrs: 24 hours daily, C-011-81-611-634-3383. **Bus (Shuttle):** Bldg 3409, Hrs: daily 0530-0030 - every 30 minutes, C-011-81-611-634-4462 (base area). **Car Rentals:** Bldg 219, Hrs: daily 0800-1730, C-011-81-611-633-0007. **Taxi (Comm):** Bldg 3409, Hrs: 24 hours daily, C-011-81-611-633-1405 on base, C-011-81-611-97-4002/97-2467. **Taxi (Gov):** Bldg 3409, Hrs: 24 hours daily, C-011-81-611-634-0030/0604(duty Pax only). **Parking:** Bldg 3409, Hrs: 24 hours daily, C-011-81-611-634-2475 (short term-2 hours in front of Pax Term; long term-hill above Pax Term).

**TML:** Lodging Office (Bldg 332): Hrs: 24 hours daily, C-011-81-611-732-1000, D-315-632-1100. All ranks. **Navy:** C-011-81-611-634-1173. **Kuwae Lodge:** C-011-81-611-634-0214/3656. DV/VIP: C-011-81-611-634-1273 (06+).

**TRAVELERS AID: American Red Cross:** Bldg 99, Hrs: Mon-Fri 0730-1630, C-011-81-611-634-1294; after hours, C-011-81-611-634-4611. **Chaplain:** Bldg 9800, duty hours, C-011-81-611-634-1288; after hours, C-011-81-611-634-4274. **Emergency Relief:** Bldg 99, Hrs: Mon-Fri 0730-1630, C-011-81-611-634-3366 (AF Aid Society). **Lost/Found:** Bldg 3409, Hrs: Mon-Fri 0730-1630, C-011-81-611-634-4221. **Security Police:** Main gate, Hrs: 24 hours daily, C-011-81-611-633-3333 (Desk Sgt). **USO:** Bldg 337, Hrs: daily 0730-2100, C-011-81-611-634-0473/0438.

**OTHER SERVICES: Exchange:** Bldg 3409, Hrs: 24 hours daily, C-011-81-611-633-4570. Main BX, Bldg 413, Hrs: Mon-Sun 1000-2000, C-011-81-611-633-4570. **Bank/Exchange:** National Bank: Bldg 409, Hrs: Mon-Thu 0900-1500, Fri 0900-1700, C-011-81-611-634-3347. **Hair Styles:** Barber: Bldg 3409, Hrs: Mon-Sat 0900-1700, C-011-81-611-634-4927; Beauty: Bldg 409, Hrs: daily 0900-1800, C-011-81-611-633-4176. **Laundry/Dry Cleaning:** Bldg 409, Hrs: daily 1000-1800, C-011-81-611-633-1568 (service mall). **Medical:** Bldg 703, Hrs: 24 hours daily, C-011-81-611-631-7555, D-315-630-3333 (emergency care). **Postal:** Bldg 160, Hrs: Tue-Fri 0900-1700, Sat 0900-1500, C-011-81-611-634-2237.

**ATTRACTIONS:** Naha JA, Okuma Rec Center, White Beach Rec Center.

| ORIGINATING SCHEDULES | | | |
|---|---|---|---|
| | **PPM/DNA-1 3rd SUN DC862** | | |
| **Location ID** | **Airport (Station)** | **Country/State** | **Days Out** |
| DNA | Kadena AB | JA | +0 |
| **BKK** | **Don Muang APT** | **TH** | **+1** |
| DNA | Kadena AB | JA | |
| | **PPM/DNA-2 1st/3rd TUE DC862** | | |
| DNA | Kadena AB | JA | +0 |
| **FUK** | **Fukuoka/Itazuke APT** | **JA** | **+0** |
| IWA | Iwakuni MCAS | JA | +0 |
| OKO | Yokota AB | JA | |
| | **PPM/DNA-3 1st SUN DC862** | | |
| DNA | Kadena AB | JA | +0 |
| **DJK** | **Halim Perdanakusuma IAP** | **IE** | **+1** |
| DNA | Kadena AB | JA | |
| | **PCM/DNA-4 1st/3rd TUE DC862** | | |
| DNA | Kadena AB | JA | +0 |
| **IWA** | **Iwakuni MCAS** | **JA** | **+0** |
| FUK | Fukuoka/Itazuke APT | JA | +0 |
| OKO | Yokota AB | JA | |

| IN ROUTE SCHEDULES | | | |
|---|---|---|---|
| **Altus AFB** | PCC/LTS-1 | PCC/LTS-3 | |
| **Lambert St. Louis IAP** | PPP/STL-1 | | |
| **McChord AFB** | PPM/TCM-6 | | |
| **Travis AFB** | PCC/SUU-6 | | |
| **Yokota AB** | PPM/OKO-3 | PPM/OKO-4 | PPMOKO-6 |
| | PPM/OKO-7 | PCM/OKO-8 | PPM/OKO-9 |
| | PPM/OKO-10 | PCM/OKO-11 | PPM/OKO-12 |
| | PCM/OKO-20 | PPM/OKO-21 | PCM/OKO-22 |

**JAPAN**

# MISAWA AIR BASE (MSJ)

Det 1, 316th APS/TROP
APO AP 96319-5008

**LOCATION:** On the northeast portion of the Island of Honshu, 400 miles north of Toyko. *ML-ARM: (141°30'E/40°45'N).* NMC: Hachinohe City, 17 miles southeast. Main installation numbers: C-011-81-176-53-5181, D-315-226-1110.

**PAX TERM INFO: C-011-81-3117-66-2444/5, D-315-226-2444/5.** Bldg 943, Hrs: Mon-Fri 0730-1630, Sat/Sun as mission requires. Directions: From main gate drive down Friendship Blvd. At the intersection turn left on Falcon Dr and go approximately .75 miles until you come to a passenger terminal direction sign. At that intersection turn right and drive .25 miles to the Pax Term. Bldg 943 is on the right. **Pax Recorder:** C-011-81-3117-66-2852, D-315-226-2852. **Pax Info (other services):** Bldg 961, Hrs: Mon-Fri 0800-1630, EX-226-3125 (Navy Operations). **Pax Paging:** Same as Pax Term, EX-226-2445.

**PAX LOUNGES:** Small **DV/VIP** lounge and nursery for families. **General:** Bldg 943, Hrs: daily 0730-1630, EX-226-2444. A/C, bag check, game room, nursery, telephones (local and defense), TV, restrooms. **Protocol Service:** Bldg 504, Hrs: daily 0730-1630, D-315-226-4804.

**FOOD SERVICE: Cafeteria:** Bldg 1044, Hrs: Mon-Sat 0700-1300, EX-226-4513. **Dining Hall:** Bldg 624, EX-226-3889. **Consolidated Club:** Hrs: Mon-Fri 0800-1700, EX-226-3217. **Food Court:** Bldg 325: Sun-Thu 1100-1930, Fri-Sat 1100-2000, EX 226-2378/77. **In-flight Meals:** Bldg 624, Hrs: 24 hours daily, EX-226-3889 (24 hours notification). **O'Club:** Bldg 22, Hrs: Mon-Fri 0800-1600, EX-226-4724. **Burger King:** Bldg 526, Hrs: daily 0500-2400, EX-226-5905. **Snack Bar:** Bldg 961, Hrs: Mon-Fri 0700-1300, EX-226-5619. **Vending:** Bldg 431, Hrs: Mon-Fri 0800-1700, EX-226-5491.

**TRANSPORTATION: Air Tickets:** Bldg 943, Hrs: Mon-Fri 0730-1600, EX-226-5555. **Bus (Gov):** Bldg 987, Hrs: 24 hours daily, EX-226-4062. **Bus (Shuttle):** Bldg 987, Hrs: 24 hours daily, EX-226-4062. **Car Rentals:** Bldg 325, Hrs: Mon-Fri 0800-1630, EX-226-7222. **Taxi (Comm):** Bldg 14, Hrs: 24 hours daily, EX-226-5438/9. **Taxi (Gov):** Bldg 987, Hrs: 24 hours daily, EX-226-4062. **Parking:** Front of the Pax Term, EX-226-2444 no overnight/reserved parking. Long term next to Pax Term.

**TML:** Lodging Office (Misawa Inn), C-011-81-176-53-5181-EX-3526, 24 hours daily. Check in billeting. DV/VIP: C-011-81-176-53-5181-EX-4804, 06+. Retirees Space-A.

**TRAVELERS AID: American Red Cross:** Bldg 1082, EX-226-3772. **Chaplain:** Bldg 358, EX-226-4630. **Emergency Relief (CBPO):** Bldg 961, EX-226-3721. **Lost/Found:** Bldg 943, EX-226-2444/45. **Security Police:** Bldg 648, Hrs: 24 hours daily, EX-226-4358.

**OTHER SERVICES: Exchange:** Bldg 325, EX-226-5959. **Bank/Exchange:** Bldg 470, EX-226-5412. **Barber:** Bldg 325, EX-226-6186. **Beauty:** Bldg 325, EX-226-5755. **Laundry/Dry Cleaning:** Bldg 325, EX-226-5521. **Medical:** Bldg 1000, Hrs: 24 hours daily, EX-226-2985 (Emergency 911). **Postal:** Bldg 519, EX-226-3492/93. **Valet/Dry Cleaning:** Bldg 325, EX-226-5521 (main Exchange). **Wire:** Bldg 320, EX-226-3880/5412.

**ATTRACTIONS:** Ski area, lodge on base. Skeet shooting, deep sea fishing trips.

| IN ROUTE SCHEDULES | | | |
|---|---|---|---|
| **Yokota AB** | PCM/OKO-13 | PPM/OKO-14 | PPM/OKO-15 |
| | PPM/OKO-16 | PPM/OKO-17 | PPM/OKO-18 |

## YOKOTA AIR BASE (OKO)

316th APS/TRO
APO AP 96328-5114

**LOCATION:** Take Rt-16 South from Tokyo. AB is 1 mile west of Fussa JA. Clearly marked. *ML-ARM: (139°45'E/35°25'N)*. NMC: Tokyo JA, 35 miles northeast. Main installation numbers: C-011-81-425-52-2511, D-315-225-9540.

**PAX TERM INFO: C-011-81-425-52-2511-X-7119, D-315-225-7119, REC: D-315-225-7111, FAX: D-315-225-9768.** Bldg 80, Hrs: daily 0400-2200. Directions: From Gate #5 straight on Bobzien Ave to Terminal on the right or across from Main Gate. **Pax Service Information:** Bldg 80, Hrs: daily 0400-2200 C-EX 7119/9540, D-315-225-7119/9540 2200-0400 REC C-EX-7111, D-315-225-7111. **Pax Paging:** Bldg 80, Hrs: 24 hours daily, C-EX-7119, D-315-225-7119.

**PAX LOUNGES:** Bldg 80, Hrs: 24 hours daily. USO provides both accompanied and unaccompanied lounges. **General:** Bldg 80, Hrs: 24 hours daily, EX-9540. A/C, bag check/lockers, coffee/tea served, game room, restrooms, showers, TV, P/C seats. No sleeping in the Terminal overnight. **DV/VIP:** Bldg 80, Hrs: 24 hours daily, EX-9540 (06+), A/C, restrooms, read/write rooms, TV, O/S seats. Not staffed. Protocol Service: Bldg 714, Hrs: Daily 24 hrs, EX-4141.

**FOOD SERVICE: Cafeteria:** Bldg 80, Hrs: 24 hours daily, EX-7146. **Dining Hall:** Bldg 427, EX-8870. **Enlisted Club:** Bldg 2066, EX-7-8820, O'Club: Bldg 31 EX 8341. Restaurants: Bldg 442 Yokota Burger EX-8837.

**TRANSPORTATION: Air Tickets:** Bldg 80, EX-6430. **Bus (Comm):** Bldg 80, EX-9520(local area). **Bus (Gov):** Bldg 80, EX-7750/0519. Service to New Sanno and Narita - adults $6/24, children $4/12. **Bus (Shuttle):** Bldg 529, Hrs: 24 hours daily, EX-9121 (schedule at Space-A counter). **Car Rentals:** Bldg 1296, EX-8070. **Taxi (Comm):** Hrs: Daily 24 hrs EX-5901. **Taxi (Gov):** Bldg 409, EX-9121. **Trains:** Gate 2,

*JAPAN*
***Yokota Air Base, continued***

Hrs: Daily: 24 hrs, Fussa station TOKYO. **Parking:** Bldg 80, short-term at Pax Term; long term-across Rt-16.

**TML:** Lodging Office (Bldg 10 at Bobzien Ave. and 1st St.), C-011-81-425-52-2511-EX-5-7712, FAX C-011-81-425-52-3499, D-315-225-9270. Hrs: 24 hours daily, EX-5-7794. All ranks. DV/VIP: C-011-81-425-52-2511-EX-5-4141 06+.

**TRAVELERS AID: American Red Cross:** Bldg 4018, EX-7522; after hours, EX-9901. **Chaplain:** Bldg 345, EX-7009/8009. **Emergency Relief:** Bldg 535, EX-8725 (AF Aide). **Lost/Found:** Bldg 80, Hrs: daily 0400-2200, EX-9543 (Pax Service NCOIC). **Security Police:** Bldg 555, Hrs: 24 hours daily, EX-116 (Desk Sgt). **USO:** Bldg 4018, Hrs: 24 hours daily, EX-2087/2093.

**OTHER SERVICES: Exchange:** Bldg 4018, EX-7236. **Bank/Exchange:** Bldg 4018, EX-3828, **Hair Styles:** Bldg 416, EX-8379. **Laundry/Dry Cleaning:** Bldg 436, EX-9878. **Medical:** Bldg 4408, Hrs: 24 hours daily, C-011-81-0425-225-7740 (emergency). **Postal:** Bldg 538, EX-7220.

**ATTRACTIONS:** Tokyo, Mount Fuji, New Sanno US Forces Center, Hakone National Park, Central Alps, Toshimien Water Park, Ueno Zoo, Disneyland, Seibu Lions Professional Baseball Stadium, Imperial Palace, The Ginza, Akihabara Electronic Districk, Tokyo Tower, The Ski Dome, Tama Lodge and Golf Course, Tama Tech amusement park, Tama Zoo, Tokyo Dome, Yokohama Indoor water park, Roppangi.

| ORIGINATING SCHEDULES | | | |
|---|---|---|---|
| **PPM/OKO-1 WED C-130E** | | | |
| **Location ID** | **Airport (Station)** | **Country/State** | **Days Out** |
| OKO | Yokota AB | JA | +0 |
| **UAM** | **Andersen AFB** | **GU** | **+2** |
| OKO | Yokota AB | JA | |
| **PPM/OKO-2 2nd/4th MON, 1st/3rd TUE DC862** | | | |
| OKO | Yokota AB | JA | +0 |
| UAM | Andersen AFB | GU | +1 |
| HIK | Hikam AFB | HI | +1 |
| **SUU** | **Travis AFB** | **CA** | |
| **PPM/OKO-3 1st SAT DC862** | | | |
| OKO | Yokota AB | JA | +0 |
| FUK | Fukuoka/Itazuke APT | JA | +1 |
| **DNA** | **Kadena AB** | **JA** | |
| **PPM/OKO-4 3rd SAT DC862** | | | |
| OKO | Yokota AB | JA | +0 |
| IWA | Iwakuni MCAS | JA | +1 |
| FUK | Fukuoka/Itazuke APT | JA | +1 |
| **DNA** | **Kadena AB** | **JA** | |

| | **PPM/OKO-5 2nd/4th SUN DC862** | | |
|---|---|---|---|
| OKO | Yokota AB | JA | +0 |
| IWA | Iwakuni MCAS | JA | +0 |
| FUK | Fukuoka/Itazuke APT | JA | +0 |
| OKO | Yokota AB | JA | +1 |
| **FUK** | **Fukuoka/Itazuke APT** | **JA** | **+1** |
| IWA | Iwakuni MCAS | JA | +1 |
| OKO | Yokota AB | JA | |
| | **PPM/OKO-6 2nd/4th THU, 1st/3rd/5th FRI C-141B** | | |
| OKO | Yokota AB | JA | +0 |
| IWA | Iwakuni MCAS | JA | +1 |
| DNA | Kadena AB | JA | +1 |
| **OSN** | **Osan AB** | **RK** | **+1** |
| OKO | Yokota AB | JA | |
| | **PPM/OKO-7 TUE C-130E** | | |
| OKO | Yokota AB | JA | +0 |
| DNA | Kadena AB | JA | +1 |
| BKK | Don Muang APT | TH | +1 |
| VBU | U-Tapao RTN | TH | +2 |
| **BKK** | **Don Muang APT** | **TH** | **+2** |
| DNA | Kadena AB | JA | +3 |
| OKO | Yokota AB | JA | |
| | **PCM/OKO-8 3rd SUN C-141B** | | |
| OKO | Yokota AB | JA | +0 |
| DNA | Kadena AB | JA | +0 |
| **DJK** | **Halim Perdanakusuma IAP** | **IE** | **+2** |
| DNA | Kadena AB | JA | +2 |
| OKO | Yokota AB | JA | |
| | **PPM/OKO-9 3rd MON C-141B** | | |
| OKO | Yokota AB | JA | +0 |
| DNA | Kadena AB | JA | +0 |
| DJK | Halim Perdanakusuma IAP | IE | +2 |
| DNA | Kadena AB | JA | +2 |
| OKO | Yokota AB | JA | |
| | **PPM/OKO-10 1st/3rd/5th THU C-141B** | | |
| OKO | Yokota AB | JA | +0 |
| DNA | Kadena AB | JA | +1 |
| KHE | Kimhae IAP | RK | +1 |

*JAPAN*
*Yokota Air Base, continued*

| **OSN** | **Osan AB** | **RK** | **+1** |
|---|---|---|---|
| OKO | Yokota AB | JA | |
| | **PCM/OKO-11 2nd/4th MON C-141B** | | |
| OKO | Yokota AB | JA | +0 |
| DNA | Kadena AB | JA | +1 |
| **OSN** | **Osan AB** | **RK** | **+1** |
| OKO | Yokota AB | JA | |
| | **PPM/OKO-12 TUE C-130E** | | |
| OKO | Yokota AB | JA | +0 |
| DNA | Kadena AB | JA | +1 |
| **OSN** | **Osan AB** | **RK** | **+1** |
| OKO | Yokota AB | JA | |
| | **PCM/OKO-13 THU C-130E** | | |
| OKO | Yokota AB | JA | +0 |
| **KUZ** | **Kunsan AB** | **RK** | **+1** |
| FUK | Fukuoka/Itazuke APT | JA | +1 |
| MSJ | Misawa AB | JA | +1 |
| OKO | Yokota AB | JA | |
| | **PPM/OKO-14 SUN, TUE, THU C-130E** | | |
| OKO | Yokota AB | JA | +0 |
| **KUZ** | **Kunsan AB** | **RK** | **+1** |
| MSJ | Misawa AB | JA | +1 |
| OKO | Yokota AB | JA | |
| | **PPM/OKO-15 THU C-141B** | | |
| OKO | Yokota AB | JA | +0 |
| **MSJ** | **Misawa AB** | **JA** | **+0** |
| OKO | Yokota AB | JA | |
| | **PPM/OKO-16 MON, 1st/3rd/5th FRI C-141B** | | |
| OKO | Yokota AB | JA | +0 |
| MSJ | Misawa AB | JA | +1 |
| **OSN** | **Osan AB** | **RK** | **+1** |
| KUZ | Kunsan AB | RK | +1 |
| OKO | Yokota AB | JA | |
| | **PPM/OKO-17 2nd/4th FRI C-141B** | | |
| OKO | Yokota AB | JA | +0 |
| MSJ | Misawa AB | JA | +1 |
| **KUZ** | **Kunsan AB** | **RK** | **+1** |
| OKO | Yokota AB | JA | |

| | **PPM/OKO-18 SAT C-141B** | | |
|---|---|---|---|
| OKO | Yokota AB | JA | +0 |
| MSJ | Misawa AB | JA | +1 |
| KUZ | Kunsan AB | RK | +1 |
| **OSN** | **Osan AB** | **RK** | **+1** |
| OKO | Yokota AB | JA | |
| | **PPM/OKO-19 SUN C-130E** | | |
| OKO | Yokota AB | JA | +0 |
| OSN | Osan AB | RK | +1 |
| **CJU** | **Cheju IAP** | **RK** | **+1** |
| OSN | Osan AB | RK | +2 |
| OKO | Yokota AB | JA | |
| | **PCM/OKO-20 TUE C-130E** | | |
| OKO | Yokota AB | JA | +0 |
| **OSN** | **Osan AB** | **RK** | **+1** |
| DNA | Kadena AB | JA | +1 |
| OKO | Yokota AB | JA | |
| | **PPM/OKO-21 WED C-130E** | | |
| OKO | Yokota AB | JA | +0 |
| **OSN** | **Osan AB** | **RK** | **+1** |
| DNA | Kadena AB | JA | +1 |
| OKO | Yokota AB | JA | |
| | **PCM/OKO-22 THU C-141B** | | |
| OKO | Yokota AB | JA | +0 |
| **OSN** | **Osan AB** | **RK** | **+1** |
| KHE | Kimhae IAP | RK | +1 |
| DNA | Kadena AB | JA | +1 |
| OKO | Yokota AB | JA | |
| | **PCM/OKO-23 2nd/4th WED C-130E** | | |
| OKO | Yokota AB | JA | +0 |
| **OSN** | **Osan AB** | **RK** | **+1** |
| KUZ | Kunzan AB | RK | +1 |
| OKO | Yokota AB | JA | |
| | **PCM/OKO-24 SUN DC862** | | |
| OKO | Yokota AB | JA | +0 |
| SGP | Paya Lebar RSAF | SG | +1 |
| NKW | Diego Garcia Atoll | UK | +1 |
| **FUJ** | **Fujairah IAP** | **UA** | **+2** |

***JAPAN***
***Yokota Air Base, continued***

| | | | |
|---|---|---|---|
| NKW | Diego Garcia Atoll | UK | +2 |
| SGP | Paya Lebar RSAF | SG | +3 |
| OKO | Yokota AB | JA | |
| | **PPM/OKO-25 WED C-141B** | | |
| OKO | Yokota AB | JA | +0 |
| SGP | Paya Lebar RSAF | SG | +1 |
| NKW | Diego Garcia Atoll | UK | +2 |
| **FUJ** | **Fujairah IAP** | **UA** | **+3** |
| NKW | Diego Garcia Atoll | UK | +4 |
| SGP | Paya Lebar RSAF | SG | +5 |
| OKO | Yokota AB | JA | |
| | **PPM/OKO-26 TUE KC10A** | | |
| OKO | Yokota AB | JA | +0 |
| SGP | Paya Lebar RSAF | SG | +1 |
| **NKW** | **Diego Garcia Atoll** | **UK** | **+2** |
| SGP | Paya Lebar RSAF | SG | +3 |
| PKP | Yokota AB | JA | |
| | **PPM/OKO-27 THU DC862** | | |
| OKO | Yokota AB | JA | +0 |
| SGP | Paya Lebar RSAF | SG | +1 |
| **NKW** | **Diego Garcia Atoll** | **UK** | **+1** |
| SGP | Paya Lebar RSAF | SG | +2 |
| OKO | Yokota AB | JA | |
| | **PPM/OKO-28 MON KC10A** | | |
| OKO | Yokota AB | JA | +0 |
| SGP | Paya Lebar RSAF | SG | +1 |
| NKW | Diego Garcia Atoll | UK | +2 |
| **FUJ** | **Fujairah IAP** | **UA** | **+3** |
| NKW | Diego Garcia Atoll | UK | +4 |
| OKO | Yokota AB | JA | |
| | **PCM/OKO-29 2nd THU C-141B** | | |
| OKO | Yokota AB | JA | +0 |
| VBU | U-Tapao RTN | TH | +1 |
| NKW | Diego Garcia Atoll | UK | +3 |
| **FUJ** | **Fujairah IAP** | **UA** | **+3** |
| NKW | Diego Garcia Atoll | UK | +4 |
| VBU | U-Tapao RTN | TH | +5 |
| OKO | Yokota AB | JA | |

| | PCM/OKO-30 | 1st/3rd/4th/5th FRI | C-141B | |
|---|---|---|---|---|
| OKO | Yokota AB | | JA | +0 |
| VBU | U-Tapao RTN | | TH | +0 |
| NKW | Diego Garcia Atoll | | UK | +2 |
| **FUJ** | **Fujairah IAP** | | **UA** | **+2** |
| NKW | Diego Garcia Atoll | | UK | +3 |
| VBU | U-Tapao RTN | | TH | +4 |
| OKO | Yokota AB | | JA | |

| | IN ROUTE SCHEDULES | | |
|---|---|---|---|
| **Altus AFB** | PCC/LTS-3 | | |
| **Bangor IAP** | PCC/BGR-2 | | |
| **Fairchild AFB** | PCC/SKA-2 | | |
| **Kadena AB** | PPM/DNA-2 | PCM/DNA-4 | |
| **Lambert St. Louis IAP** | PPP/STL-1 | PPP/STL-2 | |
| **Lincoln MAP** | PCC/LNK-1 | | |
| **Malmstrom AFB** | PCC/GFA-1 | | |
| **March AFB** | PCC/RIV-2 | PCC/RIV-3 | |
| **McChord AFB** | PCC/TCM-3 | PCC/TCM-4 | PCC/TCM-5 |
| | PPM/TCM-6 | PPM/TCM-8 | |
| **McConnell AFB** | PCC/IAB-1 | | |
| **McGuire AFB** | PCC/WRI-23 | PCC/WRI-24 | |
| **O'Hare IAP** | PCC/ORD-1 | | |
| **Robins AFB** | PCC/WRB-2 | | |
| **Travis AFB** | PCC/SUU-1 | PCC/SUU-2 | PCC/SUU-3 |
| | PCC/SUU-4 | PCC/SUU-5 | PCC/SUU-6 |
| | PPM/SUU-7 | PCC/SUU-8 | PCC/SUU-11 |
| **Wright-Patterson AFB** | PCC/FFO-3 | | |

## JAPAN AIR BASES & AIRPORTS

(Not listed separately in this book)

The bases listed below have Space-A air opportunities. Base support facilities are very limited.

**CHITOSE APT - JA (CTS)** *ML-ARM: (141°40'E/42°50'N).* c/o Yokota Air Base, 316th APS/TRO, APO AP 96328-5114. For information: **C-011-81-425-52-2511-X-7119, D-315-225-7119.** Very limited support facilities available. No Government TML.

*JAPAN*

**OBIHIRO APT - JA (OBO)** *ML-ARM: (143°10'E/42°50'N).* 630 AMSS/TRP, Unit 5114, APO AP 96328-5114. For information: **USA C-011-81-3117-5-X-7119, JAPAN C-52-2511-5-7119, D-315-225-7119, FAX 315-225-9768.** Very limited support facilities available. PAX TERM INFO: PSC 225-9526, Dispatch D- 315-225-9466, Lost & Found D-315-225-9543. No Government TML.

**UNSCHEDULED FLIGHTS**

Flights to Misawa AB, JA (MSJ), Yokota AB, JA (OKO) & other JA bases.

# JORDAN

## KING ABDULLAH AIR BASE (AMM)

American Embassy USDAO, Unit 70208
APO AE 09892-0208

**LOCATION:** In Amman, Jordan, capital city of Hashemite Kingdom of Jordan. *ML-ARM: (36°00'E/32°15'N)*. NMC: Amman, 3 miles west. Main installation numbers: C-011-962-6-820-101-EX-2537.

**PAX TERM INFO: C-011-962-6-820-101-EX-2647, D-none, FAX: C-011-962-6-820-160.** Pax Term, Hrs: During flight processing. Contact AMC/American Embassy personnel for Pax processing. No US Base support facilities. $15 departure tax for out-bound pax through civilian airport. NOTE: *Active duty and retired military personnel on leave are required to obtain country clearance through the USDAO, Amman upon arrival. Consult Appendix B - Personnel/Entrance Requirements.*

| IN ROUTE SCHEDULES | |
|---|---|
| **Andrews AFB** | ACC/ADW-2 |
| **McGuire AFB** | ACC/WRI-10 |

# KOREA (SOUTH)

## KIMHAE AIR BASE (KHE)

AMC PAX Terminal, OL-D, 611th ALSS
APO AP 96214-0006

**Location:** On the southern coast, southeast sector of South Korea. *ML-ARM: (129°00'E/35°00N).* NMC: Pusan, 15 miles southeast. Main Installation Numbers: C-011-82-51-801-1110, D-315-763-1110.

**PAX TERM: C-011-82-51-801-3584, D-315-763-3584.** Bldg 2005, Hrs: Mon-Fri: 0730-1630. Directions: Approximately 1 and 1/2 miles from main gate on main blvd. USAF compound located on left side of road prior to T on main Blvd. No food service available at Kimhae AB. Commercial snack bar and restaurants available at Kimhae IAP.

**TML:** Lodging Office (Camp Hialeah, Pusan), C-011-82-51-801-3462.

| IN ROUTE SCHEDULES | | |
|---|---|---|
| **Yokota AB** | PPM/OKO-10 | PCM/OKO-22 |

## KUNSAN AIR BASE (KUZ)

631 AMSS OL-B
APO AP 96264-3414

**LOCATION:** On the southwest coast of the Korean peninsula at the terminus of RK-26 pipeline. *ML-ARM: (126°45'E/35°59'N).* NMC: Kunsan, 10 miles west. Main installation numbers: C-011-82-654-470-1110, D-313-782-1110.

**PAX TERM INFO: C-011-82-654-470-4666, FAX C-011-82-654-470-5616, D-315-782-4666/5403, D FAX 315-782-5616.** Bldg 2858, Hrs: Mon-Fri 0715-1630, Sat 0715-1330. Directions: Three miles from main gate on Ave B, west. Adjacent to Base Ops and weather tower. **Pax Service Office:** Same as Pax Term, C-011-82-654-470-4666, D-315-782-4666 (also Pax Paging/lost & found).

**PAX LOUNGES: General:** Same info as Pax Service. A/C, restrooms. **DV/VIP:** OL Chief's office, C-011-82-654-470-4901.

**FOOD SERVICE: Cafeteria: Bldg 1004, C-011-82-279-1-4736, D-315-782-4736. Dining Hall:** Bldg 550, C-011-82-654-470-5104. **NCO/CPO Club:** Seabreeze: Bldg 1104, C-011-82-654-470-4312. **O'Club:** Bldg 387, C-011-82-654-470-4494. **Restaurants:** Oriental House: Bldg 565, C-011-82-654-470-4100. **Snack Bars:** Bldg 2858, C-011-82-654-470-4666.

**TRANSPORTATION: Air Tickets:** Bldg 814, C-011-82-654-470-4027. **Taxi (Comm):** Bldg 724, C-011-82-654-470-4318. **Taxi (Gov):** Bldg 804, Hrs: 24 hours daily, C-011-82-654-470-5317. **Parking:** No long term available. Ground transportation to Osan and Seoul consists of commercial bus and/or train. One commercial bus leaves Kunsan for Osan at 8am daily and returns to Kunsan leaving Osan at 1600 daily (tickets sold 0730-0800 daily). Commercial transportation requires Korean money. Osan is approximately 3.5 hours north by bus or train. Seoul is three hours by bus and four by train.

**TML:** Lodging Office (Bldg 392), C-011-82-654-470-4604, D-315-782-4604. All ranks. DV/VIP: C-011-82-654-470-4604. O6+.

**TRAVELERS AID: American Red Cross:** Bldg 1051, C-011-82-7-3596-4601. **Chaplain:** Bldg 301, C-011-82-7-3596-4300/4511. **Lost/Found:** Bldg 2858, C-011-82-7-4666. **Security Police:** Bldg 590, C-011-82-654-470-4291.

**OTHER SERVICES: Exchange:** Bldg 1102, C-011-82-654-470-4520. **Medical:** Bldg 405, C-011-82-654-470-4333, D-315-782-4333. **Postal:** Bldg 1058, C-011-82-654-470-5514. Also Federal Credit Union, Hair styles, laundry and dry cleaning.

**ATTRACTIONS:** Yellow Western Sea.

| IN ROUTE SCHEDULES | | | |
|---|---|---|---|
| **Yokota AB** | PCM/OKO-13 | PPM/OKO-14 | PPM/OKO-16 |
| | PPM/OKO-17 | PPM/OKO-18 | PCM/OKO-23 |

## OSAN AIR BASE (OSN)

611th ALSS/TRO
APO AP 96278-5000

**LOCATION:** At Song Tan city, 6 miles west of Seoul-Pusan North/South Expressway. Directions to AB from expressway are marked. *ML-ARM: (127°00'E/37°00'N)*. NMC: Seoul RK, 38 miles north. Main installation numbers: C-011-82-333-661-1110, D-315-784-1234.

**PAX TERM INFO: C-011-82-333-661-1854/6809, FAX 011-82-333-661-4897, D-315-784-1854/6809. D FAX 315-784-4897.** AFKN broadcast next days schedule at 1815 hours daily. Bldg 884, Hrs: daily 0630-2100. Directions: From main gate straight on Songtan Blvd, at football field turn right on Alabama Road, go one block, turn left on Texas Road. Terminal is next to flightline on the right. **Pax Service Office:** Same as Pax Terminal (Space-A desk). **Pax Paging:** Same as Pax Terminal (Pax Service NCO).

*KOREA*
***Osan Air Base, continued***

**PAX LOUNGES:** Bldg 884. No family lounge. **General:** Bldg 884, Hrs: daily 0630-2100, C-011-82-333-661-1854/6809. A/C, bag check, telephones (local and defense), TV, restrooms, O/S seats, flight monitors. No smoking. **USO Lounge:** Hrs: daily 0800-1700, C-011-82-333-661-3491, D-315-784-3491. Limited dependent care items. Free beverages and movies. **DV/VIP:** Bldg 884, Hrs: daily 0800-1700, C-011-82-332-284-1854/6809. A/C, telephones (local and defense), TV, restrooms, O/S seats. **Protocol Service:** 7th AF, duty hours, C-011-82-333-661-5669, D-315-784-5669 (see Pax Service NCO).

**FOOD SERVICE: Dining Facilities:** Bldgs: 773 and 1343, Hrs: daily 0600-2100. **NCO Club:** Bldg 342, Hrs: daily 0600-2100. Bldg 1313, Hrs: daily 1100-2400. **O'Club:** Bldg 910, Hrs: daily 1100-2100. **Snack Bars:** REC Center: Bldg 948, Hrs: daily 24 hrs. Bowling Center: Bldg 977, Hrs: daily 1100-2230. Burger Bar: Bldg 920, Hrs: daily 0630-2130.

**TRANSPORTATION: Air Tickets:** Bldg 955, Hrs: Mon-Fri 1000-1800, C-011-82-333-661-3043/3236. **Bus (Comm):** Bldg 980, Hrs: daily 0700-2100, OSN-Yongsan $1.50, Kunsan 1600 daily $3. **Bus (Shuttle):** Bldg 884, Hrs: 24 hours daily, C-011-82-333-661-1843 (OSN Base); 0600-2300 daily (OSN main gate). **Car Rentals:** Kimpo IAP arrival lobby. Major rent-a-car companies. **Taxi (Comm):** Bldg 884, Hrs: 24 hours daily, C-011-82-333-661-4121/2/3 (AAFES). **Taxi (Gov):** Bldg 1310, Hrs: 24 hours daily, C-011-82-333-661-5841 (duty Pax only). **Trains:** TMO building, duty hours, C-011-82-333-661-4997. **Parking:** Bldg 884, Hrs: 24 hours daily, C-011-82-332-284-5515, short term-NO OVERNIGHT. Long term-72 hours at main gate (notify Security Police).

**TML:** Lodging Office (Bldg 771), Hrs: 24 hours daily, C-011-82-331-661-1841/4597, D-315-784-1841. (Limited space on AB. See Yongsan Seoul, C-011-82-331-661-4842).

**TRAVELERS AID: American Red Cross:** Bldg 944, Hrs: Mon-Fri 0730-1630, C-011-82-333-661-4140/1855. **Chaplain:** Bldg 779, Hrs: 24 hours daily, C-011-82-333-661-4184. **Emergency Relief:** Bldg 936, duty hours, C-011-82-333-661-5826 (AF Aid). **Lost/Found:** Bldg 884, Hrs: daily 0700-1700, C-011-82-333-661-4720 (Pax Svc NCO). **Security Police:** Bldg 363, Hrs: 24 hours daily, C-011-82-333-661-5515. **USO:** Yongsan, Hrs: daily 0800-2200, C-011-82-332-793-3478.

**OTHER SERVICES: Exchange:** Bldg 920, Hrs: daily 1000-2000, C-011-82-333-661-3371. **Bank/Exchange:** Merchants National: Bldg 952, Hrs: Tue-Fri 0930-1730, Sat 0930-1500, C-011-82-333-661-4185. **Hair Styles:** Barber: Bldg 954, Hrs: daily 1000-1700, C-011-82-333-661-3133; Beauty: Bldg 957, Mon-Sat 1000-1800, C-011-82-333-661-3285. Laundry/Dry Cleaning: Bldg 958, Hrs: Tue-Sun 1030-1700, C-011-82-333-661-3144. **Medical:** Bldg 76B, Hrs: 24 hours daily, C-011-82-333-661-4732, D-315-784-4732. **Postal:** Bldg 959, Hrs: Tue-Sat 1000-1800, C-011-82-333-661-4394/4658.

**ATTRACTIONS:** DMZ, Korean customs & culture, Seoul, Inchon.

| IN ROUTE SCHEDULES | | | |
|---|---|---|---|
| **Altus AFB** | PCC/LTS-3 | | |
| **Lambert St. Louis IAP** | PPP/STL-2 | | |
| **McChord AFB** | PCC/TCM-5 | PPM/TCM-6 | |
| **Travis AFB** | PCC/SUU-4 | | |
| **Yokota AB** | PPM/OKO-6 | PPM/OKO-10 | PCM/OKO-11 |
| | PPM/OKO-12 | PPM/OKO-16 | PPM/OKO-18 |
| | PPM/OKO-19 | PCM/OKO-20 | PPM/OKO-21 |
| | PCM/OKO-22 | PCM/OKO-23 | |

## Other Korean Installations with Limited Space-A Air Opportunities.

**CHEJU INTERNATIONAL AIRPORT (CJU)**, APO AP 96220-5000. *ML-ARM: (126°50'E/33°10'N)*. **PAX TERM: C-011-82-641-2472, D-315-262-1101 (ask for Cheju Do).** Bldg AMC Desk, Hrs: During flight processing. **Location:** Cheju IAP is 15 miles SW of Cheju City, on the subtropical island of Cheju, which is 50 miles south of the South Korean Peninsula.

| IN ROUTE SCHEDULES | |
|---|---|
| **Yokota AB** | PPM/OKO-19 |

# KUWAIT

## KUWAIT INTERNATIONAL AIRPORT (KWI)

P.O. Box 77 SAFAT, Kuwait, Unit 69000
APO AE 09880-9000

**LOCATION:** Kuwait IAP is 5 miles SW of Kuwait City, which is located on the NW corner of the Persian Gulf. *ML-ARM: (29°00'N/47°00'E)*. NMC: Kuwait City, 5 miles NE. Also 95 miles south of Basra, Iraq.

**PAX TERM INFO:** Call U.S. Liason office in Kuwait, **C-011-965-242-4151/2/3/4//5/6/7/8/9, FAX 011-965-244-2855.** Bldg: AMC Desk, Hours: During flight processing. No US DoD support facilities.

| IN ROUTE SCHEDULES | | |
|---|---|---|
| **Charleston AFB/IAP** | ACC/CHS-7 | |
| **Dover AFB** | ACC/DOV-8 | APM/DOV-10 |
| **McGuire AFB** | ACC/WRI-11 | |
| **Stewart ANGB** | ACC/SWF-1 | |

# NEW ZEALAND

## CHRISTCHURCH INTERNATIONAL AIRPORT (CHC)

Detachment 2, 615th AMSG, USAF
PSC 467, Box 214
FPO AP 96531-5000

**LOCATION:** Near Yaldhurst. *ML-ARM: (172°30'E/43°35'S)*. NMC: Christchurch, 5 miles southeast. Main installation numbers: C-011-64-3-358-1475, D-None.

**PAX TERM INFO: C-011-64-3-358-1455.** After hours and Sat-Sun **C-011-64-3-358-1457, FAX: 011-64-3-358-5458.** Pax Term, Hrs: Mon-Fri: 0900-1600. Sign-up at USAF hangar Gate 2 Orchard Rd. **Pax Service Office:** Gate 2 Orchard Rd. Same as Pax Term C-011-64-3-358-1455. **Pax Paging:** Gate 2 Orchard Rd or Gate 9 IAP Term, C-011-64-358-1475-EX-8160.

**PAX LOUNGES:** CHC IAP. No DV/VIP or family lounges. **General:** Pax Term, Hrs: daily 0600-2300. A/C, bag check/lockers, game room, TV, telephones (local and long distance), restrooms, O/S seats. Pax Term has support facilities: bank, restaurant, cafeteria, rent-a-car, barber/beauty, book/gift shops.

**FOOD SERVICE: Enlisted Club:** US Navy, C-011-64-3-358-1475. Ask for extension. Only US facility **(except FPO)** available to Space-A Pax.

**TRANSPORTATION: Bus (Comm):** Pax Term, CHC IAP to CHC and return. **Taxi (Comm):** Pax Term, C-011-64-3-795-795/799-799.

**TML:** Lodging Office (Bldg 7), C-011-64-3-358-1475, FAX 011-64-3-358-1448, (NZ) 358-1448, 24 hrs daily.

**OTHER SERVICES: Postal:** US Navy, C-011-64-3-358-1475. Letters & post cards only.

**ATTRACTIONS:** Christchurch, sheep ranches, snow skiing and Mount Cook.

| IN ROUTE SCHEDULES | |
|---|---|
| McChord AFB | PCC/TCM-7 |

# PALAU

## U.S. LIAISON OFFICE (USLO)

P.O. Box 6028
Koror, Republic of Palau 96940-5000

**LOCATION:** Topside, Koror State about 10-15 minutes ride from the airport. *ML-ARM: (134°30'E/08°00'N)*. NMC: Airai (where airport is located). Main installation numbers: C-011-680-488-2920/2990.

**PAX TERM INFO: C-011-680-488-2920/2990. FAX 011-680-488-2911.** Civic Action team located on the other side of the airport. Palau has one airport for all commercial and non-commercial planes.

**PAX LOUNGES: General:** First floor of the terminal, open only during flight times, baggage check. **DV/VIP:** Same as General, A/C, baggage check, restrooms. **Family Lounge:** Same as General, baggage check. **Protocol Service:** Koror, 0730-1630, C-011-680-488-2408, eligibility: VIP.

**FOOD SERVICE: Cafeteria:** Terminal, Hrs: flight times, C-011-680-587-3509. **Snack Bar:**First floor terminal, Hrs: flight times.

**TRANSPORTATION: Bus (Comm):** Outside terminal, by reservations. **Car Rentals:** Terminal, during flight hours. **Taxi (Comm):** Terminal. **Parking:** Security annexed to terminal building.

**TRAVELERS AID: Chaplain:** Koror. **Security Police:** Koror, 24 hrs daily, C-011-680-488-1422. **USO:** Koror, 0730-1630, C-011-680-488-2920.

**OTHER SERVICES: Barber Shop:** Koror, 0730-2000. **Beauty Shop:** Koror, 0730-2000. **Emergency Medical:** Meyuns, Kr, 24 hrs, 911/488-2558. **Laundry:** Koror, 0600-2100. **Postal:** Koror, 0730-1630. No Government TML.

### UNSCHEDULED

Infrequent flights to : Anderson AFB, GU (UAM) and Hickam AFB, HI (HIK).

# PANAMA

## HOWARD AIR FORCE BASE (HOW)

Howard Passenger Terminal
640 AMSS/TROP, Unit 0620
APO AA 34001-5000

**LOCATION:** Adjacent to Thatcher Hwy (K-2) on the Pacific side of the Republic of Panama. *ML-ARM: (79°50'W/09°00'N)*. NMC: Panama City, 10 miles west. Main installation numbers: C-011-507-284-3010, D-313-284-3010.

**PAX TERM INFO: C-011-507-284-4306/5758/3608, D-313-284-4306/5758, FAX 011-507-84-3848.** Bldg 228, Hrs: daily 0500-2100. Directions: Main gate to 1st intersection. Terminal on right. **Pax Service Office:** Bldg 228, Hrs: Mon-Fri: 0715-1630, C-011-507-284-5703 (NCO on duty). **Pax Paging:** Bldg 228, Hrs: daily: 0500-2100, C-011-507-284-4306/3608 (see Pax NCO). Customs and Immigrations: 507-284-3204.

**PAX LOUNGES:** Bldg 228. Family Service & nursery on inbound side of Pax Term. **General:** Bldg 228, Hrs: daily 0500-2100, C-011-507-284-4306/3608. A/C, restrooms, O/S seats, telephones (defense), TV/Cable. **DV/VIP:** Bldg 228, Hrs: daily 0500-2100, C-011-507-284-5702. Coffee/tea served, separate read/write rooms, restrooms, showers, telephones, O/S seats, TV/Cable. No staff. **Protocol Service:** Quarry Hts, duty hours, D-313-282-3211/3604. Military public phones available for Pax in Term (main lobby).

**FOOD SERVICE: Cafeteria:** Bldg 709, Hrs: daily 0630-1900, C-011-507-284-3927 (AAFES, .25 miles from Term). **In-flight Meals:** Bldg 228, Hrs: daily 0500-2100 C-011-507-284-3567. **NCO/CPO Club:** Bldg 710, Hrs: daily 0600-2400, C-011-507-284-4189. **O'Club:** Bldg 113, Hrs: daily 1000-2200, C-011-507-284-4896. **Restaurants:** Anthonys Pizza, Bldg 709, Hrs: Sun-Thu: 1100-2200, Fri-Sat: 1100-2300, C-011-507-284-6744/6252. **Snack Bars:** Burger King: Hrs: daily 0630-2200, C-011-507-284-3395 (at Fort Kobbe/HOW). **Vending:** Bldg 228, Hrs: daily 0500-2100, C-011-507-284-4306.

**TRANSPORTATION:** Means and facilities available at HOW and Panama City, PN. **Bus (Comm):** Andrews Blvd, 24hrs daily (shuttle bus/limo service on HOW. **Car Rentals:** Bldg 228, Hrs: daily 1000-1800, C-011-507-284-3784 (also at AAFES). **Taxi (Comm):** Andrews Blvd, 24hrs daily, C-011-507-264-9421. **Taxi (Gov):** Bldg 6, 24hrs daily, C-011-507-284-5058/9 (duty Pax only). **Parking:** Bldg 228, 24hrs daily, C-011-507-284-4306. Short term-in front of Term; long term-across from Term.

**TML:** Lodging Office (Bldg 708), 24hrs daily, C-011-507-84-6411/5306, D-313-285-6411/5306, FAX 011-507-84-4589. All ranks. DV/VIP: Bldg 119, C-011-507-284-4601/4914, O6+.

**TRAVELERS AID:** Support for HOW & other Pacific side installations. **American Red Cross:** Bldg 519, Hrs: Mon-Fri: 0715-1615, C-011-507-287-5509; after hours, C-011-

*PANAMA*
*Howard Air Force Base, continued*

507-252-2233. **Chaplain:** Bldg 500, C-011-507-284-3948. **Lost/Found:** Bldg 228, Hrs: daily 0500-2100, C-011-507-284-5703 (see Pax NCO). **Security Police:** Bldg 726, 24hrs daily, C-011-507-284-4711 (ask for desk Sgt).

**OTHER SERVICES: Exchange:** Bldg 709, Hrs: Mon-Fri: 1000-2000, Sat-Sun: 1000-1700, C-011-507-284-3944 (many exchanges in Panama). **Bank/Exchange:** Bldg 115, Hrs: Mon-Fri: 1000-1700, Sat: 0900-1400, C-011-507-285-4005/4253. **Hair Styles:** Bldg 709, Barber: Hrs: Mon-Fri: 1000-1800, Sat: 1000-1700, Sun: 1200-1700, C-011-507-284-5385; Beauty: Hrs: Mon-Fri: 0830-1700, Sat: 0830-1500, C-011-507-284-3917. **Laundry/Dry Cleaning:** Bldg 711, Hrs: Mon-Fri: 1000-1800, Sat: 1000/1700, C-011-507-284-3182 (call for one-day service). **Medical:** Bldg 192, 24hrs daily, C-011-507-284-3562 (appointment), Emergency and after duty hours, C-011-507-284-3014. **Postal:** Bldg 711, Hrs: Mon-Fri: 1000-1300, 1500-1730, Sat: 1000-1300, C-011-507-284-3012.

**ATTRACTIONS:** Panama Canal, Panama City, beaches.

| | IN ROUTE SCHEDULES | | |
|---|---|---|---|
| **Allen C Thompson Field** | ACC/JAN-2 | | |
| **Charleston AFB/IAP** | ACC/CHS-11 | ACC/CHS-12 | ACC/CHS-20 |
| | ACC/CHS-21 | APP/CHS-22 | APP/CHS-23 |
| **Dover AFB** | ACC/DOV-1 | | |
| **Kelly AFB** | ACC/SKF-1 | | |
| **McGuire AFB** | ACC/WRI-4 | | |
| **Westover ARB** | ACC/CEF-1 | | |

# PORTUGAL

## ALVERCA PAFB (ALA)

NAV/AVN/DEPOT/OPS/CEN ERRA REP ALVERCA, PO PSC 83
APO AE 09726-5000

**LOCATION:** From Lisbon take A-1 or PO-10 North to an exit for Alverca PAFB which is 2 miles southwest of the exit. *ML-ARM: (09°02'W/38°50'N)*. NMC: Lisbon, 15 miles southwest

**PAX TERM INFO: C-011-351-1-958-2788/0771.** Bldg Base Ops, 24hrs daily. Pax processed by Navy at Alverca PAFB. Limited support facilities can be found at Reducto Gomes Freire (IBERLANT).

**OTHER SERVICES:** BX Mart C-011-351-1-726-6600.

**UNSCHEDULED FLIGHTS**

Flights to Chievres AB, BE (CHE) and Lajes Field (AZORES) PO (LGS).

## LAJES FIELD (AZORES) (LGS)

629 AMSS/TROP, Unit 7795
APO AE 09720-8010

**LOCATION:** On Terceira Island (Azores PO) 20 miles long & 12 miles wide. Lajes AB is 2 miles west of Praia da Vitoria PO, on Mason Hwy. *ML-ARM: (26°50'W/38°10'N)*. NMC: Lisbon, 850 miles east. Main installation numbers: C-011-351-95-540100, C-EUR-351-95-540100, D-314-535-1110, D-EUR-314-245-1110.

**PAX TERM INFO: C-USA-011-351-95-540-100-X-23227/23582/23199(recording), C-EUR-351-95-540100-X-23227/23582/23199(recording), D-CONUS-535-3227/3582, D-EUR-245-3227/3582, FAX 011-351-95-540-100 EX-25110, FAX EUR 351-95-540100-25110, D FAX CONUS 314-535-5110, DSN FAX EUR 245-5110.** When in Portugal, the area code for Terceira island is (95) then 540100 (on base operator). Bldg T-612, 24 hrs daily. Directions: From main gate straight for .25 mile. Pax Term on the right. **Pax Service Office:** Same as Pax Term. **Pax Paging:** Same as Pax Term.

**PAX LOUNGES:** Bldg T-612. **General:** Bldg T-612, 24 hrs daily, EX-23227/23582, 1st floor. Telephones (local and defense), TV, restrooms, P/C seats. **Protocol Service:** Base Ops, 24 hrs daily, EX-24106 (06+). **Family:** Bldg T-612, 24hrs daily, EX-23227/23582. To the right inside main door is the nursery. Same facility as above + nursery.

**FOOD SERVICE: Tradewinds Dining Facility:** Bldg T-415, Mon-Fri, breakfast: 0600-0830, lunch 1100-1330, dinner: 1600-1830, midnight meal: 2300-0100 (weekends & holidays) brunch: 0700-1300, dinner: 1500-1800 EX 24156. **Consolidated Club:** Bldg T-

***PORTUGAL***
***Lajes Field, continued***

112, Daily: breakfast: 0600-0930, lunch: 1100-1330, dinner: 1630-2200 EX 23202. **Snack Bars:** Bldg T-169, 24 hrs daily, EX-23849, T-612, 24hrs daily EX 25123.

**TRANSPORTATION: Air Tickets:** Commercial Term, Hrs: daily 0700-1900, TAP/SATA Info: C-011-351-95-52011/12, Res C-011-351-95-53013. **Bus (Comm):** Main gate, daily: 0700-1900-every hour. **Bus (Shuttle):** Bldg T-612, Hrs: daily 0715-0815; 1115-1315; 1615-1715, every half hour, C-011-351-95-540100-23151. **Car Rentals:** Commercial Term, Hrs: daily 0800-1600, C-011-351-95-52969. **Taxi (Comm):** Bldg T-612, 24 hrs daily, call operator-ask for taxi or 23488. **Taxi (Gov):** Bldg T-220, 24hrs daily, EX-23151 (duty Pax only). **Parking:** Bldg T-612, 24 hrs daily, short term.

**TML:** Lodging Office (Mid-Atlantic Lodge, Bldg T-166), 24 hrs daily, C-011-351-95-540100, FAX 011-351-95-540100 EX 3790. DV/VIP: C-011-351-95-520100, O6+.

**TRAVELERS AID: American Red Cross:** Bldg T-615, Hrs: Mon-Fri: 0800-1600, EX-23516 (other hours-EX-26252). **Chaplain:** Bldg T-305, Hrs: Mon-Fri: 0800-1700, EX-24211 (other hours-operator). **Lost/Found:** Bldg T-815, 24 hrs daily, EX-23222. **Security Police:** Bldg T-815, 24 hrs daily, EX-23222 (Desk Sgt).

**OTHER SERVICES: Exchange:** Bldg: T-323, Mon-Sat: 1000-1800, EX-23288/23280. **Bank/Exchange:** Near Bldg: T-612, BCA bank, hrs: Mon-Fri: 0830-1500, EX-23271, & NCO/O'Clubs. **Hair Styles:** Barber: Bldg: T-112, hrs: Tue-Sat: 0800-1700, EX-23386, Beauty: Bldg: T-400, hrs: Tue-Sat: 0800-1700, EX-24124. **Laundry/Dry Cleaning:** Bldg: T-331, hrs: Mon-Sat: 0800-1430, EX-23630. **Medical:** Bldg: T-241, hrs: daily: 24 hrs, EX-23237, D-314-245/535-1110-X-23237. **Postal:** Bldg: T-324, Hrs: Mon-Fri: 0800-1700, EX-23625/23338. **Wire:** PO Term, Hrs: Mon-Fri: 0900-1230, across the street from the AMC terminal.

**ATTRACTIONS:** Bull fights, caves, cliffs. CAUTION: DO NOT export scrimshaw (whale ivory) or elephant ivory to the USA.

| IN ROUTE SCHEDULES | | | |
|---|---|---|---|
| **Andrews AFB** | ACC/ADW-2 | | |
| **Bangor IAP** | ACC/BGR-1 | | |
| **Charleston AFB/IAP** | ACC/CHS-5 | ACM/CHS-8 | ACC/CHS-13 |
| | ACC/CHS-14 | ACC/CHS-15 | ACC/CHS-18 |
| **Dover AFB** | APM/DOV-2 | ACM/DOV-3 | ACC/DOV-9 |
| **McGuire AFB** | ACC/WRI-1 | ACC/WRI-2 | ACC/WRI-8 |
| | ACC/WRI-10 | APM/WRI-12 | ACM/WRI-13 |
| | ACC/WRI-14 | ACC/WRI-15 | |
| **General Mitchell IAP/ARS** | ACC/GMF-1 | | |
| **Norfolk NAS** | APP/NGU-4 | APP/NGU-5 | |
| **Philadelphia IAP** | APP/PHL-1 | | |

| | |
|---|---|
| **Stewart ANGB** | ACC/SWF-2 |
| **McGhee Tyson APT** | ACC/TYS-1 |
| **Westover ARB** | ACC/CEF-3 |
| **Wright-Patterson AFB** | ACC/FFO-2 |

# SAUDI ARABIA

## DHAHRAN INTERNATIONAL AIRPORT (DHA)

Det 1-621 AMSG PSC 1258 Box 878, Unit 66803
APO AE 09858-0878

**LOCATION:** On the Persian Gulf near the island of Bahrain. Airport is 5 miles west of the city. *ML-ARM: (50°03'E/26°15'N)*. NMC: Dhahran, 5 miles east.

**PAX TERM INFO: C-011-966-3-899-1119 EX 7726, D- 318-431-7726/7755, D FAX 318-431-4364**. AMC Desk, 24 hrs daily. Facilities of IAP available. Note: To enter/exit Saudi Arabia, you must obtain a visa before you travel. To receive a visa, you must have a sponsor within Saudi Arbia. The airfield is controlled by Saudi Arabia. Once you exit the airbase, it is not the responsibility of the air mobility command to get you back on the base.

| IN ROUTE SCHEDULES | | | |
|---|---|---|---|
| **Charleston AFB/IAP** | ACC/CHS-7 | | |
| **Dover AFB** | APM/DOV-5 | ACM/DOV-6 | ACC/DOV-8 |
| **McGuire AFB** | ACC/WRI-11 | | |
| **Philadelphia IAP** | APP/PHL-2 | APP/PHL-3 | |
| **Ramstein AB** | APM/RMS-2 | ACM/RMS-3 | |
| **Stewart ANGB** | ACC/SWF-1 | | |

## RIYADH INTERNATIONAL AIRPORT (RUH)

AMEMB, Unit 61307
APO AE 09803-1307

**LOCATION:** Riyadh Airport is 10 miles NW of Riyadh, capital of Saudi Arabia. *ML-ARM: (47°00'E/24°00'N)*. NMC: Riyadh, 10 miles SE.

**PAX TERM INFO: C-011-966-1-891-119, D-314-435-5093/5081, FAX 011-966-1-488-7360.** AMC Desk, 24hrs daily. Facilities of IAP available.

| IN ROUTE SCHEDULES | | |
|---|---|---|
| **Dover AFB** | APM/DOV-5 | ACM/DOV-6 |

# SINGAPORE

## RSAF PAYA LEBAR (SGP)

AMC Terminal Office,
c/o Air Movements Center, Bldg: 30
FPO AP 96534-5000

**LOCATION:** Tip of Malay Peninsula. Off Apt Rd. *ML-ARM: (103°55'E/01°15'N).* NMC: Singapore SG, 5 miles southwest. Main installation numbers: C-011-65-280-0624, D-None.

**PAX TERM INFO: C-011-65-280-0624.** Bldg 30, Hrs: Mon-Fri: 0800-1630. AMC Terminal Office is located next to the Air Movements Center. Turn right off Airport Rd upon seeing sign indicating Air Movements Center. Follow signs leading to AMC Terminal Office at Bldg 30. Extremely limited facility. No photos at RSAF. **Pax Service Office:** Bldg 30, Hrs: Mon-Fri: 0800-1600, C-011-65-280-0624. No passenger lounge available. No money changing avaiable.

**FOOD SERVICE: Cafeteria:** Airport Rd (breakfast, fast food).

**TRANSPORTATION: Bus (Comm):** 10 minute walk to bus at Airport Rd, (to downtown). **Taxi (Comm):** Airport Rd. (Getting a taxi to downtown hotels can take as long as two hours.) **Parking:** No parking for Space-A or other travelers, C-011-65-280-0624.

**TML:** Lodging Office (TLQ: 100 rooms), some Space-A, C-011-65-711-6848.

**TRAVELERS AID:** Consulate secretary. **Emergency Relief:** American Embassy, 30 Hill St, Hrs: Mon-Fri: 0730-1615, C-011-65-338-0251. **Security Police:** Bldg 30, 24 hrs daily, C-011-65-280-0624.

**OTHER SERVICES:** Limited at SGP. Many in Singapore. **Medical:** American Embassy, 30 Hill St, 24 hrs daily, C-011-65-338-0251 (very limited). **Postal:** American Embassy, 30 Hill St, Hrs: Mon-Fri: 0800-1600, C-011-65-338-0251 (AD only).

| IN ROUTE SCHEDULES | | | |
|---|---|---|---|
| **Yokota AB** | PCM/OKO-24 | PPM/OKO-25 | PPM/OKO-26 |
| | PPM/OKO-27 | PPM/OKO-28 | |

# SPAIN

## MORON AIR BASE (OZP)

APO AE 09643-5000

*This is a contingency Base.*

**LOCATION:** Sevilla, Spain to Alcala, Spain on N-334, pass Alcala to SE-333. At intersection of SE-342 and B-333 proceed on SE-342 to Moron AB. Base well marked. *ML-ARM: (008°30'W/037°00'N)*. NMC: Sevilla, 40 miles northwest. Main installation numbers: C-011-34-55-848111, D-314-722-1110.

**PAX TERM INFO: C-011-34-55-84-8111 (ask for air ops), D-314-722-1110 (ask for air ops).** Limited support, dining: EX-2249; medical emergency: EX-2069.

**TML:** Lodging office, (Hotel Frontera, Bldg P-303, 1st St), C-011-34-55-848089.

*Note: No scheduled flights at press time.*

## ROTA NAVAL AIR STATION (RTA)

625th AMSS, PSC 819, Box 59

FPO AE 09645-4000

**LOCATION:** On Spain's South Atlantic Coast. Accessible from A4/E5/N IV South and SP-342 West. *ML-ARM: (6°25'W/36°35'N)*. NMC: Cadiz, 22 miles south. Main installation numbers: C-011-34-56-82-2078 (within Spain 956-82-2078), D-314-727-0111.

**PAX TERM INFO: C-011-34-56-82-2411, D-314-727-2411/2171, DSN FAX 314-727-2028.** Bldg 2, main floor, 24 hrs daily. Directions: From main gate, straight on 3rd St for 6 blocks to Pax Term on right. Get Base pass from Security or at gate. **AMC Liaison Office:** C-011-34-56-82-2355/2974, D-314-727-2355/2974. **Pax Service Office/Paging:** Bldg 2, Hrs: Mon-Fri: 0800-1700, C-011-34-56-82-2411, D-314-727-2411.

**PAX LOUNGES:** In Pax Term, Bldg 2, main floor. **General:** Bldg 2, 24 hrs daily, C-011-334-56-82-2411, D-314-727-2411. A/C, baggage lockers, game/slot machine room (in cafeteria), nursery, playground, telephones (local and defense), TV, restroom. **DV/VIP:** Bldg 2, C-011-34-56-82-2725, D-314-727-2725 (06+), A/C, telephones (local), TV, restrooms, O/S seats. Key at ATOC. **Protocol Service:** Bldg 1, Hrs: Mon-Fri: 0730-1630, C-011-34-56-82-2725, D-314-727-2725 (06+); after hours contact Quarterdeck at EX-2222.

**FOOD SERVICE: Navy Exchange Cafeteria:** (Passenger Terminal) Bldg 2, 24 hrs daily, EX-2331. **Dining Hall:** Galley, Bldg 38, Hrs: daily 0600-1830 (varies), EX-2317. **Rascals Family Steak House:** Bldg 1631, Hrs: daily 1100-2400, EX-2851. **Champion's Sports Club:** Bldg 49, Hrs: daily 1100-2200. **O'Club:** Bldg 50, Hrs: daily 0600-2230, EX-2509.

**TRANSPORTATION: Air Tickets:** SATO: Bldg 52, Hrs: Mon-Fri: 0830-1700, EX-2034. **Bus (Comm):** Downtown Rota. **Bus (Govt):** Bldg 197, EX-2720. **Car Rentals:** Bldg 2, Hrs: Mon-Fri: 0830-1900, Sat: 0830-1500, closed Sun, EX-2675, (other major rental car companies in Rota). **Taxi (Comm):** Front gate, 24 hrs daily, EX-2929, **Taxi (Govt):** Bldg 149, Hrs: daily 0600-2400, EX-2403 (duty pax only). **Trains:** Puerto, 24 hrs daily, Puerto-Sevilla-Madrid Express & Rapid. **Parking:** Bldg 2, 24 hrs daily, 2 hr time limit for short term parking. Long term parking is available across the street from Bldg 583, contact security police.

**TML:** Lodging Office (Bldg 1610), 24 hrs daily, C-011-34-56-82-1750/1751. All ranks. BOQ: C-011-34-56-82-2460/2670/2680. Navy Lodge: Bldg 1674, C-011-34-56-82-2643. DV/VIP: C-011-34-56-82-2744, O6+.

**TRAVELERS AID: American Red Cross:** Bldg 52, Hrs: Mon-Fri: 0800-1630, C-011-34-56-82-2333. **Chaplain:** Bldg 204, Hrs: Mon-Fri: 0800-1700, Sun: 0900-1400, EX-2161. **Emergency Relief:** Bldg 268, Hrs: Mon-Fri: 1000-1500, C-011-34-56-82-2805. **Lost/Found:** Bldg 2, Hrs: Mon-Fri: 0600-1600, C-011-34-56-82-2816; after hours, C-011-34-56-82-2171-X-2411. **Security Police:** Bldg 207, 24 hrs daily, C-011-34-56-82-2000/2001 (Desk Sgt).

**OTHER SERVICES: Exchange:** Bldg 40, Hrs: Tue-Sat: 1000-1800, EX-2507. Retirees, DAVs, & unaccompanied dependants are only authorized use of post office, banks, clubs, hospital, air terminal, & rec facility due to SOFA. **Bank/Exchange:** Bldg 52 Hrs: Mon-Fri: 0900-1500, EX-2913. Money exchange also available at clubs and NEX. **Hair Styles:** Barber: Bldg 40, Hrs: Tue-Sat: 1000-1730, EX-2507; Beauty: Bldg 134, Hrs: Tue-Sat: 0930-1700, EX-4034. **Laundry/Dry Cleaning:** Bldg 41, Hrs: Mon-Fri: 0900-1730, Sat: 0900-1700, EX-2559; Bldg 183, 24 hrs daily, EX-2275. **Medical:** Bldg 1802, 24 hrs daily, EX-2225/4601. **Postal:** Bldg 580, Hrs: Mon-Fri: 0900-1700, EX-2518.

**ATTRACTIONS:** Andalucia area, sherry, flamenco dancing, bull fighting.

| IN ROUTE SCHEDULES | | | |
|---|---|---|---|
| **Charleston AFB/IAP** | ACC/CHS-7 | ACM/CHS-8 | ACC/CHS-17 |
| | ACC/CHS-18 | | |
| **Dover AFB** | APM/DOV-2 | ACM/DOV-3 | |
| **March AFB** | APM/RIV-1 | | |
| **McGuire AFB** | ACC/WRI-11 | ACM/WRI-13 | ACC/WRI-19 |
| | ACM/WRI-20 | | |
| **Philadelphia IAP** | APP/PHL-4 | | |

# TORREJON de ARDOZ AIR BASE (TOJ)

DET 1, 625 AMSS
Unit 6435, PSC 61
APO AE 09642-5000

**LOCATION:** Take Hwy N-11 (A2) Northeast toward Zaragoza SP, pass the IAP at Barajas on the left. AB is on the right and clearly marked. HE: p-59, D/2. *ML-ARM: (03°35'W/40°25'N).* NMC: Madrid, 11 miles southwest. Main installation numbers: C-011-34-1-675-2773/2754.

**PAX TERM INFO: C-011-34-1-675-2754, FAX 011-34-1-656-0346.** Location Bldg 420, Hrs: Mon-Fri 0800-1600. Directions: Main gate to the first traffic circle, left on 2nd St., 3rd right on Ave. Balboa, take first left toward Groupo 45 HQ Bldg. The AMC designated parking lot is on the left (for both long and short term parking, designated by parking space.) Retirees and civlian passenger's passports must be stamped by Spanish customs before leaving the base. Re-entry to base will be denied without this customs stamp. The Spanish customs office is located within a 2 minute walk of the passenger terminal.

**PAX LOUNGES: General:** Bldg 420, Hrs: Mon-Fri: 0800-1700, EX-8427. A/C, bag check/lockers, rest-rooms, showers (men only), T/V, P/C seats, max cap 15 pax. **Family:** Bldg 403, next to restrooms, Hrs: Mon-Fri: 0600-2200, same services as Pax Terminal. **DV/VIP:** Bldg 420, Hrs: daily 0800-1700, (06+), max cap 5. Same services as Pax Terminal. **Protocol Service:** Bldg 206, Hrs: Mon-Fri: 0730-1600, D-314-723-8324.

**FOOD SERVICE:** No United States Air Force services. Spanish cafeterias located on the base. They operate on a fluctuating schedule.

**TRANSPORTATION:** Passengers are responsible for their own transportation on base and to and from the main gate (about 1 mile). Taxi cabs are not allowed on base.

**OTHER SERVICES:** No USAF base services, including TML, available.

**ATTRACTIONS:** Madrid, museums, bull fights, great food & wine.

## UNSCHEDULED FLIGHTS

Infrequent flights to Aviano AB, IT (AVB), Sigonella APT, IY (SIZ), Rota NAS, SP (RTA) and Ramstein AB, GE (RMS).

# THAILAND

## DON MUANG AIRPORT (BKK)

CHJUSMAGTHAI, MAGTJS-AT, AMC Passenger Services
APO AP 96546-5000

**LOCATION:** Bangkok is on the Chao Phraya River, 20 miles north of the gulf of Thailand. Airport is 20 miles northeast of Bangkok. *ML-ARM: (100°20'E/73°15'N).* NMC: Bangkok, 20 miles southwest. Main installation numbers: C-011-66-2-287-1036-X-333, D-None.

**PAX TERM INFO: C-011-66-2-287-1036-EX-333, FAX 011-66-2-254-2990 (AMEREMB).** JUSMAGTHAI, Bldg D, Room 114, Hrs: Mon-Fri: 0700-1600. Check-in here & use commercial bus (150 Baht) to military apt. No commercial taxi at apt. Limited US facility.

**PAX LOUNGES:** Bldg D, Room 114, Hrs: Mon-Fri: 0700-1600. Telephone (commercial), restrooms, P/C seats.

**OTHER SERVICES:** Bldg A-106 (JUSMAG). Breakfast, fast food & in-flight meals, EX-274. **Barber:** Bldg C-129. **Postal:** Bldg D-109. **Marine Guard:** 24 hrs daily, C-011-66-2-252-5040-EX-2470. No Government TML.

| IN ROUTE SCHEDULES | |
|---|---|
| **Kadena AB** | PPM/DNA-1 |
| **Yokota AB** | PPM/OKO-7 |

# TURKEY

## CIGLI AIR BASE (IGL)

741st ABS/LGTA, Izmir Air Station, Unit 6870, Box 130
APO AE 09821-0130

**LOCATION:** In Western Turkey on Aegean Sea. From Izmir take E-24 N for 12 miles to W exit for Camalti & Air Base on the right.*ML-ARM: (27°10'E/38°25'N)*. NMC: Izmir, 15 miles southeast. Main installation numbers: C-011-90-232-484-5360, D-314-675-1110.

**PAX TERM INFO: C-011-90-232-484-5360-EX-3442, D-314-675-1110, FAX 011-90-232-441-7044.** Pax Term, Hrs: Mon-Fri: 0730-1630, (Sat-Sun: 0830-1030 passenger sign up only). Access to Air Base is restricted to passengers only. No US facilities at AB. US AMC rep meets all flights with bus transport directly to Passenger Terminal located at FAC 46, Downtown Izmir.

**FOOD SERVICE:** AAFES Snack Bar & Baskin Robbins. **Restaurant:** Map #13, Hrs: Daily: 0530-2200, located in Akin Bldg.

**TRANSPORTATION:** Generous & cheap public transportation: taxi, buses, & horse carriages. Most US support facilities easy walk from each other. Limited shuttle bus service to rec areas only, ie swimming, arts & crafts and tennis and raquet ball courts.

**TML:** Lodging Office, Gov leased quarters on Space-A basis avail at Etap Pullman Hotel, Ataturk Circle (2 blocks from Pax Terminal). C-011-90-232-484-5360-EX-3366/3279. Manger EX 3490, D-314-675-1110-EX-33379 for military assistance desk. Turkish 5-star hotel with rest./ lounge and casino. DV/VIP: D-314-675-1110-EX-3341, O6+/E9.

**OTHER SERVICES:** Use of Exchange and commissary restricted to active duty stationed in Turkey or TDY personnel. **Exchange:** C-011-90-232-484-5360 EX-3469 (shoppette & commissary). AAFES Bookstore, Family Services, Class VI Store. **Security Police:** C-011-90-232-484-5360 EX-3222; Rec Center. Barber/Beauty shops. **USAF Clinic:** Hrs: daily 0730-1630, C-011-90-232-484-5360. Map #12 - Chaplain's office.

**ATTRACTIONS:** Ancient biblical and historic sites, Aegean Sea. Best Bet Space-A C-9 MEDEVAC flights: Sun, Wed, Thu, Fri, Sat to Europe locations/stations.

| IN ROUTE SCHEDULES | |
|---|---|
| **Charleston AFB** | APM/CHS-6 |
| **McGuire AFB** | APM/WRI-9 |

### UNSCHEDULED FLIGHTS

Frequent flights to TU and other Mediterranean stations.

# INCIRLIK AIRPORT (ADANA) (ADA)

628th AMSS, Unit 7100, PSC 94, Box 190
APO AE 09824-0190

**LOCATION:** From Adana (in southeast Turkey, 30 miles north of Mediterranean Sea), drive east on E-5 for 3 miles, turn left at sign for Incirlik AB. Base clearly marked. *ML-ARM: (34°50'E/36°50'N).* NMC: Adana, 3 miles west. Main installation numbers: C-011-90-322-316-1110, D-314-676-1110.

**PAX TERM INFO: C-011-90-322-316-6424/6425, D-314-676-6424/25, FAX 011-90-322-316-3654, DSN FAX 314-676-3654, REC-C-011-90-322-316-8238.** Bldg 500, Hrs: daily 0600-2200. Directions: From main gate on 1st Street to a right on "A" St, .5 mile and turn left to Pax Term on the left. Recording 0700 daily on local Armed Forces Network radio. **Pax Service Office:** Bldg 500, Hrs: daily 0730-1700, C-011-90-322-316-3162 (NCO on duty). **Pax Paging:** Bldg 500, Hrs: daily 0600-2000, C-011-90-322-316-6424/5.

**PAX LOUNGES:** Bldg 500. Dependent lounge available. **General:** Bldg 500, Hrs: daily 0600-2200, C-011-90-322-316-6424/25. A/C, bag check/lockers, telephones (local, long distance and defense), TV, rest-rooms, O/S & wood seats. **Family Lounge:** Cribs, Childrens playarea. **DV/VIP:** Bldg 500, Hrs: daily 0600-2200, C-011-90-322-316-6424/25 (on left side of Term). A/C, bag check, telephones (local, long distance and defense), TV, O/S & wood seats. **Protocol Service:** Bldg 833, Hrs: Mon-Fri: 0730-1630, C-011-90-322-316-6347; other hours, EX-66424 (06+).

**FOOD SERVICE: Cafeteria:** Bldg 957, Hrs: daily 0600-2200, C-011-90-322-316-6343. **Enlisted Club:** Willows Dining Hall: Bldg 884, Hrs: daily 0500-1900, C-011-90-322-316-3194. **NCO/CPO Club:** Bldg 864, Hrs: daily 0630-1900, C-011-90-322-316-6010, **O'Club:** Bldg 950, Hrs: daily 0630-2030, C-011-90-322-316-6967. **Restaurants:** Pizza Parlor: Bldg 970, Hrs: daily 1000-0200, C-011-90-322-316-3260. **Snack Bars:** Golf Course: Bldg 6, Hrs: Tue-Sun: 1100-1500, C-011-90-322-316-6249. **Vending:** Bldg 500, Hrs: daily 0630-2130, C-011-90-322-316-6424/25 (Term Cafeteria).

**TRANSPORTATION: Air Tickets:** SATO: Bldg 430. Hrs: Mon-Fri: 1730-1630, C-011-90-322-316-6520/6763. **Bus (Comm):** Bldg 500, Hrs: daily 0610-2400, C-011-90-322-316-6424/25 (15 minutes/ADA-Incirlik $.60). **Bus (Shuttle):** Bldg 500, Limited service - Base area. **Car Rentals:** AJAX-Incirlik: Off Base, Hrs: daily 0800-1900. **Taxi (Comm):** Main gate, Hrs: daily 0600-2200, C-011-90-322-316-6461 (give your location). **Taxi (Gov):** Bldg 492, 24 hrs daily, C-011-90-322-316-6756/6284 (duty Pax only). **Parking:** Bldg 500, 24 hrs daily, C-011-90-322-316-6424. Short term-front of Pax Term, long term on right side of Pax Term. No restrictions.

**TML:** Lodging Office (Bldg 1081), 24 hrs daily, C-011-90-322-316-1774/80, D-314-676-1774/80. All ranks. DV/VIP: C-011-90-322-316-6347, 06+.

**TRAVELERS AID: American Red Cross:** Bldg 978, Hrs: Mon-Fri: 0730-1630, C-011-90-322-316-6927; after hours, C-011-90-322-316-6376. **Chaplain:** Bldg 945, Hrs: Mon-

***TURKEY***
***Incirlik Airport, continued***

Fri: 0730-1630, C-011-90-322-316-6441. **Emergency Relief:** Bldg 924, Hrs: daily 0730-1630, C-011-90-322-316-6201 (AF Aid). **Lost/Found:** Bldg 500, Hrs: daily 0600-2200, C-011-90-322-316-6424/5. **Security Police:** Bldg 649, 24 hrs daily, C-011-90-322-316-6826 (Desk Sgt).

**OTHER SERVICES: Exchange:** Bldg 912, Hrs: Mon-Fri: 1130-1730, daily: C-011-90-322-316-6009. **Bank/Exchange:** Bldg 480, Hrs: Mon-Fri: 0800-1530, C-011-90-322-316-63204 (finance office). **Hair Styles:** Bldg 957/8, Hrs: Mon-Sat: 0730-1730, C-011-90-322-316-6093. **Laundry:** Bldg 484, 24 hrs daily (self-serve). **Medical:** Bldg 3850, 24hrs daily, C-011-90-322-316-6666, D-314-676-6666. **Postal:** Bldg 977, Hrs: daily 1000-1700, C-011-90-322-316-6301.

**ATTRACTIONS:** Snow skiing, beaches, mountain climbing, fishing.

| IN ROUTE SCHEDULES | | |
|---|---|---|
| **Charleston AFB/IAP** | APM/CHS-6 | ACM/CHS-8 |
| **Dover AFB** | APM/DOV-7 | |
| **McGuire AFB** | APM/WRI-9 | ACM/WRI-13 |
| **Philadelphia IAP** | APP/PHL-1 | |
| **Westover ARB** | APM/CEF-2 | |

## TURKEY STATIONS

**(Not listed separately in this book)**

The bases listed below have Space-A air opportunities. Base support facilities at most stations are very limited.

**ATATURK/YESILKOY AIRPORT (ISTANBUL) (YES)**, OL-A/TMO, PSC 97, Box 0003, APO AE 09827-0002. C-011-90-212-663-0925/0917, FAX C-011-90-212-251-3632. *ML-ARM: (28°40'E/41°20'N).* **LOCATION:** On the European side of the Bosporus and the Marmara Denizi. FAX: 011-90-212-663-0925. No US military support.

| IN ROUTE SCHEDULES | |
|---|---|
| **Charleston AFB/IAP** | APM/CHS-6 |
| **McGuire AFB** | APM/WRI-9 |

**DIYARBAKIR AIR STATION (DIY)**, 722nd ABS/LGTT, Unit 7200, Box 50, APO AE 09825-0050. C-011-90-412-323-3463/3464, D-314-679-1110-EX-3471/3360, FAX 011-90-412-323-9567. *ML-ARM: (40°05'E/37°30'N).* **LOCATION:** 12 miles west of Diyarbakir, in southeastern TU. Also known as Pirinclik AS (USAF). No US military support.

| IN ROUTE SCHEDULES | |
|---|---|
| **Charleston AFB/IAP** | APM/CHS-6 |
| **McGuire AFB** | APM/WRI-9 |

**ESENBOGA AIRPORT (ESB),** 7217th ABG/RMQA, Ankara Air Station, APO AE 09823-5000. C-011-90-312-25-9943-EX 4118, D-314-672-1110-EX-4118, FAX C-011-90-312-467-1366. *ML-ARM: (32°55'E/40°00'N)*. **LOCATION:** In the north center of the country, 250 miles south of the Black Sea. NMC: Ankara, 16 miles southwest.

| IN ROUTE SCHEDULES | |
|---|---|
| **Charleston AFB/IAP** | APM/CHS-6 |
| **McGuire AFB** | APM/WRI-9 |

# UNITED ARAB EMIRATES

## FUJAIRAH INTERNATIONAL AIRPORT (FUJ)

USDAO - Al-Sudan St
PO Box 4009
Abu Dhabi, UAE

**LOCATION:** Fujairah IAP is on the NW corner of the Gulf of Oman. NMC: Dubayy, 75 miles west and Abu Dhabi the capital of UAE, 125 miles SW.

**PAX TERM INFO: C-011-971-2-336691-EX-404/405, after hours: C-011-971-2-338730, FAX 011-971-4-313-131.** Bldg: AMC Desk, Hrs: during flight processing. All facilities of IAP available. No military support facilities, including TML.

| IN ROUTE SCHEDULES | | | |
|---|---|---|---|
| **Charleston AFB/IAP** | ACC/CHS-17 | | |
| **Dover AFB** | APM/DOV-2 | ACM/DOV-3 | APM/DOV-10 |
| **March AFB** | APM/RIV-1 | | |
| **McGuire AFB** | ACC/WRI-19 | ACM/WRI-20 | |
| **Yokota AB** | PCM/OKO-24 | PPM/OKO-25 | PPM/OKO-28 |
| | PCM/OKO-29 | PCM/OKO-30 | |

# UNITED KINGDOM

## ASCENSION AUXILIARY AIR FIELD (ASI)

DET 2, 45 OPG/CC
PO Box 4235, Ascension Island
Patrick AFB, FL 32925-0235

**LOCATION:** In the South Atlantic Ocean approximately halfway between Recife, BR, and Luanda, Angola. A United Kingdom possession. *ML-ARM: (14°30'W/08°10'S).* NMC: Georgetown, .5 miles. Main installation numbers: Contact international operator and ask for C-011-247-2200, D-312-854-1110-EX-2219.

**PAX TERM INFO: C-407-494-5631.** Base Ops, Hrs: during flight processing. Limited support facilities. Dining Facility: Bldg 12120, Security Police: EX-2222/3, Lodging Office: Bldg Adm II: EX-2487, all ranks. Prior permission required to visit/transit ASI from Det 2, 45 OG/CC, Patrick AFB, FL 32925-0235. See appendix B for personal entrance requirements.

| | IN ROUTE SCHEDULES |
|---|---|
| **Charleston AFB/IAP** | ACM/CHS-19 |
| **McGuire AFB** | ACM/WRI-21 |

## RAF MILDENHALL (MHZ)

627th AMSS/TRP
APO AE 09459-5000

**LOCATION:** Twenty-seven miles from Cambridge in eastern UK. Follow the A-11 (M) to Newmarket, then to Barton Mills. Take the A-1101 for 2.5 miles through Mildenhall Town to Beck Row Village to RAF Mildenhall. *ML-ARM: (00°33'E/52°25'N).* NMC: Cambridge, 24 miles southwest and London is 55 miles SW. Main installation numbers: C-011-44-638-54-3000, D-314-238-1110.

**PAX TERM INFO: C-011-44-638-54-1854/2526, D-314-238-2248/1854/2526, FAX 011-44-638-54-2250, DSN FAX 314-238-2250.** Bldg 598, Hrs: Mon-Sat: 0500-2230, Sun: 0600-2230. (.25 mi inside gate 1). **Pax Service Office:** Bldg 598, Hrs: Mon-Fri: 0800-1630, EX-2526/2861. **Pax Paging:** See Pax Term, EX-1854.

**PAX LOUNGES:** Lounges for all categories of travelers. **General:** Bldg 598, same hours as Pax Term, EX-1854. TV, restrooms, lockers, P/C seats, telephones (commercial and defense). **DV/VIP:** Bldg 598, same hours as Pax Term, EX-1854 (ground floor to the left of Gate 1). Lockers, TV, telephones (commercial and defense), restrooms, O/S seats. Not staffed (O6+). **Protocol Service:** Bldg 239, Hrs: Mon-Fri: 0800-1700, EX-2132 (07+). **Family:** Bldg 598, Hrs: Same as Pax Terminal, EX-2248 (upstairs to the left - no restrictions). Game room, lockers, telephones, TV, restrooms, O/S seats, playroom, nursery.

*UNITED KINGDOM*
*RAF Mildenhall, continued*

**FOOD SERVICE: Cafeteria:** Starlifter: Bldg 423, EX-2488. **Dining Hall:** Bldg 436, (4th meal & officers' breakfast), EX-2689. **Enlisted Club:** Bldg 449, EX-2683. **NCO/CPO Club:** Galaxy: Bldg 291, EX-2633. **O'Club:** Bldg 464, EX-2606. **Restaurants:** Pizza Cove: Bldg 433, EX-2323. **Snack Bars:** Bldg 423, EX-2488; Bowling Center: EX-2348. Bldg 598, EX-2248/2526.

**TRANSPORTATION: Air Tickets:** SATO: Bldg 598, Hrs: Mon-Fri: 0800-1630, C-EX-2968/2766. **Bus (Comm):** To London Lakenheath and London Gatwick, Daily. Bury St Edmonds C-98-66171 and Cambridge C-92-343418. To London - near Gate 2, schedule in Bldg 598. **Bus (Shuttle):** Bldg 598, Hrs: daily 0630-1730. MHZ to LKZ, hourly, C-011-638-542929. **Car Rentals:** Mildenhire: C-718288, Hertz: C-717354, Budget: C-717474, Car Hire: AAFES Concession, Bldg 598, C-712455, Hrs: Mon-Sat: 1000-1700. **Taxi (Comm):** Bldg 461, 24 hrs daily, EX-2984 (Base Cab Stand). **Taxi (Gov):** Bldg 611, 24 hrs daily, EX-2339. **Trains:** Bury St Edmonds, Hrs: Mon-Sat: 0745-2138, Sun: 0924-0256, C-98-3947; Cambridge, C-92-311999. Schedule available, Bldg 598, London, etc. **Parking:** Short-term in front of Bldg 598, 12 hour limit; long-term near Security Police compound, Bldg 645, 24hrs daily, EX-2667.

**TML:** Lodging Office (Bldg 459), 24 hrs daily, reservations: C-011-44-638-54-2655, FAX 011-44-638-54-3688. DV/VIP: EX-2132, D-314-238-2777/2568. Lakenheath, C-011-44-638-52-1844/2172, D-314-226-6717 (B&B list at Pax Service), FAX 011-44-638-52-6717.

**TRAVELERS AID: American Red Cross:** Bldg 598, EX-2113; after hours, EX-2667. **Chaplain:** Bldg 474, EX-2822. **Emergency Relief:** Bldg 436, EX-2084 (AF Aid Society). **Lost/Found:** Bldg 598, (weekends, ask Shift Supervisor). **Security Police:** Bldg 645, 24 hrs daily, EX-2667.

**OTHER SERVICES: Exchange:** Bldg 998, EX-2996. (Main BX at RAF Lakenheath). **Bank/Exchange:** Merchants: Bldg 436, EX-2850. **Hair Styles:** Bldg 178, Barber: EX-2676; Beauty: EX-2977. **Laundry/Dry Cleaning:** Bldg 123, C-717906. **Medical:** RAF Lakenheath Hospital: 24 hrs daily, D-314-226-2226. **Postal:** Bldg 442, EX-2151.

**ATTRACTIONS:** New Market-13 miles south, Cambridge-24 miles southwest, London. Bury St Edmunds, 12 miles east.

| IN ROUTE SCHEDULES | | | |
|---|---|---|---|
| **Allen C Thompson Field** | ACC/JAN-1 | | |
| **Altus AFB** | ACC/LTS-1 | | |
| **Andrews AFB** | ACC/ADW-1 | ACC/ADW-2 | |
| **Charleston AFB/IAP** | ACC/CHS-3 | ACC/CHS-4 | ACM/CHS-8 |
| **Fairchild AFB** | ACC/SKA-1 | | |
| **The WM B Hartsfield, ATL, IAP** | | APP/ATL-1 | |
| **McGuire AFB** | ACC/WRI-6 | ACC/WRI-10 | ACM/WRI-13 |
| **Memphis IAP** | ACM/MEM-1 | | |

| | |
|---|---|
| **Robins AFB** | ACC/WRB-1 |
| **Tinker AFB** | ACC/TIK-1 |
| **Wright-Patterson AFB** | ACC/FFO-1 |

## NOTES

# APPENDIX A: SPACE-A PASSENGER REGULATIONS

## CHAPTER 6
## SPACE-AVAILABLE TRAVEL

### A. GENERAL POLICY

1. Definition and Scope. Space-available travel is the specific program of travel authorized by this Chapter allowing authorized passengers to occupy DoD aircraft seats which are surplus after all space-required passengers have been accommodated. Space-available travel is allowed on a non-mission interference basis only. DoD aircraft shall not be scheduled to accommodate space-available passengers. No (or negligible) additional funds shall be expended and no additional flying hours shall be scheduled to support this program. In order to maintain the equity and integrity of the space-available system, seats may not be reserved or "blocked" for use at en route stops along mission routes.

2. Purpose of the Space-Available Program Space-available travel is a privilege (not an entitlement) which accrues to Uniformed Services members as an avenue of respite from the rigors of Uniformed Services duty. Retired Uniformed Services members are given the privilege in recognition of a career of such rigorous duty and because they are eligible for recall to active duty. The underlying criteria for extending the privilege to other categories of passengers is their support to the mission being performed by Uniformed Services members and to the enhancement of active duty Service members' quality of life.

3. Leave Status for Travel. Uniformed Services members on active duty must be in a leave or pass status to register for space-available travel, remain in a leave or pass status while awaiting travel, and be in a leave or pass status the entire period of travel. DoD civilian employees, when afforded space-available privileges listed in table 6-1, below, must be in a leave or non-duty (i.e., weekend or holiday) status to register for space-available travel. If in a non-duty status, leave must have been approved for the first normal working day following the non-duty period. A leave status must then be maintained while awaiting travel and for the entire period of travel Those members in appellate leave status are not authorized space-available travel privileges.

4. In Conjunction with Space-Required Travel or to Restricted Tour Areas. Space-available travel may not be used instead of space-required travel, such as TDY, TAD and PCS travel, except emergency leave type travel (see Chapter 2, subsection A.4., above). Space-available travel may be used in conjunction with space-required travel as long as space-available travel does not substitute for any single leg for which the traveler has a space-required entitlement (except emergency leave type travel). For example, a Uniformed Services member may take leave with a TDY or TAD, as allowed by Service regulations, and may travel space-available while on leave. Travel from the PDS to the TDY or TAD location shall be space-required with the traveler in a duty status; any space-available travel from the TDY or TAD duty location shall return to the TDY or TAD location, with the traveler in a leave status; and the final leg shall be space-required from the TDY or TAD location to the PDS with the traveler in a duty status. Dependents may not use space-available travel options in this Regulation to accompany their sponsor on

*APPENDIX A, continued*

space-required travel or to travel to or from a sponsor's restricted or all others (unaccompanied) tour location.

5. Registers and Sign-Up Procedures

a. Each base, installation or post from which space-available travel is accomplished shall maintain a single space-available register and all space-available passengers accepted for airlift from that location must have been selected from the register's roll. The maintenance of such a roster shall be the responsibility of the AMC passenger activity, where established. Where no AMC passenger activity is established, it shall be the responsibility of the base, installation, or post commander to designate the Agency responsible for maintaining the space-available roster.

b. To compete for space-available travel, eligible personnel must sign up on the space- available roster in person and present all required documentation (see subsection A.6., below). The DoD Components and the USTRANSCOM may also accept sign up information in writing from eligible space-available travelers (through mail, fax transmission, or courier). When adopted, the DoD Components and the USTRANSCOM shall provide detailed guidance outlining procedures for using "remote sign up" services. Passengers shall declare their final destination when they sign up for space-available travel. The original date and time of sign-up shall be documented and stay with the traveler until his or her destination is reached. On reaching the destination, the traveler may again sign up for space-available travel to return to home station. Those registered are not required to accept any seat offered, and failure to accept an offered seat shall not jeopardize a passenger's position on the space-available register. All but Category VI passengers (see table 6-1, below) are automatically removed from the space-available register on expiration of leave, pass or after 60 days, whichever is sooner. Category VI passengers are removed from the list after 60 days. All space-available passengers dropped from the register may sign up again in their respective categories (see table 6-1, below) with a new date and time of sign-up.

c. Eligible travelers who arrive at an air terminal seeking space-available transportation shall sign a document certifying compliance with the rules for eligibility and conditions of space-available travel, and be provided access to documentation showing the date and time their request for movement was entered onto the installation space-available roster.

d. Reservations shall not be made for any space-available passenger. Travel opportunity shall be afforded on an equitable basis to officers, enlisted personnel, civilian employees, and their accompanying dependents without regard to rank or grade, military or civilian, or branch of Uniformed Service.

6. Required Documentation. Unique documentation required for specific types of individuals (e.g., Medal of Honor recipients) is cited in table 6-1, below, on a case-by-case basis. Additionally, the following types of travelers shall present the documentation

listed below to air terminal personnel, and shall have all the documentation in their possession during travel:

a. Active duty Uniformed Services Members (includes National Guard and Reserve members on active duty in excess of 30 days)

(1) DD Form 2 (Green) U.S. Armed Forces Identification Card (Active), or Form 2 NOAA (Green) Uniformed Services Identification and Privilege Card (Active), or PHS Form 1866-3 (Green) United States Public Health Service Identification Card (Active).

(2) A valid leave authorization or evidence of pass status as required by the Service concerned.

b. Retired Uniformed Services Members. DD Form 2 (Blue) U.S. Armed Forces Identification Card (Retired), or DD Form 2 (Blue) NOAA Uniformed Services Identification Card (Retired), or PHS Form 1866-3 (Blue) United States Public Health Service Identification Card (Retired).

c. National Guard and Reserve Members

(1) Authorized Reserve Component Members (National Guard and Reserve) of the Ready Reserve. and members of the Standbv Reserve who are on the Active Status List; On presentation of the following valid:

(a) DD Form 2 (Red), "Armed Forces of the United States Identification Card" (Reserve).

(b) DD Form 1853, "Verification of Reserve Status for Travel Eligibility."

(2) Retired Reservists Entitled to Retired Pay at Age 60; On presentation of the following valid:

(a) DD Form 2 (Red).

(b) A notice of retirement eligibility as described in DoD Directive 1200.15, (reference (kk)). If the automated DD Form 2 (Red) has been issued, the member is registered in his or her Service personnel system as a Reserve retiree entitled to retired pay at age 60, and a notice of retirement eligibility is not required.

(3) Retired Reservists Qualified for Retired Pay; Documentation, as prescribed in subsection A.6.b., above. For space-available travel eligibility, no distinction is made between members retired from the Reserves and members retired from active duty.

*APPENDIX A, continued*

(4) On Active Duty for 30 Days or Less; On presentation of the following valid:

(a) DD Form 2 (Red).

(b) Orders placing the Reservist on active duty.

(c) A valid leave authorization or evidence of pass status as required by the Service concerned.

(5) ROTC. Nuclear Power Officer Candidate (NUPOC). and Civil Engineer Corps (CEC) Members; When enrolled in an advanced ROTC, NUPOC, or CEC course or enrolled under the financial assistance program, on presentation of the following valid:

(a) DD Form 2 (Red).

(b) DD Form 1853.

d. Dependents of Uniformed Services Members. DD Form 1173, "United States Uniformed Services Identification and Privilege Card."

e. EML Travelers. Besides any documentation required by paragraphs A.6.a. through A.6.d., above, EML orders issued in accordance with Unified Command procedures (see paragraph B.4.a., below).

7. Categories of Travel and Priorities of Movement

a. Categories. There are six categories of space-available travel. Space-available travelers are placed in one of the six categories based on their status (e.g., active duty Uniformed Services member, and DoDDS teacher, etc.) and their situation (e.g., emergency leave, and ordinary leave, etc.). Once accepted for movement, a space-available passenger may not be "bumped" by another space-available passenger, regardless of category. See table 6-1, below, for a list of specific travelers and the category in which they fall.

b. Priority of Movement. The numerical order of space-available categories indicates the precedence of movement between categories; e.g., travelers in Category III move before travelers in Category IV. The order in which travelers are listed in a particular category in table 6-l, below, does not indicate priority of movement in that category. In each category, transportation is furnished on a first-in, first-out basis.

c. Changes to Movement Priorities. Wherever the issue may arise, the local installation commander may change the priority of movement of any space-available traveler for emergency or extreme humanitarian reasons when the facts provided fully support such an exception. The installation commander may delegate the authority to make such changes to no lower than the Chief of the Passenger Service Center or its equivalent When a movement priority is changed, the passenger shall be moved no higher than the bottom of the Category I space-available list. Where AMC units are tenants, the senior local AMC authority shall advise the installation commander of this authority and offer technical assistance, as needed.

8. Destinations and International Restrictions

a. If authorized by this Chapter for a particular traveler's status and situation (see table 6-1, below), transportation may be between overseas stations, between CONUS stations, and between overseas and CONUS stations where adequate border clearance facilities exist or can be made readily available. Theater or international restrictions shall be observed and all requirements pertaining to passports, visas, foreign customs, and immunizations shall be met.

b. Individuals traveling to or from the CONUS, and who are not otherwise eligible to travel space-available in the CONUS, may travel on any CONUS leg segment (i.e., on a flight with enroute stops) when no change of aircraft or mission is involved.

9. Conditions of Travel. There is no guaranteed space for any traveler. The Department of Defense is not obligated to continue an individual's travel or return him or her to point of origin, or any other point. Travelers shall have sufficient personal funds to pay for commercial transportation to return to their residence or duty station if space-available transportation is not available. Space-available travel shall not be used for personal gain, for a business enterprise or outside employment, when theater or international restrictions-prohibit such travel, or to establish a home overseas or in the CONUS (except for permissive TDY house hunting trips as authorized in table 6-1, below).

10. Dependent Travel. Except where specifically noted in this chapter, dependents may travel space-available only when accompanied by their sponsor.

## B. EML TRAVEL

Except as noted, unfunded EML travel is subject to the space-available travel program rules and guidance outlined in this section A., above, and table 6-l, below. Funded EML travel is discussed in Chapter 2, sections B.l.e. B.3.a.(14).

1. Definition. EML is leave granted with an EML program, as prescribed in DoD Directive 1327.5 (reference (d)), established at an overseas installation where adverse environmental conditions require special arrangements for leave in more desirable places at periodic intervals.

2. Program Description. For a complete description of the EML program, see reference (d).

***APPENDIX A, continued***

a. EML Locations and Destinations. Specified locations where adverse environmental conditions exist and at which EML is authorized, are called "EML locations". The Under Secretary of Defense (Personnel and Readiness) designates Funded EML (FEML) locations and relief destinations. Unified commanders designate locations under the unfunded EML program. Under the EML program, not more than two relief destinations shall be designated unless additional destinations are needed to provide a reasonable prospect of relief. The CONUS shall not be designated an "EML destination" except when such designation is necessary to provide a realistic opportunity for relief.

b. Priority, Timing, and Frequency. Passengers traveling space-available under the EML program are given a higher priority than those traveling on ordinary leave (see table 6-1, below). The timing and the frequency of EML is limited by DoD Directive 1327.5 (reference (d)). Transportation officials are not responsible for monitoring this timing and frequency, but rather are responsive to EML documentation issued by the commanders concerned.

3. Responsibilities. Unified commanders shall ensure that administrative controls are in place to ensure that all eligible travelers are able to participate in the EML space-available travel program on a fair and equitable basis. The unified commanders concerned shall forward two copies of each implementing directive, and of any modifications to such directive, to The Department of the Army (DAPE-MBB-C), the Commandant of the U.S. Marine Corps (LFT), the Chief of Naval Operations (N4l), HQ USAF/LGTT, NOAA Corps (NC), and the USTRANSCOM (TCJ3/J4).

4. Policy and Procedures

a. Unified command procedures shall include the issuance of a separate set of EML orders each time an individual is approved for EML.

b. Unfunded EML travelers may travel in Category II status (See table 6-1, below) to only one EML destination for each set of EML orders. This does not preclude several approved EML destinations being included in a single set of EML orders as long as procedures are in effect to ensure that the individual is provided Category II status only for travel to and from the first authorized EML destination actually reached. Subsequent space-available travel; e.g., from the EML destination to a third location and return, or from the third location to another EML location, may only be provided in Category HI status (table 6-1, below).

c. When traveling under EML orders, dependents who are 18-years of age or older may travel unaccompanied by their sponsor. Dependents who are under 18-years of age traveling under EML orders must be accompanied by an EML eligible parent or legal guardian who is traveling in an EML status.

C. ELIGIBILITY

The travelers listed in table 6-1, below, are eligible to travel space-available in the categories and over the geographical segments cited, subject to any limitations cited in table 6-1, below, under "Traveler's Status and Situation", or elsewhere in this Regulation.

*APPENDIX A, continued*

## ELIGIBLE SPACE-AVAILABLE TRAVELERS, PRIORITIES. AND APPROVED GEOGRAPHICAL TRAVEL SEGMENTS

This table lists travelers who are eligible to travel on DoD aircraft according to the space-available program outlined in paragraphs A. and B., above. "Item" is a sequential numbering and is for reference purposes only. "Cat" is the category of travel as explained in section A.7.a., above. These are used to determine priority of movement as explained in section A.7.b., above. "Traveler's Status and Situation" lists specific travelers and conditions under which space-available travel may be authorized. The approved geographical travel segments, i.e. origin and destination combinations, are C-C (CONUS to CONUS), O-O (overseas to overseas), C-O (CONUS to overseas) and O-C (overseas to CONUS) (reference section A.8.). A "yes" in the column headed by one of these abbreviations indicates that travel is authorized in that particular geographical travel segment for the particular type traveler cited in that item number, and subject to any limitations cited. Lack of a "yes" indicates travel is not authorized in that particular geographical travel segment.

| Item | Cat | Traveler's Status and Situation | C-C | O-O | C-O and O-C |
|---|---|---|---|---|---|
| 1 | | **Category I - Emergency Leave Unfunded Travel** | | | |
| 2 | | Transportation by the most expeditious routing only for bona fide immediate family emergencies, as determined by DoD Directive 1327.5 (reference (d)) and Service regulations, for the following travelers: | | | |
| 3 | I | Uniformed Services members with emergency status indicated in leave orders (for space-required option see Chapter 2, sections B.1.L and B.1.a., above) | yes | yes | |
| 4 | I | Civilians, U.S. citizens, stationed overseas, employees of: (1)The Uniformed Services; or(2) NAF activities and whose travel from the CONUS, Alaska or Hawaii was incident to a PCS assignment at NAF expense (for space-required option see Chapter 2, sections B.2.a. and B.4.a., above | | yes | yes |

***APPENDIX A, continued***

| Item | Cat | Traveler's Status and Situation | C-C | O-O | C-O and OC |
|---|---|---|---|---|---|
| 5 | I | Dependents of members of the Uniformed Services, command sponsored, accompanied or unaccompanied (for space-required option see Chapter 2, sections B.3.a.(1), B.3.a.(2), and B.3.a.(4), above) | | yes | yes |
| 6 | I | Dependents of members of the Uniformed Services, noncommand sponsored, residing overseas with the sponsor, one-way only to emergency destination (for space-required option see Chapter 2, sections 3.b.(1) and B.3.b.(2), above | | yes | C-O no<br>O-C yes |
| 7 | I | Dependents, command sponsored, of: (1) U.S. citizen civilian employees of the Uniformed Services stationed overseas;(2) U.S. citizen civilian employees of the DoD stationed overseas and paid from NAF; or (3) American Red Cross full-time, paid personnel, serving with a DoD Component overseas (for space-required option see Chapter 2, section B.3.a.(2)above) | | yes | yes |
| 8 | I | Professional Scout leaders, and American Red Cross full-time, paid personnel, serving with a DoD Component overseas (for space-required option see Chapter 2 section B.6., above) | | yes | yes |

*APPENDIX A, continued*

| Item | Cat | Traveler's Status and Situation | C-C | O-O | C-O and O-C |
|---|---|---|---|---|---|
| 9 | | **Category II - EML** | | | |
| 10 | II | Sponsors in an EML status and their dependents traveling with them, also in an EML status. "Sponsors" includes: (1) Uniformed Services members. (2) U.S. citizen civilian employees of the Armed Forces who are eligible for Government-funded transportation to the United States at tour completion (including NAF employees). (3) American Red Cross full-time, paid personnel on duty with a DoD Component overseas. (4) USO professional staff personnel on duty with the Uniformed Services. (5) DoDDS teachers during the school year and for Employer-approved training during recess periods. | | yes | yes |
| 11 | | **Category III - Ordinary Leave, Close Blood or Affinitive Relatives, House Hunting Permissive TDY, Medal of Honor Holders and Others** | | | |
| 12 | III | Uniformed Services members in a leave or pass status other than leave (use Category I) or excess appellate leave, for which space-available travel is not authorized. This includes members of the Reserve components on active duty, in a leave or pass status. | yes | yes | yes |

***APPENDIX A, continued***

| Item | Cat | Traveler's Status and Situation | C-C | O-O | C-O and O-C |
|---|---|---|---|---|---|
| 13 | III | Dependents of a member of the Uniformed Services accompanied by their sponsor in a leave status other than emergency leave (use Category I) or excess appellate leave, for which space-available travel is not authorized. | | yes | yes |
| 14 | III | Close blood or affinitive relatives who are permanent members of the household and dependent upon a Military Service member, a DoD civilian employee, or American Red Cross employee serving with a DoD Component overseas, when the sponsor is authorized transportation of dependents at Government expense. Travel must be with the sponsor's, or his or her dependent's, PCS move. | | | yes |
| 15 | III | Dependent spouses of military personnel officially reported in a missing status under 37 U.S.C. 551 (reference (II)), and accompanying dependent children and parents, when traveling for humanitarian reasons and on approval on a case by case basis by the Head of the Service concerned (Chief of Staff of the Army, the Chief of Naval Operations, the Chief of Staff of the Air Force, and the Commandant of the Marine Corps) or their designated representative. Travelers shall present an approval document from the Service concerned. | yes | yes | yes |

***APPENDIX A, continued***

| Item | Cat | Traveler's Status and Situation | C-C | O-O | C-O and O-C |
|---|---|---|---|---|---|
| 16 | III | Uniformed Services members traveling under permissive TDY orders for house hunting incident to a pending PCS. | yes | yes | yes |
| 17 | III | Uniformed Services members traveling under permissive TDY orders for house hunting incident to a pending PCS and one accompanying dependent. | | yes | yes |
| 18 | III | Medal of Honor recipients. Except for active duty, traveler shall present a copy of the Medal of Honor award certificate. | yes | yes | yes |
| 19 | III | Dependents of Medal of Honor recipients when accompanied by their sponsor. | | yes | yes |
| 20 | III | Command sponsored dependents of Uniformed Services members accompanying their sponsor on approved circuitous travel. Commanders authorized to publish circuitous travel orders for members under current policy of their Uniformed Service, where extenuating circumstances prevail, may approve requests for space-available travel of their dependents within and between overseas areas and the CONUS, incident to approved circuitous travel of the member. (For space-required option see Chapter 2, section B.3.a.(7), above). | | yes | yes |

***APPENDIX A, continued***

| Item | Cat | Traveler's Status and Situation | C-C | O-O | C-O and O-C |
|---|---|---|---|---|---|
| 21 | III | Cadets and midshipmen of the U.S. Service academies, and foreign cadets and midshipmen attending U.S. Service academies, in a leave status. Foreign cadets' and midshipmens' native countries must be identified in the leave authorization. | | | yes |
| 22 | III | Civilian U.S. Armed Forces patients who have recovered after treatment in medical facilities and their accompanying nonmedical attendants. Travel is permitted by the most expeditious routing to return the recovered patient and nonmedical attendant to the overseas post of assignment (During the death or extended hospitalization of the patient, the nonmedical attendant retains the space-available travel authority to return to the patient's overseas post of assignment). | | yes | C-O yes<br>O-C no |
| 23 | III | Foreign exchange service members on permanent duty with the Dependent of Defense, when in a leave status. | yes | yes | yes |
| 24 | III | Dependents of foreign exchange service members on permanent duty with the Department of Defense, when accompanying their sponsor. | | yes | yes |

*APPENDIX A, continued*

| Item | Cat | Traveler's Status and Situation | C-C | O-O | C-O and O-C |
|---|---|---|---|---|---|
| 25 | | **Category IV - Unaccompanied Dependents on EML and DoDDS Teachers on EML During Summer** | | | |
| 26 | IV | Dependents traveling under the EML Program, unaccompanied by their sponsor, traveling under subsection B.4.c., above ("Sponsor" as defined in item 10, above). | | yes | yes |
| 27 | IV | DoDDS teachers or dependents (accompanied or unaccompanied) traveling under the EML Program during the summer break | | yes | yes |
| 28 | | **Category V - Permissive TDY (Nonhouse hunting), Foreign Military, Students, Dependents & Others** | | | |
| 29 | V | Military personnel traveling on permissive TDY orders other than for house hunting. | yes | yes | yes |

***APPENDIX A, continued***

| Item | Cat | Traveler's Status and Situation | C-C | O-O | C-O and O-C |
|---|---|---|---|---|---|
| 30 | V | Dependents (children) who are college students attending in residence an overseas branch of an American (U.S.) university located in the same overseas area in which they reside, command sponsored, stationed overseas with their sponsor who is: (1) A member of the Uniformed Services; (2) A U.S. citizen civilian employee of the Department of Defense (paid from either appropriated funds or NAF); or (3) An American Red Cross full-time, paid employee serving with the Department of Defense. Unaccompanied travel is permitted from the overseas military passenger terminal nearest their sponsor's permanent duty station to the overseas military passenger terminal nearest the university, and to return during school breaks. Students must present written authorization from an approving authority and only one round trip each year is authorized. Unused trips may not be accumulated from school year to school year. | | yes | |

***APPENDIX A, continued***

| Item | Cat | Traveler's Status and Situation | C-C | O-O | C-O and O-C |
|---|---|---|---|---|---|
| 31 | V | Dependents, command sponsored, stationed overseas with their sponsor who is: (1) A member of the Uniformed Services; (2) A U.S. citizen civilian employee of the Department of Defense (paid from either appropriated funds or NAF); or (3) An American Red Cross full-time, paid employee serving with the Department of Defense. Unaccompanied travel is permitted to and from the nearest overseas military academy testing site to take scheduled entrance examinations for entry into any of the U.S. Service academies. | | yes | |
| 32 | V | Dependents of active duty U.S. military personnel stationed overseas who, at the time of PCS, were not entitled to transportation at Government expense. Travel is to accompany or join their sponsor at his or her duty station. Travel may be unaccompanied and is limited to travel from the APOE in the CONUS, Alaska, or Hawaii to the overseas APOD serving the sponsor's duty station. Before travel, approval of the overseas major commander is required. (For space-required option see Chapter 2, section B.3.(8), above) | | | C-O yes<br>O-C no |

***APPENDIX A, continued***

| Item | Cat | Traveler's Status and Situation | C-C | O-O | C-O and O-C |
|---|---|---|---|---|---|
| 33 | V | Noncommand sponsored dependents, acquired in an overseas area during a military member's current tour of assigned duty, not otherwise entitled to transportation at Government expense. Travel must be with the member's PCS, may be unaccompanied, and is limited to travel from the overseas APOE to the APOD in the CONUS, Alaska, or Hawaii. Member's PCS orders are required for travel. Command regulations pertaining to the acquisition of dependents must have been followed. (For space-required option see Chapter 2, section B.3.b. (2), above). | | | C-O no<br>O-C yes |
| 34 | V | Unaccompanied spouses of Uniformed Services members stationed in overseas areas in response to written requests from school officials for personal consultation on matters about the needs of family members attending school at an overseas location away from the Uniformed Service members PDS. | | yes | |
| 35 | | **Category VI - Retired, Dependents, Reserve, ROTC, NUPOC, and CEC** | | | |
| 36 | VI | Retired Uniformed Services members. | yes | yes | yes |
| 37 | VI | Dependents of retired Uniformed Services members, when accompanying their sponsor. | | yes | yes |

*APPENDIX A, continued*

| Item | Cat | Traveler's Status and Situation | C-C | O-O | C-O and O-C |
|---|---|---|---|---|---|
| 38 | VI | Dependents, command sponsored, stationed overseas with their sponsor who is: (1) A member of the Uniformed Services; (2) A U.S. citizen civilian employee of the Department of Defense (paid from either appropriated funds or NAF); or (3) An American Red Cross full-time, paid employee serving with the Department of Defense. Unaccompanied travel is permitted to the U.S. for enlisting in one of the Armed Forces when local enlistment in the overseas area is not authorized. If an applicant for Military Service is rejected, return travel to the overseas area may be provided under this eligibility. | | yes | yes |
| 39 | VI | Authorized Reserve component members and authorized Reserve component members entitled to retired pay at age 60, traveling in the CONUS and directly between the CONUS and Alaska, Hawaii, Puerto Rico, the U.S. Virgin Islands, Guam, and American Samoa (Guam and American Samoa travelers may transit Hawaii or Alaska); or traveling within Alaska, Hawaii, Puerto Rico or the U.S. Virgin Islands. | yes | | |

*APPENDIX A, continued*

| Item | Cat | Traveler's Status and Situation | C-C | O-O | C-O and O-C |
|---|---|---|---|---|---|
| 40 | VI | NUPOC, CEC, and ROTC students of the Army, Navy, or Air Force, receiving financial assistance or enrolled in advanced training, in uniform, during authorized absences from the school. Travel is authorized within and between the CONUS, Alaska, Hawaii, and the U.S. territories. | yes | | |

**Table 6-1. Eligible space-available travelers, priorities, and approved geographical travel segments.**

*APPENDIX A, continued*

## ADDITIONAL SPACE-A INFORMATION

## FROM CHAPTER 1

C. USE OF MILITARY AIRCRAFT. INELIGIBLE TRAFFIC. AND RESTRICTIONS

1. Commanders' Responsibility. The commanders at all levels shall exercise prudent judgment to ensure that only authorized traffic is transported and that they do not misuse the authority delegated to them by this Regulation. The commanders and other officials responding to requests for transportation not specifically authorized by this Regulation shall make no commitments concerning prospective travelers or cargo until they receive all required approvals.

2. Ineligible Traffic Procedures

a. When an order or authorization for movement of traffic (passenger or cargo) which is neither authorized by this Regulation nor approved according to the procedures in this Regulation is presented, transportation shall be denied. The station making the determination shall document the case and forward it through channels to USTRANSCOM TCJ3/J4-LP, 508 SCOTT DRIVE, SCOTT AFB IL 62225-5357 for necessary action.

b. Any traffic transported by DoD aircraft which is ineligible, even though documentation may have been issued, is liable for reimbursement at the non-U.S. Government rate tariff according to APR 76-28 (reference (f)) for all transportation furnished. If any passenger or cargo is challenged for eligibility or authority, every effort shall be made to provide assistance short of delaying a scheduled aircraft.

3. Restrictions on Use of Unit or Operational Support Aircraft. Unless requested and authorized under DoD Directive 4500.43 (reference (t)), unit aircraft shall not be utilized to transportation~DoD passengers and cargo. Similarly, the use of unit or operational support airlift aircraft to provide PCS transportation for DoD members or their dependents is not authorized.

4. Pregnant and Post-Partum Mothers and Newborn Infants

a. Pregnant women up to the 34th week of gestation may be accepted for air transportation unless medically inadvisable.

b. Women who are 6 weeks, or more, postpartum and infants at least 6 weeks old may be accepted for air transportation unless medically inadvisable. Infants under 6 weeks old and women who are less than 6 weeks post partum may be accepted if considered medically sound and so certified in writing by a responsible medical officer or civilian physician.

5. Unaccompanied Minors. Restrictions on travel by unaccompanied minors vary with types of travel (see Chapters 2, 5, 6, and 7).

**Appendix A, continued**

6. Passengers on "Non-Transport-Type" Aircraft. Aircraft not designed or normally configured for passenger (nonaircrew personnel) carrying capability, such as, but not limited to, fighter aircraft, are not to be used for passenger travel. This does not restrict use of these type aircraft for orientation flights, as prescribed in Chapter 4 below.

7. Disabled Passenger. Every effort shall be made to transport passengers with disabilities who are otherwise eligible to travel. Passenger service personnel and crew members shall provide assistance in lading, seating, and unloading the disabled passenger. Travel may be disapproved by the chief of the passenger travel section or the aircraft commander if there is an unacceptable risk to the safety of the disabled passenger, other passengers or the crew, or if operational necessity or equipment or manpower limitations preclude accepting disabled passengers. Such disapprovals shall be rare. In such cases, air terminal personnel must ensure that the passenger understands why air transport is not possible on the mission in question. When a disabled passenger is denied transportation for the above reasons, and when his or her sponsor or dependent, who is otherwise eligible to travel, accompanies the disabled passenger to assist in his or her needs, travel shall be approved if such assistance will eliminate the reasons for denying travel

D. BAGGAGE

1. Timeliness. Baggage must arrive at the APOE either with the traveler or sufficiently in advance to permit the owner to document and offer it for movement as "accompanied baggage.

2. Allowances

a. Normal Free Checkable Baggage Allowance. Duty and space-available passengers are authorized two pieces of checked baggage and one carry-on piece. Checked baggage may not exceed 62 linear inches (length plus width plus height) or 70 pounds for each piece. Carry-on baggage must fit under the seat and may not exceed 45 linear inches (length plus width plus height). For duty passengers only, a duffel bag, sea bag, B-4 bag, flyer's kit bag, or diver's traveling bag, any of which exceeds 62 linear inches, may be substituted for one of the 62 linear inch items.

b. Excess Baggage Allowance. When authorized by service regulations or directives, an excess baggage allowance may be included in an individual's orders. Excess baggage shall be stated in terms of number of pieces, not by weight. Use the formula of 70 pounds for each piece and round to the next highest whole piece to determine the number or pieces necessary. For example, if 100-pounds excess is needed, then two pieces of excess baggage are authorized. Excess baggage is not authorized for space-available passengers.

c. Unauthorized Excess Baggage. Baggage which exceeds the normal baggage allowance without proper authorization may be accepted for shipment at the discretion of air terminal representatives. Passengers owning such baggage will be charged the appropriate excess baggage fee. Air terminal representatives are authorized to refuse to accept baggage in excess of that authorized. Disposition of unauthorized baggage not accepted for shipment shall be the person al responsibility of the owner. Shipment may be made at personal expense through postal facilities or commercial transportation companies. If shipment is otherwise

***APPENDIX A, continued***

authorized to be made at Government expense, arrangements for forwarding may be made with the APOE transportation office~

d. Patients. Patients are limited to two pieces of baggage not to exceed 70-pounds each.

e. Baggage Allowance Restriction. To maximize seat availability, terminal personnel may further restrict passenger baggage allowances when air transportation services are provided by an activity not financed through the DBOF-T.

f. Other Modes. This Regulation limits only the baggage that may be carried by passengers traveling on DoD aircraft. It does not restrict or increase the baggage allowance that may be prescribed by other directives for shipment by other modes.

3. Firearms and Ammunition. Unloaded personal firearms and small arms ammunition may be carried as checked baggage within the authorized weight allowance as long as they are in compliance with the laws and regulations of the United States, foreign governments, the Department of Defense, and the Military Departments. The Military Departments shall establish procedures which require the passenger to identify the items to passenger service personnel or their equivalent at the time of processing for flight and which ensure that the items are in checked baggage, or otherwise adequately secured, so as to be inaccessible to passengers while they are aboard the aircraft.

E. DRESS. CONDUCT. AND STANDARD OF SERVICE

1. Dress. The wearing of the uniform on DoD aircraft by members of the Uniformed Services on active duty, members of the Reserve components not on active duty, and authorized foreign military personnel shall be governed by the directives of the Service concerned and by DoD 4500.54-6, "Foreign Clearance Guide" (reference (u)). When civilian clothing is worn, it shall be in good taste and not in conflict with accepted attire in the overseas country of departure, transit, or destination.

2. Conduct. Under no circumstances shall a passenger be accepted for transportation or be permitted to board an aircraft if he or she is unruly, under the influence of alcohol or narcotic, may create a hazard to the safety of the aircraft or passengers, or is a disruptive influence.

3. Standard of Service. The DoD Components shall establish and maintain standards of appearance, conduct, and service for flight and ground personnel who come in contact with customers of the airlift system which shall ensure professional, courteous, and responsive service.

F. ANIMALS

1. Seeing Eye Dogs

a. Transportation of a dog properly trained to lead the blind, and officially identified by a bona fide organization which trains or registers such dogs, is authorized without charge when accompanying its blind owner who is otherwise authorized transportation under this Regulation.

b. The dog must be properly harnessed to lead a blind person, muzzled to safeguard other passengers and crew members, remain at the blind person's feet, and not create a safety hazard to others by being in the aisle. The dog shall be permitted to accompany the owner in the cabin, but may not occupy a seat or be in the galley area. Sanitation must be maintained at all times.

c. Transportation of seeing eye dogs shall be subject to country quarantine procedures. When it is necessary to detain the animal pending determination of its admissibility, the owner shall provide detention facilities satisfactory to the cognizant quarantine officer. The owner shall bear the expense of such detention, including necessary examinations and vaccinations, and other expenses incurred due to the dog's accompanying the owner.

2. Pets. Passengers traveling under PCS orders may be allowed to ship their pets at their own personal expense. For this privilege, pets are defined as "dogs and cats only", and are limited to two for each family. Requests to deviate from this policy, i.e. number, type, or weight of pets, will be submitted through Service Headquarters to AMC for consideration.

a. Owner Responsibilities. The owner of the pet(s) is responsible for the preparation and care of the animal and for all documentation, immunization, and border clearance requirements including quarantine. The owner shall provide a pet shipment container approved by the international Air Transport Association of sufficient size to allow the animal to stand up, turn around, and lie down with normal posture and body movements.

b. Aircraft Operator Responsibility. The DoD Component operating the aircraft shall ascertain that the means and facilities exist at origin and destination to permit the owner to accomplish his or her responsibilities before accepting the animal for shipment The operator of the aircraft shall establish procedures to ensure that the pets accepted for movement are stowed in areas heated and pressurized adequately to sustain health and comfort according to accepted -commercial industry practice.

3. Other Animals. There is no restriction on shipping other animals aboard DoD aircraft for official purposes if they meet all criteria for shipment of official cargo established by this Regulation. Animals shall be housed, caged, and shipped in a humane fashion consistent with law and industry standards.

G. FORMS

1. DD Form 1381. "Air Transportation Agreement." Before travel aboard aircraft operated by an activity not financed through DBOF-T, the DD Form 1381 shall be executed by the non-DoD personnel specified in Chapters 2, 3, 4,5, 8, and 10, below, when their flight originates in a foreign country. NATO member national personnel traveling in the performance of official duties are exempt from this requirement. The completed DD Form 1381 shall be attached to the passenger manifest and filed at the point of origin. Sponsors will execute DD Form 1381 for minor dependents or individuals incapable of signing for themselves.

***APPENDIX A, continued***

2. DD Form 1839. "Baggage Identification." All checked and carry-on baggage shall be identified with required data clearly annotated on the DD Form 1839. When the DD Form is unavailable, substitute tags, such as those used in the commercial aviation industry, may be use&

3. DD Form 1853. "Verification of Reserve Status for Travel Eligibility." Members of the Reserve components traveling under the provisions of Chapter 6, below, shall have a completed DD Form 1853 in their possession at all times.

4. Boy Scouts of America. "Parent/Guardian Consent Form for Aviation Flights." Explorer Scouts participating in an orientation flight under the provisions of Chapter 4, below, shall present a completed Parent/Guardian Consent Form for Aviation Flights before the flight

5. Supply of Forms. DD Forms 1381, 1839, and 1853 shall be made available to users by forms management officers of the DoD Components. To ensure availability to users, forms management officers are encouraged to permit local reproduction of these forms. The Parent/Guardian Consent Form for Aviation Flights shall be obtained from the individual's Scout Troop.

**AUTHOR'S NOTE:** This Appendix (chapter 6, SPACE AVAILABLE TRAVEL, of DoD 4515.13-R and related) contains references to other related documents which are independent of DoD 4515.13-R and other chapters in DoD 4515.13-R all of which are not published here because of space limitations. In most cases, this documentation amplifies, provides background information and further explains chapter 6 of DoD 4515.13-R. Although not completely essential to the understanding of the Space Available Travel directive, persons wishing to view the entire DoD 4515.13-R and related documents may do so upon request and presentation of appropriate entitlement identification at military Space-A departure locations and Uniformed Services Personnel Offices. The following chapter 6, SPACE AVAILABLE TRAVEL and part of chapter 1, DoD 4515.13-R was released to Military Living Publications by the Office of The Under Secretary of Defense, Jan 1995.

# APPENDIX B
# PERSONNEL ENTRANCE REQUIREMENTS

The info contained in this Appendix has been extracted from the Department of Defense (DoD) *FOREIGN CLEARANCE GUIDE(S): NORTH AND SOUTH AMERICA; EUROPE; AFRICA AND SOUTHWEST ASIA; PACIFIC, SOUTH ASIA AND INDIAN OCEAN, DoD 4500.54-G*. The information extracted is largely from *SECTION II, Personnel Entrance Requirements.* Some data from other sections which we believe meet the needs of Space-A travelers has also been included in this appendix. Note: Only Countries/Areas with regular Space-Available passenger traffic are listed in this Appendix.

It should be noted that immunization requirements are established by and listed in each service's directives and are not listed in the *Foreign Clearance Guide(S).* The only immunization requirements listed in the attached pages are in addition to those required by individual services. U.S. Armed Forces immunization requirements are based on decisions by the World Health Organization (WHO). U.S. requirements are stated in *AR 40-562, NAVMEDCOMINST 6230.3, AFR 161 13, CG COMDTINST M6230.4D, Immunization Requirements & Procedures*. Additional information may be obtained from the **Centers for Disease Control International Travelers Hotline at Tel: 404-332-4559 in Atlanta, GA.** Additional immunization requirements may be levied based on the requirements of local foreign governments.

The data in this appendix is subject to change without notice as political situations change and new developments occur in foreign countries. When in doubt about Personnel Entrance Requirements, Space-A travelers should call or write to the anticipated departure location or military personnel office (which issues official duty orders) for current Personnel Entrance Requirements.

**Please NOTE** abbreviations below: (**ID/C:** Identification Credentials, **ICQI:** Immigration/Customs/Quarantine Inspections, **IR:** Immunization Requirements, & **OTHER**).

AMERICAN (EASTERN) SAMOA (AS)
**ID/C:** ***AD:*** ID Card, Leave orders. ***Ret/Civ:*** ID Card.
**ICQI:** Normal US
**IR:** None
**Other:** ***All:*** Samoa Air Svc (& PanAm on request) handle in-transit AMC aircraft at Pago Pago IAP, AS is US Territory & includes Manua, Tutuila, & Swains Islands.

ANTIGUA & BARBUDA (AN & BD)
**ID/C:** ***AD:*** ID Card, Leave orders. ***Ret/Civ:*** ID Card or Passport. Passport & Visa for 6 + mos.
**ICQI:** Embark/Debark Card if arriv on civ aircraft.
**IR:** Yellow Fever, if arriving from an infected area (IAFIA).
**Other:** ***AD:*** No uniform restric. ***All:*** No currency restric. Declare all currency. 2.72 ECC=$1. Currency export requires license.

ARGENTINA (AG)
**ID/C:** ***All:*** ID Cards, Passport. ***AD:*** Leave orders.
**ICQI:** None
**IR:** Yellow Fever

***APPENDIX B, continued***

**Other:** *AD:* Civ clothing. ***All:*** **Declare all currency.** No limit on currency imports. Exports ltd to imported amt - expenses. **Chk local photographic restric.** Military personnel notify USDAO of planned travel.

ASCENSION ISLAND (United Kingdom) (AI)
**ID/C:** ***AD:*** ID Card, Leave orders. ***Ret/Civ:*** ID, Passport.
**ICQI:** Yes
**IR:** Service
**Other:** ***AD:*** No data avail on uniform restric. ***All:*** Transient pax confirm avail + qtrs prior to travel fm ASCENSION/RAF/CC info copy ESMC Patrick AFB/FL/FA. Sterling imports ltd 10 pounds. Exports 10 pounds sterling. Mess + ltd lodging avail only @ arpt.

AUSTRALIA (AU)
**ID/C:** ***AD:*** ID Card, Leave orders. ***Ret/Civ:*** ID Card, Passport, Visa.
**ICQI:** Yes
**IR:** Service
**Other:** ***AD:*** Uniforms OK, except to
and from Woomera & Alice Springs. No import of animals, animal products and germinable vegetables. Notify your svc. USDAO by phone 61-6-270-5805/5811 of leave address & length of stay and follow-up by letter with leave orders. ***All:*** $20.00 AU depart tax pd @ arpt. Do not use cameras in prohibited areas. No currency import restric. Export limit $100 AU. $1.28 AU = $1 US.

AZORES (See Portugal (PO)
**ID/C:** ***AD:*** ID Card, Passport, Leave orders. ***Ret/Civ:*** ID Card, Passport. 60 day ICQI: Yes, if aircraft 24 hrs delay.
**IR:** Yellow Fever if arriv fm infected area.
**Other:** ***AD:*** Leave orders bilingual in Portuguese & Eng or French & Eng. No data avail on uniform restric. ***All:*** 150 escudos = $1 US.

BAHRAIN (BA)
**ID/C:** ***All:*** ID Cards, Passport, Visa (if leaving apt).
**ICQI:** Yes
**IR:** Yellow Fever if arriv fm infected area.
**Other:** ***All:*** No uniforms. 72 hr landing visa issued @ arpt. 90 day Visa issued Washington DC. **No evidence of entry into Israel or South Africa admitted.** No currency restric. 1 Bahrain dinar = $2.65 US. No liquor. **Chk Amer Emb for other restric items. No photography of local women or religious act.**

BELGIUM (BE)
**ID/C:** ***AD:*** ID Card, Leave orders. ***Ret/Civ:*** ID Card, Passport, Visa aft 3 mo.
**ICQI:** No
**IR:** Services
**Other:** ***AD:*** Civ clothing recommended. ***All:*** Register w/ local "police entrangers" w/in 8 days of arriv. **Declare all currency.** No limit on imports. Export limit 50,000 BF. 31 BF = $1 US. **Photography of canals, bridges, & mil installations is restricted.**

***APPENDIX B, continued***

BERMUDA (BM)
**ID/C:** ***AD:*** Proof of citizenship, ID Card, Leave orders. ***Ret/Civ:*** ID Card, Proof of Citizenship or Passport, Visa for stay 6+ mo.
**ICQI:** Yes
**IR:** Services
**Other:** ***AD:*** No data avail on uniform restric. ***All:*** Depart tax $10 pd @ arpt. No currency restric.

BOLIVIA (BO)
**ID/C:** ***AD:*** ID Card, Passport, Leave orders, Visa stamped by im-migration at Apt on entry, for 30 days. Exit stamp is mandatory. Visa not approved if passport expires within 6 mo. ***Ret/Civ:*** ID Card, Passport. Visa same as AD above.
**ICQI:** Required
**IR:** Yellow Fever
**Other:** ***AD:*** Civ clothing worn on arriving mil or comm acf. No uniforms in public places. ***All:*** No currency restric. Due to altitude, limit phy activity for 1st 48 hrs. Deaths from cholera have been reported near La Paz.

BRAZIL (BR)
**ID/C:** ***All:*** ID Card, Passport, Visa. ***AD:*** Leave orders.
**ICQI:** Yes
**IR:** Yellow Fever
**Other:** ***AD:*** Civ clothing required. ***All:*** No Visas issued @ arpt. No currency restric on import. Export ltd to 50% of import &/on conversions.

CANADA (CN)
**ID/C:** ***AD:*** ID Card, NATO Leave orders. ***Ret/Civ:*** ID Card.
**ICQI:** Yes
**IR:** Services
**Other:** ***AD:*** Civ clothing. ***All:*** No currency restric. $1.29 Canadian = $1 US.

CHAD (CD)
**ID/C:** ***All:*** ID Card, Passport, Visa.
**ICQI:** Yes
**IR:** Yellow Fever & Gamma Globulin
**Other:** ***AD:*** No data avail on uniform restric. Notify USDAO Ndjamera upon arriv. ***All:*** Visas valid for single entry (multiple entries on request). **No photo-graphy allowed w/out permission of the Pres of Chad.** No limit on foreign currency imports. 293 CFA = $1 US.

CHILE (CH)
**ID/C:** ***AD:*** ID Card, Passport, Leave orders. ***Ret/Civ:*** ID Card, Passport.
**ICQI:** Yes
**IR:** Yellow Fever
**Other:** ***AD:*** No data avail on uniform restric. ***All:*** Visas required aft 90 days. No currency restric. 300 Pesos = $1 US. **Gold exports other than jewelry are prohibited.**

COLUMBIA (CL)
**ID/C:** ***AD:*** ID Card, Passport, Leave orders. ***Ret/Civ:*** Passport and proof of onward/return ticket. Visa not required for visits of less than 90 days.
**ICQI:** Yes
**IR:** Yellow Fever

*APPENDIX B, continued*

**Other:** ***AD:*** Civ clothing. Clearance fm USDAO & contact for security briefing on arriv. ***All:*** Proof of onward/return ticket. Currency exchange illegal except at officially designated fac. 520 Pesos = $1 US. No Visas @ arpt. Visas not required for arpt transfer status. **Columbia is currently under a declared state of siege. All travelers must display a current Passport** if questioned by authorities.

<u>CRETE (CR) (Same as Greece)</u>
**ID/C:** ***AD:*** ID Card, NATO Leave orders. ***Ret/Civ:*** ID Card, Passport.
**ICQI:** Yes
**IR:** Yellow Fever if arriv fm infected area. Small Pox vac if arriv fm Israel.
**Other:** ***AD:*** Civ clothing advisable & required when traveling to/fm Greece. ***All:*** No currency restric for 200 Drachma or less. **$500 or more non-Greek currency must be declared.** 60+ days visit requires alien resident permit or police ID Card.

<u>CUBA (CU) (US Guantanamo Bay)</u>
**ID/C:** ***AD:*** ID Card, Leave orders. ***Ret/Civ:*** ID Card.
**ICQI:** Yes
**IR:** Services
**Other:** ***AD:*** Class "A" uniform worn on arriv & depart. ***All:*** US Guantanamo Bay is not considered part of the special area of Cuba. **Temporary shelters for Haitian refugees at Guantanamo Bay has placed a strain on limited facilities, requiring confirmed theater clearance prior to travel to Guantanamo NAS. Lodging must be confirmed by messages prior to arriv. No off-base lodging.**

<u>CYPRUS (CY)</u>
**ID/C:** ***AD:*** ID Card, Passport, Leave orders. ***Ret/Civ:*** ID Card, Passport.
**ICQI:** Yes
**IR:** Yellow Fever
**Other:** ***AD:*** No uniforms except in transient @ depart ramp area. Inform USDAO of arriv, duration of stay, address. ***All:*** Currency import & export ltd to 10 pounds sterling. 1 Cyprus pound = $2.30 US. Pax's Passport stamped by the "Turkish Republic of Northern Cyprus" may be denied entry to Greece if traveling on same Passport.

<u>DENMARK (DN) (Greenland)</u>
**ID/C:** ***AD:*** ID Card, Leave orders. Passport if landing at non-US base. ***Ret/Civ:*** ID Card. Passport if landing at non-US base.
**ICQI:** US aircraft exempt fm inspec
**IR:** Services. Depart med statement
**Other:** ***AD:*** No uniform data avail. ***All:*** Off-base visits require permission fm Danish liaison officer thru base commander. Qtrs confirmation required prior to arriv.

<u>DIEGO GARCIA (Chagos Archipelago) United Kingdom) (See Indian Ocean IO)</u>
**ID/C:** ***All:*** ID Card, Leave orders or PCS orders. Civilian passports.
**ICQI:** No data avail
**IR:** Services
**Other:** ***AD:*** No uniform restric data avail. Clearance required for TAD/TDY entry to Diego Garcia. ***All:*** Leave travel & Space-A travel (including circuitous travel for pers on official orders) are not authorized to or through Diego Garcia. **Access to Diego Garcia is ltd to mission-essential personnel.**

<u>DOMINICAN REPUBLIC (DR)</u>
**ID/C:** ***All:*** ID Card, Passport or Birth certificate. Purchase Tourist Card ($10 US).

**ICQI:** Yes
**IR:** Gamma Globulin recommended
**Other:** ***All:*** Civ clothing. No currency restric. 12.3 pesos = $1 US. **CAUTION .. water is not potable.**

EGYPT (EG) (United Arab Republic of)
**ID/C:** ***All:*** ID Card, Passport, Visa. AD: Leave orders.
**ICQI:** No data avail
**IR:** Yellow Fever if arriv fm an infected area. Cholera, Booster (every 6 mo) if arriv fm an infected area. Certificate of HIV(AIDS) Screenings.
**Other:** ***All:*** Civ clothing. Visas (valid for 6 mo) obtainable @ arpt banks for $2 US. **Local currency cannot be taken outside country.** Declare currency & other valuables on arriv. **Only typical tourist-type photography is allowed. The penalty in Egypt for conviction of smuggling or selling drugs is execution. Space-A travel to/fm Egypt is ltd to: a)** those eligible pers stationed in or assigned TDY to Egypt; **b)** those pers personally sponsored by US agencies or official US pers in country. Cairo East is an Egyptian mil base with strict- controlled access, no food svc, & no trans. AMC representatives cannot furnish sponsorship or trans to/fm Cairo East AB. Space-A pax must have written permission fm Chief OMC(Officer of Mil Cooperation, Amer Emb Cairo, Box 29, FPO New York, NY 09527-5000) Admin, Cairo, prior to travel. **Requests permission** (sponsorship) should be submitted to OMC Admin Sec by sponsoring in-country agency or individual. Requests **should include** names, Passport #'s; type Passport; exp dates of Visas; proposed arrival & depart dates; & local sponsor's name, address, & phone #. Request **must also include** a statement that: **1)** Sponsor will be responsible for traveler's trans & base access to/fm Cairo East pax term; & **2)** Sponsor will be avail @ Cairo East AB until aircraft is airborne. Uniforms will not be worn for Space-A travel to/fm Egypt due to GOE (Govt of EG) regulations. **3)** Because of heavy workload, it is impossible for OMC Cairo & USDAO Cairo to honor individual requests for sponsorship. Personnel arriving in Cairo by other than AMC travel will not be authorized to depart by AMC travel. A letter of permission is required for individuals to sign up for AMC Space-A travel into and out of Egypt.

GERMANY (GE)
**ID/C:** ***AD:*** ID Card, Passport, Visa,
NATO Leave orders. ***Ret/Civ:*** **ID Card, Passport.**
**ICQI:** Yes
**IR:** Services
**Other:** ***AD:*** Civ clothing in non-duty status. ***All:*** Resident permit for stays in excess of 90 days. No currency restric.

GREECE (GR)
**ID/C:** ***AD:*** ID Card, NATO Leave orders. ***Ret/Civ:*** ID Card, Passport.
**ICQI:** Yes
**IR:** Yellow Fever if arriv fm infected area. Small Pox if arriv fm Israel.
**Other:** ***AD:*** Civ clothing advisable & required on arriv & depart Greece. ***All:*** Import & export of 200 Drachma or less. **Declare $500 or more of non-Greek currency.** Boil & filter water.

GUAM (GU) (Guam is US Territory)
**ID/C:** ***AD:*** ID Card, Leave orders. ***Ret/Civ:*** ID Card.
**ICQI:** Yes
**IR:** Services
**Other:** ***AD:*** Summer uniform. ***All:*** No currency restric. **Chk w/ mil authorities prior to scuba diving or snorkeling.** TML ltd @ Andersen AFB & Agana NAS. Ground trans ltd. Local hotels near capacity.

***APPENDIX B, continued***

HAITI (HA)
**ID/C:** ***AD:*** ID Card, Proof of citizenship. ***Ret/Civ:*** ID Card, Tourist Card, Proof of citizenship.
**ICQI:** Yes
**IR:** Yellow Fever if arriv fm infected area.
**Other:** ***AD:*** No data avail on uniform restric. Report to USDAO, phone 011-509-2-29397 w/in 24 hrs of arriv in Haiti. ***All:*** Tourist Card avail @ arpt for $2 US (30 days or less). $20.00 US depart tax @ arpt. Haitien citizens in US mil require Passport & Exit Permit. No currency restric. 5 Gourde = $1 US.

HONDURAS (HO)
**ID/C:** ***All:*** ID Card, Passport(valid 6 mo), Visa(or Tourist Card $4 Lempira).
**ICQI:** Yes
**IR:** Yellow Fever & Gamma Globulin
**Other:** ***AD:*** Civ clothing. Register w/ USDAO, in person or phone 32-3120 ext 2310. ***All:*** If depart via commercial airline, an Exit Tax of $50 Lempira, approx $10 US. US $ used @ US mil-controlled fac. Use boiled or bottled water. **No photography of mil installations.**

HONG KONG (HK)
**ID/C:** ***AD:*** ID Card, Leave orders. ***Ret/Civ:*** ID Card, Passport.
**ICQI:** Yes
**IR:** Services
**Other:** ***AD:*** Civ clothing. ***All:*** Visa aft 30 days, not avail @ entry arpt. No currency restric. HK $7.8 = $1 US. No import into US. If merchandise originating in North Korea or Vietnam. $11 US fee is collected upon arriv by the aircraft servicing contractor for the Hong Kong govt. Air pax Depart Tax 12+ yrs $150 H.K..

ICELAND (IC)
**ID/C:** ***AD:*** ID Card, Leave orders. ***Ret/Civ:*** ID Card, Passport
**ICQI:** Yes
**IR:** Meningococcal & Adenovirus vac
**Other:** ***AD:*** Civ clothing off base. ***All:*** No currency restric except reconversion of Kroner to US $ ltd to $250 US. Visas required for 90+ days. No pets.

INDONESIA (IE)
**ID/C:** ***AD:*** ID Card, Passport, Visa, Leave order. ***Ret/Civ:*** ID Card, Passport, Visa.
**ICQI:** Yes
**IR:** Cholera:infected area
**Other:** ***AD:*** Civ clothing, and advise USDAO Jakarta, 62-21-360-360 Ex:2190. ***All:*** Visa valid for 60 days and a single entry. **Declare currency. Indonesian Rupiah imports prohibited.** Use only bottled water. Antimalarial drugs recommended outside Jakarta. **Photography of mil installations, arpts, terms prohibited.** No AD travel to Irian Jaya & Timor w/out permission.

IRELAND (IR)
**ID/C:** ***AD:*** ID Card, Leave orders. Passport. ***Ret/Civ:*** **ID Card, Passport.**
**ICQI:** Yes
**IR:** Services
**Other:** ***AD:*** Civ clothing. ***All:*** No currency restric. 1 Irish pound = $1.78 US.

ISRAEL (IS)
**ID/C:** ***All:*** ID Card, Leave Orders, Passport, Visa. (Valid 1 entry. 90 days)
**ICQI:** Yes

***APPENDIX B, continued***

**IR:** Service
**Other:** *AD:* Civ clothing. ***All:*** Visa @ Ben Gurion arpt for Tourist Passport (90 days). **Israeli currency may not be imported or exported.** Exit reconvert up to $3 US. 2.35 New Israeli Shekels (NIS) = $1 US. **Do not photograph mil installations or pers.**

ITALY (IT)
**ID/C:** ***AD:*** ID CARD, NATO Leave orders. ***Ret/Civ:*** **ID Card, Passport.**
**ICQI:** Yes
**IR:** Services
**Other:** ***AD:*** Civ clothing. ***All:*** Tourist Passport highly recommended. Visa required over 3 mos. Import & export restric to 350,000 Lire per border crossing. Bottled water in rural areas.

JAMAICA (JM)
**ID/C:** ***AD:*** ID Card, Leave orders. ***Ret/Civ:*** ID Card, Proof of citizenship.
**ICQI:** Yes
**IR:** Yellow Fever if fm infected area.
**Other:** ***AD:*** Civ clothing. ***All:*** Contact USDAO Kingston upon arriv in Jamaica. **No import & export of Jamaican $.** 7.00 Jamaican $ = $1 US. Exchange only at designated money exchanges. No firearms imported or used

JAPAN (JA)
**ID/C:** ***AD:*** ID Card, Leave orders. ***Ret/Civ:*** **ID Card, Passport.**
**ICQI:** Yes
**IR:** Services
**Other:** ***AD:*** Mil uniform. ***All:*** Visa for stay over 90 days. Reconversion of Yen to US currency 500,000 Yen per day. 110-120 Yen per $1 US.

JOHNSTON ATOLL (JO) (Johnston Atoll is US Territory)
**ID/C:** ***AD:*** ID Card, Leave orders, Entrance approval. ***Ret/Civ:*** ID Card, Entrance approval.
**ICQI:** No
**IR:** Services
**Other:** *AD:* Summer uniform. ***All:*** Pax not permitted to RON w/out approval of Commander. **No pers allowed to RON w/ beards or facial hair which preclude the proper wearing & sealing of a M17A1 protective mask or its equivalent.** Fac avail @ term to remove excess hair.

JORDAN (JR)
**ID/C:** ***AD:*** ID Card, Passport, Visa. ***Ret/Civ:*** ID Card.
**ICQI:** Yes
**IR:** No data avail
**Other:** ***AD:*** Civ clothing. **Must** contact USDAO on arriv. **Require** clearance fm USDAO Amman. ***All:*** **Travelers refused entry to Jordan if Passport contains Israeli stamp or issued in TelAviv.** (Use 2 Passports or request Israeli authorities not to stamp Passport .. stamp clear page outside Passport.) Exit via civ arpt, exit fee of $30 US. Boil & filter water. Pers traveling via King Hussein/Allenby Bridge between Israel & Jordan can cross bridge one way in either direction, but travel must commence in Jordan to make a round-trip. Commence travel in the Moslem countries. 1 Jordan Dinar=$1.00 U.S.

KENYA ( KE)
**ID/C:** ***All:*** ID Card, Passport, Visa.
**ICQI:** Yes
**IR:** Yellow Fever, Cholera, Malaria prophylaxis

***APPENDIX B, continued***

**Other:** ***AD:*** Civ clothing, casual slacks, shirt w/ collar (coat & tie evenings). Ordinary leave to Kenya via AMC is not authorized except for pers residing in area w/ permission fm Kenya U.S. Liaison Office. ***All:*** Transit Visas avail for stays up to 7 days. Kenya admission allowed if traveler stayed less than 3 mo in S Africa. No export of Kenyan Shillings. 17 KE Shillings = $1 US. Chk source of water. $20.00 U.S. departure tax paid in U.S. dollars.

KOREA (Republic of) (RK)
**ID/C:** ***AD:*** ID Card, Leave orders. ***Ret/Civ:*** ID Card, Passport, Visa, (for 15+ days visit).
**ICQI:** Yes
**IR:** Cholera if fm an infected area
**Other:** ***AD:*** Mil & Civ clothing. ***All:*** No import of Korean Won. Boil or chlorinate water. Clearance required to visit Panmunjom. Airport departure tax of 6,000 Won or approx $8.40 US, except EML leave, funded emerg leave & overseas tour leave.

KWAJALEIN ATOLL (U.S. Army) (KA) (USAKA) (Republic of the Marshall Islands)
**ID/C:** ***AD:*** ID Card, Leave orders, Entry approval. ***Ret/Civ:*** ID Card, Entry approval.
**ICQI:** No
**IR:** Services
**Other:** ***AD:*** Command restric on uniforms. ***All:*** First aid recommended for all burns, bites, etc.

LIBERIA (LI)
**ID/C:** ***AD:*** ID Card, Passport, Visa, Leave orders. ***Ret/Civ:*** ID Card, Passport, Visa.
**ICQI:** Yes
**IR:** Cholera:infected area. Malaria prophylaxis strongly recommended.
**Other:** ***AD:*** Civ clothing & rainwear. ***All:*** Visas not avail @ arpt. Travelers must report to immigration Hqs in Monrovia w/in 48 hrs of arriv to obtain permit to stay for planned visit. Depart AMC aircraft consult w/ AMC to determine aircraft rte & Visa requirements. Exit Visa fm immigration required to depart. 7 day delay in issuing Exit Visa. Register w/Amer Emb if stay is a wk+. Maximum stay is 3 mos. US $ legal currency in denominations up to $20. **Do not carry or use cameras**. Travelers notify local authorities before entering interior. Delay & search @ mil roadblocks.

MALAYSIA (MA)
**ID/C:** ***AD:*** ID Card, Passport, Leave orders. ***Ret/Civ:*** ID Card, Passport. No VISA for less than 6 mo.
**ICQI:** Yes
**IR:** Yellow Fever if arriv fm infected area. Cholera infected.
**Other:** ***AD:*** No uniform restric. Civ clothing recommended. ***All:*** Limit of currency import & export is M $10,000. M $2.60 = $1 US. Boil water or treat w/ halazone tablets in rural areas.

MARSHALL ISLANDS (MI) (Republic of) (RMI)
*[Includes Ailinglapalap Atoll, Arno Atoll, Bikini Atoll, Ebon Atoll, Enewetak Atoll, Jaluit Atoll, Kili Island, Kwajalein Atoll (except US) Army Kwajalein Atoll), Majuro Atoll, Maloelap Atoll, Mili Atoll, NamorikAtoll, Ralik Chain, Ratak Chain, Rongelap Atoll, Taongi Atoll, Ujelang Atoll, Utirik Atoll, Wotje Atoll]*
**ID/C:** ***AD:*** ID Card, Leave orders. ***Ret/Civ:*** ID Card.
**ICQI:** No
**IR:** Services
**Other:** ***All:*** Command restric, if any, apply. No currency restric. **Water outside major hotels & restaurants not potable.**

*APPENDIX B, continued*

MIDWAY ISLAND (MW)
**ID/C:** ***All:*** ID Card.
**ICQI:** No data avail
**IR:** No data avail
**Other:** ***All:*** Clearance is required - COMNAVBASE Pearl Harbor, HI 96860-5020.

NEW ZEALAND (NZ)
**ID/C:** ***AD:*** ID Card, Passport (valid for 6 mos), Leave orders. ***Ret/Civ:*** ID Card, Passport.
**ICQI:** Yes
**IR:** Services
**Other:** ***AD:*** No uniform restric. ***All:*** Visa required when stay exceeds 90 days. ID Card is accepted in lieu of usual outward ticket requirement for Space-A traveler. Maximum currency export is $100 NZ. 1 NZ $ = .58 US. No US - NZ SOFA. Drug offenders receive sentences up to life imprisonment

NORWAY (NO)
**ID/C:** ***AD:*** ID Card, NATO Leave orders. ***Ret/Civ:*** ID Card, Passport.
**ICQI:** Yes
**IR:** Services
**Other:** ***AD:*** Civ clothing. ***All:*** Export up to 5,000 Kroner. US currency larger than $20 US must be cashed at banks. **Rigid laws on DWI.** Shortage of hotel rooms in Oslo.

OMAN (OM)
**ID/C:** ***AD:*** ID Card, Passport, Visa. ***Ret/Civ:*** ID Card, Passport, Visa.
**ICQI:** Yes
**IR:** Yellow Fever if arriv fm infected area.
**Other:** ***All:*** Civ clothing. ***AD:*** Visa (validation for 7 - 90 days) not avail @ arpt. Advise USDAO of travel plans. No entry for travelers to or fm Israel or w/ Israeli Visa in their Passport. Travelers may transit Oman w/out FCG compliance provided they do not disembark the aircraft. **Liquor & adult-only literature are prohibited.** No currency restric. Boil water. **Photography of ports & arpts prohibited.**

PANAMA (PN) (Republic of)
**ID/C:** ***AD:*** ID Card, Leave orders. ***Ret/Civ:*** ID Card, Passport, Visa.
**ICQI:** Yes
**IR:** Yellow Fever
**Other:** ***AD:*** Summer uniform, civ clothing off base. ***All:*** Country clearance required fm USDAO, Box E, APO AA 34002. Visa for Panama obtained fm Panamanian Consulate in Tampa, FL. No currency restric. 1 Balboa = $1 US.

PARAGUAY (PG)
**ID/C:** ***AD:*** ID Card, Passport, Visa or Tourist Card, Leave orders. ***Ret/Civ:*** ID Card, Passport, Visa or Tourist Card.
**ICQI:** Yes
**IR:** Yellow Fever
**Other:** ***AD:*** Mil uniforms. Contact USDAO on arriv, phone 201-041 ext 265. ***All:*** No currency restric. 1330 Guaranie = $1 US. Outside Asuncion, use bottled water. Rabies is a problem in Paraguay. Visits less than 90 days require Tourist Card ($3 US) @ arpt.

PERU (PE)
**ID/C:** ***AD:*** ID Card, Passport, Leave orders. ***Ret/Civ:*** ID Card, Passport.

***APPENDIX B, continued***

**ICQI:** Yes
**IR:** Yellow Fever and cholera.
**Other:** *AD:* Summer uniforms. Consult w/ USDAO, APO AA 34031. ***All:*** Contact USDAO to arrange security briefing. Tel. 33800, ex. 360-3. Exit Tax @ Lima arpt = $15 US. No currency restric. Use bottled water. **Photography of infrastructure & mil installations is prohibited.**

PHILIPPINES (RP) (Republic of)
**ID/C:** ***AD:*** ID Card, Leave orders. Passport. ***Ret/Civ:*** ID Card, Passport, Visa (59 days).
**ICQI:** Yes
**IR:** Services
**Other:** *AD:* Arriv & depart (in civclothes) @ Manila IAP. Civ clothing for arriv & depart through Manila IAP.
***All:*** **No Visa issued in country.** Space-A pax's manifested thru & to outside destinations auth to transit Philippines only when no other alternate routing is available. No more than 500 Pesos on entering or leaving, other instruments not ltd. 20.20 Pesos = $1 US (rates vary).

PORTUGAL (PO)
**ID/C:** ***AD:*** ID Card, Passport, NATO Leave orders. ***Ret/Civ:*** ID Card, Passport.
**ICQI:** Yes
**IR:** Services
**Other:** *AD:* Civ clothing. ***All:*** Visa aft 60 days. No currency restric. Water in Lisbon unsafe to drink. Pers stationed in Azores may visit w/out Passport & Visa up to 60 days.

PUERTO RICO (PR) Puerto Rico is US Territory)
**ID/C:** ***AD:*** ID Card, Leave orders. ***Ret/Civ:*** ID Card.
**ICQI:** No
**IR:** Yellow Fever
**Other:** *AD:* Uniforms allowed.

SAUDI ARABIA (SA)
**ID/C:** ***AD:*** ID Card, Passport, Visa, Leave orders. ***Ret/Civ:*** ID Card, Passport, Visa.
**ICQI:** Yes
**IR:** Yellow Fever, Small Pox
**Other:** *AD:* Civ clothing. Notify USDAO, Riyadh & CHUSMTM/MR Dhahran. ***All:*** Transit Visa required to change between AMC & civ aircraft. Visa required prior to arriv. Visa of any type will not be granted by Saudi Arabian Emb w/out proof that visit is of an official nature. All Space-A pax attempting thru passage must have a valid Transit Visa in case they are removed for duty pax. Transit Visa may be extended up to 10 days if applied for w/in 72 hrs of validity period. Visa valid for 3 Saudi months or 87 days. **Alcoholic bevs, pornographic materials, or items offensive to Moslem religion prohibited.** Use bottled water. **No photography of women, mil installations, or ports.**

SENEGAL (SE) (Republic of)
**ID/C:** ***AD:*** ID Card, Passport, Visa, Leave orders. ***Ret/Civ:*** ID Card, Passport, Visa.
**ICQI:** No
**IR:** Malaria Prophylaxis, Yellow Fever
**Other:** *AD:* No uniform restric. ***All:*** Import of CFA Francs ltd to 10,000. 293 CFA Francs = $1 US. Boil all water or use purification tablets.

SINGAPORE (SG)
**ID/C:** ***AD:*** ID Card, Leave orders. ***Ret/Civ:*** ID Card, Passport.**ICQI:** Yes
**IR:** Services. ***All:*** Valid records required.

*APPENDIX B, continued*

**Other:** ***AD:*** Mil uniform recom-mended. ***All:*** Entry valid for 14 days. Visa aft 14 days required. Physician must sign & authenticate w/ stamp Int'l Certificate of Vaccination. Currency declared. $1.82 Singapore = $1 US. **No adult literature. No cameras exhibited or used on mil installations.** Coordinate taxi w/ AMC terminal manager.

SOMALIA (SM) (Democratic Republic)
**ID/C:** ***AD:*** ID Card, Passport, Visa, Leave orders. ***Ret/Civ:*** ID Card, Passport, Visa.
**ICQI:** Yes
**IR:** Yellow Fever, Cholera, Malaria Prophylaxis, Gamma Globulin
**Other:** ***AD:*** Mil uniform or civ clothing. ***All:*** **Declare all currency.** Export of currency must be less than import. Use bottled or treated water. **No photography of arpt or local populace.**

SPAIN (SP)
**ID/C:** ***AD:*** ID Card, NATO Leave orders. ***Ret/Civ:*** ID Card, Passport.
**ICQI:** Yes
**IR:** Yellow Fever
**Other:** ***AD:*** Civ clothing. ***All:*** AD & Ret mil pers on leave who are not permanently assigned w/in Spain are not authorized Base Exchange, Commissary, or Class VI privileges. **Declare currency.** Import of Bank of Spain notes ltd to 50,000 Pesetas & export of 3,000 Pesetas. 95 Pesetas = $1 US. Fr Torrejon AB AMC Gram ... Re: Spanish Immigration Requirements .. **Ret/DoD Civ & their dependents:** (Entering Spain thru Torrejon AB) **Must obtain** a **"Ltr of Entrada"** & a **Base Pass** fm pax svc pers if desiring to go on or off Base. **Passports must have an "Entrada" stamp** before re-entering the Base. "Entrada" stamps can be obtained fm Spanish customs located @ Barajas IAP in Madrid or at the Spanish Nat'l Police Station (COMISARIA) In Torrejon (2 mi fm Base) located on Hilados Street, # 15, in an area known as Parque Cataluna. Spanish customs will not issue "Entrada" stamps w/out the presentation of a "Ltr of Entrada." **AD & their dependents: Are not required to obtain the "Ltr of Entrada" or Base Pass.** ID Cards are sufficient to re-enter Base. The **"Ltr of Entrada" is required only if dependents plan to exit the country via commercial means.**

SUDAN (SU) Republic of)
**ID/C:** ***AD:*** ID Card, Passport, Visa. ***Ret/Civ:*** ID Card, Passport, Visa.
**ICQI:** No data avail
**IR:** Yellow Fever. Malaria suppressants 2 wks prior to arriv.
**Other:** ***AD:*** Civ clothing. Contact USDAO ASAP aft arriv. Tel. 74700, 74611, 75680, ex. 4215-6. ***All:*** Israeli or South African stamp in Passport will prevent entry. No Visa avail @ arpt. Visa valid for 90 days. **Declare foreign currency.** 12.2 Sudanese pounds = $1 US. **Alcoholic bev & pornographic material prohibited.** Register w/ police w/in 3 days of arriv. Chk w/ Amer Emb for travel advisories. 100 Sudanese pounds departure tax.

THAILAND (TH)
**ID/C:** ***All:*** ID Card, Passport, Visa
**ICQI:** No
**IR:** Cholera infected area
**Other:** ***AD:*** Civ clothing. ***All:*** Visa not required for 15 day (or less) visit. Stamp, in lieu of Visa, good for 15 days & not extendable. Non-immigration Visa (valid up to 90 days) can be extended to 1 yr. Exchange money only at licensed
money changers (10% loss). 24 to 26 Baht per $1 US. **No photography at mil arpts.** Pers desiring follow-on US mil air trans contact AMC Rep, Bangkok, phone 287-1027 @ JUSMAGTHAI Compound, 7 South Sathorn Rd (1 mi so of Amer Emb). Only APO & snack bar avail.

***APPENDIX B, continued***

TURKEY (TU)
**ID/C:** ***AD:*** ID Card, Passport, NATO Leave orders. ***Ret/Civ:*** ID Card, Passport.
**ICQI:** Yes
**IR:** Yellow Fever if arriv fm infected area
**Other:** ***AD:*** Civ clothing. Must inform USDAO Ankara, & info to CJUSMMAT/TDAI of arriv & place of residence. ***All:*** Visa for visit of 90+ days. **Declare currency & valuables.** Import & export limit is 50,000 TL. 1365 Turkish Lira = $1 US. Boil or chlorinate water. **No photography of Turkish mil installations.** Chk w/ Amer Emb on special travel restric.

UNITED KINGDOM (UK)
*[England, Northern Ireland, Scotland, & Wales]*
**ID/C:** ***AD:*** ID Card, NATO Leave orders. ***Ret/Civ:*** ID Card, Passport.
**ICQI:** Yes
**IR:** Services
**Other:** ***AD:*** Civ clothing. Uniform is appropriate for visits to US & British mil installations outside London. No currency restric. No govt trans avail in London.

URUGUAY (UG)
**ID/C:** ***AD:*** ID Card, Passport, Leave orders. ***Ret/Civ:*** ID Card, Passport.
**ICQI:** Yes
**IR:** Yellow Fever
**Other:** ***AD:*** Civ clothing. ***All:*** **Photography of mil installations or equip prohibited.**

US VIRGIN ISLANDS (VI) (The US Virgin Islands are US Territory)
**ID/C:** ***AD:*** ID Card, Leave orders. ***Ret/Civ:*** ID Card.
**ICQI:** Yes
**IR:** Yellow Fever if arriv fm infected area
**Other:** ***All:*** Boil water unless sure of source.

WAKE ISLAND (WK) (Wake Island is US Territory)
**ID/C:** ***AD:*** ID Card, Leave orders. ***Ret/Civ:*** ID Card.
**ICQI**: Normal US customs
**IR:** None
**Other:** ***All:*** Enter & depart Wake Island Airfield. Ltd billeting for RON pers. Billeting, food svc, grd trans, & medical svcs are austere & severely ltd. No off base qtrs.

ZAIRE (ZA) (Republic of)
**ID/C:** ***AD:*** ID Card, Passport, Visa, Leave orders. ***Ret/Civ:*** ID Card, Passport, Visa.
**ICQI:** Yes
**IR:** Cholera & Yellow Fever (7 days prior to arriv)
**Other:** ***AD:*** Civ clothing. ***All:*** Enter Zaire only at Kinshasa. Arpt Visa not avail. Visa for other than official business requires approval fm Foreign Ministry Kinshasa (3 wks delay). **US mil Space-A travel is highly discouraged** & must be approved in advance in writing by the Chief, US Mil Mission to Zaire (ZAMISH), APO AE 09662-0006. Lead time is 1 mo prior to travel. Travel by non-sponsored AD/Ret pers on leave or unofficial status is highly discouraged. Such travelers must have an in-country sponsor while in Zaire. Pax arriv via AMC Space-A trans **must obtain clearance** fm USDAO prior to entry, in addition written clearance fm Chief ZAMISH. **Request** for clearance **must include** a brief description of the **purpose** of the travel & the name of an **in-country sponsor** who can be contacted by USDAO or ZAMISH. Travelers w/ Tourist Passport require a return/onward ticket. **Declare all currency. Keep records.** 301 Zaires = $1 US. **No Zaires**

**taken out of country.** Drink boiled or treated water. **Photography prohibited of arpt or infrastructure. No travel in some areas** w/out govt authorization.

## PROOF OF US CITIZENSHIP (POC)

The following documents are considered valid proof of US citizenship:

a) United States of America Passport
b) Birth or Baptismal Certificate
c) State ID Card
d) Naturalization Certificate
e) Voter ID Card
f) US Mil ID Card (regardless of true citizenship of mil member)
g) US Mil Dependent ID Card (regardless of true citizenship of mil member)

# APPENDIX C

## LOCATION IDENTIFIERS AND CROSS-REFERENCE INDEX

The location Identifiers (LIs) used in this book are the Federal Aviation Administration coordinated **three letter** LIs for the United States, its possessions and Canada. Foreign Country LIs have been coordinated by the Department of Defense. An LI represents the name/location of an airport/airbase. They are considered permanent (changes are made for air safety only) and cannot be transferred. The original LI remains in effect even if it becomes necessary to change the name of a given facility.

The International Civil Aviation Organization (ICAO) has established an international location indicator which is a **four letter** code used in international telecommunications. The ICAO/LIs listed below are primarily used to identify military stations/locations around the world.

This appendix has been cross-referenced so that each LI is followed by the page numbers on which the LI appears as the destination of a scheduled flight possibility. The number in bold face indicates the page number the main base listing for the given LI. The four stars (****) indicates that ICAO have not been assigned.

*APPENDIX C, continued*

BLV/KBLV = *Scott Air Force Base, IL:* 33, 34, 36, **66**, 83, 95, 170.
BNA/KBNA = *Nashville International Airport, TN:* **163.**
BOG/SKBO = *El Dorado Airport, CL:* **218.**
BQN/**** = *Borinquen Coast Guard Air Station, PR:* **208.**
BSB/SBBR = *Brasilia Airport, BR:* 112, 151, **218.**
BUE/SAEZ = *Buenos Aires, AR:* 151, **218.**
*Ezeiza Airport, AG:* 151, **219**.
BZZ/**** = *Belize City, BZ:* **218.**
CAE/**** = *Columbia Metropolitan Airport, SC:* **157.**
CAI/HECA = *Cairo International Airport, EG:* 113, 115, 135, 152, **225.**
CEF/KCEF = *Westover Air Force Base, MA:* **89.**
CHC/NZCH = *Christchurch International Airport, NZ:* 188, **265.**
CHE/**** = *Chievres Air Base, BE:* **217.**
CHS/KCHS = *Charleston Air Force Base, SC:* 42, 83, 90, 112, 113, **149,** 170.
*Charleston International Airport, SC:* **157.**
CJU/RKPC = *Cheju International Airport, RK:* 255, **263.**
CLT/KCLT = *Charlotte/Douglas International Airport, NC:* **125.**
COF/KCOI = *Patrick Air Force Base, FL:* **53**, 67, 117, 154.
COS/KCOS = *Peterson Air Force Base, CO:* **38.**
CPD/**** = *Otis Air National Guard Base, MA:* **88.**
CRW/KCRW = *Yeager Airport, WV:* **190.**
CTS/RJCJ = *Chitose Airport, JA:* **257.**
CVS/**** = *Cannon Air Force Base, NM:* 33, 69, **119**.
CYS/KCYS = *Cheyenne Municipal Airport, WY:* **194.**
DAA/**** = *Davison Army Airfield, VA:* **176.**
DFW/**** = **Dallas/Fort Worth IAP, TX: 167.**
DHA/OEDR = *Dhahran International Airport, SA:* 43, 44, 114, 123, 145, 152, 228, **272.**
DIY/LTCC = *Diyarbakir Air Station, TU:* 114, 152, **280.**
DJK/WIIH = *Halim Perdanakusuma International Airport (Jarkarta Airport), IE:* **236**, 249, 253.
DKR/GOOY = *Dakar Yoff Airport, SE:* 153, 154, **211.**
DLF/**** = *Laughlin Air Force Base, TX:* **171.**
DMA/**** = *Davis-Monthan Air Force Base, AZ:* **6**, 32, 68.
DNA/RODN = *Kadena Air Base, JA:* 32, 99, 138, 187, **247**, 252, 253, 254, 255.
DOV/KDOV = *Dover Air Force Base, DE:* **41**, 61, 82, 83, 90, 93, 113, 114, 115, 123, 124, 135, 138, 140, 151, 152, 153, 154, 161, 170, 184.
DYS/KDYS = *Dyess Air Force Base, TX:* **167.**
ECG/**** = *Elizabeth City Coast Guard Air Station, NC:* **126.**
EDF/PAED = *Elmendorf Air Force Base, AK:* 24, 31, 32, 61, 65, 72, 78, 103, 104, 117, 136, 138, 184, 186, 187, **197.**
EDW/**** = *Edwards Air Force Base, CA:* **16,** 32.
EFD/**** = *Ellington ANGB / Houston CGAS, TX:* **168.**
EIL/PAIE = *Eielson Air Force Base, AK:* 186, **196**.
ESB/LTAC = *Esenboga Airport, TU:* 114, 152, **281.**
FFO/**** = *Wright-Patterson Air Force Base, OH:* 68, **134.**
FHU/**** = *Fort Huachuca, AZ:* **7.**
FIH/FZAA = *Kinshasa N'Djili Airport, ZA:* 153, 154, **211.**
FOE/**** = *Forbes Field Air National Guard Base, KS:* **71.**
FOK/**** = *Suffolk County Air National Guard Base, NY:* **124.**

*APPENDIX C, continued*

**FRF/EDAF** = ***Rhein-Main Air Base, GE:*** 56, 145, 153, 167, **230.**
**FRI/****** = ***Marshall Army Airfield, KS:*** 69, **71.**
**FSI/****** = ***Henry Post Army Airfield, OK:*** **139.**
**FTK/****** = ***Godman Army Airfield, KY:*** **73.**
**FUJ/OMFJ** = ***Fujairah IAP, UAE:*** 24, 42, 43, 44, 116, 117, 154, 255, 256, 257, **283.**
**FUK/RJFF** = ***Fukuoka Airport, JA:*** **244**, 249, 252, 253, 254.
**GAL/PAGA** = ***Galena Airport, AK:*** **200.**
**GAO/MUGM** = ***Guantanamo Bay Naval Station, CU:*** 83, 116, 161, 179, **223.**
**GFA/****** = ***Malmstrom Air Force Base, MT:*** 34, 68, **102.**
**GMF/****** = ***General Billy Mitchell Field, WI:*** **192.**
**GRF/****** = ***Gray Army Airfield, WA:*** **184.**
**GRK/KGRK** = ***Robert Gray Army Airfield, TX:*** **169.**
**GSB/KGSB** = ***Seymour Johnson Air Force Base, NC:*** **129.**
**GUA/****** = ***Guatemala City Airport, GT:*** **219.**
**HIF/****** = ***Hill Air Force Base, UT:*** 34, 68, **174.**
**HIK/PHIK** = ***Hickam Air Force Base, HI:*** 24, 31, 32, 33, 117, 138, 187, 188, **204,** 252.
**HOP/****** = ***Campbell Army Airfield, KY:*** 68, **73.**
**HOW/MPHO** = ***Howard Air Force Base, PN:*** 42, 90, 93, 112, 153, 155, 156, 170, **267.**
**HRT/****** = ***Hurlburt Field, FL:*** **49.**
**HUA/****** = ***Redstone Arsenal, AL:*** **4**, 95.
**IAB/****** = ***McConnell Air Force Base, KS:*** 36, 68, **72.**
**IAG/****** = ***Niagara Falls International Airport, NY:*** **122.**
**IGL/LTBL** = ***Cigli Turkey Air Base, TU:*** 113, 152, **278.**
**ILG/KILG** = ***New Castle County Airport, DE:*** **45.**
**IWA/RJOI** = ***Iwakuni Marine Corps Air Station, JA:*** **246,** 249, 252, 253.
**JAN/KJAN** = ***Jackson Municipal Airport, MS:*** **93.**
**JON/PJON** = ***Johnston Atoll, JO:*** 24, 32, 205, **207.**
**KEF/BIKF** = ***Keflavik Airport, IC:*** 43, 44, 83, 90, 93, 112, 114, 116, 152, 154, 180, **233**.
**KHE/RKPK** = ***Kimhae IAP, RK:*** 253, 255, **260.**
**KIN/MKJP** = ***Kingston, JM:*** 12, 179, **219.**
***Norman Manley, JM:*** 12, 179, **221.**
**KRT/HSSS** = ***Khartoum Airport, SU:*** 155, **211.**
**KUZ/RKJK** = ***Kunsan Air Base, RK:*** 254, 255, **260.**
**KWA/PKWA** = ***Kwajalein Atoll, KA:*** 24, 32, 205, **207.**
**KWI/OKBK** = ***Kuwait IAP, KW:*** 44, 114, 123, 152, **264.**
**LAX/KLAX** = ***Los Angeles International Airport, CA:*** **21**, 99, 100.
**LCK/****** = ***Rickenbacker Air National Guard Base, OH:*** **133.**
**LFI/KLFI** = ***Langley Air Force Base, VA:*** **176.**
**LGS/LPLA** = ***Lajes Field (Azores), PO:*** 42, 43, 44, 78, 83, 90, 112, 113, 114, 115, 124, 135, 145, 152, 153, 154, 160, 180, 192, **269.**
**LIM/SPIM** = ***Jorge Chavez International Airport, PE:*** 113, **219.**
***Lima, PE:*** 112, **220**.
**LNK/****** = ***Lincoln Municipal Airport, NE:*** **104.**
**LPB/SLLP** = ***J. F. Kennedy, BO:*** 113, **219.**
**LPZ/****** = ***La Paz, BO:*** **220.**
**LRF/KLRF** = ***Little Rock Air Force Base, AR:*** **68.**
**LSF/****** = ***Lawson Army Airfield (Fort Benning), GA:*** **58**, 62, 82.

***APPENDIX C, continued***

**LSV/****** = *Nellis Air Force Base, NV:* 33, **107**.
**LTS/****** = *Altus Air Force Base, OK:* **137.**
**LUF/****** = *Luke Air Force Base, AZ:* **8**, 32, 68.
**MCC/****** = *McClellan Air Force Base, CA:* **25.**
**MCF/****** = *MacDill Air Force Base, FL:* **51**, 66.
**MCO/****** = *Orlando International Airport, FL:* **52,** 66.
**MDT/KMDT** = *Harrisburg International Airport, PA:* **143.**
**MEI/****** = *Key Field Airport, MS:* **96.**
**MEM/KMEM** = *Memphis International Airport, TN:* **160.**
**MFD/KMFD** = *Mansfield Lahm Airport, OH:* **133.**
**MGA/****** = *Managua, NU:* **221.**
**MGE/****** = *Dobbins Air Reserve Base, GA:* **57**, 94.
**MHZ/EGUN** = *RAF Mildenhall, UK:* 56, 61, 82, 93, 113, 114, 115, 135, 141, 151, 152, 153, 161, 184, **283.**
**MIB/****** = *Minot Air Force Base, ND:* 34, 37, 68, **131.**
**MIQ/****** = *Maiquetia, VE:* **221.**
**MMT/****** = *McEntire National Guard Base, SC:* **157.**
**MOB/****** = *Mobile Coast Guard Aviation Training Center, AL:* **4.**
**MRB/KMRB** = *Eastern West Virginia Regional Airport, WV:* **190.**
**MRY/****** = *Presidio of Monterey Airport, CA:* 34, **36.**
**MSJ/RJSM** = *Misawa Air Base, JA:* **250**, 254, 255.
**MSP/KMSP** = *Minneapolis-St. Paul International Airport, MN:* **92.**
**MTC/****** = *Selfridge Air National Guard Base, MI:* **91.**
**MTN/KMTN** = *Martin State Airport, MD:* **84.**
**MUO/****** = *Mountain Home Air Force Base, ID:* **63,** 68.
**MVD/SUMU** = *Carrasco International Airport, UG:* 151, **219.**
*Montevideo, UG:* 151, **220.**
**MXF/****** = *Maxwell Air Force Base, AL:* **3**, 94.
**NAP/LIRN** = *Capodichino Airport (Naples), IT:* 116, 145, 146, 154, 155, 228, 229, **239.**
**NBC/****** = *Beaufort Marine Corps Air Station, SC:* **149.**
**NBE/KNBE** = *Dallas Naval Air Station, TX:* **165.**
**NBG/****** = *New Orleans Naval Air Station, LA:* **75**.
**NBO/HKNA** = *Embakasi Airport, KE:* 155, **212.**
**NDJ/FTTJ** = *N'Djamena IAP, CD:* 154, **212.**
**NEL/****** = *Lakehurst Naval Air Warfare Center, NJ:* **110.**
**NFL/****** = *Fallon Naval Air Station, NV:* **106.**
**NFO/****** = *Futenma Marine Corps Air Station, JA:* **245.**
**NGP/****** = *Corpus Christi Naval Air Station, TX:* **164.**
**NGU/KNGU** = *Norfolk Naval Air Station, VA:* 12, 23, 24, 42, 43, 59, 67, 83, 93, 114, 116, 117, 128, 152, 154, 155, 161, **178.**
**NGZ/****** = *Alameda Naval Air Station, CA:* **14.**
**NHK/****** = *Patuxent River Naval Air Warfare Center, MD:* **84.**
**NHZ/****** = *Brunswick Naval Air Station, ME:* **79**, 82.
**NID/****** = *China Lake Naval Weapons Center, CA:* **16.**
**NIP/KNIP** = *Jacksonville Naval Air Station, FL:* **49,** 179.
**NJA/RJTA** = *Atsugi Naval Air Facility, JA:* **244.**
**NJK/****** = *El Centro Naval Air Facility, CA:* **17.**

*APPENDIX C, continued*

**NKT/****** = *Cherry Point Marine Corps Air Station, NC:* 67, 83, **125.**
**NKW/FJDG** = *Diego Garcia Atoll, IO:* 180, **235**, 255, 256, 257.
**NKX/****** = *Miramar Naval Air Station, CA:* **26**, 32.
**NLC/****** = *Lemoore Naval Air Station, CA:* **19.**
**NMM/****** = *Meridian Naval Air Station, MS:* **96.**
**NPA/****** = *Pensacola Naval Air Station, FL:* **54.**
**NQA/KNQA** = *Memphis Naval Air Station, TN:* **161**, 170.
**NQX/****** = *Key West Naval Air Station, FL:* **50**, 66.
**NRR/TJNR** = *Roosevelt Roads Naval Air Station, PR:* 12, 59, 83, 116, 128, 161, **208.**
**NSF/****** = *Washington Naval Air Facility, WASH DC:* **85.**
**NTD/****** = *Point Mugu Pacific Missile Test Center, CA:* **28**.
**NTU/****** = *Oceana Naval Air Station, VA:* **131.**
**NUW/****** = *Whidbey Island Naval Air Station, WA:* **185.**
**NXX/****** = *Willow Grove Naval Air Station, PA:* **146.**
**NZC/****** = *Cecil Field Naval Air Station, FL:* **46.**
**NZJ/****** = *El Toro Marine Corps Air Station, CA:* **18.**
**NZW/****** = *South Weymouth Naval Air Station, MA:* **88.**
**NZY/****** = *North Island Naval Air Station, CA:* **27.**
**OBO/RJCB** = *Obihiro Airport, JA:* **258.**
**OCO/****** = *San Jose, CS:* **222.**
**OFF/****** = *Offutt Air Force Base, NE:* 68, **104.**
**OKC/KOKC** = *Will Rogers Air National Guard Base, OK:* **141.**
**OKO/RJTY** = *Yokota Air Base, JA:* 24, 31, 32, 33, 61, 65, 72, 99, 100, 103, 104, 117, 136, 138, 184, 187, 188, 249, **251.**
**OLB/LIEO** = *Olbia/Costa Smeralda Apt, IT:* 228, 229, **241.**
**OQU/****** = *Quonset Point State Airport, RI:* **148.**
**ORD/****** = *O'Hare Air Reserve Forces Facility, IL:* **65.**
**OSN/RKSO** = *Osan Air Base, RK:* 31, 100, 138, 187, 253, 254, 255, **261.**
**OZP/*** *** = *Moron Air Base, SP:* **274.**
**OZR/****** = *Cairns Army Airfield, AL:* **2.**
**PAP/MTPP** = *Francois Duvalier IAP, HA:* 153, **219.**
*Port Au Prince, HA:* 153, **221.**
**PAS/****** = *Port of Spain, Trinidad & Tobago:* **221.**
**PDX/****** = *Portland International Airport, OR:* **142.**
**PHL/KPHL** = *Philadelphia International Airport, PA:* 56, **144**, 180.
**PHX/****** = *Sky Harbor International Airport, AZ:* **9.**
**PIA/****** = *Greater Peoria Regional Airport, IL:* **66.**
**PIE/****** = *Clearwater Coast Guard Air Station, FL:* **47.**
**PIT/****** = *Pittsburgh International Airport, PA:* **143.**
**PLA/MHSC** = *Soto Cano Air Base, HO:* 155, **222.**
**POB/KPOB** = *Pope Air Force Base, NC:* 67, 83, **127.**
**POE/****** = *Polk Army Airfield, LA:* **77**, 170.
**PPG/NTSU** = *Pago Pago IAP, AS:* 33, 188, **201.**
**PSM/****** = *Pease Air Force Base, NH:* **109.**
**PTY/****** = *Tocumen/Torrijos, PN:* 113, 156, **222.**
**RCA/****** = *Ellsworth AFB, SD:* 37, 68, **159.**
**RCM/ASRI** = *Richmond RAAFB, AU:* 33, 188, **213.**
**RDR/****** = *Grand Forks Air Force Base, ND:* 37, 68, **130.**

*APPENDIX C, continued*

**REE/****** = ***Reese AFB, TX:*** **172.**
**RIO/SBGL** = ***Rio de Janeiro IAP, BR:*** 112, 151, **222.**
**RIV/KRIV** = ***March Air Force Base, CA:*** **22**, 32.
**RME/****** = ***Griffiss Air Force Base, NY:*** 70, **121.**
**RMS/EDAR** = ***Ramstein Air Base, GE:*** 43, 44, 82, 83, 90, 93, 112, 113, 114, 115, 116, 123, 124, 135, 151, 152, 153, 154, **227.**
**RND/****** = ***Randolph AFB, TX:*** **171.**
**RTA/LERT** = ***Rota Naval Air Station, SP:*** 23, 24, 42, 43, 114, 115, 116, 117, 145, 146, 152, 153, 154, 155, **274.**
**RUH/****** = ***Riyadh International Airport, SA:*** 43, **272.**
**SAL/****** = ***San Salvador, ES:*** **222.**
**SAV/KSAV** = ***Savannah International Airport, GA:*** **61.**
**SCH/KSCH** = ***Schenectady County Airport, NY:*** **122.**
**SCL/SCEL** = ***Pudahel IAP, CH:*** 112, 113, **221.**
***Santiago, CH:*** 112, 113, **222.**
**SDF/KSDF** = ***Standiford Field Air National Guard Base, KY:*** 68, **74.**
**SDQ/MDSI** = ***San Isidro Air Base, DR:*** **22.**
**SGP/WSAP** = ***RSAF Paya Lebar, SG:*** 255, 256, **273.**
**SIT/****** = ***Sitka Coast Guard Air Station, AK:*** **200.**
**SIZ/LICZ** = ***Sigonella Airport (Sicily), IT:*** 23, 24, 42, 43, 44, 114, 115, 116, 117, 135, 145, 152, 153, 154, 155, 180, 228, 229, **241.**
**SKA/****** = ***Fairchild Air Force Base, WA:*** 34, 68, **133.**
**SKF/KSKF** = ***Kelly Air Force Base, TX:*** 33, 68, 69, 93, 95, 153, **169.**
**SLC/****** = ***Salt Lake City International Airport, UT:*** **175.**
**SLI/****** = ***Los Alamitos Army Airfield, CA:*** **20**, 34.
**SOC/LGSA** = ***Souda Bay Naval Air Facility (Crete), GR:*** 116, 155, 228, 229, **232.**
**SPS/****** = ***Sheppard AFB, TX:*** **173.**
**STJ/KSTJ** = ***Rosecrans Memorial Airport, MO:*** **100.**
**STL/KSTL** = ***Lambert-St. Louis International Airport, MO:*** **98,** 167.
**STX/TISX** = ***Alexander Hamilton Apt, VI:*** 59, **210.**
**SUU/KSUU** = ***Travis Air Force Base, CA:*** 7, 8, 17, 21, 24, 27, **30**, 35, 36, 38, 60, 64, 68, 72, 78, 84, 95, 103, 108, 116, 118, 132, 136, 138, 164, 170, 175, 184, 186, 188, 198, 202, 204, 211, 212, 213, 249, 252, 257, 263, 266, 267.
**SWF/KSWF** = ***Stewart Air National Guard Base, NY:*** 70, **123.**
**SYA/PASY** = ***Eareckson Air Station, AK:*** **200.**
**SZL/****** = ***Whiteman Air Force Base, MO:*** **100.**
**TBN/****** = ***Forney Army Airfield, MO:*** 69, **98.**
**TCM/KTCM** = ***McChord Air Force Base, WA:*** 34, 68, **185.**
**TGU/****** = ***Tegucigalpa, HO:*** **222.**
**THU/BGTL** = ***Thule Air Base (Greenland), DN:*** 117, **225.**
**TIK/KTIK** = ***Tinker Air Force Base, OK:*** 69, **139.**
**TLV/LLBG** = ***Ben Gurion International Airport, IS:*** 43, **237.**
**TOJ/LETO** = ***Torrejon de Ardoz Air Base, SP:*** **276.**
**TYS/****** = ***McGhee Tyson Airport, TN:*** **160.**
**UAM/PGUA** = ***Andersen Air Force Base, GU:*** 32, 138, 187, **202**, 252.
**UIO/****** = ***Quito, EC:*** **222.**
**UMR/APWR** = ***Woomera Air Station, AU:*** 188, **214.**
*****/USLO** = ***Palau, U.S. Liaison Office:*** **266.**

*APPENDIX C, continued*

## NOTES

# APPENDIX D: A BRIEF DESCRIPTION OF AIRCRAFT ON WHICH MOST SPACE-A TRAVEL OCCURS

The following transport, tanker, and special mission aircraft are used by the military services (USPHS and NOOA do not have aircraft which are suitable for Space-A travel) for missions having Space-A air opportunities. **Only the major channel and support aircraft are listed.** We have not listed minor, some special mission, and helicopter (rotary wing) aircraft due to space limitations. **We have provided for you a brief description of each aircraft with emphasis on performance and passenger accommodations.** The total number of each aircraft changes in the inventory due to acquisitions, conversions, reconfiguration, and attrition. **Our best estimate of current specific aircraft inventories are listed below.**

## C-5A/B GALAXY

The C-5A/B is a long-range, air-refuelable, heavy logistics transport which is capable of airlifting loads up to 291,000 pounds. This aircraft was developed, designed and configured to meet a wide range of military airlift missions. This is the "Free World's" largest aircraft.

**PROGRAM/PROJECT CONTRACTOR:** Lockheed Aeronautical Systems Company.
**POWER SOURCE:** Four General Electric TF39-GE-1C turbofan engines.
Each engine has 43,000 lbs of thrust.
**DIMENSIONS:** Wing span is 222 ft, 8.5 in. Length is 247 ft, 10 in. Height is 65 ft, 1.5 in.
**WEIGHTS:** Empty weight is 374,000 lbs. Maximum payload is 261,000 lbs. Gross weight is 837,000 lbs.
**PERFORMANCE:** Maximum speed at 25,000 ft is 571 mph. Service ceiling with 615,000 lbs gross weight is 35, 750 ft. Range with maximum payload is 3,434 miles and range with maximum fuel is 6,469 miles. Between 1982-1987 the 77 C-5A's were upgraded to C-5B capabilities. From 1985-1989, 50 C5B's were acquired.

**FACILITIES:** Aircraft crew of six. Relief crew/rest area of 15. **Seating for 75 passengers, 2nd deck airline type seats facing to the rear of the aircraft for safety purposes.** cargo, 1st deck, 36 standard 463L pallets or mounted weapons and vehicles or a maximum of 340 passengers in a wide-body jet configuration. There is a program to repaint all USAF C-5A/B's flat grey. AMC has control of all C-5A/B's.
**INVENTORY: Total USAF 127.**

## C-009A/E NIGHTINGALE

This aircraft was designed as a commercial airliner. The DC-9 Series 30 commercial aircraft was reconfigured, modified and equipped to perform aeromedical (air ambulance) airlift transport missions. The C-009A/C performs aeromedical missions in CONUS, and in the European and Pacific Theaters.

**PROGRAM/PROJECT CONTRACTOR:** Douglas Aircraft Company. Division of McDonnell Douglas Corporation.
**POWER SOURCE:** Two Pratt & Whitney JT8D-9 turbofan engines. Each engine produces 14,500 lbs of thrust.
**DIMENSIONS:** Wing span is 93 ft, 3 in. Length is 119 ft, 3 in. Height is 27 ft, 6 in.
**WEIGHT:** Gross weight 108,000 lbs.
**PERFORMANCE:** The maximum cruising speed at 25,000 ft is 565 mph. Ceiling is 35,000 ft. Range is in excess of 2,000 miles.
**FACILITIES:** Aircraft crew of three (includes flight mechanic and spare parts) and five medical staff. There can be a combination of 40 litter (stretcher) or 40 ambulatory patients. Most MEDEVAC patients are ambulatory, that is, they can walk but may be put in a litter for comfort. The ambulatory seats are spacious airline type seats. These are the seats used by Space-A passengers.
**INVENTORY:** Twenty-one in CONUS, four in Europe, three in Pacific, for a total inventory of 28 aircraft configured for aeromedical missions. Three are specifically configured C-9C's which are assigned for Presidential and related missions. **The USN has**

*APPENDIX D, continued*

**29 each C-9B SKYTRAIN II aircraft procured in FY 1985 to meet major Navy logistics requirements. This aircraft is configured for cargo and passenger (airline type seats, up to approximately 100). Total 60.**

## C-17A GLOBEMASTER III

This is a new aircraft which is now undergoing initial operational testing. It is a heavy-lift, air-refuelable, cargo transport designed to meet inter-theater and intra-theater airlift for all types of cargo and passengers. This aircraft will be capable of using unimproved landing facilities (runways - 90 ft wide x 3,000 ft long). The initial operational capability (IOC) date is scheduled for FY 1994. A total of 40 aircraft have been funded through FY 1995. The planned total acquisition is 120 aircraft. **The passenger configurations for this aircraft have not been established.**

**PROGRAM/PROJECT CONTRACTOR:** McDonnell Douglas Aerospace Transport Aircraft Division of McDonnell Douglas Aerospace.
**POWER SOURCE:** Four Prat & Whitney F117-PW 100 turbofans; each 40,000 lbs of thrust on each aircraft.
**DIMENSIONS:** Wing span is 169 ft 10 in. Lenght is 174 ft. Height is 55ft 1 in.
**WEIGHT:** Payload 172,000 lbs, Gross weight 585,000 lbs.
**PERFORMANCE:** Cruising speed (estimated) 518 mph, range with 160,000 lbs payload is 2,765 miles.
**FACILITIES: The passenger and cargo configurations for this aircraft have not been determined.**
**INVENTORY: Total USAF 26.**

*APPENDIX D, continued*

# C-21A EXECUTIVE AIRCRAFT

There is a group of executive type aircraft in use in all of the Military Services. The C-21A is typical of these aircraft. **We will list the data for the C-21A and then list the inventory and passenger capacity of executive type aircraft in the Military Services.**

**PROGRAM/PROJECT CONTRACTOR:** Learjet Corporation.
**POWER SOURCE:** Two Garrett TFE731-2-turbojet engines. Each engine has 3,500 lbs thrust.
**DIMENSIONS:** Wing span is 39 ft, 6 in. Length is 48 ft, 8 in. Height is 12 ft, 3 in.
**WEIGHT:** Gross 18,300 lbs.
**PERFORMANCE:** Cruising speed is Mach 0.81. Service ceiling is 45,000 ft. Range with maximum passengers is 2,420 miles and with maximum cargo load is 1,653 miles.
**FACILITIES:** Aircraft crew of two. **Eight passengers in airline type seats,** or cargo of 3,153 lbs. Also convertible to aeromedical (MEDEVAC) configuration.
**INVENTORY: Total 498.**

C-12A-J HURON (8 Passengers (PAXs): USAF-77

HU-25A GUARDIAN (APPROX 12 PAXs): USCG-41,

C-20A/B GULFSTREAM III/IV (14-18 PAXs): USAF-22

C-21A EXECUTIVE AIRCRAFT (8 PAXs): USAF-88,

C 22B (BOEING 727 (APPROX 100 PAXs): USAF-4,

C-23A SHERPA (APPROX 8 PAXs): USAF-13,

VC-25A Presidential Transport, USAF-2, (53 ON ORDER), C-27A s

C-26-A FAIRCHILD METRO III (19-20 PAXs): USAF -13

***APPENDIX D, continued***

(53 ON ORDER), C-27A STOL (53 PAXs): USAF-5,

C-29A (125-800 BUSINESS JET, APPROX 8 PAXs): USAF-6.

The U.S. Army operates a fleet of C-12, U-21 and older aircraft of approximately 200 in number. Each aircraft can seat approximately 8 passengers.

## C130A-H HERCULES

The C-130 Hercules is a very versatile aircraft which is used to perform a wide range of missions for all of the military services. The aircraft has been used mainly in a cargo and passenger role. It has also been used in specialized combat, electronic warfare, Arctic ice cap resupply, aerial spray, aeromedical MEDEVAC, and aerial refueling among many similar missions. This aircraft is found in the inventory of all the military (Armed) services.

**PROGRAM/PROJECT CONTRACTOR:** Lockhead Aeornautical Systems Company.
**POWER SOURCE:** Four Allison T-56-A-15 turboprop engines. Each engine has 4,508 ehp.
**DIMENSIONS:** Wing span is 132 ft, 7 in. Length is 97 ft, 9 in. Height is 38 ft, 3 in.
**PERFORMANCE:** The maximum cruising speed at 20,000 ft is 374 mph. The service ceiling for 130,000 lbs is 33,000 ft. The range with maximum payload is 2,356 miles.
**FACILITIES:** Aircraft crew of five, **92 passengers in commercial airline type seats,** 74 litter patients, five 463L standard pallets, and assorted mounted weapons and vehicles. Seating ranges from side "bucket" seats along the sides of the aircraft to airline type seating with aisles and facing to the rear. The noise level is extremely high in this aircraft. Ear plugs are highly recommended for all passengers and crew.
**INVENTORY: Total 1,271.** C-130A-H and HC-130H/N/P: USAF-APPROX 1,100. USN-97, USMC-42 (KC-130), USCG-30 (HC-130), USA-1 (EW MISSIONS).

*APPENDIX D, continued*

## KC-135A-R STRATOTANKER

This stratotanker was designed to military specifications. The aircraft is similar in size and design appearance to the commercial 707 aircraft but there the similarity ends. The KC-135 has different internal structural designs and materials which stress the ability to operate at high gross weights. The fuel carried in this tanker is located in the "wet wings" and in the fuel tanks below the floor in the fuselage. Passengers traveling on this aircraft are allowed, subject to mission restraints, to observe the Air to Air Refueling Operations which usually take place over the world's oceans.

**PROGRAM/PROJECT CONTRACTOR:** Boeing Military Airplanes.
**POWER SOURCE:** Four CFM international F108-CF-100 turbofan engines. Each engine has 22,224 lbs of thrust.
**DIMENSIONS:** Wing span is 130 ft, 10 in. Length is 136 ft, 3 in. Height is 38 ft, 4 in.
**WEIGHT:** Empty weight is 119,231 lbs. Gross 322,500 lbs.
**PERFORMANCE:** The maximum speed at 30,000 ft is 610 mph. Service ceiling 50,000 ft. Range with 12,000 lbs of transfer fuel is 11,192 miles.
**FACILITIES:** Aircraft crew of 4 or 5. **Maximum of 80 passengers in airline type seats facing to the rear of the aircraft.**
**INVENTORY: USAF 552.**

*APPENDIX D, continued*

## C-135B STRATOLIFTER

This aircraft is similar to the KC-135 Stratotanker without the refueling equipment. These aircraft were initially purchased as an interim cargo/passenger aircraft placed in service before delivery of the C-141's. The appearance of this aircraft is similar to the KC-135.

**PROGRAM/PROJECT CONTRACTOR:** Boeing Military Airplanes.
**POWER SOURCE:** Four CFM international F108-CF-100 turbofan engines. Each engine has 22,224 lbs of thrust.
**DIMENSIONS:** Wing span is 130 ft, 10 in. Length is 134 ft, 6 in. Height is 38 ft, 4 in.
**WEIGHT:** Empty 102,300 lbs. Gross 275,000 lbs.
**PERFORMANCE:** Maximum speed 600 mph. Range with 54,000 lb payload is 4,625 miles.
**INVENTORY: USAF 48**

## VC-137B/C STRATOLINER

This is a special mission aircraft which has been modified from the commercial Boeing 707 transport. Two of these aircraft were the original "Air Force One" aircraft used by past United States Presidents.

**PROGRAM/PROJECT CONTRACTOR:** The Boeing Company.
**POWER SOURCE:** Four Pratt & Whitney JT3D-3 turbofan engines. Each engine has a 17,200 lb thrust.
**DIMENSIONS:** VC-137B: Wing span is 130 ft, 10 in. Length 144 ft, 6 in. Height 42 ft, 10 in. VC137-C: Wing span is 145 ft, 9 in. Length is 152 ft, 11 in. Height is 42 ft, 5 in.
**WEIGHT:** VC-137B: Gross 258,000 lbs. VC-137C: Gross 322,000 lbs.
**PERFORMANCE:** VC-137C: Maximum speed 627 mph. Service ceiling 42,000 ft. Range 5,150 miles.
**FACILITIES:** This is a special mission aircraft with a variety of configurations. There are full-service galleys, dining, sleeping berths, and airline type seating.
**INVENTORY: USAF 7.**

## C-141A/B STARLIFTER

*APPENDIX D, continued*

The C-141A/B STARLIFTER transport has undergone extensive modification to extend the airframe and modernization to all aspects of the aircraft. The result is a modern air transport which is fully capable of performing many missions from routine cargo and passengers to inter-theater MEDEVAC and humanitarian missions around the world. All of the C-141A/B fleet are scheduled for repainting to a flat grey.

**PROGRAM/PROJECT CONTRACTOR:** Lockheed-Georgia Company.
**POWER SOURCE:** Four Pratt & Whitney TF33-P-7 turbofan engines. Each engine has 21,000 lbs of thrust.
**DIMENSIONS:** Wing span is 159 ft, 11 in. Length is 168 ft, 3.5 in. Height is 39 ft, 3 in.
**WEIGHT:** operating 149,000 lbs. Maximum payload 89,000 lbs. Gross 343,000 lbs.
**PERFORMANCE:** Maximum cruising speed is 566 mph. Range with maximum payload is 2,293 miles without air refueling.
**FACILITIES:** Air crew of five. **200 passengers in commercial airline seats facing to the rear of the aircraft.** 103 litter patients plus attendants. Cargo on 13 standard 463L pallets or alternate mounted weapons, vehicles or other cargo.
**INVENTORY: USAF 270.**

## KC-10A EXTENDER

This advanced tanker/cargo aircraft is based on the commercial DC-10 Series, 30 CF. It has been modified to include fuselage fuel cells, aerial refueling operator station and boom. Military avionics have been added. The aircraft is fit to perform a role of extending and enhancing worldwide military mobility. The latest modifications to this aircraft are wing-mounted air-refueling pods designed to supplement the basic system and increase capability.

*APPENDIX D, continued*

**PROGRAM/PROJECT CONTRACTOR:** Douglas Aircraft Company, Division of McDonnell Douglas Corporation.
**POWER SOURCE:** Three General Electric CF-6-50C2 turbofan engines. Each engine has 52,500 lbs of thrust.
**DIMENSIONS:** Wing span is 165 ft, 4.5 in. Length is 181 ft, 7 in. Height is 58 ft, 1 in.
**WEIGHT:** Gross 590,000 lbs.
**PERFORMANCE:** Cruising speed Mach 0.825. Service ceiling 42,000 ft range with maximum cargo 4,370 miles.
**FACILITIES:** Aircraft crew of four. **75 passengers in commercial airline seats facing to the rear of the aircraft.** 27 standard 463L pallets. Maximum cargo payload 169,409 lbs.
**INVENTORY:** USAF 59.

## P-3C-ORION

This is a propeller-driven aircraft which has been used by the U.S. Navy since 1958 in an Anti-Submarine Warfare (ASW) role. Many improvements have been incorporated in the basic airframe over the years. The latest improvements allow the aircraft to detect, track and attack quieter new generation submarines. **The replacement P-7A program with Lockheed as the contract was terminated in July 1990. The USN is investigating alternative programs.**

**PROGRAM/PROJECT CONTRACTOR:** Lockheed.
**POWER SOURCE:** Four Allison T-56-A-14 turboprop engines. Each engine has 4,900 ehp.
**DIMENSIONS:** Wing span is 100 ft. Length is 117 ft. height is 34 ft.
**WEIGHT:** Gross wieght is 139,760 lbs.
**PERFORMANCE:** Maximum speed 473 mph. Cruise speed 377 mph. Ceiling 28,300 ft.
**FACILITIES:** Aircraft crew of 10. **18 passengers in airline seats.**
**INVENTORY:** USN-133. Seventy-three older aircraft are to be retired in the very near future, thus reducing the number of aircraft in regular and reserve P-3 squadrons. **Total-247.**

# APPENDIX E :

**VERIFICATION OF RESERVE STATUS FOR TRAVEL ELIGIBILITY**
(Part B may be completed by the requester's commander, First Sergeant, or a DoD personnel official with access to the Personnel Data System.)

1. Date Prepared (YYMMMDD)
94 Nov 10

**PRIVACY ACT STATEMENT**

AUTHORITY: 10 USC 8102, 44 USC 3101 and EO 9397.
PRINCIPAL PURPOSE: Use of your SSN is necessary to positively identity you.
ROUTINE USE: Used by Reserve personnel to verify eligibility for space available transportation on DoD-owned or controlled aircraft.
DISCLOSURE: Voluntary; however, failure to disclose will prevent the applicant from traveling on a DoD-owned or controlled aircraft.

**PART A - TO BE COMPLETED BY APPLICANT**

| 2. NAME *(Last, First, Middle Initial)* | 3. PAY GRADE | 4. BRANCH OF SERVICE | 5. SSN |
|---|---|---|---|
| Smith, John C. | E-3 | USAFR | 123-45-6789 |

| 6. UNIT/COMMAND NAME | 7. UNIT COMMAND ADDRESS |
|---|---|
| 459 APS | Andrews AFB, MD 20331 |

| 8. SIGNATURE | 9. DATE SIGNED *(YYMMMDD)* |
|---|---|
| | |

**PART B - TO BE COMPLETED BY VERIFYING OFFICIAL**

The Reservist named above is an active reserve component member and is eligible for space available transportation on DoD-owned or controlled aircraft in accordance with DoD Regulation 4515.13-R, and is authorized to so travel *(not to exceed six months)*.

| 10. FROM *(YYMMMDD)* | 11. TO *(YYMMMDD)* |
|---|---|
| 95 NOV 10 | 96 JAN 10 |

| 12. NAME OF VERIFYING OFFICIAL | 13. PAY GRADE | 14. TITLE |
|---|---|---|
| Jones, Jane M. | O-5 | Commander |

| 15. ORGANIZATION | 16. SIGNATURE | 17. DATE SIGNED *(YYMMMDD)* |
|---|---|---|
| 459 APS | | 95 NOV 10 |

DD FORM 1853, AUG 94 PREVIOUS EDITIONS MAY BE USED.

# APPENDIX F

| SPACE AVAILABLE TRAVEL REQUEST<br>*This form is affected by the Privacy Act of 1974 - See below.*<br><br>This information is required for space available travel registration. Upon completion, place the upper right corner of this form and the back of you leave form into the Date Time validator. Be sure to deposit one copy of this request into the box; retain carbon copy for the Space Available roll call. Space-A sign-up is good for a 60-day period, or when your leave expires, whichever comes first. For facsimile (fax) requests, telefax header will establilsh date time of sign-up. | INSERT HERE | |
|---|---|---|
| PLEASE PRINT CLEARLY | | |
| 1. NAME (*Last, First, MI*) | | |
| 2. RANK, GRADE | 3. SSN | 4. SEATS REQUIRED |
| 5. TRAVEL STATUS (*Type of leave*) | FOR OVERSEAS TRAVEL: | |
| CATEGORY I - Civ or Mil Dependent on Emergency Leave | | |
| CATEGORY II - Environmental Morale Leave (EML) | Border Clearance<br>Document Current? | |
| CATEGORY III - Active Duty on Ordinary Leave / House Hunting | YES NO | |
| CATEGORY IV - (EML) Unaccompanied Dependents | (See note on reverse) | |
| CATEGORY V - Permissive TDY or TAD / Student Travel | | |
| CATEGORY VI - Retired Military / Reserves | | |

| 6. SERVICE: | | ARMY | | NAVY | | AF | | MARINES | | OTHER |
|---|---|---|---|---|---|---|---|---|---|---|

| 7. DATE LEAVE BEGINS (*Active Duty Only*) | 8. DATE LEAVE ENDS (*If extended, you must notify us before this date*) |
|---|---|
| 9. COUNTRY CHOICES (*List up to 5, one choice may be all*) | |
| 10. LIST NAMES OF DEPENDENTS TRAVELING AND TYPE OF PASSPORT (*US or Foreign*) | |
| | |
| | |
| | |

11. I CERTIFY THAT I AM ON LEAVE OR PASS STATUS AT THE TIME I REGISTER FOR SPACE AVAILABLE TRAVEL AND WILL REMAIN IN SUCH STATUS WHEN AWAITING AND/OR HAVE BEEN ACCEPTED FOR SPACE AVAILABLE TRAVEL. IF ACCOMPANIED BY DEPENDENTS, I FURTHER CERTIFY THAT MY TRAVEL IS NOT IN CONJUNCTION WITH TDY/TAD AND THAT I AM NOT USING SPACE AVAILABLE TRAVEL TO TRANSPORT MY DEPENDENTS TO OR FROM MY RESTRICTED DUTY STATION OR ALL OTHER (UNACCOMPANIED) TOUR LOCATION STATIONS. I CERTIFY THAT MY REQUEST FOR AND ACCEPTANCE OF TRANSPORTATION VIA DOD OWNED OR CONTROLLED AIRCRAFT IS NOT FOR PERSONAL GAIN NOR FOR, OR IN CONNECTION WITH BUSINESS OF ANY NATURE AND THAT THIS TRIP WILL NOT RESULT IN ANY FORM OR RENUMERATION TO MYSELF OR TO MY FAMILY. I UNDERSTAND VIOLATION OF ANY OF THE ABOVE COULD RESULT IN BILLING AND OR PUNITIVE ACTION.

| 12. DATE | 13. SIGNATURE |
|---|---|

PRIVACY ACT STATEMENT

AUTHORITY 10 U.S.C. 8013; EO 9397, 22 November 1943.
PRINCIPAL PURPOSE: To apply for air travel. SSN is needed for positive ID.
ROUTINE USEIS: Records from this system of records may be disclosed for any of the blanket routine uses published by the Air Force.
DISCLOSURE IS VOLUNTARY: Failure to provide the information may result in member not being accepted for travel on military aircraft. Disclosure of SSN is voluntary.

**AMC FORM 140, FEB 95** ***(EF) (PerFORM PRO)*****AMC COPY**

# APPENDIX G

## STATE ABBREVIATIONS

AK-Alaska
AL-Alabama
AR-Arkansas
AZ-Arizona
CA-California
CO-Colorado
CT-Connecticut
D C - D is t r i c t of Columbia
DE-Delaware
FL-florida
GA-Georgia
Hi-Hawaii
IA-Iowa
ID-Idaho
IL-Illinois
IN-Indiana
KS-Kansas
KY-Kentucky
LA-Louisiana
MA-Massachusetts
MD-Maryland
ME -Maine
MI-Michigan
MN-Minnesota
MO-Missouri
MS-Mississippi
MT-Montana
NE-Nebraska
NC-North Carolina
ND-North Dakota
NH-New Hampshire
NJ-New Jersey
NM-New Mexico
NY New York
NV-Nevada
OH-Ohio
OK-Oklahoma
OR-Oregon
PA-Pennsylvania
RI-Rhode island
SC-South Carolina
SD-South Dakota
TN-Tennessee
TX-Texas
UT-Utah
VA-Virginia
VT-Vermont
WA-Washington
WI-Wisconsin
WV-West Virginia
WY-Wyoming

## POSSESSION ABBREVIATIONS

AS-American Samoa
GU-Guam
PR -Puerto Rico
KA-Kwajalein Atoll
WK-Wake Isand
VI-U.S.Virgin Islands
JO Johnston Atoll

## COUNTRY ABBREVIATIONS

AF-Africa
AG-Argentina
AN-Antigua
AI-Ascension Island
AU-Australia
BA-Bahrain
BE-Barbados
ED-Barbuda
BE-Belgium
BH-Bahamas
BM-Bermuda
BO-Bolivia
BR-Brazil
BZ-Belize
CD-Chad
CH-Chile
CL-Columbia
CN-Canada
CR-Crete
CS-Costa Rico
CU-Cuba
CY-Cyprus
DN-Denmark
DR-Dominican Republic
DJ-Djibouti
E-Ecuador
EG-Egypt
ES-El Salvador
GE-Germany
GL-Greenland
GR-Greece
GT-Guatemala
GY-Guyana
HA-Haiti
HO-Honduras
HK-Hong Kong
IC-Iceland
IE-Indonesia
IO-Indian Ocean (Diego Garcia UK)
IR-Ireland
IS-Israel
IT-Italy
JA-Japan
JM-Jamaica
JR-Jordan
KE-Kenya
KW-Kuwait
LI-Liberia
MA-Malaysia
MC-Micronesia
Mi-Marshall islands
N-Niger
NI-Nicaragua
NO-Norway
NT-Netherlands
NZ-New Zealand
OM-Oman
PE-Peru
PG-Paraguay
PN-Republic of Panama
PO-Portugal
RK-Republic of Korea
RP-Republic of the Philippines
SE-Senegal
SF-South Africa
SG-Singapore
SM-Somalia
SP-Spain
SU-Sudan
TH-Thailand
TU-Turkey
UAE-United Arab Emirates
UG-Uruguay
UK-United Kingdom
US-United States
V-Venezuela
ZA-Zaire

# APPENDIX H

## General Abbreviations Used in this Book

This appendix contains general abbreviations used in this book. Commonly understood abbreviations and standard abbreviations found in addresses have not been included in order to save space.

Days of the Week:
Mon, Tue, Wed, Thu, Fri, Sat, Sun.
lst/Mon - i.e. First Monday of Month
1st/2nd/3rd/Tue - i.e First, Second and Third Tuesdays of the Month.
2 Monthly - 2 flights monthly, call for dates.
3 Weekly -3 flights weekly, call for days.

A
AAF-Army Airfield
AAFES-Army/Air Force Exchange System
AB-Air Base
AC-Air Conditioning
ACC-Atlantic Cargo Cargo
ACM-Atlantic Cargo Mixed
ACS-Army Community Service
AD-Active Duty
AF-Air Force
AFB-Air Force Base
AFRO-Air Force Reserve Center
AFRC-Armed Forces Recreation Center
AAF-Air Force Auxiliary Field
AFRES-Air Force Reserve
AFS-Air Force Station
AMC-Air Mobility Command
AMEN-American Embassy
ANGB-Air National Guard Base
APO-Army Proving Ground
APP-Atlantic Passenger Passenger
APM-Atlantic Passenger Mixed
APT -Airport
APO-Army Post Office
AS-Air Station
ATC-Air Traffic Control

B
BEQ-Bachelor Enlisted Quarters
BOQ-Bachelor Officers' Quarters
BART-Bay Area Rapid Transit

C
C-Cargo Mission
CG-Coast Guard
CGAS-Coast Guard Air Station
CMDR-Commander
CO-Commanding Officer
C-Commercial Telephone System
CPO-Chief Petty Officer
CSM-Command Sergeant Major
CONUS-Continental United States
CQ-Charge of Quarters

D
D-Defense Switched Network
DAVs-Disabled American Veterans
DO-Duty Officer
DoD-Department of Defense
DV-Distinguished Visitor
DVQ-Distinguished Visitor Quarters
DVOQ-Distinguished Visitor Officer's Quarters

E
ETS-Estimated Time of Separation
ETS-European Telephone System
EX-Telephone Extension

F
FPO Fleet Post Office
FTS-Federal Telephone System

G
GAFB-German Air Force Base
GH-Guest House

H
Hq-Headquarters

I
WSMR-White Sands Missile Range
ITT-Information, Tickets & Tours
ITR-Information,Ticketing and Registration

K
Km-Kilometer

***APPENDIX H, continued***

L
LI-Location Identifier
LSD-Local Standard Time

M
MAC-Military Airlift Command
MC-Marine Corps
MCAS-Marine Corps Air Station
MCAS-Marine Corps Air Station
MCAS-Marine Corps Air Station
MCBX-Marine Corps Exchange
MCRC-Marine Corps Recruiting Station
MWR-Morale, Welfare and Recreation

N
NAB -Naval Amphibious Base
NAF~Non~appropriated Funds
NAS-Naval Air Station
NB-Naval Base
NCO-Noncommissioned Officer
NG-National Guard
NMC-Nearest Major City
NMI-Nearest Military Installation
NS-Naval Station
NSB-Navy Submarine Base
NSO-Navy Security Office
NSWC-Naval Surface Weapon Center
NTC-Naval Training Center
NWC-Naval Weapons Center

O
O'Club-Officers' Club
OCONUS-Outside Continental US
OD-Officer of the Day
OIC-Officer in Charge
OAFS-Oman Air Force Base

P
P-Passenger Mission (contract)
PAO-Public Affairs Officer
PCC-Pacific Cargo Cargo
PCS-Permanent Change of Station
PERS-Person
PMO-Provost Marshall's Office

R
Rec-Recreation
RON-Remain over night
RTN-Royal Thailand Navy

SAC-Strategic Air Command
SATO-Scheduled Airline Ticket Office
SDO-Staff Duty Officer
SDNCO-Senior Duty Non-Com Officer
Space-A~Space available
SNCO-Senior Non-Commissioned Officer
SEBQ-Sailors' Enlisted Bachelors Quarters

T
TAD-Temporary Attached Duty
TAQ- Temporary Airmens' Quarters
TD -Temporary Duty
TLF-Temporary Facility Lodging
TEQ-Temporary Enlisted Quarters
TLA-Temporary Lodging Allowance
TLQ-Temporary Living Quarters
TM-Temporary Military Lodging
TO-Transient Officer.' Quarters
TVEQ-TemporaryVisitingEnlisted Quarters
TVOQ-TemporaryVisitingOfficers'Quarters

U
US- United States
USA-United States Army
USAF-United States Air Force
USCG United States Coast Guard
USDAO-U.S Defense Attache Office
USEUCOM-U.S European Command
USM-U.S Military Installation Road Map
USMA-U.S. Military Academy
USMRA-U.S Military Road Atlas
USMC-United States Marine
USNCOQ-Unaccompanied Senior Non-Commissioned Officers' Quarters
USN-United States Navy
USO-United Service Organization

V
VAQ-Visiting Airmens' Quarters
VEQ-Visiting Enlisted Quarters
VIP-Very Important Person
VHA-Variable Housing Allowance
VOQ-Visiting Officer Quarters
VQ-Visiting Quarters, all ranks

W
WSMR-White Sands Missile Range

# CENTRAL ORDER COUPON

Military Living Publications
P.O. Box 2347, Falls Church, VA 22042-0347
**TEL: (703) 237-0203 FAX: (703) 237-2233**

| Publications | | QTY |
|---|---|---|
| **R&R Space-A Report®.** *The worldwide travel newsletter.* 6 issues per year. 1 yr/$15.00 - 2 yrs/$24.00 - 3 yrs/$33.00 - 5 yrs/$49.00 (Shipped by 3rd class bulk rate) | | |
| **Military Space-A Air Basic Training.** | $12.95 | |
| **Military Space-A Air Opportunities Air Route Map.** | (Folded) $13.95 | |
| **Military Space-A Air Opportunities Around the World.** | $17.95 | |
| **Temporary Military Lodging Around the World.** | $15.95 | |
| **Military RV, Camping & Rec Areas Around the World.** | $12.95 | |
| **U.S. Forces Travel and Transfer Guide, USA and Caribbean Areas.** | $13.95 | |
| **U.S. Military Museums, Historic Sites & Exhibits.** | (Soft Cover) $17.95 | |
| **United States Military Road Atlas** | $18.95 | |
| **U.S. Military Installation Road Map.** | (Folded) $7.95 | |
| **United States Military Medical Facilities Map** | (Folded) $7.95 | |
| **COLLECTOR'S ITEM! Desert Shield Commemorative Maps.** | (Folded) $8.00<br>(2 unfolded wall maps in a hard tube) $18.00 | |
| **Assignment Washington Military Road Atlas.** | $10.95 | |
| **California State Military Road Map -**<br>**Florida State Military Road Map -**<br>**Mid-Atlantic States Military Road Map -**<br>**Texas State Military Road Map -** | (Folded) $5.95<br>(Folded) $5.95<br>(Folded) $5.95<br>(Folded) $5.95 | |
| **Military Living Magazine, Camaraderie Washington.** *Local Area magazine.* | 4 seasonal issues, $8.00 per issue | |
| **Virginia Addresses add 4.5% sales tax (Books, Maps, & Atlases only)**<br>**ALL ORDERS SHIPPED BY 1ST CLASS MAIL TOTAL $** | | |

*If you are an R&R Space-A Report® subscriber, you may deduct $1.00 per book. (No discount on the R&R Report itself or on the maps or atlas.) Mail Order Prices are for U.S. APO & FPO addresses. Please consult publisher for International Mail Price. Sorry, no billing.
We're as close as your telephone...by using our Telephone Ordering Service. We honor American Express, MasterCard, and VISA. Call us at **703-237-0203 (Voice Mail after hours)** or **FAX 703-237-2233** and order today! Sorry, no collect calls. Or...fill out and mail the order coupon below.

NAME:_______________________________________________

STREET:_____________________________________________

CITY/STATE/ZIP:______________________________________

PHONE:________________ SIGNATURE:__________________

RANK (or rank of sponsor):______Branch Of Service:______________

Active Duty:_Retired:_Widow/er:_100% Disabled Veteran:_Guard:_Reservist:_Other:

Card # Card Expiration Date:

Mail check/money order to Military Living Publications, P.O. Box 2347, Falls Church, VA 22042-0347 - **Tel: 703-237-0203 - FAX: 703-237-2233.**

Save $$$s by purchasing any of our books, Maps, and Atlases at your military Exchange.

Prices subject to change. Please check here if we may ship and bill difference. __

# *How Long Has It Been Since YOU Flew Space-A ??*

*Whether the answer is NEVER or a year or so ago, you may find our sister book,* ***Military Space-A Air Basic Training*** to be of great help. Numerous rules have changed in Space-A travel -in fact, this fringe benefit has gotten even better and more user-friendly than ever before! This is the **HOW TO DO IT BOOK ON FLYING SPACE-A.**

# How to Go About Space-A Air Travel Step by Step

Our Space-A Basic Training book has helpful letters from military personnel, active, retired, Guard and Reserve.

Detailed conversion and documentation charts.

Latest Space-A rules, necessary forms and FAX numbers.

Sample trips for active, retired, Guard and Reserve.

Look for Military Living's ***Space-A Air Basic Training*** at your military exchange. If not available, the book may be ordered from Military Living Publications by phone with Visa, MasterCard or American Express. Phone **(703) 237-0203**. Mail orders - PO Box 2347, Falls Church, VA 22042-0347. The cost is $12.95 including our first class service.